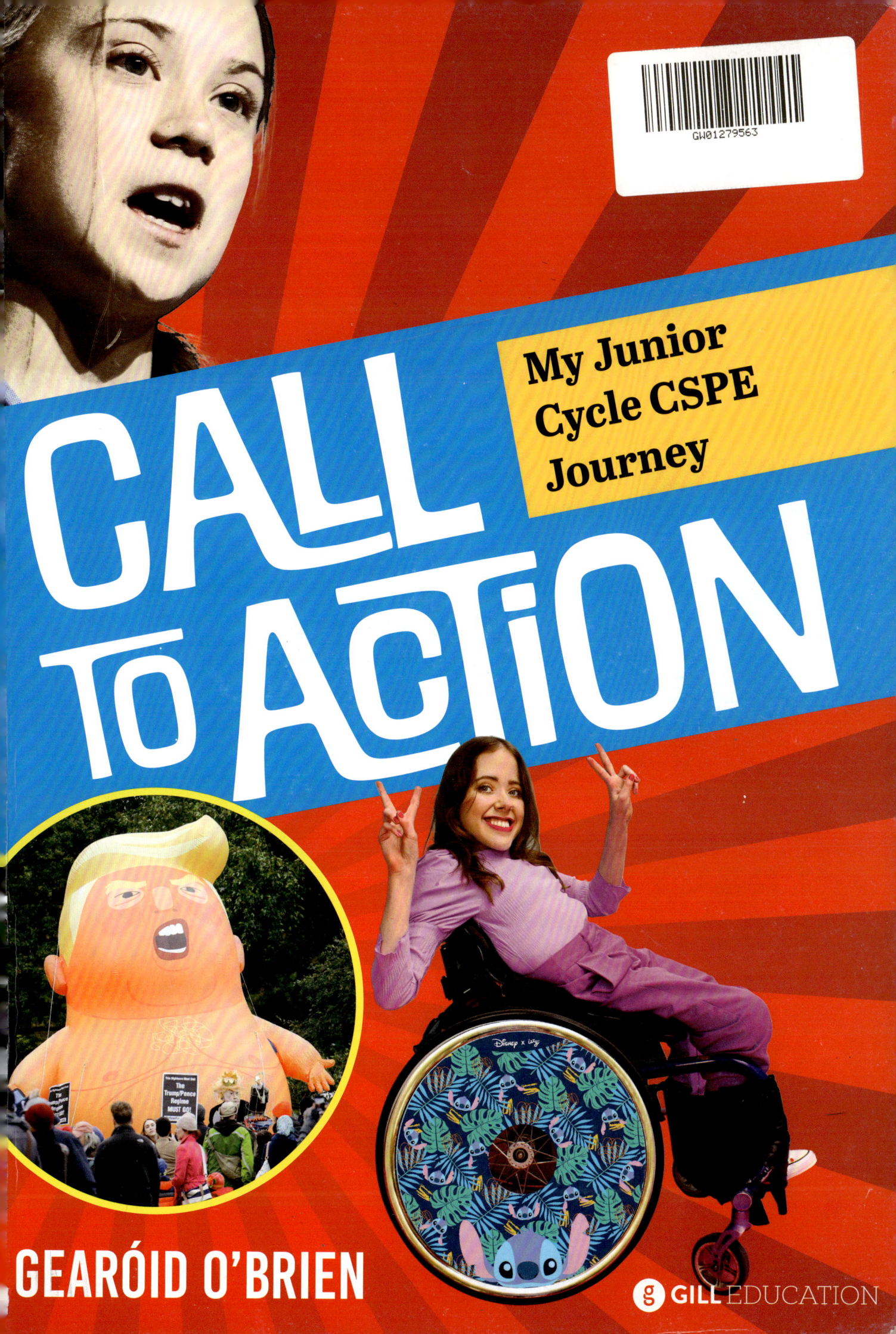

Gill Education
Hume Avenue
Park West
Dublin 12
www.gilleducation.ie

Gill Education is an imprint of M.H. Gill & Co.

© Gearóid O'Brien 2022

ISBN: 978-0-7171-93905

All rights reserved. No part of this publication may be copied, reproduced or transmitted in any form or by any means without written permission of the publishers or else under the terms of any licence permitting limited copying issued by the Irish Copyright Licensing Agency.

Design: Síofra Murphy
Illustrations: Andriy Yankovskyy and Katie Allen

At time of going to press, all web addresses were active and contained information relevant to the topics in this book. Gill Education does not, however, accept responsibility for the content or views contained on these websites. Content, views and addresses may change beyond the publisher or author's control. Students should always be supervised when reviewing websites.

For permission to reproduce photographs, the authors and publisher gratefully acknowledge the following:
© Adobe Stock: 2T, 5T, 9T, 12T, 15, 18, 20T, 23T, 27T, 32, 42, 47T, 56T, 64T, 66, 73, 75, 83, 89, 99, 105T, 107T, 111, 115, 119, 124T, 281, 302, 322TR, 314, 315TC, 315TL, 315C, 322BL, 325BL, 328T, 332, 341, 344, 350T, 364C, 369, 416T, 415TR, 425; © Age Action Ireland: 45Ra; © Alamy: 5Be, 5Bg, 19Cb, 27Bb, 27Bc, 28Ta, 28Te, 28Tg, 28Th, 57Bb, 57Bd, 57Be, 57Bf, 105B, 120La, 122, 139, 153, 165Be, 190, 199C, 201, 205, 237, 253, 256, 274L, 284, 287, 291B, 298T, 300, 321BR, 325BR, 328Ca, 328Cb, 328Bb, 328Bd, 329TC, 329TR, 329BL, 329BR, 350Bb, 366B, 371, 379, 393B, 401CR; © Amnesty International: 37B, 60C; © Amnesty International and Afrewatch: 86BR; © APAImages/Shutterstock: 120Lc, 120Ld; © BBDO: 401TL; © BeLonG To Youth Services: 45Re; © Ben Garrison, Grrr Graphics: 335BR; © Carbon Trust: 162C; Photograph of Mary Elmes, c. 1940. © Courtesy of Caroline and Patrick Danjou: 58; © Central Statistics Office: 22, 31C, 37C, 141; © Children's Commissioner for Wales and Children's Commissioner for England: 85; © Citizen's Information: 391L; © Civil Rights Defenders/Isabel Verner: 57Bg; © Conradh na Gaeilge: 10T; © Cyprus Mail: 81; © David Trilling/Eurasianet: 325BC; © Department of Health and Social Care, UK. This image is subject to Crown copyright (Open Government Licence v3.0): 401TR; © Department of the Taoiseach: 309; © Environmental Protection Agency: 172; Copyright © Environmental Working Group, www.ewg.org. Reproduced with permission: 168C; © Fairtrade Ireland, www.fairtrade.ie: 203C; © HRD Memorial Project data, via Front Line Defenders, Global Analysis, www.frontlinedefenders.org: 56B; © GDS Infographics (Flikr): 169; GETTY IMAGES © Popperfoto via Getty Images: 27Ba; © RDB/ullstein bild via Getty Images: 328Ba. © Gil Khabar: 407BL; © Copyright Guardian News & Media Ltd 2022: 335TR; © Horse.com: 401CL; © HSE: 407C; © Ian Berry/Magnum Photos: 328Bc; © 2017 - 2022 ILGA World - The International Lesbian, Gay, Bisexual, Trans and Intersex Association: 102; © Irish Council for Civil Liberties: 45Rd; © iStock/Getty Premium: 1, 2C, 3, 5C, 5Ba, 5Bc, 5Bf, 7, 10B, 12Ca, 12Cc, 12Ce, 12Cf, 12Cg, 12Cd, 19Ca, 19Cc, 19Cd, 23B, 31T, 60T, 64B, 79C, 365, 107C, 117, 121Ta, 124B, 130, 131, 134, 136, 137, 140, 145, 148T, 151, 157, 158, 162T, 165Ba, 165Bb, 165Bc, 165Bd, 178, 181, 182, 187, 192, 199T, 199B, 203T, 208, 213, 214, 219T, 224, 227, 229, 240, 246, 250, 255T, 258, 261, 265, 266, 267, 268, 270, 282, 283, 286, 290, 294, 295T, 295C, 296, 312, 316T, 319, 321BL, 322TL, 322CL, 322CR, 324, 324B, 340, 343, 355, 366T, 373, 387T, 387B, 393T, 406, 398, 404, 410; Comprehensive Assessment of Water Management in Agriculture © IWMI, http://www.iwmi.cgiar.org: 189; © Izzy Wheels and © Disney: 28Tb; © Jens Hage: 335BL; © JOE.ie: 391BR; © Keep Kilkenny Beautiful: 298B; © Kerry Ford (Pinterest): 252; © Luigi Scuotto/Fotomovimiento: 408B; © Mirrorpix: 400BC, 400CL; © Mywaste.ie: 175; © National Women's Council of Ireland: 45Rb; © National Youth Council of Ireland, youth.ie: 45Rc; © Used with permission of The NEED Project, www.need.org: 28; © Numan Afifi: 57Ba; © Office Congresswoman of Doris Matsui and UPI/Newscom: 5Bd; © Oireachtas.ie: 347; © OPHI Multidimensional Poverty Index - Alkire and Robles (2016), https://ourworldindata.org/grapher/share-multi-poverty: 215; © Pavee Point Traveller & Roma Centre: 45Rf; © PovCal (2021), https://ourworldindata.org/income-inequality: 44; © Reduce Carbon Footprint - Go Green: 168T; © Referendum Commission: 310; © Republic of Kirabati: 219B; © Reuters: 400CC; © Rollings News: 308C, 350Ba, 350Bc; © RSPCA: 415TL; © RSPO: 255C; © Sam Tarling/Oxfam: 35; © United Nations Sustainable Development Goals, https://www.un.org/sustainabledevelopment. The content of this publication has not been approved by the United Nations and does not reflect the views of the United Nations or its officials or Member States: 155T, 156T, 156C; © Shutterstock: 5Bh, 9C, 12Ch, 12Cb, 28Tf, 120Lb, 121Tb, 144, 148B, 166, 171, 235, 241, 242, 243, 273, 274R, 291T, 303, 305, 308T, 316B, 329TL, 329BC, 346, 349, 350Ca, 350Cb, 350Cc, 352, 358, 359T, 364T, 415BR, 416; © Statista: 389; © Statista/Walk Free Foundation: 70; © The Capital/Capital Daily: 407BR; © The Courts Service: 361; © The Courts Service/Fotofast Sligo: 359C; © The Independent/ESI Media: 400BR; © The Irish Mail on Sunday: 400CR; © The Irish Times: 391TR; © The Sun: 335TL; © Tramore Valley Park managed by The Glen Resource & Sports Centre on behalf of Cork City Council: 154; © UCA News, globalslaveryindex.org: 69; © UNICEF/UNI195222/Khuzaie: 86BL; © 2022 Waterlovers Australia: 179; WIKIMEDIA COMMONS: Commonwealth of Australia/National Archives of Australia (CC BY 3.0 au): 328Cd; Ensaf Haidar/PEN International (CC BY-SA 3.0): 57Bc; Israel Defence Forces (CC BY-SA 3.0): 415BL; Leon A. Perskiedigitization: FDR Presidential Library & Museum (CC BY 2.0): 28Td; Oireachtas.ie (CC BY 2.0): 59; SbwO1f (CC BY-SA 3.0): 210; Wikimedia Commons: 5Bb, 27Bd, 28Tc, 47B, 49, 407T. © WWF EU: 259; © WWF/TBWA: 407BC.

The authors and publisher have made every effort to trace all copyright holders. If, however, any have been inadvertently overlooked, we would be pleased to make the necessary arrangement at the first opportunity.

The paper used in this book comes from the wood pulp of sustainably managed forests.

Contents

Introduction for Students vi
Introduction for Teachers viii
Acknowledgements viii

STRAND 1 Rights and Responsibilities — LO 1

Chapter 1 Human Dignity: The Basis for Human Rights — 2

		LO	Page
1	What it means to be human	1.1	2
2	Human dignity	1.1, 1.2	5
3	Community	1.1	9
4	Rights, wants and needs	1.3	12
5	Maslow's hierarchy of needs	1.3	15
6	My rights, wants and needs	1.3	18
7	What is a home?	1.1	20
8	Human dignity of people without a home	1.1	23
9	Human dignity of people with disabilities	1.1, 1.3	27
10	Human dignity of refugees and asylum seekers	1.1, 1.3	32
11	Creating an infographic	1.1, 1.2	37
12	Inequality in Ireland	1.4	42
13	Global inequalities	1.4	47
Reflection	Reflecting on my learning about human dignity	1.11	52
Action	Organising a celebration of International Human Rights Day		53

Chapter 2 Human Rights Instruments — 56

		LO	Page
14	Human rights activists	1.5	56
15	Researching human rights activists	1.5	60
16	Presentation on human rights activists	1.5	64
17	The history of human rights	1.6	66
18	Timeline of human rights	1.6	73
19	The Universal Declaration of Human Rights	1.7	75
20	The European Convention on Human Rights	1.7	79
21	The United Nations Convention on the Rights of the Child	1.7, 1.8	83
22	Ireland and the UNCRC	1.7	89
23	Rights in conflict	1.9	95
24	Human rights abuses	1.9	99
25	Simulated debate on disadvantage	1.9	105
26	My responsibilities	1.10	107
27	The importance of responsibility	1.10	111
28	My human rights actions	1.10	115
29	Case study: Human rights in the West Bank	1.9	119
30	Probable and possible futures	1.9	124
Reflection	Reflecting on my learning about human rights	1.11	127
Action	Organising a fundraiser		128

STRAND 2 Global Citizenship — 130

Chapter 3 Sustainability — 131

31	Global citizenship	2.1	131
32	Interdependence	2.1	136
33	International trade	2.1	140
34	Development	2.2	145
35	Sustainability	2.2	151
36	My carbon footprint	2.3	157
37	Tackling carbon footprint	2.3	162
38	Carbon footprint infographic	2.3	169
39	The 4 Rs	2.4	171
40	Plastic bottles	2.4	178
41	Plastic	2.4	182
42	Water	2.4	187
43	My sustainability actions	2.4	192

Reflection Reflecting on my learning about sustainability 2.12 195

Action Organising a guest speaker 196

Chapter 4 Local and Global Development — 199

44	Case study: Kenya	2.5	199
45	Fairtrade	2.5	203
46	Causes of poverty	2.6	208
47	Global poverty	2.6	214
48	Case study: Kiribati	2.6	219
49	Local development	2.7	224
50	A development proposal	2.7	227
51	Simulated debate on a development proposal	2.7	229

Reflection Reflecting on my learning about local and global development 2.12 231

Action Organising a visit to a successful sustainable development 232

Chapter 5 Effecting Global Change — 235

52	Muhammad Yunus	2.8	235
53	The United Nations	2.8	241
54	Causes of deforestation	2.9	246
55	Consequences of deforestation and its impacts on humans	2.9	250
56	Solutions to deforestation	2.9	255
57	Case study: Indonesia's palm oil industry	2.9	261
58	My response to deforestation	2.10	265
59	Case study: Google Camp	2.11	268
60	Case study: Fridays for Future	2.11	273

Reflection Reflecting on my learning about effecting global change 2.12 278

Action Creating an awareness campaign 279

STRAND 3 Exploring Democracy — 281

Chapter 6 The Meaning of Democracy — 282

#	Topic	Ref	Page
61	Power and influence	3.1	282
62	Creating a visual image of power and influence	3.1	285
63	Democracy	3.2	286
64	Decision-making	3.2	290
65	Voting	3.3	294
66	Local government	3.3	298
67	The government	3.3	302
68	The Oireachtas	3.4	305
69	The Constitution and the President	3.4	309
70	EU institutions	3.4	314
71	Systems of democratic government	3.5	319
72	Case study: Turkmenistan	3.5	324
73	Strengths of democracy	3.6	328
74	Weaknesses of democracy	3.6	332

Reflection Reflecting on my learning about democracy 3.14 337
Action Running a mock election 338

Chapter 7 The Law and the Citizen — 340

#	Topic	Ref	Page
75	Rules or laws	3.7	340
76	Laws that relate to young people	3.7	343
77	How laws are made	3.8	346
78	Policing laws	3.8	350
79	Criminal and civil cases	3.9	355
80	The role of Irish courts	3.9	359
81	International courts	3.9	364
82	Changing laws	3.8	369
83	The nine grounds of discrimination	3.10	373
84	Legal case studies	3.11	379

Reflection Reflecting on my learning about law 3.14 384
Action Taking part in a mock trial 385

Chapter 8 The Role of Media in a Democracy — 387

#	Topic	Ref	Page
85	What is media?	3.12	387
86	Types of media	3.12	393
87	Different perspectives	3.12	398
88	Bias, propaganda and fake news	3.12	404
89	My media actions	3.12	410
90	Case study: 2020 US presidential election	3.13	416

Reflection Reflecting on my learning about the role of media in a democracy 3.14 421
Action Conducting a survey 422

Chapter 9 Classroom-Based Assessment: My Citizenship Action Record — 425

■ CALL TO ACTION

Introduction for Students

Welcome to *Call to Action*, your Junior Cycle CSPE journey. Civic, Social and Political Education (CSPE) is a course in citizenship. This book will help you on your path through the course.

There are three types of citizens:

1. Personally responsible citizens live in a way that is helpful to others in society and to the world.
2. Participatory citizens organise and help lead when they see a problem – they are action focused.
3. Justice-oriented citizens look at the causes of problems and how to deal with them.

An example of how all three work would be if a town was badly damaged by flooding. The personally responsible citizens would donate food, clothes and money for the people who lost their homes. The participatory citizens would organise a collection of money and food. The justice-oriented citizens would ask why the flood had happened and what must be done to prevent it recurring. A person can be all three types of citizen in one. This book will help you develop all three elements.

Throughout the book the focus is on learning by doing. Each chapter is divided into short lessons. The lessons contain many different types of activities such as quizzes; group work; video assignments; designing posters; memes and infographics; and researching information. Completing the lessons will help you to become more aware of what is happening in the world and to use this to increase your ability to understand why it is happening. Each lesson deals with at least one learning outcome. Each exercise covers the learning intention and success criteria. The success criteria allow you to measure what you have learned.

Classroom-Based Assessment

As part of the Junior Cycle, you will have to complete a Classroom-Based Assessment (CBA). The CBA in CSPE is a Citizenship Action Record. For each chapter of the book, you will complete an action such as conducting a mock election or a mock trial, designing and promoting a survey, inviting a guest speaker and organising a field trip. You can develop one of these into your Citizenship Action Record in Chapter 9.

Key Skills

Throughout the book, you will have the opportunity to engage with each of the eight Key Skills of the Junior Cycle. When you see one of the icons below, it means you will be developing that skill as you complete the exercise:

1. **Being creative** involves imagining things and then presenting them in a way you decide, such as designing a poster.

2. **Being literate** is being able to read and understand what a text means. You will have the opportunity to read passages from reports, books and newspapers, as well as developing your media literacy, including online media literacy.

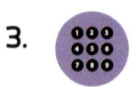

3. **Being numerate** is about understanding numbers, such as analysing graphs and statistics.

4. **Communicating** involves discussing and debating with others. It includes areas such as pair and group work, walking debates and simulated debates.

5.  **Managing information and thinking** includes understanding and being able to explain information that you have read, heard, etc. It involves activities such as report writing and taking part in debates.

6.  **Managing myself** involves being able to reflect on your own learning. There is a reflection section at the end of each chapter.

7.  **Staying well** – this involves being social and able to understand how to stay safe. You will look at areas such as online media.

8.  **Working with others** is the idea of being able to work with other people to make a difference. This is covered especially in the actions, but also in day-to-day problem-solving tasks in class.

Wellbeing

CSPE is part of the Wellbeing programme. The aim is to help you understand how your wellbeing and the wellbeing of others are connected. Because of the focus on human rights and global citizenship, CSPE helps you to see the links between individual wellness, the wellness of others and the wellbeing of the environment. Each lesson shows you which wellbeing indicator you have achieved.

There are six indicators of wellbeing shown by the following icons:

1.  **Active** aims to develop your confidence and skills in physical activity.

2.  **Resilient** aims to develop your coping skills and understanding of how to seek help.

3.  **Responsible** aims to develop skills to protect and promote your wellbeing and that of others, and to make healthy and safe choices.

4.  **Respected** aims to develop your sense of being valued and listened to and to develop positive friendships and relationships.

5.  **Connected** aims to make connections between your school, local area, country and the world.

6.  **Aware** aims to make you more aware of your thoughts, feelings and behaviours, and of what is going on in the world.

Reflection

Each chapter contains a reflection section where you can think about, analyse and show what you have learned.

Actions

Each chapter also contains an action that will allow you to put your developing skills and knowledge into practice.

■ CALL TO ACTION

Each element in the book – the lessons, reflections and actions – is designed to develop your skills, wellbeing and knowledge. They will help you to understand the importance of personal responsibility in actions such as conserving water or reusing products. The actions show how you can participate in your community, and the reflections allow you to consider what the situation is and how you could develop it further.

Wishing you the best of luck as you embark on an exciting journey to develop your citizenship!

Introduction for Teachers

Call to Action has been written with the aim of developing personally responsible, participatory and justice-oriented citizens. These are often treated as distinct types of citizenship. I do not think that they should be distinct citizen types as all are valuable attributes in the citizens of the future. As such, the book includes exercises based on developing skills to instil each CSPE element in students.

Often, too much of a teacher's time is spent sourcing materials, trying to adapt them to the learning outcomes and updating them. The specification's focus on learning outcomes can make it difficult to decide what content to cover. The aim of the *Call to Action* package is to do that work for you.

As well as this book, the *Call to Action* package includes digital lessons on GillExplore and a Teacher's Resource Book. The material in this package is designed to deliver the learning outcomes and develop the range of skills. For example, being numerate is developed and assessed by use of charts and statistics; being creative by designing posters, memes and infographics; and working with others by completing class actions.

Additional exercises are available to you, the teacher, within the lessons on GillExplore. These will be supplemented annually with more up-to-date exercises and case studies. The textbook includes everything your students need for classwork, homework and assessment, reducing the need for students having to bring different books for different tasks. Students can also complete the CBA in the book itself.

The answers to activities and guidance for the teacher are available in the Teacher's Resource Book.

I hope you enjoy using *Call to Action* and find it useful, stimulating and enjoyable and that it assists you greatly in teaching CSPE.

Gearóid O'Brien

Acknowledgements

A huge thank you to all the Gill Education team, including Margaret Burns, Anita Ruane, Shannagh Rowland, Kirstin Campbell and Grace O'Doherty, whose expertise helped me enormously in producing *Call to Action*. Thanks to Síofra Murphy for the wonderful design. A special thanks to everybody involved in editing the book, especially Ciara McNee and Emma O'Donoghue. Finally, I especially wish to thank my commissioning editors Emily Holly and Emily Lynch for their expert guidance and encouragement throughout.

STRAND 1
Rights and Responsibilities

Chapter 1   Human Dignity: The Basis for Human Rights   2

Chapter 2   Human Rights Instruments   56

Chapter 1 Human Dignity: The Basis for Human Rights

LESSON 1

What it means to be human

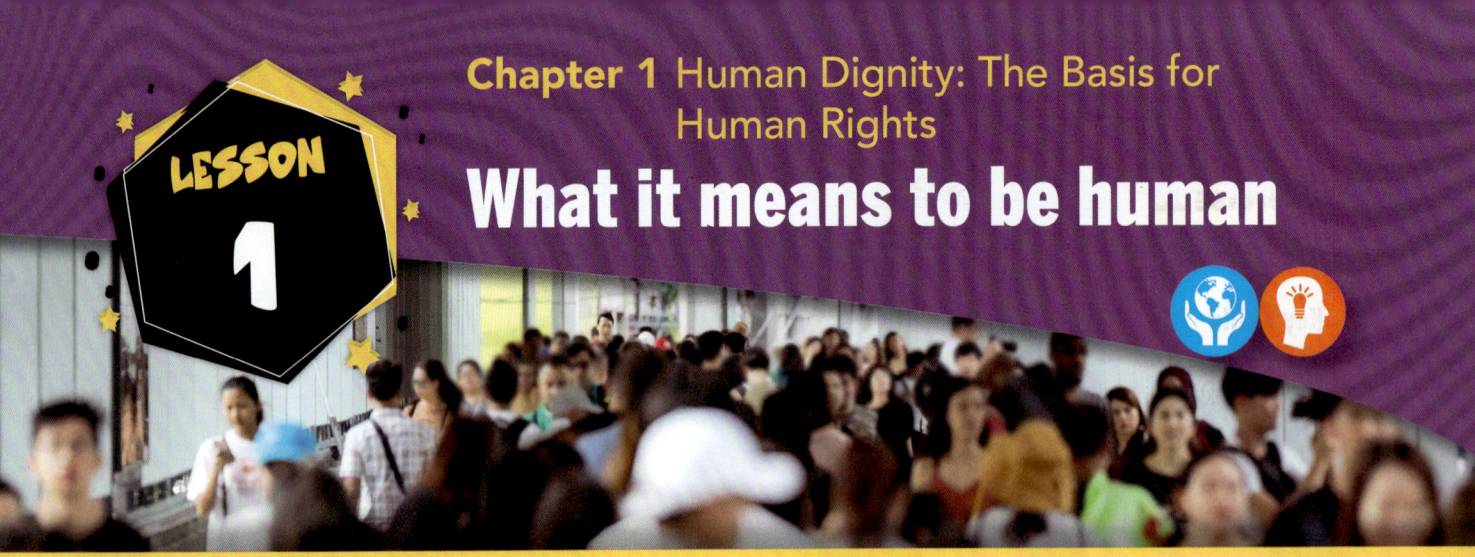

Learning outcome 1.1
Students should be able to discuss what it means to be human and to live in a community with rights and responsibilities.

According to the Oxford English Dictionary, a human being is a man, woman or child of the species Homo sapiens, distinguished from other animals by:

- having superior mental development
- being able to speak clearly
- and having upright stance.

Article 1 of the Universal Declaration of Human Rights says that:

> *All human beings are born free and equal in dignity and rights. They are endowed with reason and conscience and should act towards one another in a spirit of brotherhood.*

Exercise 1A — Understanding how human behaviours can be shared by other species

Key Skills **Success criteria** ☐ I can name similarities and differences between human and animal behaviour.

Working in pairs, discuss whether each of the following statements is true or false (you will probably have to guess some of the answers).

Statement	True	False
1. Human teeth are as strong as shark teeth.		
2. Humans are the only species that can blush.		
3. Only humans can paint pictures and explain what they have painted.		
4. Humans are the only creatures that can recognise themselves in a mirror.		
5. Only humans can make and use tools.		
6. Humans are the only animal that respond to being tickled.		
7. Humans are the animals with the longest childhood.		
8. Humans are the best animals at long-distance running.		
9. Humans are the only animals that understand fairness.		
10. Humans are the most advanced animal.		

2

Lesson 1: What it means to be human

Exercise 1B — Identifying whether words related to being human are positive, negative or neutral

Key Skills

Success criteria
- ☐ I can explain terms about humans in my own words.
- ☐ I can distinguish between positive, negative and neutral terms.

Working as a group, discuss the meanings of the following words and decide whether they are positive, negative or neutral terms.

Word	Meaning	Positive	Negative	Neutral
1. Humane				
2. Humanity				
3. Dehumanise				
4. Superhuman				
5. Humanitarian				
6. Non-human				
7. Human being				
8. Human nature				

Exercise 1C — Classifying human actions as beneficial or harmful

Key Skills

Success criteria
- ☐ I can explain why human actions are beneficial or harmful.

In the past, many people believed that the difference between animals and humans was that humans possessed **consciousness** (which means they are aware of what they do) whereas animals acted only from instinct. It has now been shown that all mammals, birds such as magpies and grey parrots, and other creatures, such as octopuses, are also capable of consciousness. While animals can have consciousness, human beings go one step further: we are conscious of our actions and also aware of the **impact** of those actions.

Octopuses are capable of consciousness.

Working in pairs, consider the actions on the next page and classify them as Beneficial, Harmful or It depends in the table below. Then, give a reason for each choice.

3

CALL TO ACTION | Chapter 1

| 1. Laugh and tell jokes | 2. Create medicines | 3. Plan wars |
| 4. Make tools and technology | 5. Practise a religion | 6. Participate in sporting events |

Action	Beneficial	Harmful	It depends	Reason for choice
1.				
2.				
3.				
4.				
5.				
6.				

Exercise 1D — Reflecting on my own actions

Key Skills

Success criteria ☐ I can link and explain my own actions to positive and negative things that happen in society.

Think about your own human actions and fill in the information below.

1. An action I have carried out recently

   _____

2. Something I would like to change about my actions

   _____

3. Something that angers me in society

   _____

4. Something I would like to change in society

   _____

Lesson 2: Human dignity

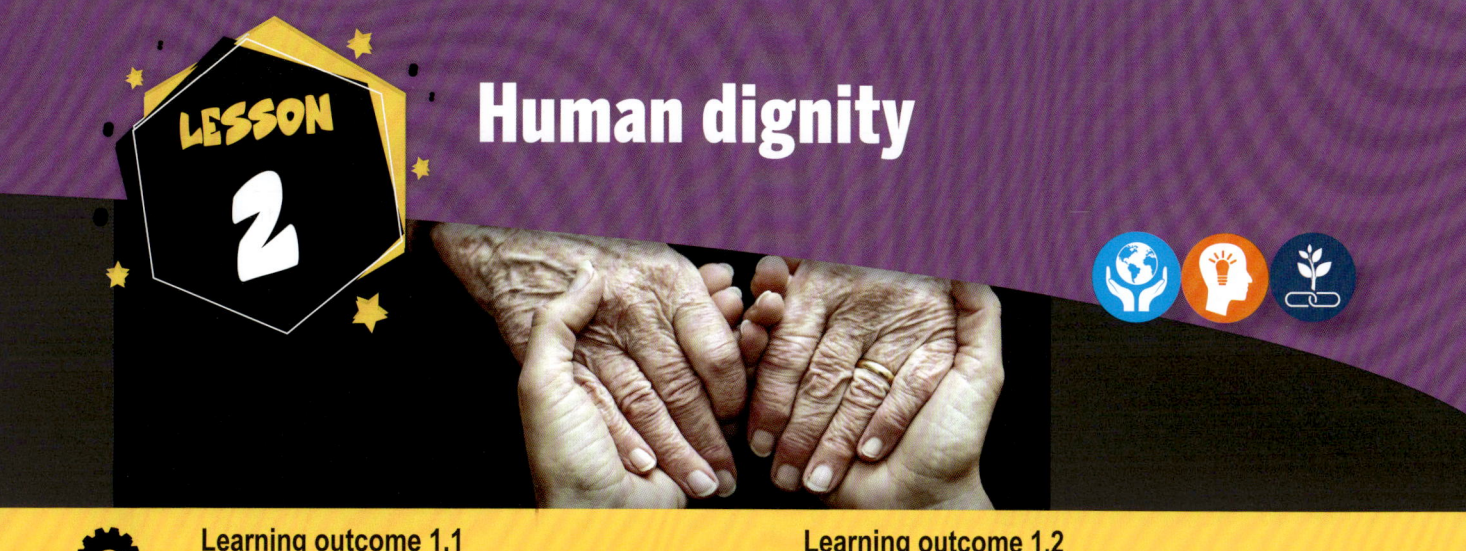

Learning outcome 1.1
Students should be able to discuss what it means to be human and to live in a community with rights and responsibilities.

Learning outcome 1.2
Students should be able to create a visual representation to communicate a situation where human dignity is not respected.

Exercise 2A — Identifying examples of human dignity not being respected

Key Skills

Success criteria  I can identify situations where human dignity is not respected, and explain how it is not respected.

Human dignity means that each person should be valued and respected as a human being. It involves treating all individuals with respect regardless of race, gender, religion, ability, social class or any other perceived difference. Having access to basic needs such as healthcare, food, water, safety and education is essential for human dignity. When these basic needs are not provided or are taken away, it leads to a loss of human dignity.

Working in pairs, look at the following photos. Find examples where human dignity is not being respected, explain in the table on the next page how it is not being respected and suggest how it could be respected.

1. A man searching for food in a rubbish bin

2. A burned-out Rohingya village, Myanmar 2017

3. An Irish primary school

4. Family separation at US/Mexico border

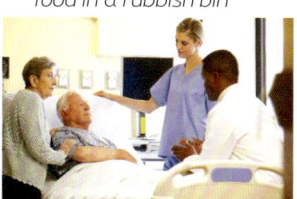
5. A patient receiving care in an Irish hospital

6. A homeless man in Dublin

7. Yazidis fleeing religious persecution from ISIS

8. A Hindu wedding

■ CALL TO ACTION | *Chapter 1*

Photo where human dignity is not respected	How it is not respected? How could it be respected?

Exercise 2B **Understanding words related to human rights**

Key Skills **Success criteria** ☐ I can identify words used when talking about human rights.

Human rights are the basic rights that a human being has, from birth to death, regardless of nationality, sex, ethnic origin, colour, religion, sexuality, language or any other status. There are five kinds of human rights:

1. Civil   2. Cultural   3. Economic   4. Political   5. Social

These rights include really important ones like the right to life as well as rights that make life better, such as working in a safe environment, education, healthcare, fair trial and asylum. Human rights are based on **human dignity**, **respect**, **fairness**, **equality** and **independence**.

Your teacher will show you one of the videos about human rights. In the box below, write the words used when referring to human rights.

Go to YouTube and search for:
1. 'The Story of Human Rights – Ultralized' (9:51)
2. 'Human rights in two minutes – Amnesty Switzerland' (2:33).

6

Lesson 2: Human dignity

Exercise 2C Understanding how people are often unaware that somebody's human dignity is not respected

Key Skills

Success criteria ☐ I can explain how others are often unaware when somebody's human dignity is not respected.

Read the extract from Sally's diary below and answer the questions that follow.

> Last Sunday I went into the city with Claire. She'd had a rough week and so we decided that we needed a little retail therapy. We got the 11.00 am train to town. When we got to the station, I saw a man by the ticket office with an empty yoghurt tub asking for spare change. I was going to throw him a euro, but Claire said not to as he'd only spend it on drink or drugs. Three hours later, €250 less in my bank account, a lunch to die for and feeling good I headed back to the station. The man who had been begging for money earlier was sitting on a bag by the door eating a sandwich and drinking a hot coffee. I bought a magazine for the journey home. There was an article about a woman working with street kids in South America and another about a movie star showing off her $22 million revamp of her mansion in Los Angeles. It was obscene, especially when $22 per month could take a child off the street and pay for them to be educated in Brazil. Maybe in the future I would like to go to help the street kids in South America.

1. What needs do the people in this passage have?	Sally and Claire	The homeless man
2. Were their needs met?	Sally and Claire	The homeless man

3. Can you suggest what Sally spent her money on?
   _____
   _____

4. Can you suggest what happened during the three hours for the homeless man?
   _____
   _____

5. In your opinion, what was Sally thinking at the end of this passage?
   _____
   _____

7

CALL TO ACTION | *Chapter 1*

Exercise 2D — Understanding stereotyping and its impact

Key Skills

Success criteria ☐ I can explain what stereotyping is, why it happens and how it makes me feel.

Stereotypes are when people believe that a particular person or group will look or behave in a certain way, just because of their age, sex, nationality or any other factor. For example, a common stereotype about Irish men in the past was that they were always drunk. Stereotypes can be positive as well as negative, such as the belief that women are kinder than men.

Discrimination is when a person or a group is treated unfairly based on race, age, religion, sex or other factors. An example would be a qualified person not getting a job because they were seen as being too old.

Prejudice is when a negative opinion is formed about a person or a group without knowing enough about them. It is not based on experience. For example, some think that people who are overweight are lazy. If people are prejudiced against a person or a group, they are more likely to have a negative attitude towards them, have a stereotypical view of them and discriminate against them.

Working as a group, choose three of the words below that are used to describe young people and answer the questions that follow.

| Responsible | Lazy | Untidy | Caring |
| Hardworking | Moody | Selfish | Loud |

	Word 1	Word 2	Word 3
1. Which people use this word to describe young people?			
2. Why do they use this word?			
3. Write how the use of this word makes you feel as a young person.			

LESSON 3 — Community

Learning outcome 1.1
Students should be able to discuss what it means to be human and to live in a community with rights and responsibilities.

Exercise 3A — Distinguishing between a community and a group

Key Skills

Success criteria ☐ I can explain whether or not a group of people is a community.

A group of people is simply a collection of individuals. However, in a **community** people share a common characteristic, interest, background or reason for being together. They also generally have a sense of responsibility to the community and its members. Examples of communities include a workplace or a sports club. While all communities are groups of people, not all groups of people are communities.

Classify the following into group or community and explain your decision.

People queueing for coffee	The local GAA club	People using the motorway
An orchestra	A book club	

Group	Community	Reason for your decision

9

■ CALL TO ACTION | *Chapter 1*

Exercise 3B — Identifying communities I belong to

Key Skills | **Success criteria** ☐ I can name communities I am a member of.

Communities can be:
- **Local**, which means they are only in your local area, for example, your village's local history society.
- **National**, which means the community can include the whole country. For example, Conradh na Gaeilge is an organisation that promotes the Irish language across the country.
- **Global**, which is a community that involves people from the whole world. For example, Amnesty International promotes human rights across the world.

Working in pairs, discuss the communities you are part of, then make a list of five of these. Tick whether the community is a local, national or global community. Decide which you enjoy the most and explain why.

Community	Local?	National?	Global?

Which I enjoy the most	
Why?	

Exercise 3C — Understanding different types of communities

Key Skills | **Success criteria** ☐ I can explain what a community is and what makes my class a community.

Schools are communities because they are composed of groups of people coming together with a specific purpose. Classes are also groups of people who come together for a specific purpose, such as to learn maths. This means a class is also a community.

1. What do you have in common with other members of your class community? _____

2. How do you contribute to your class community? _____

Lesson 3: Community

3. What responsibilities do you have to your class community? _____
   _____

4. How could you improve your class community? _____
   _____

Exercise 3D Designing a crest that identifies the main aspects of our class community

Key Skills **Success criteria** ☐ I can create a visual representation of the things that are important for our class community.

Working in groups, design three symbols and find two words that sum up the type of community you want your class to be.

Symbols		
Words		

Your teacher will write each group's symbols and words on the board. The two most common words will be selected to be used for a class crest and motto.

Working on your own, you will each create a class crest and motto using the symbols and words chosen to represent the class.

Lesson 4: Rights, wants and needs

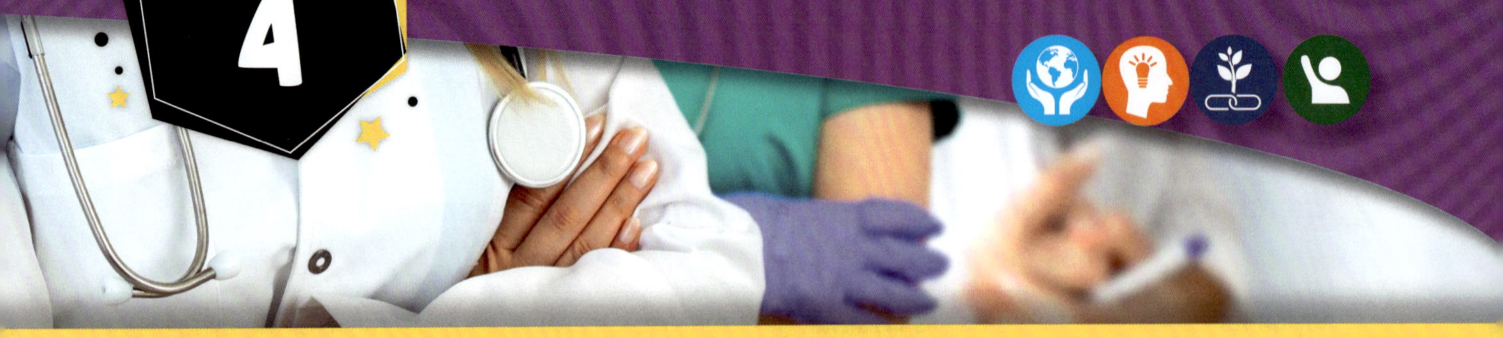

Learning outcome 1.3
Students should be able to explain the hierarchy of human needs and how this relates to human rights.

Exercise 4A Identifying the difference between a want and a need

Key Skills   **Success criteria**   ☐ I can explain the difference between a want and a need.

The difference between a **want** and a **need** is that wants are something you would like to have, but they are not essential for survival. A need is necessary for survival and is protected as **right**. Being safe is an example of a right because it is needed for survival. Getting a new bike is a want because it is nice to have but not needed to survive.

Look at the following pictures and classify them as needs or wants. Explain your decisions.

School

Netflix account

Healthcare

Fashionable clothes

Healthy food

Expressing opinions

Sun holiday

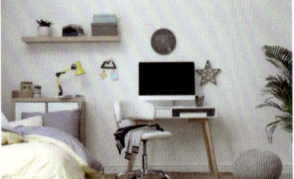
Own bedroom

Need: why?	Want: why?

Lesson 4: Rights, wants and needs

Exercise 4B — Identifying what I need to survive

Key Skills

Success criteria ☐ I can list key the main things I need in order to survive.

Working in pairs, decide on the five most important things you would need to survive. Once you have this done, rank them in order of importance by writing them into the spider diagram.

Things I need to survive

1.
2.
3.
4.
5.

Exercise 4C — Identifying three rights I need to survive

Key Skills

Success criteria ☐ I can name three rights essential for my survival and identify those who do not have them.

Answer the questions in the box below.

	Right 1	Right 2	Right 3
1. Name three human rights that you think every person needs to survive.			
2. Give examples of people who do not have these rights.			
3. Where do these people live?			

CALL TO ACTION | Chapter 1

Exercise 4D Identifying the impact of rights not being respected

Key Skills

Success criteria ☐ I can explain why rights must be protected, by giving examples of what happens when they are not.

Working in groups, read the stories below and fill in the grid that follows.

A.	My brothers go to the local school, but I am the only daughter. My family needs me to help out with work in our home, so I cannot go to school. I am seven years old.
B.	I am nine years old, and my family doesn't have much money. We live in two small rooms; we have to carry our water from a well a kilometre away. The houses in our village don't have indoor toilets, so we use a pit in the ground at the end of our street.
C.	I am 13 years old, and my country has been fighting over a border with another country for three years. A captain from the army came to my home to tell me that because I am big and strong, I should join the army and fight for my country.
D.	I am 10 years old, and I speak the language that my parents and grandparents and all my family have always spoken. In the local school, none of the teachers speak my language, and they don't allow me to speak it either – they say we must all learn how to speak their language.
E.	I started to work at a carpet factory for 12 hours a day when I was nine years old. Now I am 12 years old, and the factory wants me to work even more hours every day.

Source: *The Rights, Wants & Needs* Activity Kit, produced by the UNICEF Canada Global Classroom team

	A	B	C	D	E
1. Is a need (right) or a want denied in this story?					

2. Why was this right denied to the child?	
A	
B	
C	
D	
E	

3. How could this right be better protected?	
A	
B	
C	
D	
E	

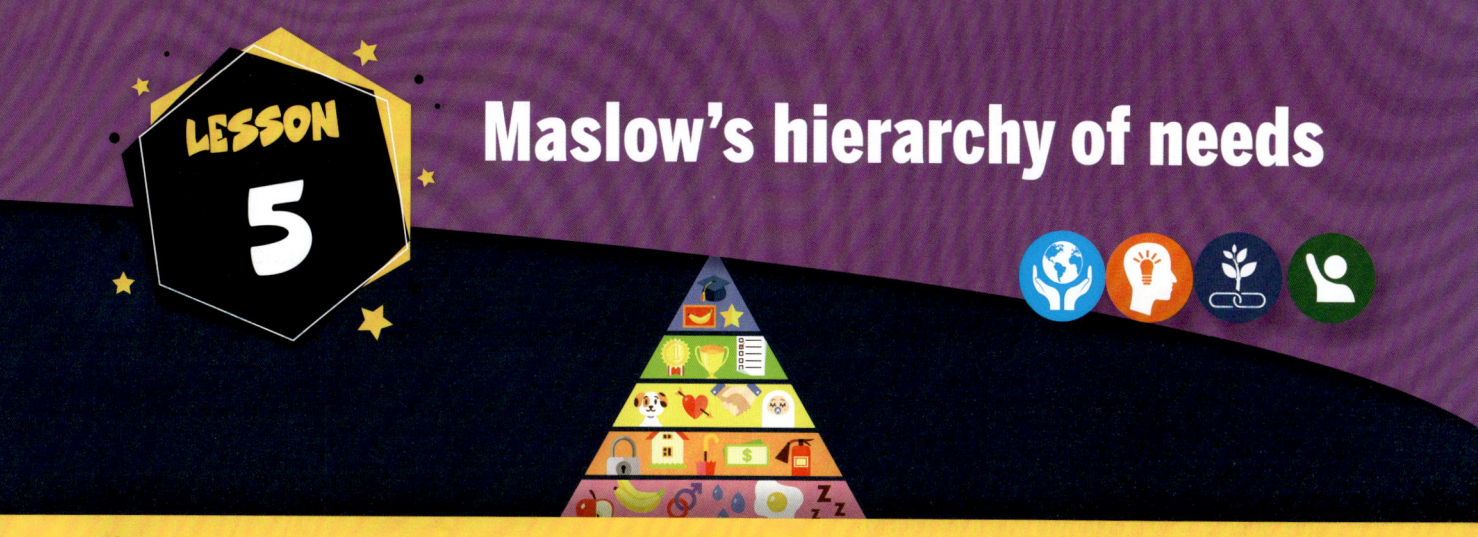

Lesson 5: Maslow's hierarchy of needs

Learning outcome 1.3
Students should be able to explain the hierarchy of human needs and how this relates to human rights.

Exercise 5A Classifying needs according to Maslow's hierarchy

Key Skills  **Success criteria** ☐ I can place needs in the correct category.

In 1943, **Abraham Maslow** wrote that, in order for people to meet their full potential, they must satisfy a series of needs. Maslow called this a **hierarchy of needs**. These are shown in the diagram. Maslow's hierarchy suggested that people need to fulfil basic needs (at the bottom of the pyramid), before moving on to more advanced needs, at the top of it.

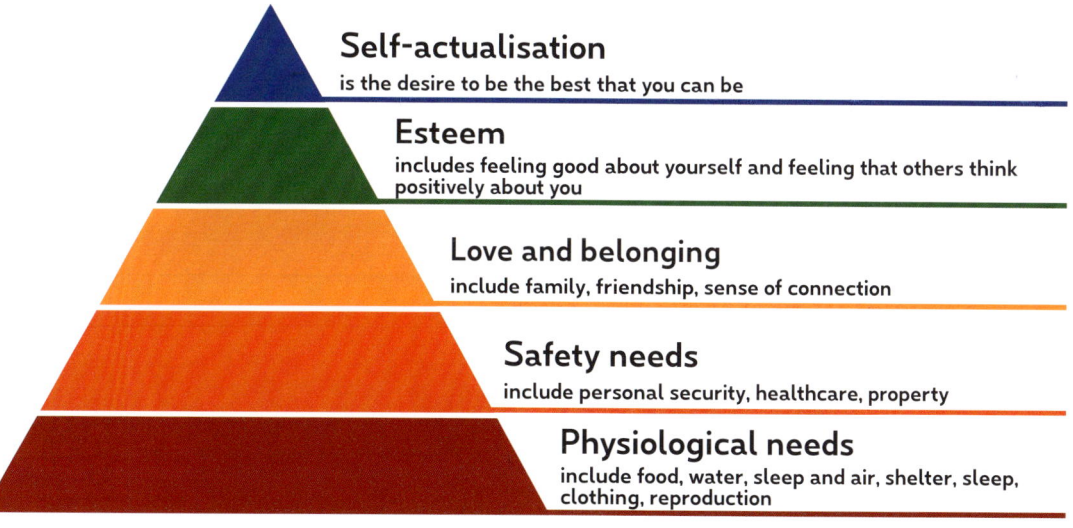

Self-actualisation is the desire to be the best that you can be

Esteem includes feeling good about yourself and feeling that others think positively about you

Love and belonging include family, friendship, sense of connection

Safety needs include personal security, healthcare, property

Physiological needs include food, water, sleep and air, shelter, sleep, clothing, reproduction

Look at Maslow's hierarchy of needs pyramid. Write the number of the statements beside the correct level.

Self-actualisation	
Esteem	
Love and belonging	
Safety	
Physiological	1

Statements

1. I bring my water bottle to class.
2. I meet my friends in school.
3. I am afraid walking home in the dark.
4. They are going to Conor's party and they haven't invited me.
5. I am running for the student council and I expect to win.

■ CALL TO ACTION | *Chapter 1*

Exercise 5B   Understanding the impact of not having basic needs met

Key Skills **Success criteria** ☐ I can give examples of the impact of not having basic needs met.

Read Michael's story and answer the questions that follow.

Michael is 36 and he lives in Dublin. He has a little girl, Sophie, who is eight and who lives with Michael's ex-partner. Michael is originally from Wexford and was a good student in school, but his father drank a lot and was violent, so Michael left school early to get a job and move out of the home. His father often called to his house looking for money, so Michael left Wexford and found a job in a factory in Dublin.

Michael met Ciara, Sophie's mother, shortly after arriving in Dublin and they were happy for a few years. But when they split up, Michael was very short of money. He moved into a tiny flat in a rundown part of the city. It was very old and poorly maintained, but it was cheap and was close to Ciara's house. It meant he could take Sophie to the local park at weekends.

Michael is always short of money, so he works long shifts. He used to play football with a few friends, but this was not suited to shift work, so he doesn't meet his friends anymore. Michael's flat has no central heating, but he wears warm clothes when it is cold.

Michael works in the warehouse at the factory. There is only one other person working with him, but this man is nearly retired and does not have the same interests as Michael. Michael never really has any dealings with his manager, beyond sending him a text of the hours he is available per week. Michael has a driving licence but had to sell his car because it was too costly. He walks the 40 minutes to work now. When he gets home, he is too tired to think of shopping or cooking so he gets a takeaway from the chip shop under his flat. Luckily, it is cheap. Michael likes reading and loves history. He would love to become a history teacher or work in a museum.

1. Which of Michael's needs from the hierarchy are being met?
   _____

2. Can you suggest ways in which his needs might be improved?
   _____
   _____

3. Do you think Michael's story is a common one?
   _____
   _____

4. How do you think Michael's needs not being met will affect his future? Why?
   _____
   _____

Exercise 5C   Identifying needs for a specific task

Key Skills **Success criteria** ☐ I will be able to list the needs required for a set task and place them on Maslow's hierarchy.

16

Lesson 5: Maslow's hierarchy of needs

As part of an effort to collect information on Mars, your class is being sent on a trip across the galaxy in a spaceship. The journey will take a year to complete. In the ship, you will be able to live as you would normally, but you will need to create a list of five things your group should bring on the journey. They should be a mix of different need types.

1. Write a list of the five items you would bring with you.

   _____
   _____
   _____
   _____
   _____

2. Now place these items on the hierarchy pyramid.

3. Are any of the categories fuller or emptier than others? Why do you think this is?

   _____
   _____

Exercise 5D Placing a home on Maslow's hierarchy

Key Skills   **Success criteria**   ☐   I can understand how having a home is an essential need.

Answer the following questions:

1. Note five needs that a person experiencing homelessness would have.

2. Place these needs on the hierarchy.

3. In which category of the hierarchy are the most needs? Why?

   _____
   _____

17

Lesson 6: My rights, wants and needs

Learning outcome 1.3
Students should be able to explain the hierarchy of human needs and how this relates to human rights.

Exercise 6A Classifying my wants and needs

Key Skills

Success criteria ☐ I can name my own wants and needs.

In the box below, list five needs and wants that you have. For each need, tick Yes if it is protected as a right and No if it is not. If you do not know, tick Not sure.

Needs	Is this need protected as a right?			Wants
	Yes	No	Not sure	

Exercise 6B Identifying my medium-term and long-term wants and needs

Key Skills

Success criteria ☐ I can name my medium-term and long-term wants and needs.

Think about your wants and needs for the future. In the box on the next page, note your needs for next year, and for when you leave school. Are there differences between the two sets of needs?

Lesson 6: My rights, wants and needs

My needs and wants in the next year	
Needs	Wants

My needs and wants when I leave school	
Needs	Wants

Is there a difference between your needs next year and when you leave school? Why/Why not?

_____

_____

Exercise 6C   Considering other wants and needs

Key Skills   **Success criteria**   ☐   I can identify other wants and needs.

Look at the photos below. How many of these would you like? Would you consider them a want or a need?

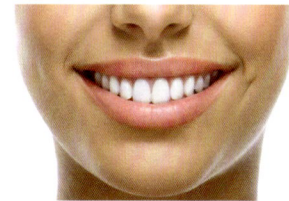

White teeth    *Branded sports gear*    *Sun holiday*    *Latest smartphone*

	White teeth	Branded sports gear	Sun holiday	Latest smartphone
1. Do you consider it a want or a need?				
2. If it is a want, are there cases where you could see it as a need?				
3. Are any of these items protected as a right?				

19

What is a home?

Learning outcome 1.1
Students should be able to discuss what it means to be human and to live in a community with rights and responsibilities.

Exercise 7A Creating a definition of home

| Key Skills | Success criteria | ☐ I can explain what a home is in two sentences. |

A **home** is a physical structure like a house or an apartment where a person or people live. It can be a permanent residence (where you live all the time) or a semi-permanent residence (where you live some of the time). A home is not just a building, it is also a place where a person feels safe and comfortable. Most people have a sense of belonging in a home. Homes differ hugely: they can be tiny apartments, boats, mansions, hotels or igloos.

In the box below, write all the words you can think of that describe what a home is. Then circle the ones that you think are the most important and use these to write two sentences explaining what a home is.

Home

A home is _____
_____
_____

20

Lesson 7: What is a home?

Exercise 7B Defining terms relating to home

Key Skills

Success criteria ☐ I can explain terms related to home and explain whether they have positive and negative meanings.

Explain the meaning of the expressions related to home. Is each term positive or negative?.

Expression	Meaning	Positive or negative?
1. Homework		
2. Home-school		
3. Homesick		
4. Make yourself at home		
5. Nursing home		

Exercise 7C Creating a picture of an ideal home

Key Skills

Success criteria ☐ I can identify the elements required for an ideal home.

Draw and label five things that you would find in the ideal home.

21

■ CALL TO ACTION | *Chapter 1*

Exercise 7D — Understanding statistics about families and what this means about Irish homes

Key Skills

Success criteria ☐ I will be able to explain census statistics and what they mean about Irish families.

Every five years, the government arranges for the Central Statistics Office (CSO) to carry out a **census** of the population. The census is a detailed count of every person in the country on a particular date. The census collects information about age, sex, occupation, religion and what type of accommodation people live in. This helps the government to plan for areas such as education. If the government knows that there are more young people living in a town than there are school places available, it can plan for new schools in that town.

Look at the infographic, which gives information about findings in the 2016 census. Then answer the questions below.

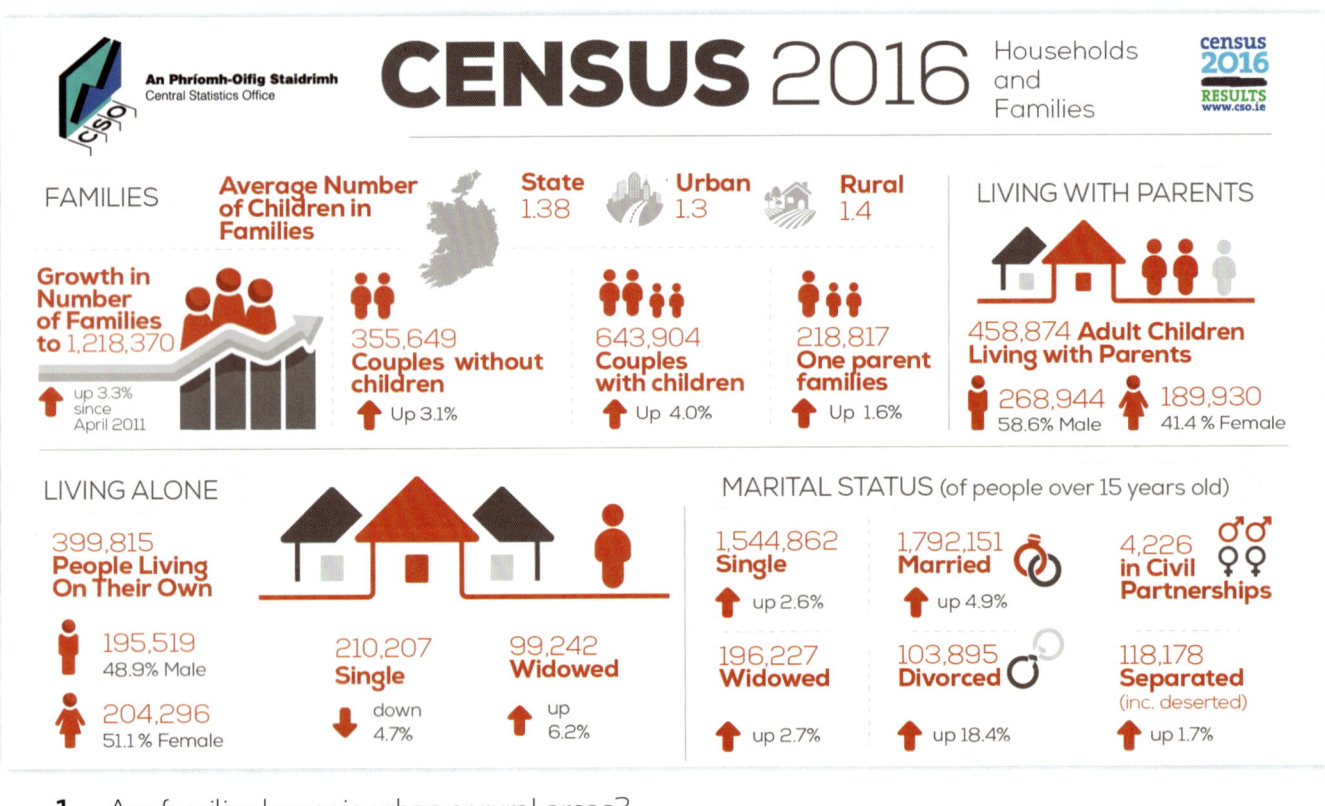

1. Are families larger in urban or rural areas?
   _____

2. Are adult children living with parents more likely to be male or female?
   _____

3. Do more men or women live alone?
   _____

4. What is the most common marital status?
   _____

5. What does all the information given in this lesson tell you about Irish homes?
   _____
   _____

Lesson 8: Human dignity of people without a home

Learning outcome 1.1

Students should be able to discuss what it means to be human and to live in a community with rights and responsibilities.

Exercise 8A — Identifying words I associate with homelessness

Key Skills

Success criteria ☐ I can identify some aspects of homelessness.

The Department of Housing, Local Government and Heritage must ensure that there is a supply of good-quality housing in the country. The Department's figures on homelessness are based on the number of people staying in emergency accommodation. According to homeless charity Focus Ireland, there are three types of homelessness:

1. The **visible homeless** are people who are sleeping rough or staying in emergency accommodation paid for by the State.

2. The **hidden homeless** are people sleeping in insecure accommodation, such as staying with friends.

3. The **at risk of homelessness** are people who have housing at the moment but risk losing it. They may no longer be able to afford to pay rent or they may be in State care and will soon be leaving it.

People lose their human dignity when they lose their home. Their basic human rights are not met, and this can cause them to lose their sense of self-identity and self-confidence.

In each box, write one word that comes to mind when you think of homelessness.

23

● CALL TO ACTION | *Chapter 1*

Exercise 8B   Identifying whether or not somebody is homeless

Key Skills   **Success criteria**   ☐ I can identify instances of homelessness.

People lose their home for different reasons.
- They lose their job or have to work reduced hours and can no longer afford to pay their rent or mortgage.
- The cost of childcare is so much that a parent must give up their job to mind the children.
- There is an unexpected cost such as medical care, a new boiler or paying for a car to be repaired.
- A member of the family becomes too ill to work or requires full-time care.
- The house is damaged and there is no home insurance to pay for the cost of repairs.
- A group of people are sharing a house and one person moves out, making the rent too costly for the others to afford.
- There is a shortage of accommodation in the area and a rent increase is too much to afford.
- A person moves to a new area to search for work but cannot afford to pay a deposit and rent until they start working.

Read the following situations and identify who is homeless.

Person	Homeless	Not homeless
Carla is 20 years old. She left home and moved to Galway when she was 17 and had a job and a flat. She was made redundant earlier this year and lost her flat because she could not keep up the rent. She is now staying with friends and sleeping on their sofa.		
Tom is 38. For the past few years, he has been drinking heavily and has not been able to hold down a job. He was not able to pay his mortgage and lost his house last year. Since then, he has been sleeping rough or staying in emergency accommodation.		
Martin is 45. His marriage broke down three years ago. Martin became depressed and was unable to work. Last year, his landlord asked Martin to leave his flat as he was behind in his rent. He is now living in a hostel.		
Erin is 17. She was living with her mother and her mother's partner, but she did not get along with her mother's partner. When she was 13, she was taken into care, and she has been in and out of different foster homes since. Next month she will turn 18.		
Mark is 15. His dad has been a wheelchair user since an accident and the family have been promised an adapted home. However, two years later, after various delays, they are still living in a single hotel room.		

Lesson 8: Human dignity of people without a home

Exercise 8C — Understanding how people can become homeless and how they can escape homelessness

Key Skills **Success criteria** ☐ I can name causes of, effects of and solutions to homelessness.

Read the following story and answer the questions below.

> My name is Conor, and I am 23. My grandmother brought me up and was really good to me. Her house was small but comfortable and I still remember the smell of her baking every day when I came in from school. Unfortunately, when I was 18 my grandmother died suddenly. She had not made a will, so her house was sold and the money divided amongst her six children. I had no family to stay with as nobody wanted me to move in with them. At first, I stayed with some friends I knew from school, but they were all living at home and their parents didn't want me there all the time. One summer's night, I had nowhere to stay so I slept out in the local park. After that, I started sleeping rough.
>
> It was frightening. I was always scared of being beaten up or attacked. I got very thin and lost all contact with my friends. Winter was the worst. Life outdoors was so cold that I moved to a homeless shelter. I was terrified there. I knew nobody and I was awake all night. A lot of the people in the hostel were drunk and I didn't feel safe. Since then, I made contact with a homeless charity, and they organised appointments for me with a doctor and a counsellor. For the past year, I have been living in an apartment owned by the charity. I have started an apprenticeship and, when I can earn enough money, I will rent my own apartment.

1. How did Conor become homeless?
   _____
   _____

2. In what ways did homelessness affect Conor?
   _____
   _____

3. When did his situation improve?
   _____

4. What problems do you think Conor may face in the future?
   _____
   _____
   _____

Exercise 8D — Considering the challenges for people who were homeless or in danger of homelessness

Key Skills **Success criteria** ☐ I can write about the challenges of people facing homelessness.

Several organisations work to help people without a home in Ireland. These include Focus Ireland, the Simon Community and the Peter McVerry Trust. These organisations advise people in danger of homelessness and support people who are homeless by providing emergency, temporary and long-term accommodation. They also help people by providing education and training and support with addiction issues. They advise vulnerable people on how to get social protection benefits and to set up bank accounts.

Watch the two videos from Focus Ireland and the Simon Community.

> Go to YouTube and search for:
> 1. 'Without Your Home Your Life Develops Differently' (0:41).
> 2. 'Unsilent Night – Dublin Simon Community' (1:00).

Imagine that you are one of the people in the adverts. Write a diary entry about your future plans.

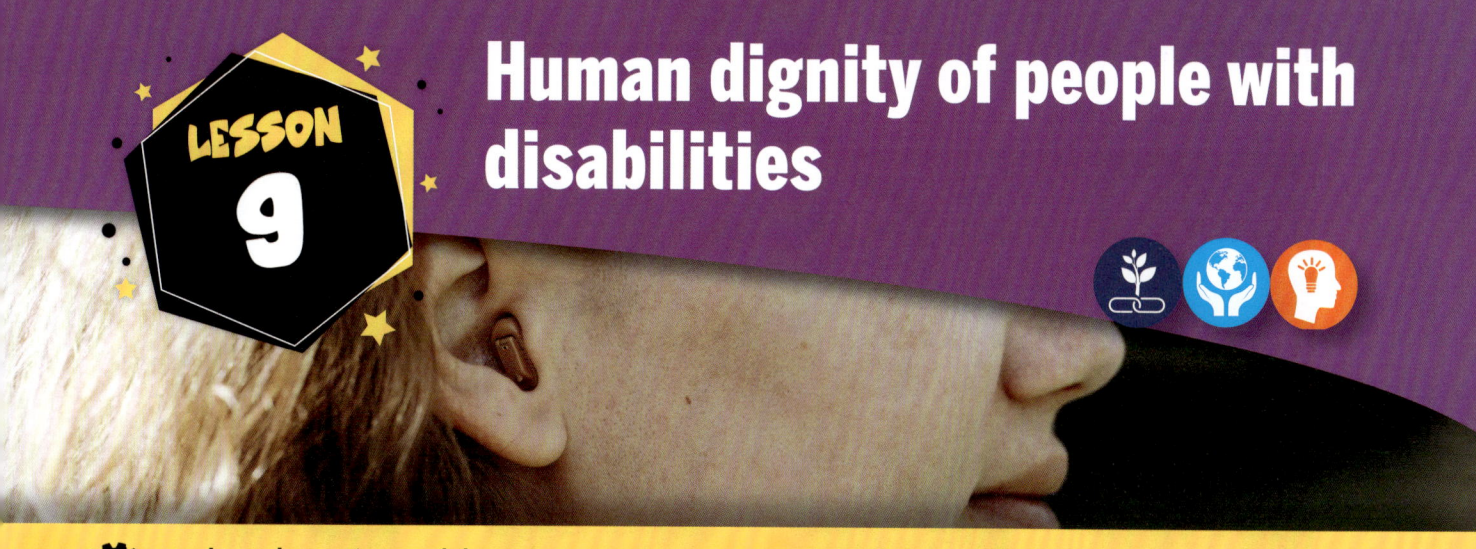

Lesson 9: Human dignity of people with disabilities

 **Learning outcome 1.1**
Students should be able to discuss what it means to be human and to live in a community with rights and responsibilities.

Learning outcome 1.3
Students should be able to explain the hierarchy of human needs and how this relates to human rights.

Exercise 9A Understanding how people with disabilities can achieve despite their disability

Key Skills **Success criteria** ☐ I can name people with disabilities who have achieved and explain their achievements.

A **disability** is a medical condition that can be:

- **Intellectual** – the person may have difficulties in communicating, in learning or with social skills, for example, Down syndrome
- **Developmental** – the person has a condition which causes physical, language or behavioural difficulties, for example, ADHD or cerebral palsy
- **Mental health** – the person's condition causes a behaviour that distresses them, for example, anxiety disorders or anorexia
- **Physical** – the person's condition prevents them being able to move the same as others, for example, wheelchair users
- **Sensory** – the person's disability affects the senses, for example, blindness and deafness.

Disabilities can restrict a person's ability to participate on an equal basis with others in social or cultural activities. With suitable services and aids, many people with disabilities can overcome these restrictions.

Look at the photos below and on the next page, and match the people with the names on the next page (search online for any you do not know). Then write the correct name in the biographies which follow.

1    2   3   4

27

CALL TO ACTION | Chapter 1

(a) Evelyn Glennie (b) Ludwig van Beethoven (c) Natalie du Toit (d) Anne Hegerty
(e) Samuel L. Jackson (f) Francisco Goya (g) Stephen Hawking (h) Andrea Bocelli
(i) Franklin D. Roosevelt (j) Izzy Keane (k) Francesca Martinez (l) Christy Brown

1	2	3	4	5	6	7	8	9	10	11	12

Biographies

(i) _____ (b. 1997) is a successful entrepreneur who has spina bifida. With her sister Ailbhe, she created a company that designs and sells colourful wheelchair covers in over 35 countries. Together they were named on Forbes 30 under 30 list of promising entrepreneurs in 2017 and won the 2021 EU Women Innovators Rising Star Award.

(ii) _____ (b. 1948) is an American film and television actor. In childhood, he had a speech impediment, which he conquered. He has won multiple awards throughout his career and has appeared in films and on television series and has released music.

(iii) _____ (1770–1827) was one of Germany's greatest composers. He had a severe hearing impairment, which made playing at concerts difficult. He was almost totally deaf when he composed his 9th Symphony.

(iv) _____ (1746–1828) was a Spanish painter and printmaker. At 46, an illness left him deaf. He went on to create the most famous Spanish art of the nineteenth century and inspired Picasso and Dali.

(v) _____ (1882–1945) was the longest-serving president of the United States. His New Deal helped pull the US economy out of depression in the 1930s. He also led the US through World War II. During his time as US president, he was unable to walk without assistance and in private he relied on a wheelchair.

(vi) _____ (b. 1958) is a star in *The Chase* television quiz show's UK and Australian versions. She also presents *Britain's Brightest Families* and has appeared on other television shows such as *I'm a Celebrity*. In 2007, she was diagnosed with Asperger's syndrome.

(vii) _____ (b. 1958) is a famous Italian opera tenor. He became blind after a football accident at the age of 12. He is world famous and has sold over 7 million records. His 2018 album *Sì* reached the number-one spot in the US and UK charts.

Lesson 9: Human dignity of people with disabilities

(viii) _____ (b. 1965) is a Scottish percussionist. She has been deaf since the age of 12. Despite this, she is a highly successful musician and often plays barefoot during her performances in order to feel the music through ground vibrations.

(ix) _____ (1942–2018) was a physicist and a mathematician. In 1988, he wrote *A Brief History of Time: From the Big Bang to Black Holes*. In 1979, he was appointed Lucasian Professor of Mathematics at Cambridge, a post held by Sir Isaac Newton 300 years earlier. He had Lou Gehrig's Disease, which meant he had to use a wheelchair and needed a computer to talk.

(x) _____ (b. 1978) is a stand-up comedian and actress who has cerebral palsy. She became the first female winner of the Daily Telegraph Open Mic Award at the Edinburgh Festival in 2000.

(xi) _____ (1932–1981) was an Irish writer who had cerebral palsy. His autobiography, *My Left Foot*, was an international bestseller, with a film of the same name winning Oscars. He also wrote poetry and novels, including *A Shadow on Summer*.

(xii) _____ (b. 1984) is a South African swimmer. At the age of 17, she was in a traffic accident and had to have her left leg amputated. She competed in the Paralympic Games in 2004, 2008 and 2012, the Commonwealth Games in 2002, 2006 and 2010 and in the Olympics in Beijing in 2008.

Exercise 9B — Understanding the impact of a disability

Key Skills   **Success criteria** ☐ I can tell if a comment about disability is true or false.

Working in pairs, discuss whether each of the following statements is true or false.

Statement	True	False
1. Wheelchairs are used only by people who cannot walk.		
2. Over 1 billion people in the world have some form of disability.		
3. People with disabilities work as politicians, engineers, doctors and teachers, as well as in many other professions.		
4. Public places, such as cinemas and restaurants, are easy for people who use wheelchairs to enjoy.		
5. It is impossible for people with disabilities to live on their own.		
6. Most disabilities are caused by accidents.		
7. People can become disabled at any point in their lives.		
8. People with disabilities are more likely to be unemployed than people without disabilities.		
9. In 2016, Irish people living with deafness or a severe hearing impairment were more likely to have a job than people living with any other disability.		
10. People with disabilities have no legal protection in access to services and employment in Ireland.		

CALL TO ACTION | *Chapter 1*

Exercise 9C — Identifying challenges associated with disabilities and how they differ in their impact

Key Skills

Success criteria ☐ I can give examples of how disabilities can limit people's lives and how these limitations can be overcome.

Divide into pairs. Your teacher will assign each pair a disability, such as blindness or cerebral palsy. Discuss whether, with your disability, you could do the activities listed below and, if not, what you would need to be able to do them. Write your answers below.

Can I?/Could I?	No, because	Yes, if
1. Dress myself without difficulties		
2. Read a book		
3. Travel by public transport without difficulties		
4. Travel on a plane without difficulties		
5. Paint a picture		
6. Cycle on a greenway		
7. Go on a hike		
8. Play the piano		
9. Play rugby for Ireland		
10. Use a computer		

Lesson 9: Human dignity of people with disabilities

Exercise 9D — Learning how disability impacts people's ability to work

Key Skills | **Success criteria**
☐ I can understand data represented on a bar chart and explain what types of disability are most likely to cause people to be unemployed.

Unfortunately, sometimes people with disabilities do not have their needs met. This results in a loss of human dignity. In the previous exercises, you saw how in some cases people can overcome their disability with proper assistance, but this is not always available.

Look at the chart below from the Central Statistics Office and answer the questions that follow.

Unemployment rates by type of disability, 2016

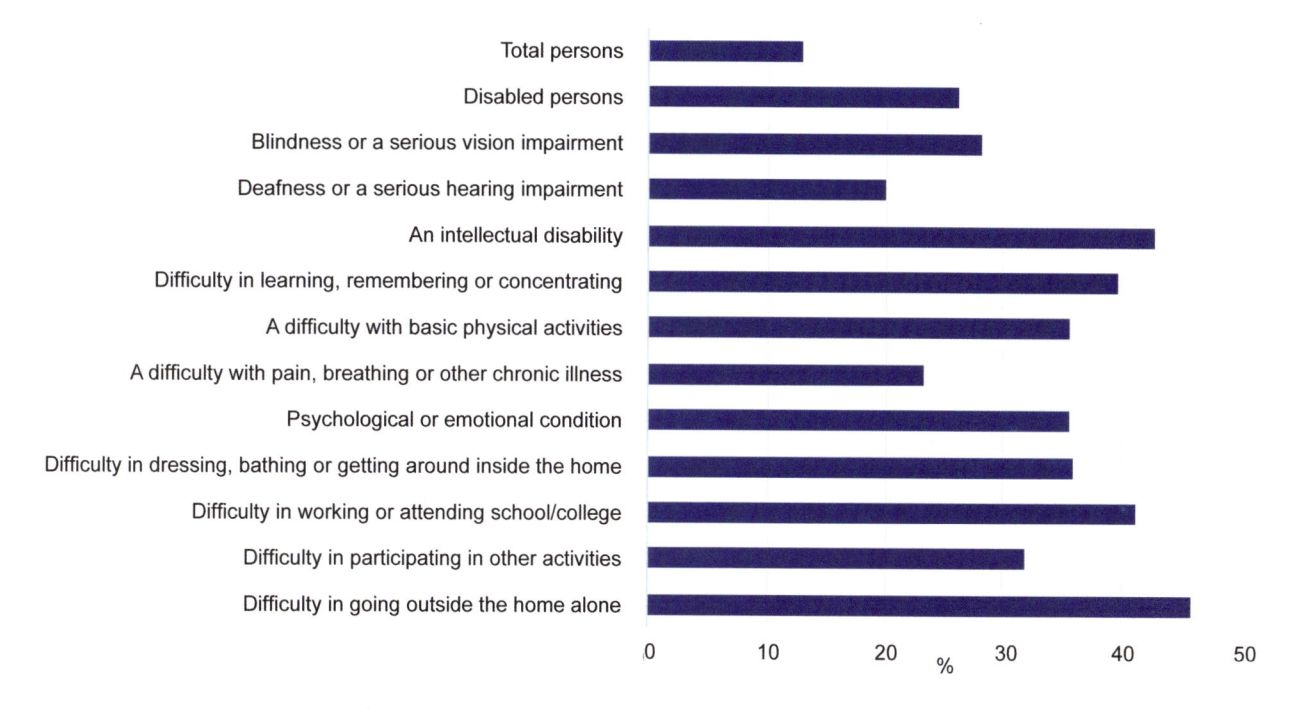

Category	%
Total persons	~13
Disabled persons	~26
Blindness or a serious vision impairment	~28
Deafness or a serious hearing impairment	~20
An intellectual disability	~42
Difficulty in learning, remembering or concentrating	~40
A difficulty with basic physical activities	~35
A difficulty with pain, breathing or other chronic illness	~23
Psychological or emotional condition	~35
Difficulty in dressing, bathing or getting around inside the home	~35
Difficulty in working or attending school/college	~41
Difficulty in participating in other activities	~31
Difficulty in going outside the home alone	~45

1. Which types of disability are most likely to lead to people being unemployed?

   _____
   _____

2. Which disability is least likely to lead to being unemployed?

   _____
   _____

3. Why do you think there are different rates of unemployment for each of these disabilities?

   _____
   _____

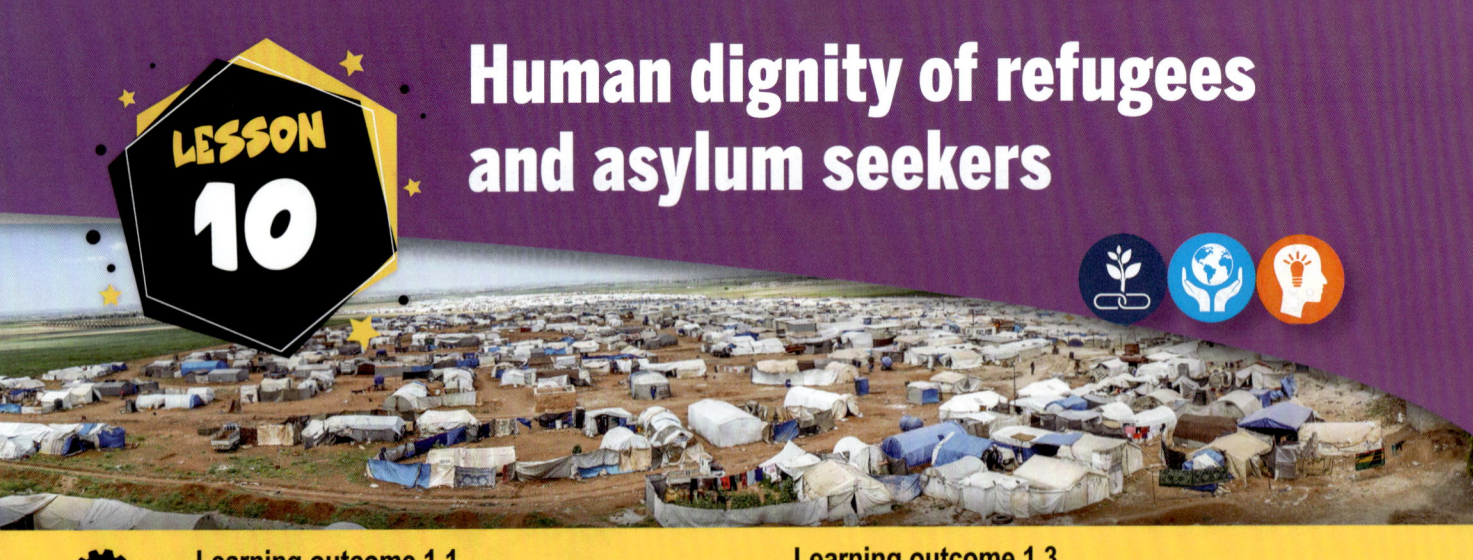

Lesson 10: Human dignity of refugees and asylum seekers

Learning outcome 1.1
Students should be able to discuss what it means to be human and to live in a community with rights and responsibilities.

Learning outcome 1.3
Students should be able to explain the hierarchy of human needs and how this relates to human rights.

Exercise 10A Understanding the push and pull factors that cause migration

Key Skills

Success criteria ☐ I can name factors responsible for pushing people to leave their home and factors that pull people to move to other places.

Human migration is when a person or a group of people move permanently or temporarily to live in another place. It can include movement from one country to another and movement within a country. People seeking asylum, refugees, displaced persons, economic migrants or people moving to be reunited with family are all examples of human migration (these terms are explained later on page **34**). Migration does not include travel such as commuting to work or tourism. In some cases, people choose to migrate, such as those looking for a job in another country, but in other cases people are forced to migrate, to escape war, for example. **Emigration** describes people leaving a country, whereas **immigration** is the term for when people move into a country.

Look at the following reasons for migrating and classify them into push factors or pull factors.

- Unemployment
- Environmental disasters
- Safety
- Educational opportunities
- Flooding
- Famine
- Religious persecution
- War
- Good housing
- A failing economy
- Food
- Fear of torture
- Healthcare
- A warm climate
- Ability to practise religion freely
- Fertile land
- Poverty
- Job opportunities

Push	Pull

Lesson 10: Human dignity of refugees and asylum seekers

Exercise 10B Developing my knowledge about refugees and asylum seekers

Key Skills   **Success criteria** ☐ I can identify facts about human migration.

Working in pairs, tick the correct answers in the quiz below (you will probably have to guess some of the answers).

Quiz

1. 67% of the world's asylum seekers come from how many countries?
   (a) 5 ☐   (b) 10 ☐   (c) 15 ☐   (d) 20 ☐

2. Which country below is one of the top five from which asylum seekers come?
   (a) China ☐   (b) Afghanistan ☐   (c) Namibia ☐   (d) Nauru ☐

3. The number of asylum seekers who arrived in Ireland in 2019 was:
   (a) 20,150 ☐   (b) 10,254 ☐   (c) 4,781 ☐   (d) 1,061 ☐

4. Most asylum seekers:
   (a) travel to European countries ☐
   (b) travel to North American countries ☐
   (c) travel to Australia ☐
   (d) travel to the nearest safe country ☐

5. A person who leaves their own country to get a better job is:
   (a) a refugee ☐
   (b) an internally displaced person ☐
   (c) an economic migrant ☐
   (d) an asylum seeker ☐

6. 4.5 million people were displaced abroad from which South American country between 2014 and 2019:
   (a) Brazil ☐   (b) Peru ☐   (c) Colombia ☐   (d) Venezuela ☐

7. Since 2017, 1.1 million people from which ethnic group have fled their homes in Myanmar?
   (a) Uighur ☐   (b) Tamil ☐   (c) Rohingya ☐   (d) Sikh ☐

8. What percentage of refugees are hosted by developing countries?
   (a) 20% ☐   (b) 45% ☐   (c) 72% ☐   (d) 85% ☐

9. The top three host countries for refugees are:
   (a) US, Germany and France ☐
   (b) Canada, UK and US ☐
   (c) Turkey, Pakistan and Lebanon ☐
   (d) Lebanon, Jordan and Israel ☐

10. What percentage of the world's population has been displaced?
    (a) 20% ☐   (b) 10% ☐   (c) 5% ☐   (d) 1% ☐

33

CALL TO ACTION | *Chapter 1*

Exercise 10C — Distinguishing between different types of migration

Key Skills **Success criteria** ☐ I can explain the differences between categories of migrant.

- According to the Geneva Convention, a **refugee** is someone who has applied for asylum in another country because they fear being persecuted due to their religion, race or political opinion. A person becomes a refugee when their request for asylum has been granted.
- An **asylum seeker** is someone who has applied for refugee status in another country because they fear they will be persecuted in their own country. Asylum seekers can remain in a country until their case for refugee status is decided. Since July 2018, asylum seekers in Ireland can apply for permission to work.
- Some asylum seekers do not meet the criteria for refugee status. Others spend years waiting for their application to be decided. Sometimes these people are given **leave to remain**.
- Sometimes people flee their homes but remain within the borders of their own country. These people are described as **internally displaced people**.
- Unlike asylum seekers, **legal immigrants** are granted visas because they have skills that are lacking in the country that they move to. An **illegal migrant** is somebody who does not have permission to live and work in a country. They do not make themselves known to the authorities in case they are deported.
- **Economic migrants** are people who move to another country to earn more money or to escape poverty.
- **Seasonal migrants** are people who move to another country for a short period of time to earn money doing seasonal jobs such as fruit picking.

Look at the explanations above, and classify the people according to the category.

1. My name is Rachel. I am from Ireland. However, I live and work in Boston. Two years ago, I applied for and was given a green card that allows me to legally work in America.
2. My name is Joyce. I am from Malawi. I applied for refugee status in Ireland but was refused. Since arriving in Ireland, I have been diagnosed with a serious illness. I applied for and got permission to stay here because I would not receive treatment for it at home.
3. My name is Georgi. I am from Bulgaria. I spend the harvest months in Ireland, away from my family. The pay I get in Ireland is much better than what I get at home.
4. My name is Efrem. I am from Eritrea. I looked for asylum when I arrived in Ireland. In Eritrea, anybody suspected of being against the government is put in prison and tortured or disappeared. At 18, all Eritreans must join the army for military service. I was allowed to remain here under the Geneva Convention.
5. My name is Paulo. I am from Brazil. My family and I moved to Ireland in search of a better quality of life. There are more jobs here and they are better paid. My children can also get a better education.
6. My name is Zoya and because of a civil war in Ethiopia my life was in danger. We had to leave our home in Tigray and cross the border to live with relatives of my mother in neighbouring Sudan. We have applied to become refugees.

7. My name is Rory. I am 24 and from Sligo. I have been working in construction in Chicago for the past two years. I came here on a holiday visa but stayed on afterwards. I hope I will not be caught because I could be deported.

8. My name is Martha. I am from South Sudan. I used to live in Yei in the south west of the country, but we were attacked by an armed group and are now living in a camp in Pibor in the east of the country.

What type of migrant is each person above?

1.	Legal immigrant	5.	
2.		6.	
3.		7.	
4.		8.	

Exercise 10D — Understanding how forced migration leads to a loss of human dignity

Key Skills — **Success criteria**: ☐ I can name challenges faced by people forced to migrate.

Watch the video and read the passage below from Oxfam Ireland. Then answer the questions that follow.

YouTube: Go to YouTube and search for 'From Beirut to Birr, Ireland: The journey of one Syrian family' (1:27).

Reema's story – a 12-year-old Syrian refugee in Lebanon

Posted by: Jane Beaseley

Reema (12) lives on the first floor of a house still under construction in Lebanon. There are piles of rubble and concrete all around. There are no windows, no comfort. She sleeps in a small 'room' with her parents and four siblings. Rats are frequent visitors. A year ago her home in Syria was destroyed by the bombings. In the time that followed she moved with her family from place to place, one of the 1.6 million Syrians who have fled their war-torn country in search of refuge in Lebanon, Jordan and further afield. By the end of the year, close to 3.5 million Syrians are expected to have fled. 'I used to enjoy writing before but since coming here, after this tragedy,' says Reema, 'I wake up in the morning and I see children going to school and I cry. Why don't I have the right to go to school and I sit here and I remember our home back in Syria before the fighting.'

'I don't want my photograph to be taken because I'm afraid that when we go back something might happen to us.' Reema (not her real name) has been writing moving poetry about her situation and desire to return to Syria.

A year ago it was destroyed by the bombings. Now she is one of 750,000 young Syrian refugees. 'I miss my friends,' she says, 'I miss my teachers. I miss my classes, my English classes, my Arabic classes, my music classes. Now I'm just sitting here every day.'

■ CALL TO ACTION | *Chapter 1*

1. What is life in Lebanon like for both these families?

2. Why does Reema not use her real name and not want her photo taken?

3. What does Reema miss about Syria?

4. What does the father in the video say are the benefits of living in Ireland?

5. Why are both these stories examples of how people lost their human dignity?

6. How did the family in the video regain their human dignity?

Lesson 11: Creating an infographic

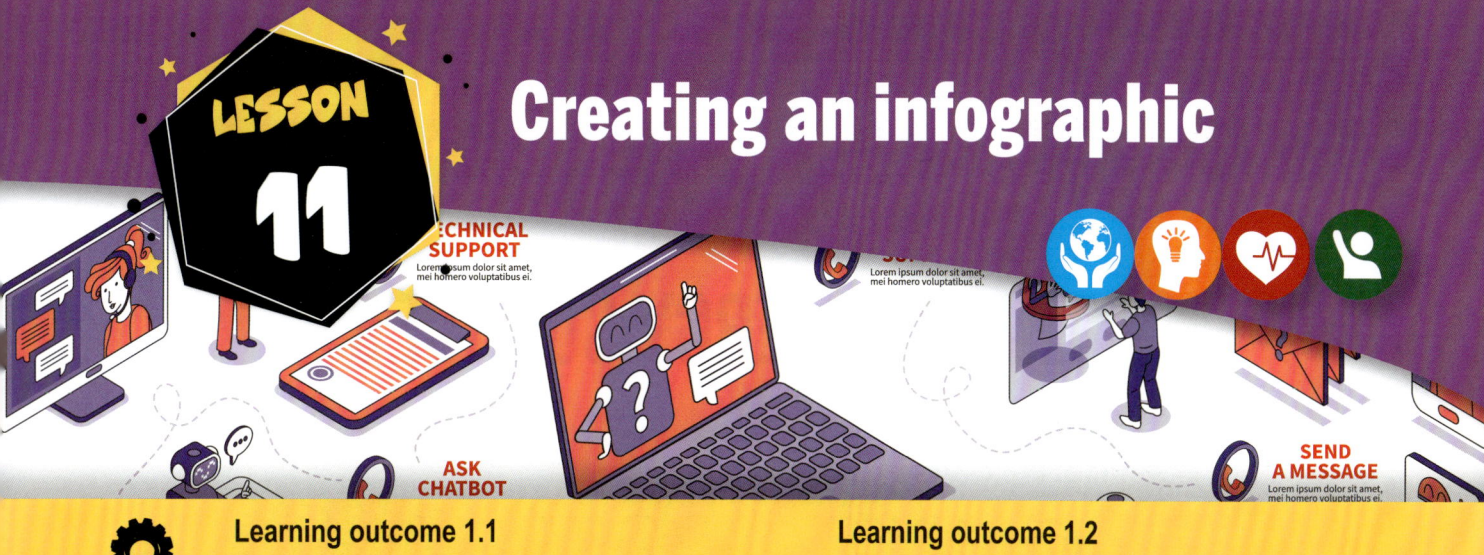

Learning outcome 1.1
Students should be able to discuss what it means to be human and to live in a community with rights and responsibilities.

Learning outcome 1.2
Students should be able to create a visual representation to communicate a situation where human dignity is not respected.

What is an infographic?

An **infographic** (short for information graphic) is information or data shown using pictures, data, maps, charts and a small amount of text. It is meant to sum up detailed information in a visual format that is easy to understand. An infographic makes information easier to explain. Good infographics attract people's attention and encourage people to read them. The infographic above was produced by the Central Statistics Office to show the impact of Covid-19 on people.

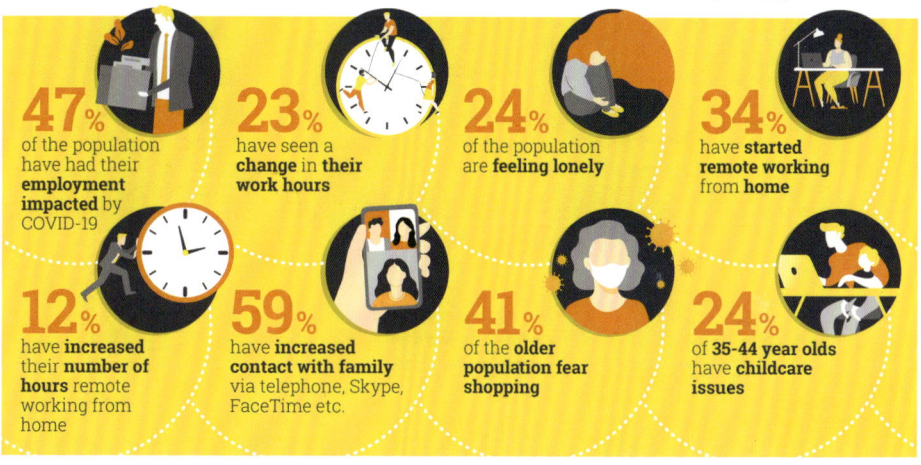

Why are infographics used?

Infographics are a very helpful way to:

- Share complicated information in a way that is easy to understand. For example, a government infographic could be used to explain the main findings of a census.
- Raise awareness about an issue. The human rights charity Amnesty produced this infographic to highlight the danger of guns as in the US city of Chicago.
- Promote a campaign on social media, as an infographic is more likely to be shared, read and understood than a report.

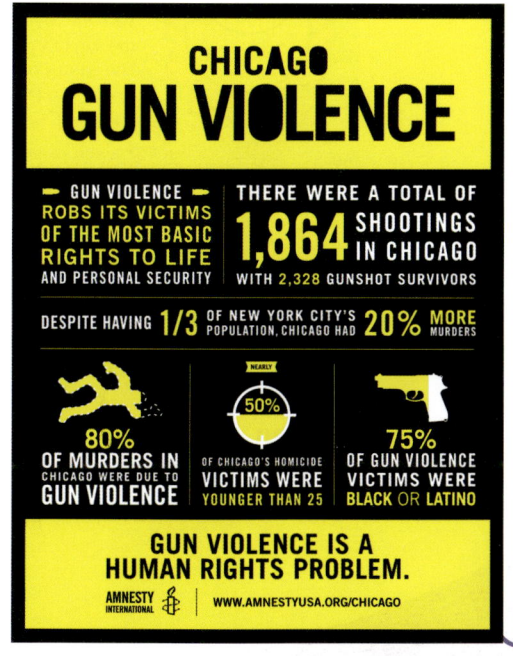

■ CALL TO ACTION | *Chapter 1*

- List reasons for doing or not doing something, for example, a public health campaign.
- Compare and contrast two or more different positions, such as the one below showing the differences between renewable and nonrenewable energy.

THE 10 ENERGY SOURCES

RENEWABLE
Fuels that can be easily made or replenished; we can never use up renewable fuels.

BIOMASS
Anything that is alive, or anything that was alive a short time ago is called biomass. Trees, crops, garbage, and animal waste are all biomass. Most of the biomass we use for energy today is wood.

GEOTHERMAL
Geothermal energy is heat from inside the Earth. The inside of the Earth is very hot. Sometimes this heat comes near the surface. We can use this heat to warm our houses. We can generate electricity with it.

HYDROPOWER
Hydropower is energy created by moving water. Moving water has a lot of energy. We use that energy to generate electricity.

SOLAR
The sun provides lots of energy to the Earth. We call it solar energy. It travels from the sun to the Earth in rays. The energy from the sun makes rain fall, wind blow, and plants grow.

WIND
Wind is moving air. We can use the energy in wind to do work.

NONRENEWABLE
Fuels that cannot be easily made or replenished; we can use up nonrenewable fuels.

COAL
Coal was formed millions to hundreds of millions of years ago from plants. Coal is often shiny, black rock. Coal is a fossil fuel that we burn for energy.*

NATURAL GAS
Natural gas is a mixture of gases you can't see, smell, or taste. We often add an odor to it so we can smell it. It has a lot of energy in it. You can burn it to make heat. Natural gas is a fossil fuel.*

PETROLEUM
Petroleum is a liquid that is found underground. Sometimes we call it oil. Oil can be as thick and black as tar or as thin as water. Petroleum is a fossil fuel* that has a lot of energy we release when we burn it.

PROPANE
Propane is the gas we use to fuel our backyard grills and operate machines in warehouses. You cannot see it, smell it, or taste it, but you can burn it to produce heat energy. Propane is fossil fuel.*

URANIUM
Uranium is a mineral found in rocks in the ground. We split uranium atoms to release energy in nuclear power plants.

*FOSSIL FUEL: Formed millions to hundreds of millions of years ago from the remains of living organisms. The plants and animals received their energy when they were alive from the sun. It was stored in them when they died.

NEED
Putting Energy into Education
www.NEED.org

Lesson 11: Creating an infographic

How do I create an infographic?

- Decide what you want people to learn from your infographic.
- Select a title.
- Consider the type of infographic style you will use, for example, lists, statistics, compare and contrast, timelines, process infographics (a series of numbered steps). Then select the information you want to include and how you will present it, for example,. in charts, pictures, or a mixture of both.
- Keep it simple and have a clear message. If it is too detailed, people will be less likely to read it.
- Use font and text colour that are easy to read.
- Consider the colours you will use. It is a good idea to contrast the colours to bring out the main information.
- Include your data sources, e.g. www.un.org.

Exercise 11A Identifying the key points I need to put in my infographic

Key Skills   **Success criteria**   ☐ I can gather key points and summarise them for my infographic.

You are going to produce an infographic to show how the human dignity of one of the groups you have studied – people without a home, people with disabilities or refugees – is not respected. In each of the lessons, you used or watched material such as statistics from the CSO or information provided by an **NGO** working with the people affected. An NGO is a non-governmental organisation, such as Oxfam or Trócaire, that works for a cause independently of governments. Research the information you need to create your infographic using these and other sources. In the box below, name your sources of information and note the key points you want to put in your infographic.

Name of source one	Name of source two	Name of source three

Key points I want to put in my infographic

CALL TO ACTION | Chapter 1

Exercise 11B — Identifying the data and pictures I want to use in my infographic

Key Skills

Success criteria ☐ I can gather suitable data and show it using charts and pictures to support my points.

Create or collect suitable charts and pictures to use in your infographic. Print them out and stick them in the box below.

Lesson 11: Creating an infographic

Exercise 11C Creating an infographic

Key Skills   **Success criteria**   ☐ I can create an infographic that communicates how the human dignity of people without a home/refugees/people with disabilities is not respected.

Your teacher will show you how to produce an infographic. Now create your infographic. Print it out and stick it in the box below.

Exercise 11D Promoting my infographic

Key Skills   **Success criteria**   ☐ I can make people aware of how human dignity is not respected by promoting my infographic.

With your teacher's help, promote your infographic. You could give a class presentation, put up posters, launch a social media campaign or send it to an NGO or to a government department.

41

Lesson 12: Inequality in Ireland

Learning outcome 1.4
Students should be able to access and interpret numerical data showing local and global distribution of basic resources and patterns of inequalities.

Exercise 12A Assessing my knowledge about inequality in Ireland

Key Skills

Success criteria ☐ I can identify the correct responses on inequality in Ireland.

Inequality is when money, property or other resources and opportunities are distributed unequally among different members of society. Some types of inequality include:

- **Income inequality**, which means there are large differences between the amount of money people earn for doing their job. Some rich people earn enormous incomes, whereas other people in poorly paid jobs might work very hard but receive only a tiny income in comparison.
- **Educational inequality**, which means that some people will have more education or a better education than others.
- **Gender inequality**, which means that a person will experience inequality because they are male or female.

Equality of opportunity means that everybody has an equal chance to do as well as others. Rich and powerful people and their families will not have an unfair advantage.

Working in pairs answer the following quiz on inequality (you will probably have to guess some of the answers).

Quiz

1. In 2019, which Irish counties formed the third richest area of the EU?
   - (a) Cavan, Monaghan and Donegal ☐
   - (b) Galway, Mayo and Roscommon ☐
   - (c) Waterford, Cork and Limerick ☐
   - (d) Dublin, Meath and Kildare ☐

2. In 2019, residents of which Irish counties were earning below the average EU income?
   - (a) Monaghan and Donegal ☐
   - (b) Kerry and Clare ☐
   - (c) Dublin and Kildare ☐
   - (d) Kilkenny and Carlow ☐

3. In which county are people most likely to have completed third-level education?
   - (a) Wexford ☐
   - (b) Wicklow ☐
   - (c) Cork ☐
   - (d) Dublin ☐

Quiz

Lesson 12: Inequality in Ireland

4. In which region did the most people leave school before the age of 15?
   - (a) Midlands ☐
   - (b) Border ☐
   - (c) South-east ☐
   - (d) South-west ☐

5. In 2019, what percentage of company chairpersons were male?
   - (a) 55% ☐
   - (b) 68% ☐
   - (c) 81% ☐
   - (d) 93% ☐

6. In 2018, the EU average for the number of women in parliament was 31.2%. What was the percentage of female members of the Dáil and Seanad?
   - (a) 10% ☐
   - (b) 22% ☐
   - (c) 28% ☐
   - (d) 38% ☐

7. In July 2021, how many of the 15 members of the Irish cabinet were women?
   - (a) 2 ☐
   - (b) 4 ☐
   - (c) 6 ☐
   - (d) 8 ☐

8. Which group experienced the highest rate of discrimination in Ireland in 2019?
   - (a) elderly people ☐
   - (b) LGBTI+ people ☐
   - (c) women ☐
   - (d) ethnic minorities ☐

9. In 2018, which age group earned the highest income in Ireland?
   - (a) 15-24 ☐
   - (b) 24-39 ☐
   - (c) 40-49 ☐
   - (d) 50-59 ☐

10. Which was the highest paid sector in 2018 in Ireland?
    - (a) food and accommodation ☐
    - (b) construction ☐
    - (c) ICT ☐
    - (d) education ☐

Exercise 12B — Analysing income inequality in Ireland

Key Skills

Success criteria ☐ I can explain figures about income inequality in Ireland.

Look at the video and answer the questions that follow.

Go to YouTube and search for 'Ireland's Great Wealth Divide poll – RTÉ One' (1:27).

1. How many people took part in this poll? _____
2. What percentage of the country's wealth did people think the wealthiest 20% owned? _____
3. What percentage of the country's wealth did people think the poorest 20% owned? _____
4. What is the actual percentage owned by the wealthiest 20%? _____
5. What is the actual percentage owned by the poorest 20%? _____
6. How much do the wealthiest 5% own? _____

■ CALL TO ACTION | *Chapter 1*

Exercise 12C Analysing statistics on income inequality

Key Skills

Success criteria ☐ I can understand income inequality in Ireland and other countries.

The Gini index is used to measure income inequality within countries. If a country has a score of 100 on the index, it means that all the income goes to just one person. On the other hand, if a country gets 0 it means that everyone gets an equal share of the country's income. So, a lower score on the Gini index means a country's income is shared in a fairer way.

Working in pairs, look at the chart below which shows the Gini index for six countries between 1995 and 2015. Then answer the questions that follow.

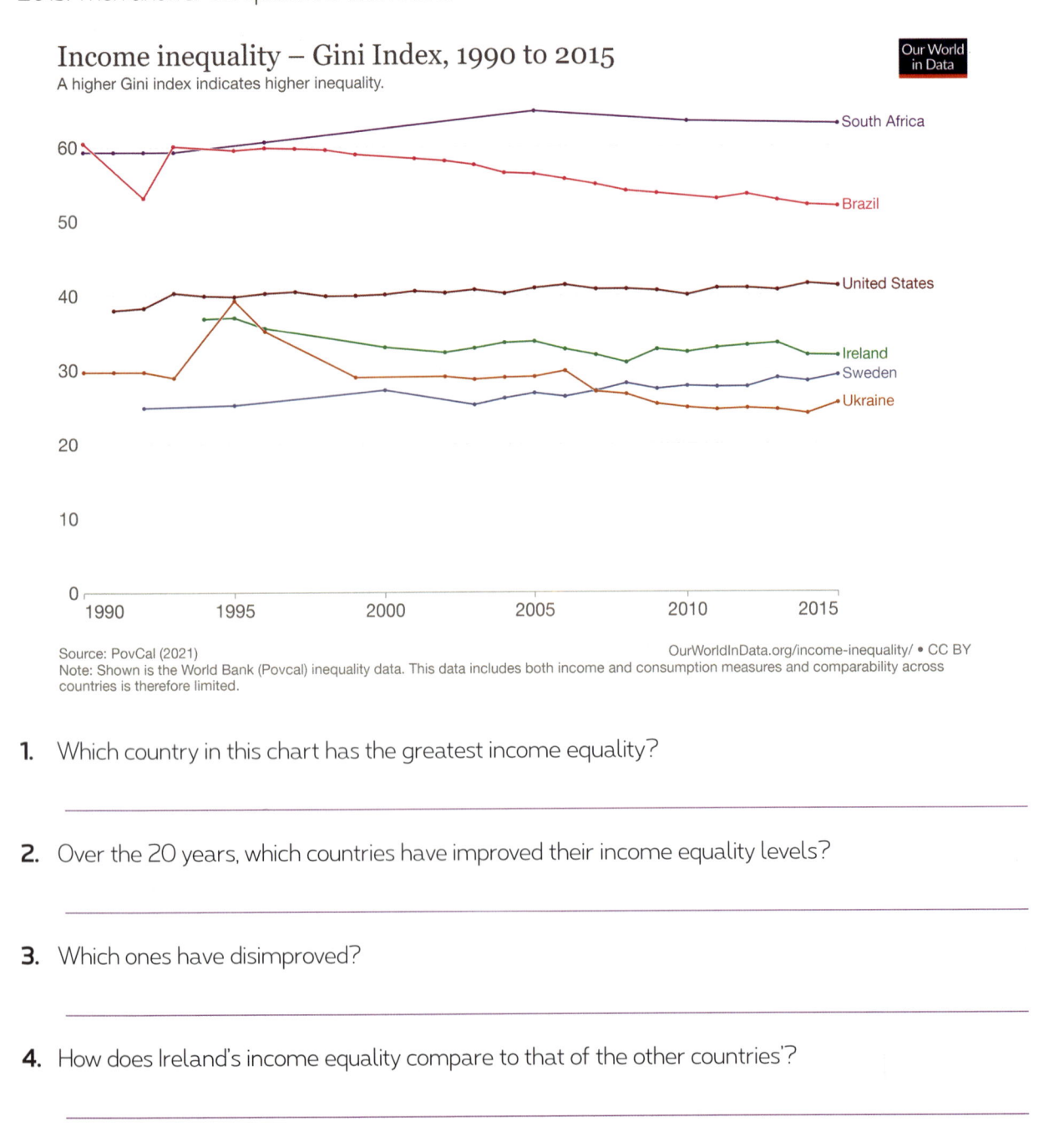

Income inequality – Gini Index, 1990 to 2015
A higher Gini index indicates higher inequality.

Our World in Data

- South Africa
- Brazil
- United States
- Ireland
- Sweden
- Ukraine

Source: PovCal (2021)
OurWorldInData.org/income-inequality/ • CC BY
Note: Shown is the World Bank (Povcal) inequality data. This data includes both income and consumption measures and comparability across countries is therefore limited.

1. Which country in this chart has the greatest income equality?

   _____

2. Over the 20 years, which countries have improved their income equality levels?

   _____

3. Which ones have disimproved?

   _____

4. How does Ireland's income equality compare to that of the other countries'?

   _____

Exercise 12D — Identifying organisations working for equality in Ireland

Key Skills

Success criteria ☐ I can identify organisations working to achieve equality in Ireland.

Working in pairs, look at the descriptions of organisations that work for equality in Ireland. Match the organisation with its description.

Description	Organisation
1. This organisation acts on issues that affect young people and tries to ensure that all young people can participate as active citizens on an equal basis.	(a) Age Action — Age Equality
2. This organisation supports policies and services that promote equality for older people.	(b) nWc — National Women's Council
3. This organisation campaigns and advocates for young LGBTI+ people to create a society in which they are equal, safe and valued.	(c) nYci — national youth council of ireland — COMHAIRLE NÁISIÚNTA NA NÓG
4. This organisation is made up of Travellers, Roma and members of the majority population working to achieve equality of outcomes and full human rights for Travellers and Roma.	(d) Irish Council for Civil Liberties
5. This organisation aims to achieve women's equality in Irish society by representing women's views in policies and by organising research to allow women to participate equally in society.	(e) belong to — Supporting LGBTI+ Young People in Ireland
6. This organisation aims to bring about equality for everyone in Ireland. They work with groups affected by inequality, including LGBTI+ people, Travellers, asylum seekers and people with disabilities.	(f) Pavee Point — Traveller and Roma Centre

1	2	3	4	5	6

■ CALL TO ACTION | *Chapter 1*

Exercise 12E — Analysing the impact of inequality on a person

Key Skills

Success criteria ☐ I can identify how unequal distribution of wealth can affect a person.

Read Mary's Story from a St Vincent de Paul case study and answer the questions that follow.

Case Study

Mary's Story

Mary is in her early 70s and lives alone in a local authority house just outside the small town centre. She receives the non-contributory pension (€237), the living alone allowance (€14) and fuel allowance (€24.50 per week during winter months). She has difficulty moving about easily, and her town has no public transport. She has an old petrol car which she uses to get to the supermarket and hospital appointments and to visit her grandchildren who live 45 km away. But she is worried it might break down as she couldn't afford for it to be fixed and she struggles to afford a tank of petrol. Her home is very old and poorly insulated, and the gas boiler is inefficient so she has to spend more than she should for energy. She has a large gas bill from March and April when the Covid restrictions were in place and she was at home more. Usually, in wintertime she has to rely on the open fire to keep her warm and on very cold nights she sleeps in the sitting room.

1. What is Mary's main need?

   _____
   _____

2. Why is Mary's situation harder than if she were a younger person?

   _____
   _____

3. What changes could be put in place to allow Mary enjoy life in a more equal way?

   _____
   _____
   _____

Lesson 13: Global inequalities

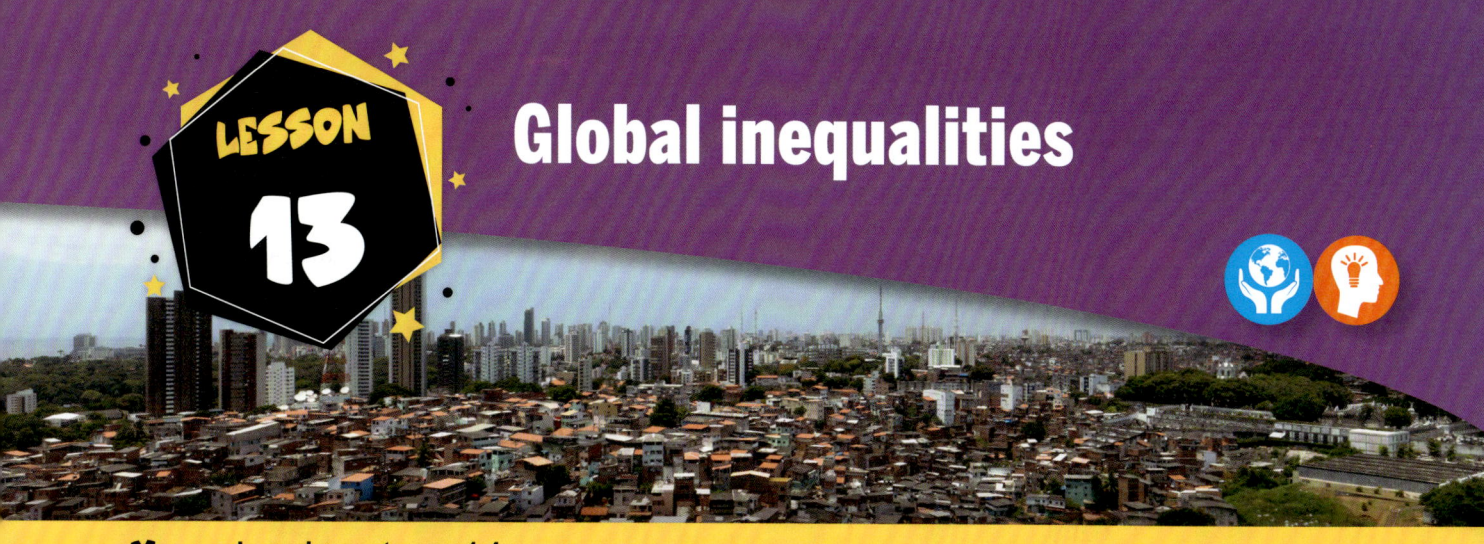

Learning outcome 1.4
Students should be able to access and interpret numerical data showing local and global distribution of basic resources and patterns of inequalities.

Exercise 13A Using statistics to identify differences between the Global North and the Global South

Key Skills

Success criteria ☐ I can name and explain differences between the Global North and Global South.

The terms '**Global North**' and '**Global South**' or 'developed countries' and 'developing countries' are often used when talking about global inequality. Countries in the Global North tend to be wealthy, more economically developed, with less inequality in how wealth is shared. Countries in the Global South tend to be poorer, have less developed economies, more inequalities in how the wealth is shared and are more recent democracies or are not democratic. Many of these countries are also former **colonies** of northern countries. A colony is an area controlled by another country. Many European countries had colonies in Africa, Asia, America and Oceania during the nineteenth and twentieth centuries.

A 2014 Oxfam report found that the richest 85 people in the world control the same amount of wealth as the poorest half of the world's population (almost 4 billion people). The population of the Global North is only about 25% of the total population of the world, yet it controls about 80% of global income.

The map shows the Global North countries in blue and the Global South countries in red.

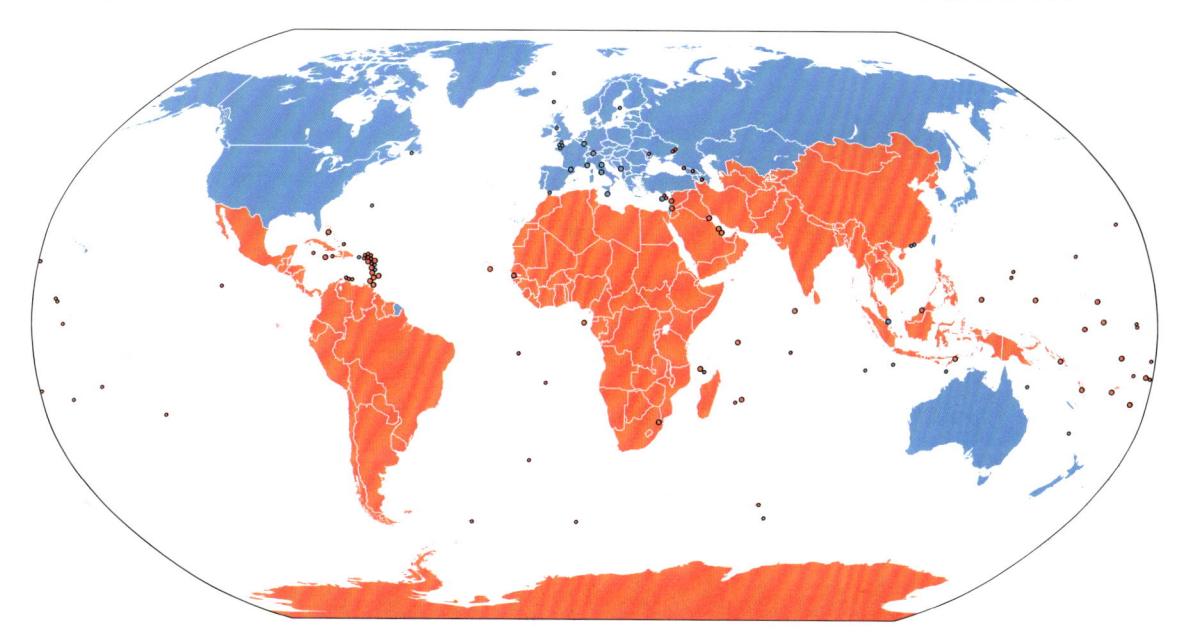

■ CALL TO ACTION | *Chapter 1*

Look at the statistics in the bar chart below and answer the questions that follow.

Bar chart: Proportion of the population
- Africa: 41% under 15, 3% over 65
- World: 26% under 15, 9% over 65
- Latin America, Caribbean: 24% under 15, 9% over 65
- Asia: 24% under 15, 9% over 65
- Oceania: 23% under 15, 12% over 65
- North America: 18% under 15, 17% over 65
- Europe: 16% under 15, 19% over 65

Legend: People under 15 years of age; People over 65 years of age

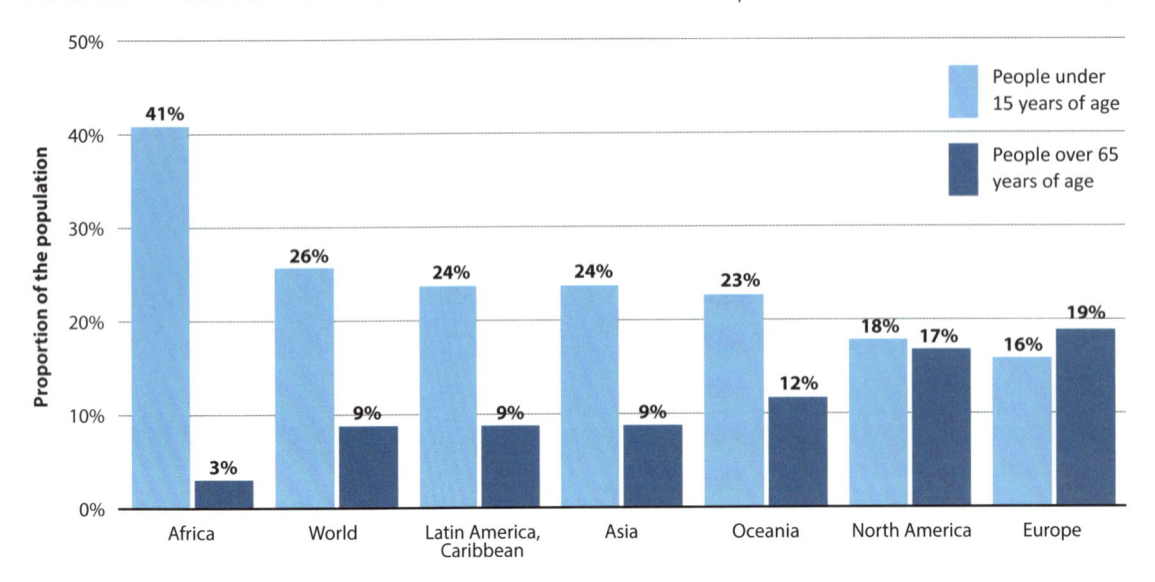

1. Which continent has the highest proportion of young people?

2. Is this continent in the Global North or Global South?

3. Which continent has the highest proportion of old people?

4. Is this continent in the Global North or Global South?

5. Which continent has the most equal balance between young and old?

6. Can you think of any consequence of the differences in population? List them.

Exercise 13B   Identifying differences within the Global North and Global South

Key Skills   **Success criteria**   ☐ I can name countries in the Global North and Global South that do not fit easily into the overall category.

Look at the maps on the next page and answer the questions that follow. The map on the left shows the countries with the highest income, with dark blue indicating the wealthiest. The map on the right shows countries' GDP (which measures the size of a country's economy) in relation to the world average GDP. The countries in blue have a GDP above the world average GDP and those in orange have a GDP that is below.

Lesson 13: Global inequalities

■ High income economies
■ Former high-income economies

■ Above world average GDP
■ Below world average GDP

1. What do you notice about the countries with the highest incomes?
   _____
   _____

2. Are any of these countries in the Global South? Explain your answer.
   _____
   _____

3. Write down the names of as many countries as you can identify in the Global South which have a GDP above the world average GDP.
   _____
   _____

Exercise 13C Identifying indicators of wealth in the Global North and Global South

Key Skills

Success criteria ☐ I can use statistics to show differences in wealth between Global North and South countries.

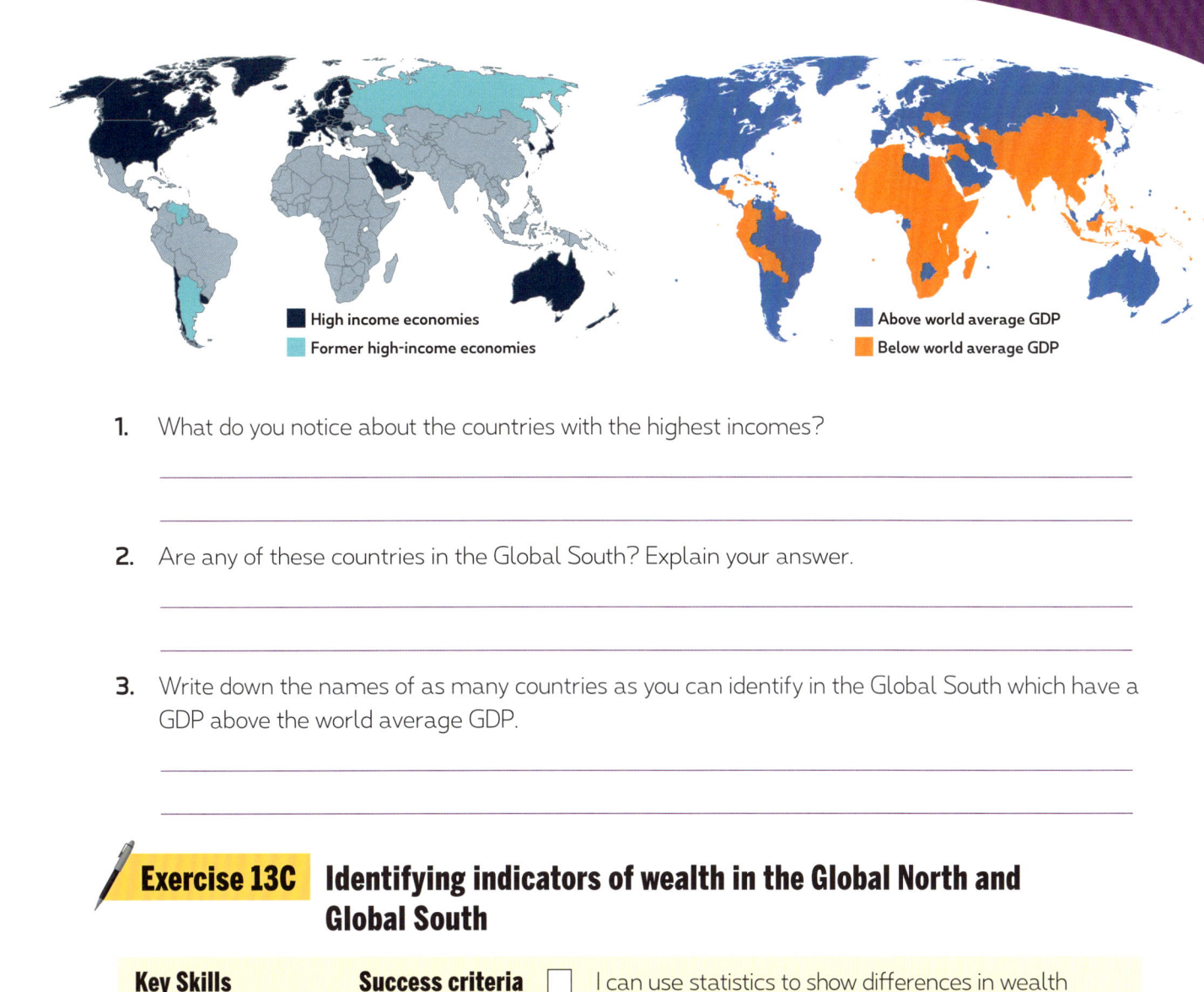

Read the article and answer the questions that follow.

The World's Richest and Poorest Countries 2021

Author: Luca Ventura

Would you rather be rich in a poor country or poor in a rich one? Measuring how rich you are depends to a large degree on how rich and poor countries are defined.

If we simply consider a nation's GDP, then we would have to conclude that the richest nations are exactly the ones with the largest GDP: United States, China, Japan, Germany. A problem with GDP is that it does not measure wealth distribution. That is why a more accurate representation of people's living conditions begins with dividing a nation's GDP by the number of people that live there. This is called per capita GDP but using per capita GDP still poses a problem: the very same income can buy very little in some countries and go much further in others where basic necessities – food, clothing, shelter, or healthcare – cost far less.

© Global Finance Media 2021

■ CALL TO ACTION | *Chapter 1*

Rank	Country	Per capita GDP in US dollars	Rank	Country	Per capita GDP in US dollars
1	Luxembourg	118,001	78	Botswana	16,893
2	Singapore	97,057	85	Brazil	14,916
3	Ireland	94,392	95	Ukraine	13,110
7	USA	63,416	98	Moldova	12,811
19	Germany	54,076	108	Kosovo	11,274
20	Australia	51,680	153	Papua New Guinea	3,833
28	UK	44,117	192	Somalia	925
53	Russia	27,903	193	South Sudan	791
64	Argentina	20,751	194	Burundi	760
77	China	17,192			

Source: International Monetary Fund, World Economic Outlook April 2021

1. Why is GDP per capita a useful way of telling how wealthy residents of a country are?

2. In what way does it not give the full picture?

3. Where does Ireland come on the list?

4. How does Ireland's GDP per capita compare to:
   (a) the US's
   (b) China's
   (c) Brazil's
   (d) Somalia's?

5. Are all the countries in the top 97 of the list in the Global North? If not, what Global South countries can you identify?

6. Are there any countries in the Global North in the bottom 97 of the list? If so, which ones?

Exercise 13D **Identifying the impact of inequality in the Global South**

Key Skills **Success criteria** ☐ I can name impacts of inequality in the Global South.

Read Madris's story and answer the questions below.

Madris's Story

Kenya has high levels of economic growth, but has a lot of social and economic inequality. Over one third of Kenyans live below the poverty line and 80 per cent of the country is very dry making it difficult to grow vegetation. Chronic malnutrition rates among children aged six to nine months stand at 26 per cent.

Madris Nginya is forty-three years old and lives with her children in the countryside near Iria-itune, a community south of Ishiara, Embu County, Kenya. Her home is small and basic, made of wooden poles and mud, with a corrugated iron roof. There are only two small rooms for her and her children and there is no running water or electricity. She and her family, like many in Kenya, are struggling to make ends meet, given the failed rains. As the planet warms, drought is becoming more frequent in the arid areas of this country. Madris can no longer depend on food or income from farming to survive. She has to rely on rearing chickens and goats and engaging in casual labour such as collecting and selling firewood. Without a steady income she struggles to feed her family and to pay their school fees.

Madris has been supported by Trócaire's local partner, Ishiara parish. This support has enabled her to learn new methods of zero-waste organic farming. She learns how to harvest rainwater, prepare sunken beds, use waste from animals to fertilise the crops and grow crops together that can maximise yields and keep the soil nourished in this harsh environment. She breeds chickens that supply her family with nutritious eggs and provide an income.

Madris has been supported to join a savings and loans group, which enables her to receive an additional income during the dry months and to get support and help from other women. For Madris, the support that she gets from the group goes beyond the economic impact. The group comes together to help each other in a communal spirit; for example, during times of planting and harvest, they will work together on each other's farms. They also sometimes help the elderly people in the village by bringing them firewood and water.

Source: The Development Education Team in Trócaire

1. What factors make Madris's life difficult?

    _____

2. From where has she received help?

    _____

3. What have been the benefits of this?

    _____

4. List two benefits of NGOs (private, not for profit, non-government owned organisation) getting involved in countries like Kenya.

    _____

5. List two disadvantages of NGOs getting involved in countries like Kenya.

    _____

6. Research the causes of inequalities in countries like Kenya.

    _____

    _____

Reflection: Reflecting on my learning about human dignity

Learning outcome 1.11

Students should be able to reflect on their ongoing learning and what it means for them.

Key Skills **Success criteria**

☐ I can give examples of the skills I use to show how I understand issues such as needs, wants, rights, discrimination and prejudice.

☐ I can give examples of how my thinking about human dignity has developed.

Look back at the skills and knowledge you have developed in this chapter. It is important to identify what you have learned and where you could learn more. Use the following worksheet to guide your reflection on human dignity. Then working in groups, discuss your responses to each of the questions.

1. Before looking at human dignity, I thought …	
2. Things I learned about human dignity	
3. Where I got my information from	
4. How I know the information was reliable	
5. The different types of sources I got my information from	
6. The most interesting thing I learned was …	
7. How the new information I have learned will change what I do	

Action: Organising a celebration of International Human Rights Day

International Human Rights Day is celebrated on **10 December** every year. This date was chosen because it was the day when the United Nations General Assembly adopted the Universal Declaration of Human Rights in 1948.

✓ Action 1 Producing a short video on what International Human Rights Day means for us

Key Skills

Success criteria ☐ I will create a video explaining what human rights mean for me.

Watch this video of South African students discussing what human rights means for them.

> **YouTube** Go to YouTube and search for 'Celebrating Human Rights Day University of the Free State' (4:10).

After watching the video, answer these questions.

1. Which comment about human rights did you find the most interesting?
   _____
   _____

2. Why?
   _____
   _____

Work in groups to discuss and decide what human rights means for your group. Think about how human rights issues have had a role in your life. Sum this up in a few sentences.

What human rights means for us
_____
_____
_____
_____
_____

Finally, record what human rights means for all of your group. Use the same format as the video you watched. Each group will do a recording and may speak as a group or as individuals. Once every group has recorded their video, all the recordings can be added together to create a film.

CALL TO ACTION | *Chapter 1*

✓ Action 2 — Creating a poster that raises awareness of human rights and our video

Key Skills

Success criteria ☐ I can produce a poster that informs people of International Human Rights Day and encourages them to mark it.

Design a poster to promote your International Human Rights Day video. Your poster must consist of a picture, a heading and some information on human rights and how to access your video. Fill in the grid below to plan your poster.

1. What heading will I use in my poster?	
2. What facts will I add to my poster?	
3. What picture or pictures will I use?	
4. What have we done that I want the poster to inform others about?	
5. Include a photo of your poster.	

54

✓ Action 3 Promoting our video

Key Skills **Success criteria** ☐ I can ensure that our video celebrating International Human Rights Day is seen by as many people as possible.

Working as a class group, decide the best means of promoting your video celebrating International Human Rights Day. This could involve showing it to other classes, launching it on the school website, organising a lunchtime screening or sharing it on social media.

In the box below, decide on the advantages and disadvantages of each method.

Advantages	Disadvantages
Presentation to classes	
Launching the video on the school website	
Lunchtime screenings	

Once you have that completed, discuss as a class the best method and what tasks need to be done to promote your video using that method. Organise committees to run and complete each task.

55

Lesson 14

Chapter 2 Human Rights Instruments
Human rights activists

Learning outcome 1.5
Students should be able to share stories of individuals or groups who inspire them because of their work for human rights.

A **human rights activist**, or defender, is a person who works on their own or as part of an organisation to protect human rights. Activists also make others aware when human rights are being threatened or not being respected. They can do this as a volunteer or as a paid employee of an organisation. In many countries, human rights activists are threatened, punished, imprisoned, tortured or even disappeared because they are seen as being a threat to the government.

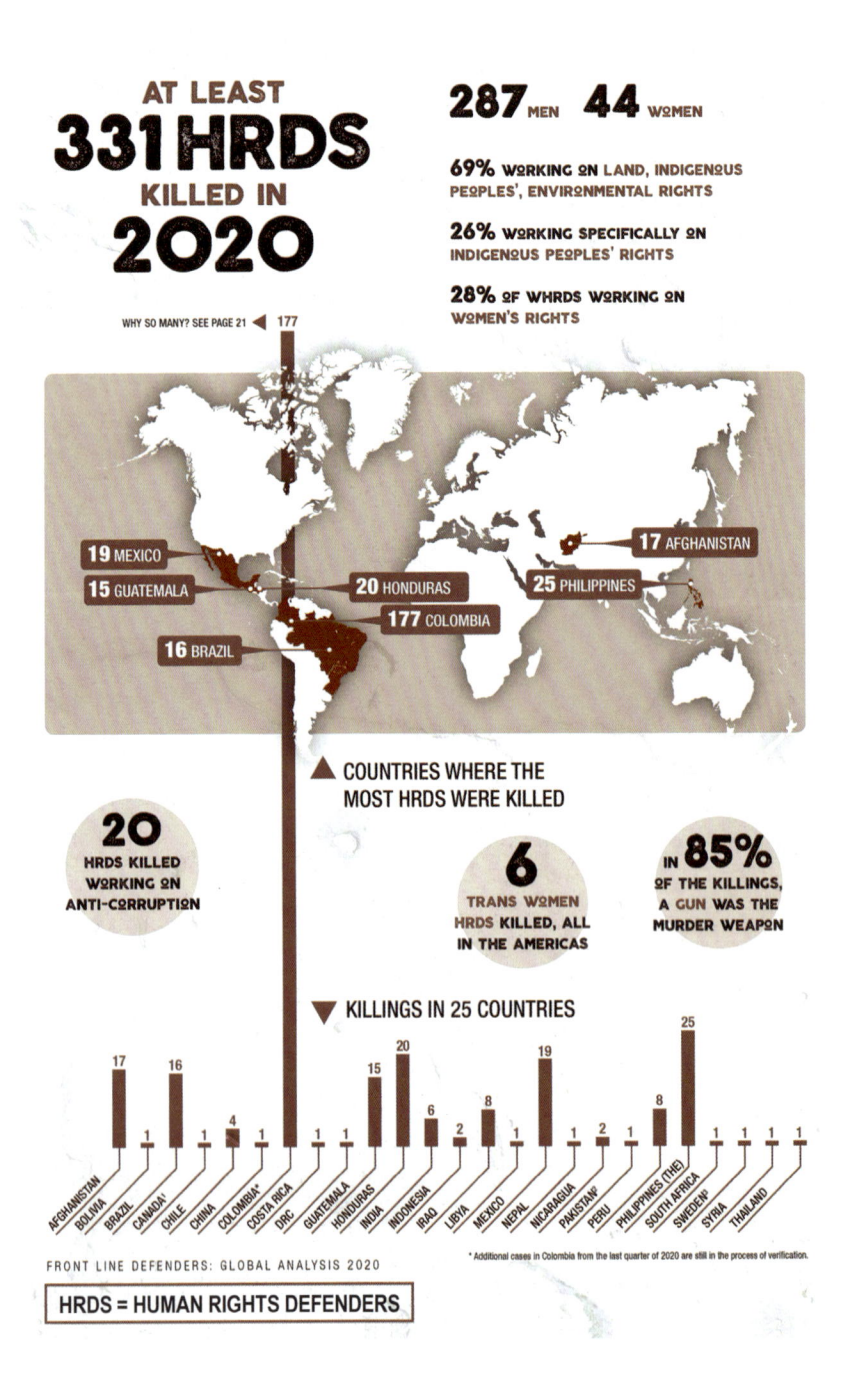

AT LEAST 331 HRDS KILLED IN 2020

287 MEN 44 WOMEN

69% WORKING ON LAND, INDIGENOUS PEOPLES', ENVIRONMENTAL RIGHTS

26% WORKING SPECIFICALLY ON INDIGENOUS PEOPLES' RIGHTS

28% OF WHRDS WORKING ON WOMEN'S RIGHTS

WHY SO MANY? SEE PAGE 21 ◀ 177

- 19 MEXICO
- 15 GUATEMALA
- 20 HONDURAS
- 177 COLOMBIA
- 16 BRAZIL
- 17 AFGHANISTAN
- 25 PHILIPPINES

▲ COUNTRIES WHERE THE MOST HRDS WERE KILLED

20 HRDS KILLED WORKING ON ANTI-CORRUPTION

6 TRANS WOMEN HRDS KILLED, ALL IN THE AMERICAS

IN **85%** OF THE KILLINGS, A GUN WAS THE MURDER WEAPON

▼ KILLINGS IN 25 COUNTRIES

AFGHANISTAN	17
BOLIVIA	1
BRAZIL	16
CANADA*	1
CHILE	1
CHINA	4
COLOMBIA*	1
COSTA RICA	1
DRC	1
GUATEMALA	15
HONDURAS	20
INDIA	6
INDONESIA	2
IRAQ	8
LIBYA	1
MEXICO	19
NEPAL	1
NICARAGUA	2
PAKISTAN	1
PERU	8
PHILIPPINES (THE)	25
SOUTH AFRICA	1
SWEDEN	1
SYRIA	1
THAILAND	1

FRONT LINE DEFENDERS: GLOBAL ANALYSIS 2020

* Additional cases in Colombia from the last quarter of 2020 are still in the process of verification.

HRDS = HUMAN RIGHTS DEFENDERS

Lesson 14: Human rights activists

Exercise 14A — Understanding the dangers of being a human rights activist

Key Skills **Success criteria** ☐ I can look at an infographic and give examples of the impact of being a human rights defender.

Look at the infographic from the organisation Frontline Defenders on the previous page and answer the questions below.

1. Which country is the most dangerous for human rights activists?
   _____

2. What cause were most human rights activists working for?
   _____

3. Does the inclusion or exclusion of any country on this list surprise you? Why/why not?
   _____
   _____

Exercise 14B — Understanding the range of human rights activism and the dangers involved

Key Skills **Success criteria** ☐ I can identify people with their human rights work.

Working in pairs, see if you can match each of these human rights activists with their biography.

A. Numan Afifi **B.** Vian Dakhil **C.** Raif Badawi **D.** Patrisse Cullors **E.** Malala Yousafzai

F. Shirin Ebadi  **G.** Befeqadu Hailu

Activist	1	2	3	4	5	6	7
Person							

1. This Saudi Arabian activist created a website about free speech and questioned practices such as women needing a male guardian to go out in public. In 2012, he was arrested for insulting Islam. In 2014, he was sentenced to 1,000 lashes and ten years in prison. In 2015, the first 50 lashes were carried out in public.

2. This Pakistani woman began writing a blog at the age of 11 and became famous for promoting education for girls. In 2012, the Taliban attempted to kill her, but she survived and the attack made her more famous. She won the Nobel Peace Prize in 2014 and now lives in the UK. She continues her activism and set up a fund that invests in education for girls.

3. This American woman set up Dignity and Power Now to fight for changes in law enforcement in Los Angeles in 2012. She succeeded in having a civilian oversight board introduced. In the same year, she and two friends founded Black Lives Matter. She created the #BlackLivesMatter hashtag in 2013. She believes in nonviolent direct action.

4. This human rights activist is a member of the Iraqi parliament and a member of a minority religion in Iraq, the Yazidis. During the Yazidi genocide at the hands of ISIS, she memorably pleaded for the Iraqi government to help stop her people being wiped out. Since then, she has worked to help return and rehabilitate Yazidi women who were kidnapped, held as slaves and forced to marry ISIS fighters.

5. This Ethiopian writer and blogger co-founded the Zone 9 bloggers group, which allows people to speak out against human rights abuses in Ethiopia. He was arrested in 2014 and has been imprisoned for his activities. He continues to write about human rights abuses.

6. This Iranian human rights activist was Iran's first female judge. After the Islamic Revolution in 1979, she was dismissed. She began to defend people who were being persecuted by the authorities. In 2000, she was imprisoned for criticising the government. She set up organisations and wrote books demanding better conditions for women and children. In 2003, she won the Nobel Peace Prize for her work.

7. This Malaysian man is an advocate for human rights for LGBTI+ people in Malaysia. He worked as a press aide for the Minister of Sports but was forced to resign because of his sexuality. He made a speech to the United Nations in Geneva about Malaysia's poor record on the human rights of LGBTI+ people. He faced police questioning because of this.

Exercise 14C Understanding how people become human rights activists

Key Skills   **Success criteria**   ☐ I can explain how people become effective human rights activists.

Ishmael Beah is a human rights activist from Sierra Leone. From the age of 13 to 16, Ishmael was forced to become a child soldier before eventually being rescued by UNICEF. In 1997, he moved to New York and in 2004 gained a degree in political science. Ishmael has spoken and written about his experiences as a child soldier, including how he was drugged and brainwashed. He was appointed as UNICEF's first Advocate for Children Affected by War in 2007. In the same year, he founded the Ishmael Beah Foundation, which is dedicated to reintegrating children affected by war into society and improving their lives.

YouTube
Go to YouTube and search for:
1. 'Ishmael Beah's Story: From Child Soldier to Human Rights Activist UNICEF USA' (3:04).
2. 'Mary Elmes: A silent hero' (1:53).

In 2013, Cork woman **Mary Elmes** (1908–2002) became the first Irish person honoured by Yad Vashem, the World Holocaust Remembrance Center, as **Righteous Among the Nations**. This award is given to non-Jewish people who risked their lives to save Jews during the Holocaust. Mary was recognised for her work saving Jewish children from the Nazi gas chambers during World War II.

Watch the videos about Ishmael Beah and Mary Elmes. Then answer the questions on the next page.

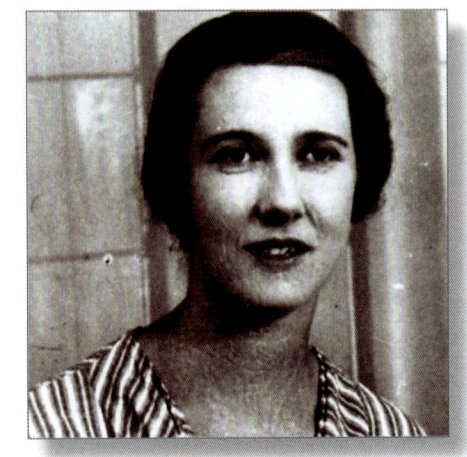

1. Do you think Ishmael is an effective human rights activist? Why/why not?

2. List three things you learn about the life of a child soldier from this piece.

3. In what ways is Mary Elmes like other human rights activists you have looked at?

4. In what ways is she different?

5. How might her story be different if it happened today?

Exercise 14D — Understanding how human rights issues are raised by politicians

Key Skills

Success criteria ☐ I can explain how human rights issues are raised in the Oireachtas and list the impacts of these.

Senator Eileen Flynn studied at Trinity College in Dublin and later earned a BA from NUI Maynooth. She has worked as an activist and community worker and campaigned on other issues such as marriage equality. In 2020, she was nominated to the Seanad by Taoiseach Micheál Martin, becoming the first Traveller to be a member of the Oireachtas.

Watch the video of Senator Flynn speaking in the Seanad and answer the questions that follow.

YouTube Go to YouTube and search for 'Senator Eileen Flynn – Travellers' Health & Human Rights' (1:53).

1. Why do you think Senator Flynn's speech is a helpful contribution regarding human rights?

2. What examples are given that would convince people to support her stance?

Lesson 15: Researching human rights activists

Learning outcome 1.5
Students should be able to share stories of individuals or groups who inspire them because of their work for human rights.

Exercise 15A — Researching a human rights activist

Key Skills

Success criteria ☐ I can find information about a human rights activist by researching NGO websites.

Choose a human rights activist that you are familiar with or that you have an interest in. You could consider people working with NGOs or full-time activists, journalists, academics, medical and science professionals, politicians or people with personal experience such as former prisoners or refugees. The following websites are useful to find out about human rights activists:

- www.amnesty.ie
- www.un.org
- www.hrw.org
- www.humanrights.com

AMNESTY INTERNATIONAL

Answer the following questions:

1. What country does this person live in?

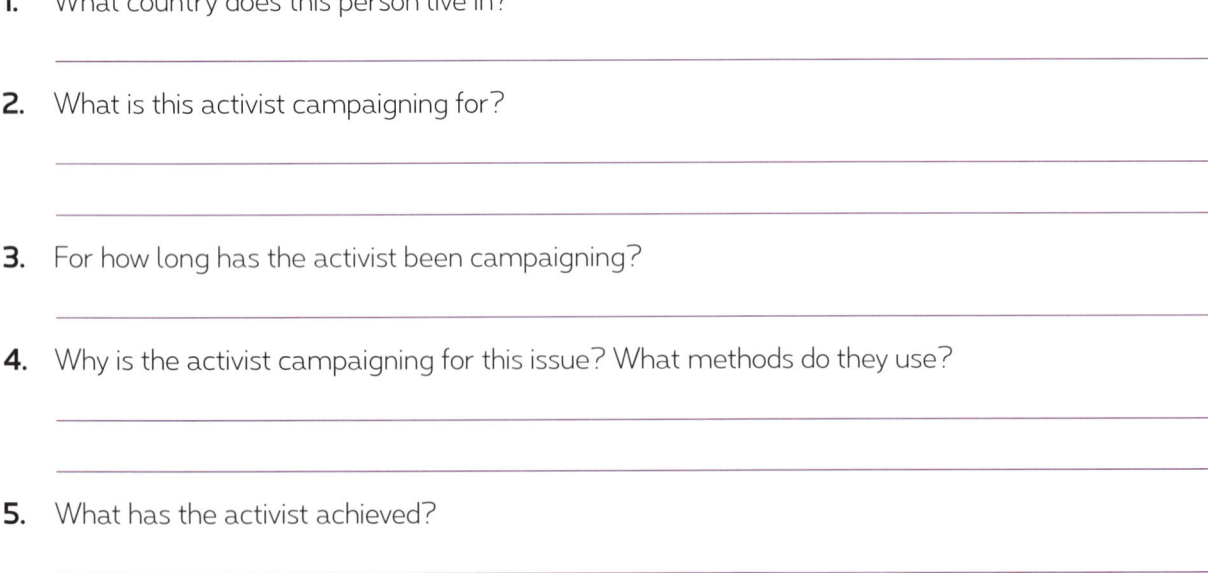

2. What is this activist campaigning for?

3. For how long has the activist been campaigning?

4. Why is the activist campaigning for this issue? What methods do they use?

5. What has the activist achieved?

Lesson 15: Researching human rights activists

6. Has the activist faced danger because of their activism?

7. Are you inspired by this activist? Why/why not?

8. List the websites you used for your research.

Exercise 15B — Researching a named human rights activist using news media

Key Skills

Success criteria ☐ I can identify the differences in how an activist is presented in the media and on NGO websites.

Continue your research into your chosen human rights activist by searching for this person in news media (TV news, newspapers, online news). Choose a number of different news websites, such as www.rte.ie/news, www.cnn.com, www.bbc.com/news, www.theguardian.co.uk or www.dailymail.co.uk, and answer the following questions.

1. Is there a difference in how this person is presented between different news media? If so, what is it?

2. Does this person use the media to raise awareness of their work or do they avoid media attention?

3. Did you come across any sensationalist (designed to cause a reaction like excitement or anger) stories involving this person? If so, what were they?

4. Do you think this activist is respected by the general population?

5. Has your opinion of this activist changed in any way as you researched the news media? Why/why not?

6. List the news sources you used for your research.

● CALL TO ACTION | *Chapter 2*

Exercise 15C — Researching a named human rights activist using video

Key Skills

Success criteria ☐ I can identify and name differences in how an activist is presented in videos and the different information such videos can give.

Continue your research into your chosen human rights activist by searching www.youtube.com for videos about them. You will probably find long documentaries and shorter pieces. The shorter pieces are generally good for a summary, but you may prefer to look at a longer documentary for more detail. Once you have finished watching the videos answer the following questions.

1. Did you learn anything different about this person from the videos? If so, what?

   _____
   _____

2. Was it an interview or a day-in-the-life-style video?

   _____

3. In what way was the video more useful for learning about the person than the other resources?

   _____

4. Was the video one-sided or did it give a fair account? Explain your answer.

   _____
   _____

5. Has your opinion of this activist changed in any way having watched the video? Why/why not?

   _____
   _____

6. List the videos you watched.

   _____
   _____

Exercise 15D — Creating a presentation on a human rights activist

Key Skills

Success criteria ☐ I can sum up the key facts and information about the activist's life and work and present it to the students in my class.

You are now ready to create your presentation on a human rights activist, using the notes you have researched. You can use either PowerPoint or create a poster. In either case, follow the headings in the box. Focus on the key points, so do not go into too much detail. For example, if you want to add an extract from one of the videos, use a short piece and only use it to show something that can be explained better by watching a video.

Lesson 15: Researching human rights activists

Name of activist	
Area the activist works in and the human rights they promote	
Early life/reason for becoming involved in this area	
Human rights that are not being respected	
How the activist has fought for the rights and the difference they have made	
The dangers of fighting for the rights	
Why I chose this person and what I think of them having researched them in greater detail	
Something that surprised me in my research	
The references I used	

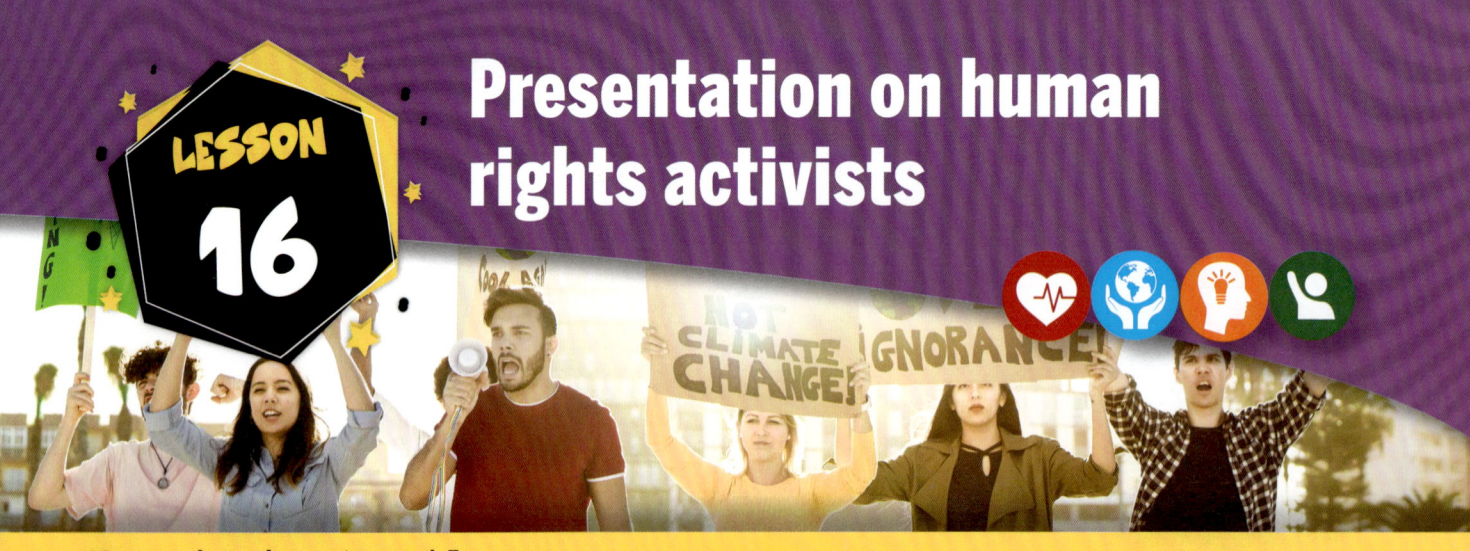

Lesson 16: Presentation on human rights activists

Learning outcome 1.5
Students should be able to share stories of individuals or groups who inspire them because of their work for human rights.

Exercise 16A — Reflecting on my presentation

Key Skills

Success criteria
☐ I can identify strengths and areas for improvement in my presentation.

In this lesson, you will make your presentation to the class. When preparing, remember the following:

- **Practise** the presentation before delivering it in front of the class. Begin by reading it aloud, then practise it while standing, then make the presentation to yourself in front of a mirror or to your family.
- **Keep a copy** of your presentation in front of you to help you, but refer to it only if you get stuck.
- Note the **pronunciation** of key words, spelling them phonetically in your notes, for example, Uyghur is pronounced *oy guh*.
- **Speak slowly**. Sometimes people rush a presentation and the audience cannot understand them.
- Allow **time for questions** at the end of the presentation.

64

Lesson 16: Presentation on human rights activists

After you have given your presentation, complete the following reflection:

1. Overall, how do I feel my presentation went?
   _____

2. What went well? How do I know?
   _____
   _____

3. What would I do differently the next time?
   _____
   _____

4. Were there any very difficult questions? If so, was I happy with the answers I gave? If I was not happy with my answers, how would I answer them now?
   _____
   _____
   _____
   _____

Exercise 16B — Identifying strengths and weaknesses of presentations

Key Skills

Success criteria ☐ I can name the effective points of a presentation and those areas that can be improved.

As you listen to your classmates' presentations, consider what impresses you about their presentations. Note any questions that you have related to the topic.

1. What features of my classmates' presentations impressed me?
   _____
   _____
   _____
   _____

2. Questions I have for presenters:
   _____
   _____
   _____
   _____
   _____

LESSON 17

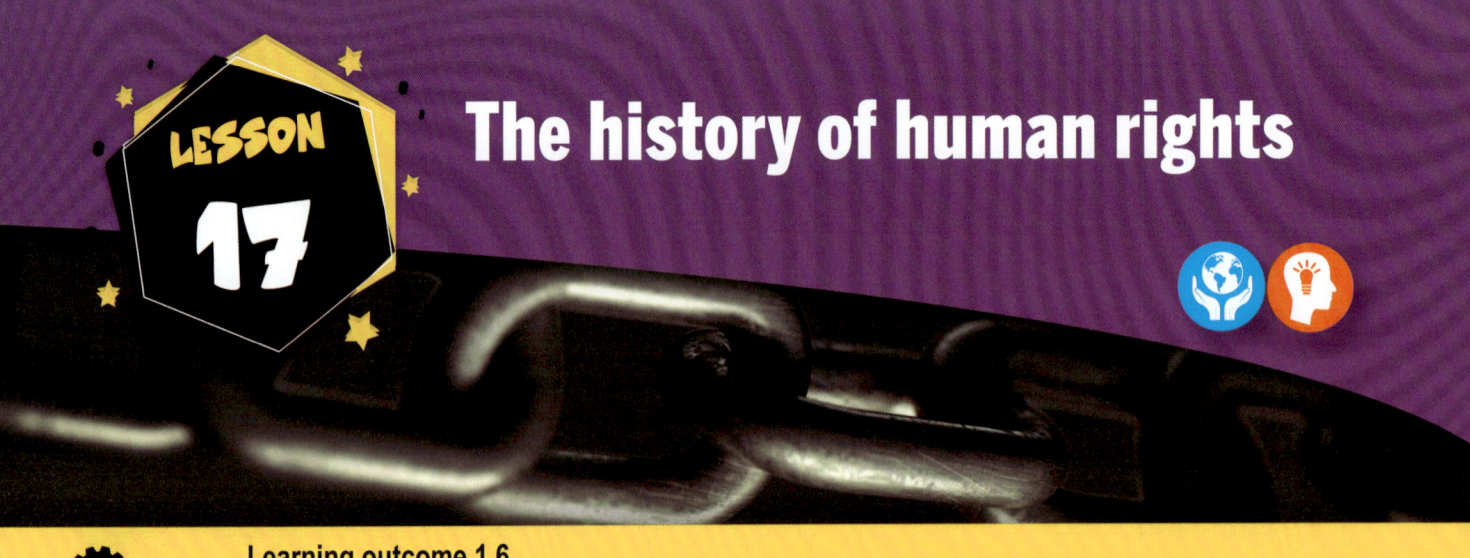

The history of human rights

Learning outcome 1.6
Students should be able to create a timeline tracing the origin of the concept of human rights, showing five or more key dates, events, people and documents.

Exercise 17A — Identifying the benefits of Cyrus's declaration on human rights

Key Skills **Success criteria**
☐ I can name the benefits of decisions taken by Cyrus on human rights.

The oldest known charter of human rights dates from 539 BC when Cyrus the Great, the first king of ancient Persia, conquered the city of Babylon. He freed the slaves, allowed all people to choose their own religion, and brought about racial equality. These decrees were recorded on a baked clay cylinder, known as the Cyrus Cylinder, which is today kept in the British Museum in London. Other ancient civilisations, such as Egypt, Greece and Rome, also gave their citizens rights, but not everyone was a citizen and the civilisations allowed slavery.

Watch the video on the Cyrus Cylinder and answer the questions that follow.

> **YouTube** Go to YouTube and search for 'The Cyrus Cylinder: An Artifact Ahead of Its Time' (3:03).

1. What type of society was Babylon?
   _____
   _____

2. Why was Cyrus's decision unusual?
   _____
   _____

3. Why is his decision relevant to today's big cities?
   _____
   _____

4. Who was influenced by Cyrus?
   _____
   _____

5. How might this decision have affected individual people?

_____

_____

6. Do you think Cyrus's view of how an empire should be run applies everywhere today? Why/why not?

_____

_____

Exercise 17B — Understanding how citizens' rights are denied in a dictatorship

Key Skills

Success criteria ☐ I can name the impacts of living in a dictatorship.

In the Middle Ages, most European countries had **monarchs** (kings or queens) who ruled by decree. A decree is when a law is made by the monarch without having to consult parliament or anybody else. From the time of the French Revolution, the power of monarchs in Europe began to weaken and they had to share this power with parliament. At the time, members of parliaments came from the wealthy and powerful classes only.

The transfer of monarchs' powers to the people took place over a long period and included the following events:

- In 1215, King John of England and his barons signed the **Magna Carta**, which limited the king's power.
- In 1791 the **Bill of Rights** was adopted in the USA. The bill protects freedom of speech, assembly and religion, bans cruel and unusual punishment, and prevents the government from depriving any person of life, freedom or property without due process of law.
- In 1789, in France, the **Declaration of the Rights of Man and of the Citizen** guaranteed the rights of liberty, property, security and resistance to oppression to all citizens. The special rights of the clergy and nobles were removed and all citizens were seen as equal in the eyes of the law.

The 20th century saw the rise of **dictators**, such as Hitler and Stalin. They ruled by decree and had total power over their country – just as the absolute monarchs had. To get a sense of what life might have been like under a dictatorship, look at the decree that the dictator (school principal) has released below. Working in groups, discuss how these rules would impact you and answer the questions that follow.

1. Students who have not completed their assigned homework will be beaten at 9:00 in front of the class.
2. Teachers can go through the students' bags at any time and remove their property.
3. Anyone who criticises these rules will be punished.
4. Students cannot talk to each other or stand in groups of more than two during school hours.

CALL TO ACTION | Chapter 2

> **5.** Students can be given a detention at any time without reason. They are not allowed to argue with this decision.
>
> **6.** Teachers can take students' phones, can go through their messages, call history, social media and search histories and keep them for their own use.
>
> **7.** Students whose surnames start with the letters A to D cannot come to class ever again and will instead clean the school toilets and tidy the canteen after breaks.
>
> **8.** Students whose surnames start with the letters M and O will have an extra hour free during the day and can take it at a time that suits them. They will also be entitled to share 30% of any property confiscated.
>
> Source adapted from 'Right Here, Right Now', created by the British Institute of Human Rights and Amnesty International

1. How many of these rules do you agree with?
   _____

2. Do these rules affect everybody in the group equally?
   _____

3. Are some rules more unfair than others? If so, which ones?
   _____
   _____

4. Why do you think rule 8 is included?
   _____
   _____

5. Name three ways that these rules would affect you.
   _____
   _____
   _____

6. Is there any way that you could overturn these rules?
   _____
   _____

7. Could these rules apply only in a dictatorship?
   _____
   _____

Lesson 17: The history of human rights

Exercise 17C **Identifying how people are impacted by slavery in modern times**

Key Skills **Success criteria** ☐ I can name places where slavery is still in existence.

In the Middle Ages, a **serf** belonged to the land and had to work on it for their lord. If a lord was selling land, the serfs could be sold with it. Serfdom came to an end in France in 1318, in England in 1574 and in Russia as late as 1861.

Slavery was abolished (ended) in 1833 in the UK and in 1865 in the US. Unfortunately, there are still many forms of slavery today. These include human trafficking, child slavery, bonded labour (being forced to work to pay back a debt), forced labour, domestic slavery and forced marriage.

Working in pairs, look at the two sources of information on slavery below and answer the questions that follow.

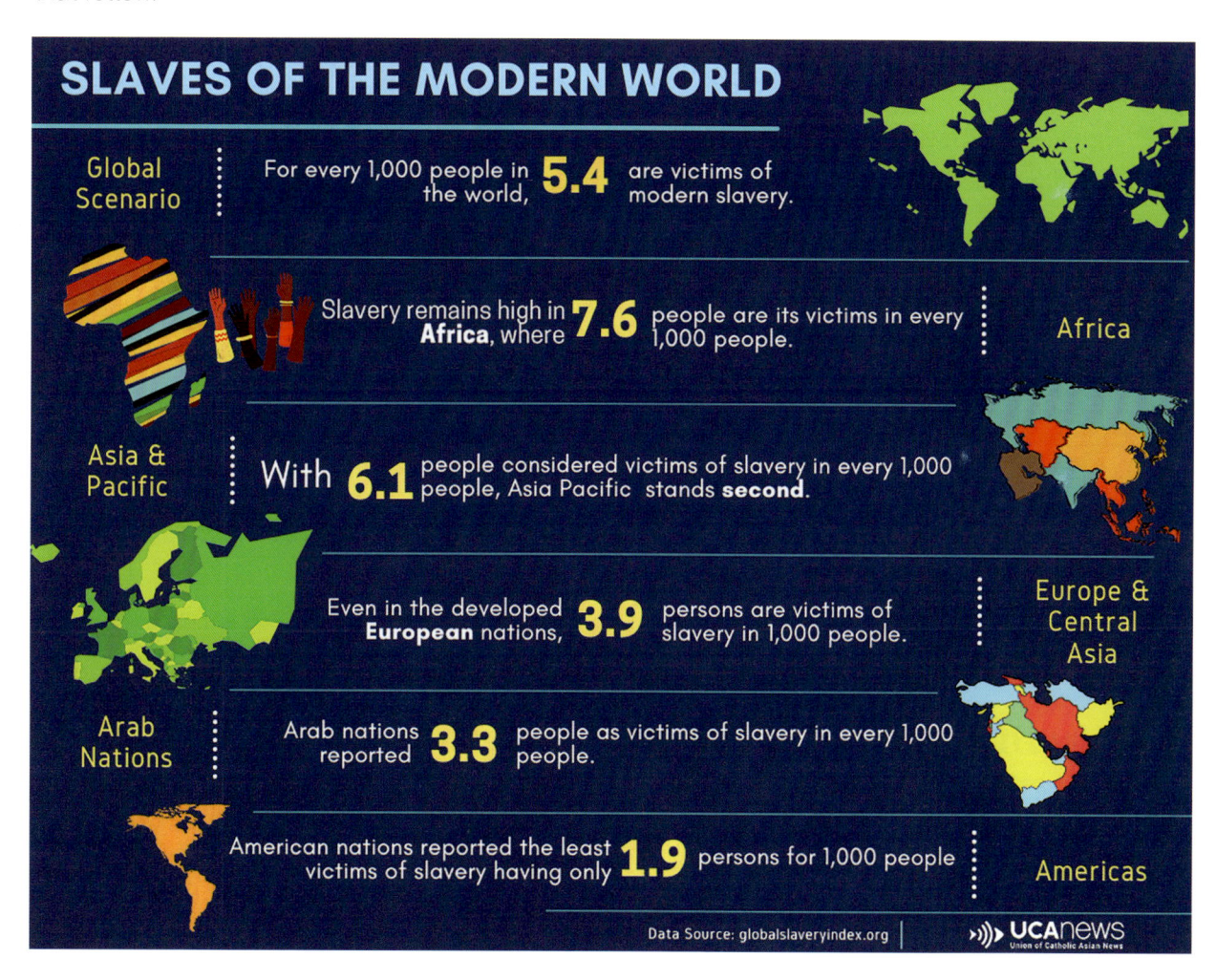

SLAVES OF THE MODERN WORLD

Global Scenario: For every 1,000 people in the world, **5.4** are victims of modern slavery.

Africa: Slavery remains high in **Africa**, where **7.6** people are its victims in every 1,000 people.

Asia & Pacific: With **6.1** people considered victims of slavery in every 1,000 people, Asia Pacific stands **second**.

Europe & Central Asia: Even in the developed **European** nations, **3.9** persons are victims of slavery in 1,000 people.

Arab Nations: Arab nations reported **3.3** people as victims of slavery in every 1,000 people.

Americas: American nations reported the least victims of slavery having only **1.9** persons for 1,000 people.

Data Source: globalslaveryindex.org | UCAnews (Union of Catholic Asian News)

69

■ CALL TO ACTION | *Chapter 2*

Modern Slavery Is A Brutal Reality Worldwide

Estimated number of people living in modern slavery in 2018*

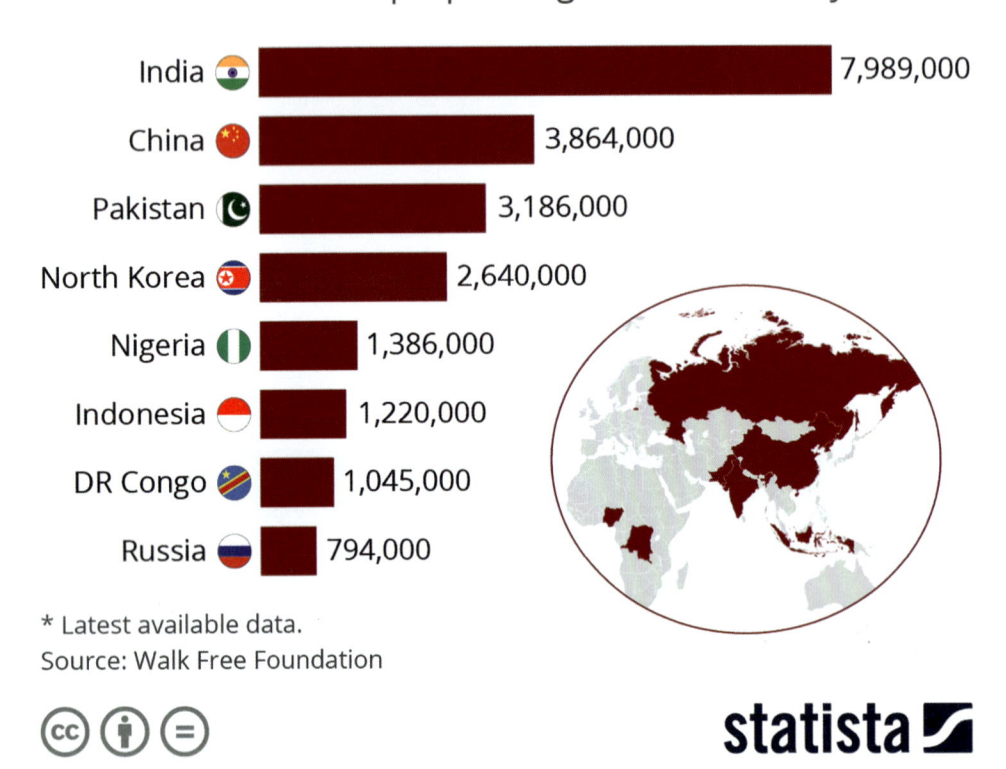

India	7,989,000
China	3,864,000
Pakistan	3,186,000
North Korea	2,640,000
Nigeria	1,386,000
Indonesia	1,220,000
DR Congo	1,045,000
Russia	794,000

* Latest available data.
Source: Walk Free Foundation

statista

1. Which continent is most affected by slavery?
   _____

2. Which continent is least affected?
   _____

3. Which Asian country has the largest number of enslaved people?
   _____

Exercise 17D — Looking at human rights advances in the 20th century

Key Skills — **Success criteria** ☐ I can identify developments in human rights in the 20th century.

The **United Nations** was established in 1945 to prevent any future wars and to promote peace in the world. The UN Human Rights Commission chaired by Eleanor Roosevelt drafted the **Universal Declaration of Human Rights (UDHR)**, which was adopted by the United Nations in 1948. This was the first international document to apply human rights to all people regardless of race, gender, religion or any other difference. In 1950, the **European Convention on Human Rights** was signed and in 1989 the **United Nations Convention on the Rights of the Child** was passed.

Lesson 17: The history of human rights

There have been many advances in human rights during the 20th century, but there is still much work to be done:

- In 1919, child labour was outlawed in the UK, but it is still widespread in many parts of the world.
- During the 19th century, many parts of the world were **colonised** by European powers. These people lost their power and land. Many of these countries did not gain their independence until the 1950s, 1960s and 1970s.
- A system called **apartheid** existed in South Africa (a former colony of Great Britain and the Netherlands) until 1994. Under this system non-white South Africans were treated as second-class citizens.
- Throughout the 20th century, other rights were won in many countries, such as improved working conditions and welfare for people too old or sick to work or not in a position to work. These developments were largely due to trade unions and political parties representing poorer citizens.
- In 1893, New Zealand gave women the right to vote but not the right to sit in parliament. In the UK, the **suffragettes** campaigned to get the right to vote for women. They used tactics such as breaking windows, hunger strikes and handcuffing themselves to railings to raise awareness of their cause. The Irish Women's Franchise League, led by Hanna Sheehy-Skeffington, began its campaign in Dublin in June 1912. Eight members broke windows in the GPO, the Custom's House and Dublin Castle as a protest. The women were arrested and sentenced to between a month and six months in jail. In 1918, when World War I ended, women in the UK over the age of 30 who owned property or wives of men who owned property were given the right to vote. This rule applied in Ireland as it was part of the UK, but when Ireland got independence in 1922, all women over the age of 21 were given the right to vote and to sit in the Dáil. British women were not given that right until 1928! The right of women to vote was introduced in most countries during the 20th century. In Switzerland women did not get the right to vote until 1971, and in Saudi Arabia, women only got the vote in 2015.

Read the information above and answer the questions below.

1. Name three human rights documents.
   _____
   _____
   _____

2. Why was colonisation against human rights?
   _____
   _____

3. What was the aim of the suffragettes?
   _____
   _____

4. What tactics did the suffragette campaign use?
   _____
   _____

5. Why do you think they chose these tactics?
   _____
   _____

CALL TO ACTION | *Chapter 2*

Exercise 17E Assessing my knowledge on the history of human rights

Key Skills   **Success criteria**   ☐ I can complete a crossword on the history of human rights.

Working in pairs, complete the crossword below using information learned in this lesson.

Across

2   Country that freed all serfs in 1861
6   Organisation founded in 1945 to promote peace and prevent future wars
8   The first country to give women the right to vote
9   Declaration of the Rights of Man and of the _____
10 An English charter of liberties signed in 1215

Down

1   They campaigned for the right of women to vote in Britain
3   European country which only gave women the right to vote in 1971
4   Apartheid was used in this country to discriminate against the non-white majority until 1994.
5   Countries that were once controlled by other countries
7   Abolished in the US in 1865

Lesson 18: Timeline of human rights

Learning outcome 1.6
Students should be able to create a timeline tracing the origin of the concept of human rights, showing five or more key dates, events, people and documents.

Exercise 18A — Identifying key dates in human rights development that are important for me personally, nationally and globally

Key Skills

Success criteria ☐ I can research these dates and say when they came about.

A **timeline** is used to present a series of events in **chronological** order, that is the order in which they happened. It allows the person looking at it to see the main events that happened and how far apart they were in time. A timeline does not usually include a lot of information, just the main events that happened. Pictures can be included.

The timeline below is from the Oireachtas website and shows the history of parliament in Ireland. It does not have pictures and the space between dates is not to scale with the time that elapsed.

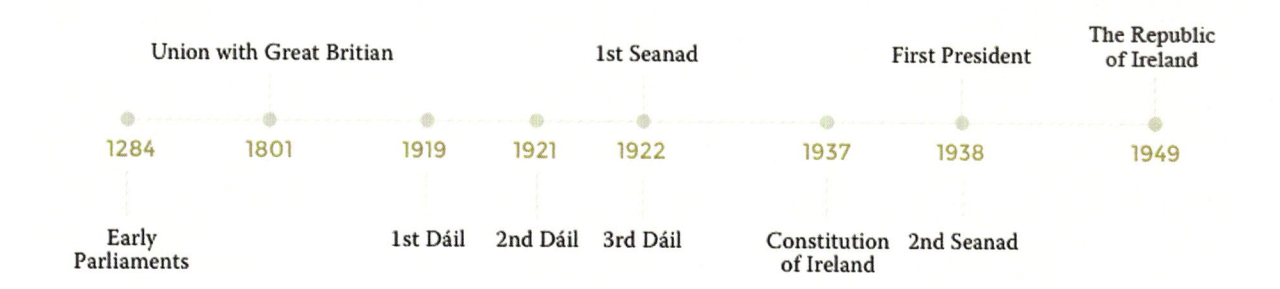

1284	1801	1919	1921	1922	1937	1938	1949
Early Parliaments	Union with Great Britian	1st Dáil	2nd Dáil	3rd Dáil / 1st Seanad	Constitution of Ireland	2nd Seanad / First President	The Republic of Ireland

In the next exercise, you are going to create your own timeline on the development of human rights. Before beginning your own timeline, identify the key dates, people, events and documents you want to include. This may involve some research. For example, you might want to find out when Catholics were allowed to sit in the British parliament. Sites such as www.wikipedia.org or www.britannica.com will be useful for your research, as will websites of organisations working in human rights, such as www.amnesty.ie or www.un.org. Include international elements such as the UDHR, but try to cover some important developments in human rights in Ireland. Finally, include some that are personally important for you. Write these in the box on the next page. The first one has been done for you.

CALL TO ACTION | *Chapter 2*

Event	Year	International, national or personal?
Women got the right to vote in Saudi Arabia	2015	International

Exercise 18B — Producing a timeline showing the development of human rights

Key Skills

Success criteria ☐ I can produce a timeline using a clear heading, key dates in chronological order and pictures.

Based on your research and the information contained in Lesson 17, create a timeline showing the development of human rights. You can create your timeline by writing it or typing up a Word document. You can also use free timeline templates available online. Include the dates, pictures and a heading explaining what the timeline is showing. When you have completed your timeline, you can add it to the box below.

74

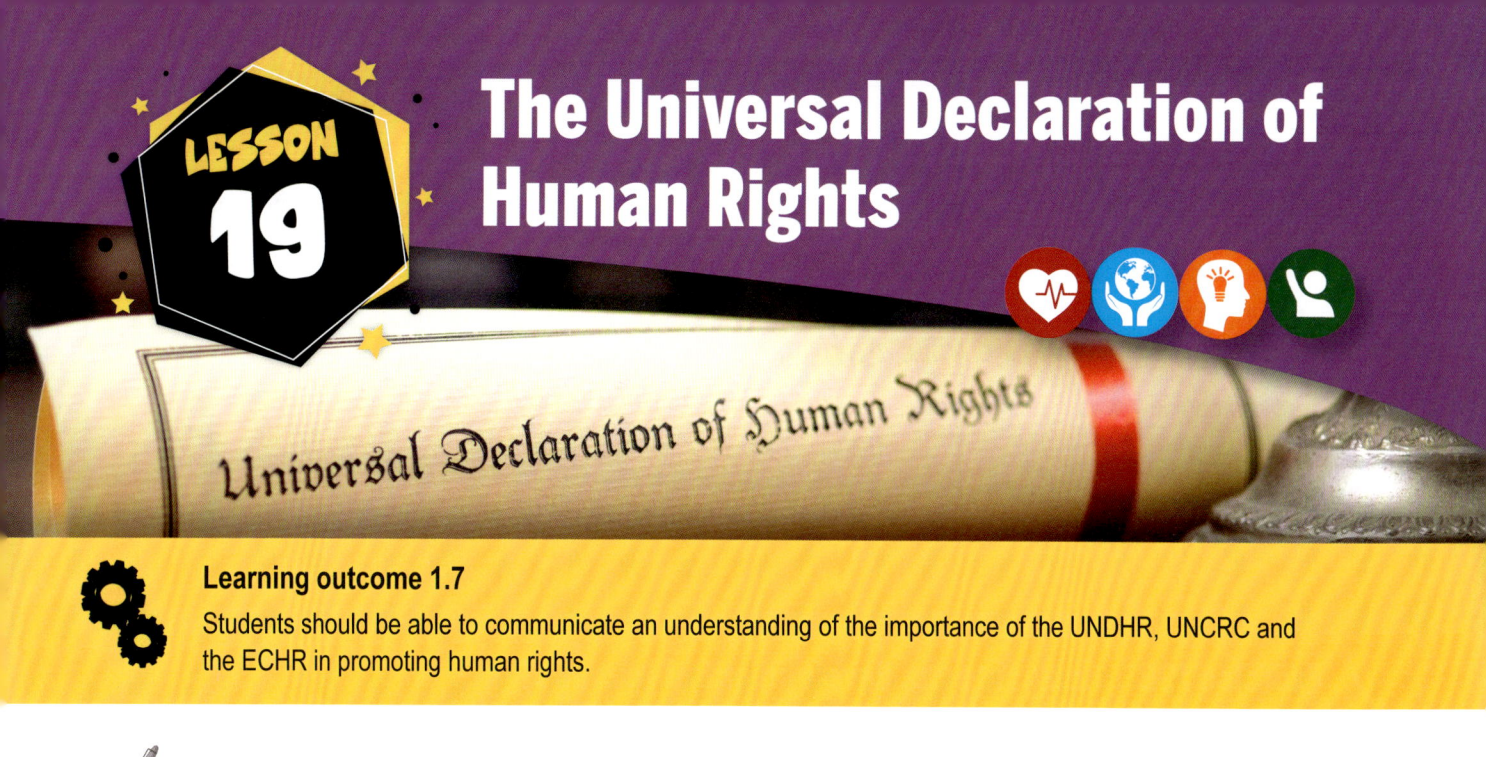

Lesson 19: The Universal Declaration of Human Rights

Learning outcome 1.7
Students should be able to communicate an understanding of the importance of the UNDHR, UNCRC and the ECHR in promoting human rights.

Exercise 19A Assessing my knowledge about the UDHR

Key Skills

Success criteria ☐ I can explain facts about the UDHR.

The **Universal Declaration of Human Rights (UDHR)** was adopted by the General Assembly of the United Nations on 10 December 1948 in Paris in the aftermath of the Holocaust. It lists 30 rights that all humans have, regardless of race, sex, religion or any other characteristic. These rights cannot be taken away from people. The rights include the right to education and healthcare, and freedom from torture. The Declaration is not legally binding, but the rights it gives have been included in the national laws of many countries. All countries must apply these rights to all their citizens, regardless of their political, religious or cultural systems. The UDHR has been translated into 370 languages.

The **UN High Commissioner for Human Rights** is the person in charge of protecting and promoting human rights. They advise the Secretary-General of the UN on human rights issues. Ireland's former president, Mary Robinson, served as High Commissioner from 1997 to 2002.

Working in pairs, tick the correct answers in the quiz below (you will probably have to guess some of the answers). (*Quiz based on Amnesty International's 'Celebrating the UDHR' resource*)

Quiz

1. Leaders of the main world powers met between 1942 and 1944 to shape a new organisation. What was this organisation called?
   - (a) Amnesty International ☐
   - (b) The United Nations ☐
   - (c) NATO ☐
2. What was the first human rights treaty adopted by the United Nations?
   - (a) The UN Convention on the Rights of the Child ☐
   - (b) The Universal Declaration of Human Rights ☐
   - (c) The Declaration on the Right to Development ☐
3. How many languages has the Universal Declaration of Human Rights been translated into?
   - (a) 25 ☐
   - (b) 100 ☐
   - (c) 370 ☐

■ CALL TO ACTION | *Chapter 2*

4. When was the Universal Declaration of Human Rights adopted?
    (a) 1948 ☐   (b) 1973 ☐   (c) 2011 ☐
5. Which of the following people worked tirelessly to promote the message and implementation of the Universal Declaration of Human Rights worldwide?
    (a) Eleanor Roosevelt ☐   (b) Donald Trump ☐   (c) Abraham Lincoln ☐
6. In what country was the Universal Declaration of Human Rights initially adopted?
    (a) The UK ☐   (b) The US ☐   (c) France ☐
7. How many rights does the Universal Declaration of Human Rights contain?
    (a) 15 ☐   (b) 30 ☐   (c) 65 ☐

Exercise 19B — Analysing the development of human rights

Key Skills — **Success criteria** ☐ I can identify reasons for the creation of the UDHR and the strengths and weaknesses of it.

Watch the video about the UDHR and answer the questions below.

YouTube
Go to YouTube and search for 'UDHR @ 70: Perspective' (3:58).

1. After what conflict was the UN set up?

2. Who chaired the international committee that drafted the UDHR?

3. What negative freedoms does the UDHR refer to?

4. What positive freedoms does it refer to?

5. Give an example of a social right it refers to.

6. Does the Declaration say which rights are most important?

7. Why are human rights abused over and over again?

8. What is the role of the UN agencies in the protection of human rights?

9. Why is the European Convention on Human Rights more effective?

Lesson 19: The Universal Declaration of Human Rights

Exercise 19C — Identifying the most important rights in the UDHR

Key Skills

Success criteria ☐ I can explain why some rights are more important than others.

Read the simplified version of the UDHR. Working in pairs, select the five rights you think are the most important and write the article number of these below.

Universal Declaration of Human Rights (UDHR)

Article 1: Everybody is born free and has human dignity

Article 2: The rights in the UDHR apply regardless of race, colour, sex or any other factors

Article 3: Right to life, liberty, personal security

Article 4: Freedom from slavery

Article 5: Freedom from torture and degrading treatment

Article 6: Right to recognition as a person before the law

Article 7: Right to equality before the law

Article 8: Right to ask for legal help

Article 9: Freedom from arbitrary arrest and exile

Article 10: Right to fair public hearing

Article 11: Right to be considered innocent until proven guilty

Article 12: Right to privacy

Article 13: Right to free movement in and out of a country

Article 14: Right to asylum in other countries from persecution

Article 15: Right to a nationality and the freedom to change it

Article 16: Right to marriage and family

Article 17: Right to own property

Article 18: Freedom of thought and religion

Article 19: Freedom of opinion and expression

Article 20: Right to peaceful assembly and association

Article 21: Right to participate in government and in free elections

Article 22: Right to social security

Article 23: Right to work for a fair wage in a safe environment and to join trade unions

Article 24: Right to rest and leisure

Article 25: Right to a decent standard of living, including a home, enough food and healthcare

Article 26: Right to education

Article 27: Right to participate in the cultural life of the community

Article 28: Everyone has the right to the enjoy the rights and freedoms in this Declaration

Article 29: Everyone has a duty to other people, and we should protect their rights and freedoms

Article 30: Nobody has the right to take away any of the rights in this Declaration

The five most important rights in the Declaration				

■ CALL TO ACTION | *Chapter 2*

Exercise 19D   Identifying the impact of the UDHR

Key Skills   **Success criteria** ☐ I can name situations where human rights apply.

Working in groups, think of or research examples of each of the following and write your answers into the box. The first one has been done as an example.

A human right *The right to health*	The person in charge of human rights for the UN	An improvement in human rights in Ireland	An example of a human right abuse that would force a person to leave their own country	A right that you have that a young person does not have in another country
A country in the news at the moment for human rights abuses	An NGO that promotes human rights	A campaign to promote human rights	A right you have that your grandparents did not have	A country where people who follow certain religions are not allowed their human rights

Lesson 20: The European Convention on Human Rights

Learning outcome 1.7
Students should be able to communicate an understanding of the importance of the UNDHR, UNCRC and the ECHR in promoting human rights.

Exercise 20A Examining the ECHR

Key Skills **Success criteria** ☐ I can explain some rights and freedoms the ECHR guarantees.

The **Council of Europe (CoE)** was founded in 1949 to protect human rights, democracy and the rule of law in Europe. The CoE has 47 member states and is based in Strasbourg in France. In 1950, the **European Convention on Human Rights (ECHR)** was adopted by member states of the CoE. This is an international treaty based on the Universal Declaration of Human Rights. The ECHR protects rights, including the right to:

- Life (Article 1)
- Freedom and security (Article 5)
- A fair trial in civil and criminal matters (Article 6)
- Respect for private and family life (Article 8)
- Freedom of thought, conscience and religion (Article 9)
- Freedom of expression (Article 10)
- Freedom of assembly (Article 11)
- Marry (Article 12)
- Own property (Protocol 1, Article 1)
- Education (Protocol 1, Article 2)
- Free elections (Protocol 1, Article 3)
- Freedom of movement within a country (Protocol 2, Article 4)
- Compensation if you have been convicted of a crime you were innocent of (Protocol 7, Article 3)

And it bans:

- Torture or cruel or humiliating punishment (Article 3)
- Slavery and forced labour (Article 4)

■ CALL TO ACTION | *Chapter 2*

- Equality before the law and equal protection of the law (Article 7)
- Discrimination in protection of these rights based on colour, sex, politics, religion or other status (Article 14)
- Deportation of a state's own nationals or denying them entry (Protocol 4, Article 3)
- The collective deportation of foreigners (Protocol 4, Article 4)
- The death penalty (Protocol 6, Article 1)

Watch the video about the ECHR and answer the following questions.

YouTube
Go to YouTube and search for 'ECHR – European Convention on Human Rights (English Version)' (3:16).

1. Name four rights in the ECHR.
   _____
   _____

2. What freedoms are allowed under the ECHR?
   _____
   _____

3. What types of elections are allowed?
   _____

4. What religious rights are allowed?
   _____

5. What rights do you have if you are accused of a crime?
   _____
   _____

Exercise 20B Understanding the impact of a ruling from the European Court of Human Rights

Key Skills   **Success criteria** ☐ I can explain the practical application of the ECHR guarantees.

The **European Court of Human Rights** was set up in 1959 to guarantee that rights under the ECHR are respected for citizens of member countries. The court is based in Strasbourg. Each member state of the Council of Europe has a judge at the court but they are independent and do not represent their country in the court. Each judge serves a nine-year term. States must change any laws and practices found to be against the ECHR. This is supervised by the Committee of Ministers.

The ECHR allows cases to be brought to the court by:

- An individual or group of people against a state or states
- A member state against another member state.

The court can deal only with cases when the highest court in the member country has dismissed a complaint. The people bringing the case must do it within six months of the last court decision. The court can deal only with cases where a right protected by the ECHR is being violated.

Read the case study of Mr Aziz on the next page and answer the questions.

Lesson 20: The European Convention on Human Rights

Case Study

Cyprus

The island of Cyprus is divided between two ethnic groups, Greek and Turkish Cypriots. In the 1960s, the population of Cyprus was 77% Greek Cypriot and 18% Turkish Cypriot. In 1974, Turkey invaded and the island was divided in two – the northern part is recognised only by Turkey as an independent country. 99% of Turk Cypriots live in the north. Following the invasion, between 150,000 and 200,000 Turkish people moved to Northern Cyprus. Almost all Greek Cypriots live in the Republic of Cyprus (Southern Cyprus). Ibrahim Aziz, a Turkish Cypriot who had spent his life living in Nicosia, the capital of the Republic of Cyprus, applied to be registered to vote in the 2001 election to the Cypriot parliament. His application was refused because he was a Turkish Cypriot. He appealed this decision to the Cypriot Supreme Court and this was dismissed. In 2004, he took his case to the European Court of Human Rights on the basis that Turkish Cypriots living in the Republic of Cyprus were not allowed to vote or stand for election. The Court found that the refusal to allow him vote was a breach [*the law was not followed*] of Article 14 and Protocol 1, Article 3. After Mr Aziz's case, Turkish Cypriots living in the Republic of Cyprus were given the right to vote.

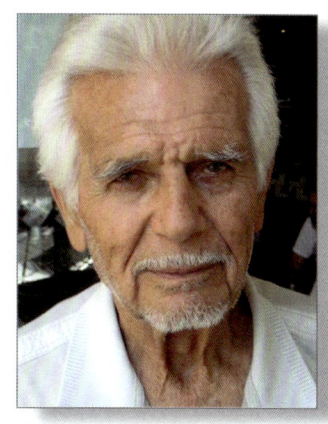

Ibrahim Aziz

1. Do you think Mr Aziz's situation was common in Cyprus? Why/why not?

2. Which articles of the ECHR were violated?

3. What has been the result of this case in Cyprus?

4. Why do you think the ECHR is able to enforce changes, but the UDHR cannot?

Exercise 20C Researching Ireland and the ECHR

Key Skills   **Success criteria**   ☐ I can research and explain Ireland's experience of the ECHR.

Member states are obliged to pass laws and to correct any existing laws to ensure human rights are protected.

Research Ireland's involvement in the ECHR to answer the questions on the next page.

■ CALL TO ACTION | *Chapter 2*

1. When did Ireland join the Council of Europe?
   _____

2. When did Ireland ratify (sign up to) the ECHR?
   _____

3. When did Ireland join the UN?
   _____

4. Name any similarities between the Irish Constitution and the rights in the ECHR.
   _____
   _____

5. Who is the Irish judge on the European Court of Human Rights?
   _____

Exercise 20D — Identifying whether the ECHR can be applied and how

Key Skills

Success criteria ☐ I can explain whether or not a case can be taken to the European Court of Human Rights and explain why or why not.

Working in a group, look at the scenario below and use the information given in this lesson to answer the questions that follow.

> Ivan has been arrested by the police in a neighbouring country (a Council of Europe member state). As his documents are not in order, the courts have ruled that he should be deported to his country of origin. Ivan is trying to appeal against this decision. He claims that he belongs to an ethnic minority which is discriminated against in his country of origin and that if he is returned there, he will most probably be tortured – or even killed – by either the official authorities or rebels.

1. Can Ivan take a case to the European Court of Human Rights against the neighbouring country to complain about the decision to send him back to his country of origin?
   _____

2. On which article(s) of the Convention could he base his application?
   _____

3. To what extent could he also submit an application against his country of origin?
   _____

Source: Rights and Freedoms in Practice: Teaching Resources © Council of Europe

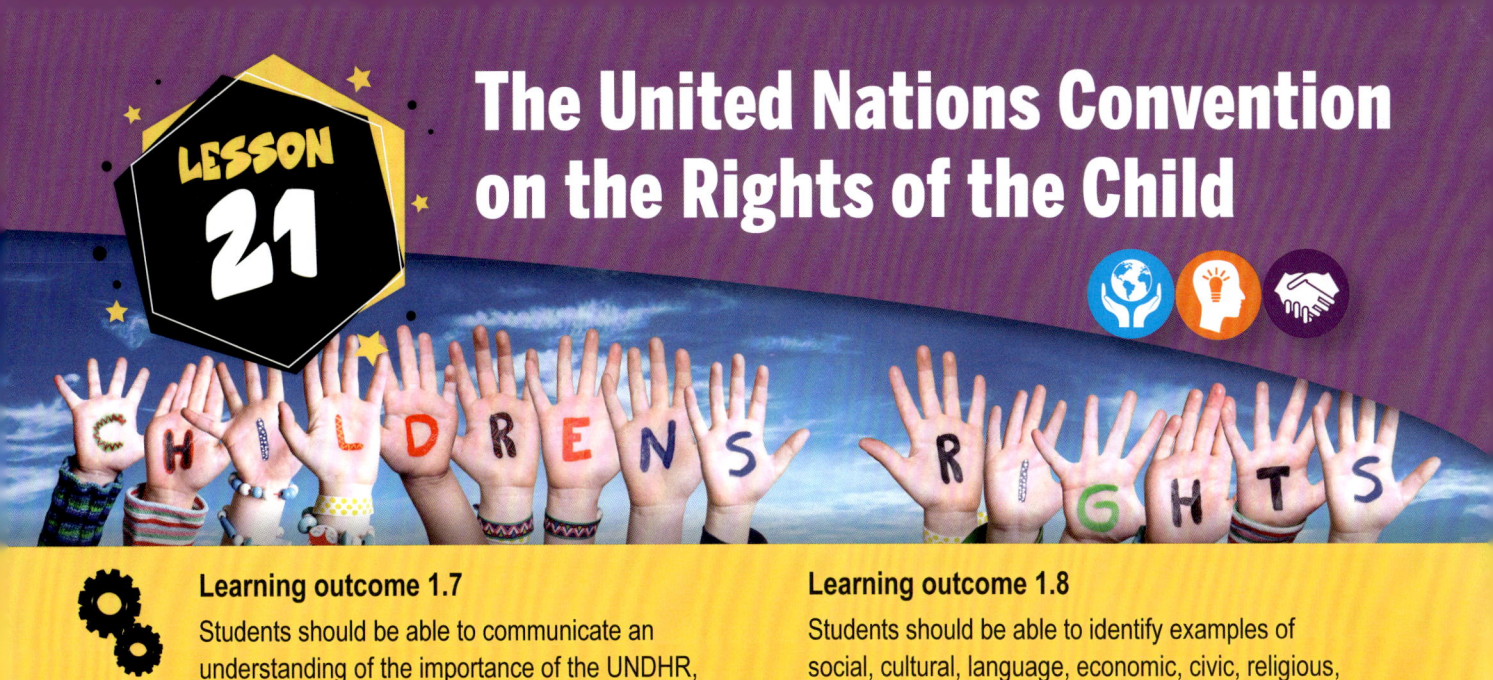

LESSON 21: The United Nations Convention on the Rights of the Child

Learning outcome 1.7
Students should be able to communicate an understanding of the importance of the UNDHR, UNCRC and the ECHR in promoting human rights.

Learning outcome 1.8
Students should be able to identify examples of social, cultural, language, economic, civic, religious, environmental and political rights.

Exercise 21A — Considering the impact of a lack of children's rights

Key Skills

Success criteria ☐ I can answer questions on children's rights.

In 1989, the **United Nations Convention on the Rights of the Child** (UNCRC) was adopted by the UN General Assembly. Like the ECHR, it is a convention and is legally binding. The US is the only country not to sign up to it. The Convention applies to all children in a country, and it describes the minimum standards every child under 18 is entitled to. If a country has higher standards than those mentioned in the Convention, the higher standards always apply.

Before looking at the rights protected by the UNCRC, work with a partner to tick the correct answers in the quiz below (you will probably have to guess some of the answers).

Quiz

1. How many primary school age children in the world have no access to education?
   - (a) 1 million ☐
   - (b) 10 million ☐
   - (c) 104 million ☐
   - (d) 1.4 billion ☐

2. How much did the US spend on its military in 2019?
   - (a) $7.2 million ☐
   - (b) $7.2 billion ☐
   - (c) $72 billion ☐
   - (d) $720 billion ☐

3. There are 27 doctors to every 10,000 people in Ireland. What is the number in Nigeria?
   - (a) 4 ☐
   - (b) 14 ☐
   - (c) 40 ☐
   - (d) 114 ☐

4. How many children under five die from hunger each year?
   - (a) 60,000 ☐
   - (b) 600,000 ☐
   - (c) 6 million ☐
   - (d) 60 million ☐

5. Of children with no access to education, what proportion are girls?
   - (a) 10% ☐
   - (b) 25% ☐
   - (c) 50% ☐
   - (d) 67% ☐

■ CALL TO ACTION | *Chapter 2*

6. Worldwide, how many children are engaged in child labour?
   (a) 15.2 million ☐   (b) 52 million ☐   (c) 152 million ☐   (d) 15.2 billion ☐

7. Which is the most common form of child labour?
   (a) Military ☐   (b) Agriculture and fishing ☐   (c) Mining ☐   (d) Transportation ☐

8. Which continent has the largest proportion of child labour?
   (a) South America ☐   (b) Asia ☐   (c) Africa ☐   (d) Europe ☐

9. How many girls under 18 are married each year?
   (a) 20,000 ☐   (b) 120,000 ☐   (c) 1,200,000 ☐   (d) 12 million ☐

10. How many of the world's children are malnourished?
    (a) 10 million ☐   (b) 20 million ☐   (c) 100 million ☐   (d) 200 million ☐

Exercise 21B Classifying children's rights

Key Skills

Success criteria ☐ I can name survival, protection, development and participation rights from the UNCRC.

There are four categories of rights in the Convention.
- **Survival rights** are the most basic rights that a child needs in order to survive, such as shelter, nutrition and access to medicine.
- **Development rights** are those rights needed for a child to develop to their full potential, such as education.
- **Protection rights** are those rights needed to keep children safe, such as from harmful drugs.
- **Participation rights** are those rights needed to play a role in society, such as the freedom to express opinions.

The **UN Committee on the Rights of the Child** receives regular progress reports on children's rights from each government and from other organisations like NGOs. In Ireland, the Children's Rights Alliance submits reports.

Working in pairs, look at the rights contained in the UNCRC on the following page and select four rights for each category. Write the number of the right in the correct category below.

Survival rights	Development rights	Protection rights	Participation rights

Lesson 21: The United Nations Convention on the Rights of the Child

UN Convention on the Rights of the Child

Survival
You have a right to life, good food, water, and to grow up healthy

Development
You have a right to an education and time to relax and play

Participation
You have a right to say how you feel, be listened to, and taken seriously

Protection
You have a right to be treated well and not be hurt by anyone

1. Everyone under 18 has these rights
2. All children have these rights
3. Adults must do what's best for me
4. The Government should make sure my rights are respected
5. The Government should respect the right of my family to help me know about my rights
6. I should be supported to live and grow
7. I have a right to a name and to belong to a country
8. I have a right to an identity
9. I have a right to live with a family who cares for me
10. I have the right to see my family if they live in another country
11. I have the right not to be taken out of the country illegally
12. I have the right to be listened to, and taken seriously
13. I have the right to find out and share information
14. I have the right to have my own thoughts and beliefs and to choose my religion, with my parents' guidance
15. I have the right to meet with friends and to join groups
16. I have the right to keep some things private
17. I have the right to get information in lots of ways, so long as it's safe
18. I have the right to be brought up by both parents if possible
19. I have the right to be protected from being hurt or badly treated
20. I have the right to special protection and help if I can't live with my own family
21. I have the right to have the best care if I am adopted
22. If I am a refugee, I have the same rights as children born in that country
23. If I have a disability, I have the right to special care and education
24. I have the right to good quality health care, to clean water and good food
25. If I am not living with my family, people should keep checking I am safe and happy
26. My family should get the money they need to help bring me up
27. I have the right to have a proper house, food and clothing
28. I have the right to an education
29. I have the right to an education which develops my personality, respect for others' rights and the environment
30. I have a right to speak my own language and to follow my family's way of life
31. I have a right to relax and play
32. I should not be made to do dangerous work
33. I should be protected from dangerous drugs
34. Nobody should touch me in ways that make me feel uncomfortable, unsafe or sad
35. I should not be abducted, sold or trafficked
36. I have the right to be kept safe from things that could harm my development
37. I have the right not to be punished in a cruel or hurtful way
38. I am not allowed to join the army until I am 15
39. I have the right to help if I have been hurt, neglected or badly treated
40. I have the right to legal help and to be treated fairly if I have been accused of breaking the law
41. Where our country treats us better than the UN does we should keep up the good work!
42. Everyone should know about the UNCRC

■ CALL TO ACTION | *Chapter 2*

Exercise 21C **Understanding how different children have different experiences of human rights**

Key Skills   **Success criteria** ☐ I can name behaviours associated with stereotypical and prejudiced attitudes.

Working in groups, watch the UNICEF video. Discuss the questions below and then answer them.

> **YouTube** Go to YouTube and search for 'Would you stop if you saw this little girl on the street? UNICEF' (3:06).

1. Why was this video made?
   _____
   _____

2. What differences do you note between the way people react to the child?
   _____
   _____

3. Why do you think the people's reactions were different?
   _____
   _____

4. What does it tell us about children's rights?
   _____
   _____

5. Do you think the reactions would have been similar in Ireland? Why/why not?
   _____
   _____

Exercise 21D **Understanding how to protect rights**

Key Skills   **Success criteria** ☐ I can explain what I and other people can do to protect and improve children's rights.

Working in groups, look at the two photos below and answer the questions that follow.

Picture 1: *Syrian children in a refugee camp*

Picture 2: *Children in the DRC sifting through rock looking for cobalt used to make mobile phones*

86

Lesson 21: The United Nations Convention on the Rights of the Child

	Picture 1	Picture 2
1. What right has been denied?		
2. What right has been protected?		
3. What could the UN do to improve this right?		
4. What other groups could help?		
5. How could they help?		
6. What could you do?		

Exercise 21E **Designing an advertisement to raise awareness of how children's rights are exploited**

Key Skills

Success criteria ☐ I can create an advertisement that informs people of the abuse of children's rights and suggests what can be done to improve them.

Your group is an advertising agency which has been hired by an NGO to highlight the abuse of children's rights. Choose a case in which children's rights are being exploited and design an advertisement that will inform the public of this exploitation. The advertisement must persuade people to do something that can lead to change.

87

CALL TO ACTION | *Chapter 2*

Your campaign may focus on any of the following:

- Child labour
- Child soldiers
- Child nutrition
- War
- Lack of education
- Discrimination based on ethnic, social, religious or gender differences.

Place your completed advertisement here.

Lesson 22: Ireland and the UNCRC

Learning outcome 1.7
Students should be able to communicate an understanding of the importance of the UNDHR, UNCRC and the ECHR in promoting human rights.

Exercise 22A — Understanding the need to frequently review children's rights

Key Skills

Success criteria ☐ I can identify problems with children's rights.

Ireland ratified the UNCRC on 21 September 1992. Some of the following changes have happened because of the UNCRC:

- The Convention became Irish law.
- A **National Strategy for Children** was put in place.
- **Dáil na nÓg**, a National Children's Parliament, was set up in 2001. It meets every two years.
- In 2004, an **Ombudsman for Children** was appointed to investigate complaints and to promote the rights of children.
- In 2011, Frances Fitzgerald became the first **Minister for Children and Youth Affairs**.
- In 2012, the **Children's Rights Referendum** was passed. This recognises children as rights holders under the Constitution separate to their parents.

The UN Committee on the Rights of the Child has asked the Irish government to make improvements in some areas, especially for children from the Travelling community, children living in poverty, children with disabilities, children in care and refugee children.

Working in pairs, discuss the following statements and tick whether you think they are true or false.

	True	False
1. 93% of children continue school after the Junior Cycle.		
2. Just 8% of Traveller children complete the Leaving Certificate.		
3. Over 3,000 Irish children are homeless or are living in emergency accommodation.		
4. Children and teenagers in Ireland were placed in adult prisons until 2017.		
5. School-leavers with a disability or specific learning difficulty can get access to third-level courses on a reduced points basis.		
6. People need to be cleared by the Gardaí in order to work with children and young people under 18.		
7. In 2021, the average cost of school clothing and shoes for a secondary school student in Ireland was €235.		
8. In 2018, 10% of Irish children aged 10–17 went to bed hungry.		

■ CALL TO ACTION | *Chapter 2*

Exercise 22B Understanding the work of the OCO

Key Skills **Success criteria** ☐ I can identify how the OCO intervenes to protect children's rights.

In 2004, Ireland appointed its first **Ombudsman for Children**. The Ombudsman for Children's Office (**OCO**) has two roles:

1. To investigate complaints brought by children or adults acting for children about public organisations such as schools and hospitals
2. To promote the rights of Irish young people under the age of 18.

Read the case study from the OCO and answer the questions that follow.

Case Study

Sean was on a school trip when another child took a photo of him and shared it in a social media app accompanied with an offensive comment. Although the school managed the incident at the time, Sean's parents complained to the OCO that the school had not given them a proper explanation about why they were not informed immediately about the incident.

The OCO found that the school had provided an explanation and an apology to Sean's parents about the delay. The school had put some changes in place to prevent a similar incident from happening. They revised their mobile phone policy and arranged a lecture for parents on internet safety. Parents now sign an agreement that mobile phones and digital cameras are not allowed on school tours. New procedures were also introduced for teachers in charge of school trips on managing such incidents.

This is a sample of a complaint made to the Ombudsman for Children's Office. Visit www.oco.ie for information on the Office and children's rights.

1. Why did the OCO become involved in this case?
   _____
   _____

2. What type of organisation was at the centre of this case?
   _____

3. Mention three things that happened as a result of this case.
   _____
   _____
   _____

4. What was the advantage of the OCO's involvement in this case?
   _____
   _____

5. What rights were affected in this case?
   _____
   _____

Lesson 22: Ireland and the UNCRC

Exercise 22C — Appreciating that some people experience rights while others are excluded

Key Skills

Success criteria ☐ I can name the rights that some people are lacking and explain how to deal with this.

Working in pairs, read Matt's account of school and answer the questions that follow.

> Hi, I'm Matt, I'm 13 and I go to an all-boys school known for its great rugby teams. Unfortunately, I am not a fan of team sports. I prefer swimming, music and films. In our school, music is not taught as a subject and we never have concerts or put on musicals. In the first term, we sampled a few subjects. Italian was one of them and the teacher showed us a classic Italian film. I loved it. In my sister's school they have a film club that meets up twice a week at lunchtime to watch films and hold discussions. They even get to go to the cinema at the end of the school year. I'd love that. Every week I dread Fridays. We all have to go to the pitch for rugby, no matter what the weather is like. I don't really like soccer, but at least it is safe. I'm pretty small and although I spend most of the time trying to avoid the ball there are times when the ball is thrown to me. I hate that because I know some of the big boys are going to flatten me. I spend the hour waiting for the final whistle. The teacher in charge is okay – he doesn't make things difficult for me – but he has no interest in me because I'm useless. Last Friday we had a half day and I missed rugby. I'm trying to get my mum to organise my check-up with the dentist for next Friday.

1. Why do you think all students in the school had to play rugby?

2. What extracurricular activities did the school offer Matt?

3. What message does the school give about extracurricular activities?

4. In this story were Matt's rights denied? Explain how.

5. If Matt wanted to change things, what do you think he could do?

6. If you were Matt, what would you do?

CALL TO ACTION | Chapter 2

Exercise 22D Analysing different levels of participation

Key Skills

Success criteria ☐ I can classify situations according to the different levels of participation.

Because of the UNCRC, children and young people in Ireland are consulted more and have some involvement in decision-making.

- Schools must have **student councils**. These councils are expected to be consulted on decisions and the views of the students are expected to be considered.
- Thirty-one **Comhairlí na nÓg** (child and youth councils) give children and young people the chance to become involved in areas of interest to young people in local development and policies. Local organisations often consult the Comhairlí na nÓg to get the view of young people when making decisions. The views of Comhairlí na nÓg members are also taken into account when preparing Ireland's report to the UN Committee on the Rights of the Child.
- Every two years, the **Dáil na nÓg** is elected from the Comhairle na nÓg councils. The representatives meet in the Dáil chamber to debate issues decided by the delegates, such as actions young people in Ireland could take to prevent climate change.
- The National Strategy on Children and Young People's Participation in Decision-making was launched in 2015. It aims to give children and young people a voice in their local community and in early education, school, health, social services and the legal system.

Including children and young people does not always give them a chance to make a meaningful contribution or even play a role in decisions. Professor Roger Hart's **Ladder of Participation** shows the different levels of participation. The higher up you go on the ladder, the greater your level of participation.

1. At the **manipulation** level, the adults decide everything and the children or young people are told what to do without needing to understand it.
2. At the **decoration** level, the children or young people understand but have no role in making decisions. They are there only to make it look like they are included.
3. At the **tokenism** level, the children or young people may be consulted, but their views are not considered.
4. At the **assigned but informed** level, the children or young people are told what to do by adults, but the role is explained to them and they may have some input in decision-making.

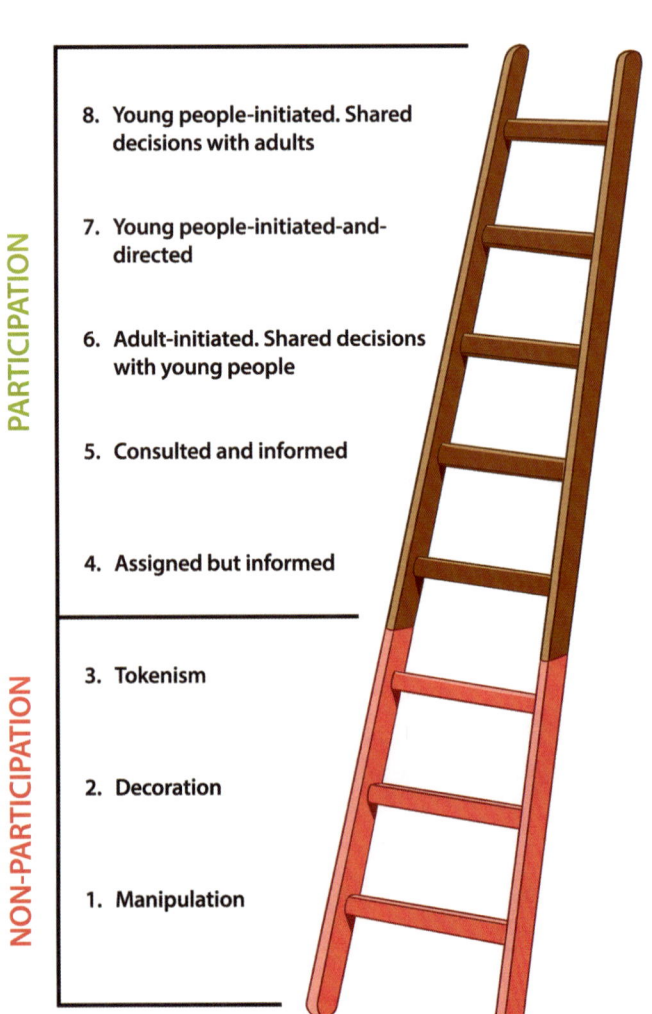

PARTICIPATION
8. Young people-initiated. Shared decisions with adults
7. Young people-initiated-and-directed
6. Adult-initiated. Shared decisions with young people
5. Consulted and informed
4. Assigned but informed

NON-PARTICIPATION
3. Tokenism
2. Decoration
1. Manipulation

Lesson 22: Ireland and the UNCRC

5. The **consulted and informed** level is still led by adults, but they have consulted with the children or young people before starting the process. The adults have explained the role and may have involved the children or young people in some decision-making.

6. At the **adult-initiated shared decisions** level, the adults start the process but decisions are shared with the children or young people.

7. At the **young people-initiated and directed** level, children or young people start the process and run it with little adult input.

8. At the **young people-initiated, shared decisions with adults** level, the children or young people run the process and final decisions are made between them and adults.

Working in pairs, look at the ladder of participation on the previous page and then decide on which rung to place the situations below. Write your answers in the column on the right, explaining your decision.

Situation 1: Your school was asked to provide a young person to represent the school on a panel to discuss changes to the local park. **Action taken**: The principal chose a student who was always neatly dressed and well-behaved, but did not live in the area.	
Situation 2: The First Year classrooms were always messy and students were often given detention at lunchtime. **Action taken**: The students decided to organise a rota of people in each class to make sure the classrooms were tidy. Two people were in charge of each classroom every week.	
Situation 3: The local mayor was hosting a reception for businesspeople who were attending a conference in your area. **Action taken**: The choir from a local school, which had won a national competition, was asked to sing for them at the reception.	
Situation 4: Some senior students heard about a programme for training students about online safety. They wanted to set up a similar scheme in your school. **Action taken**: First, the senior students told other students about the scheme. They then spoke to the guidance counsellor, principal and chaplain, who helped the students to set up a similar scheme.	

CALL TO ACTION | Chapter 2

Situation 5: Your local council brought in planners to design a new park in your area. **Action taken**: Everyone in the community was invited to a meeting to discuss what should be included. They especially wanted to know what children of all ages wanted and set up working groups of young people to work with the planners. When the plans were drawn up, all the young people in the area were given a copy of what the council proposed to do.	
Situation 6: Your school wanted to improve break and lunchtime facilities for its students. **Action taken**: All pupils got to elect a committee which found out what students wanted. They then organised the carrying out of the work by students and workers.	
Situation 7: Your school needed some students to take important visitors around the building and asked some First Year students to help them. **Action taken**: The principal explained that they wanted the visitors to see the school and explained to the students what to show the visitors and why.	
Situation 8: Parents from a growing suburb organised a demonstration in front of Leinster House asking for a new primary school to be opened in their area. **Action taken**: The parents took their young children and gave them posters and placards to carry which had slogans like 'I want to go to school'.	

LESSON 23

Rights in conflict

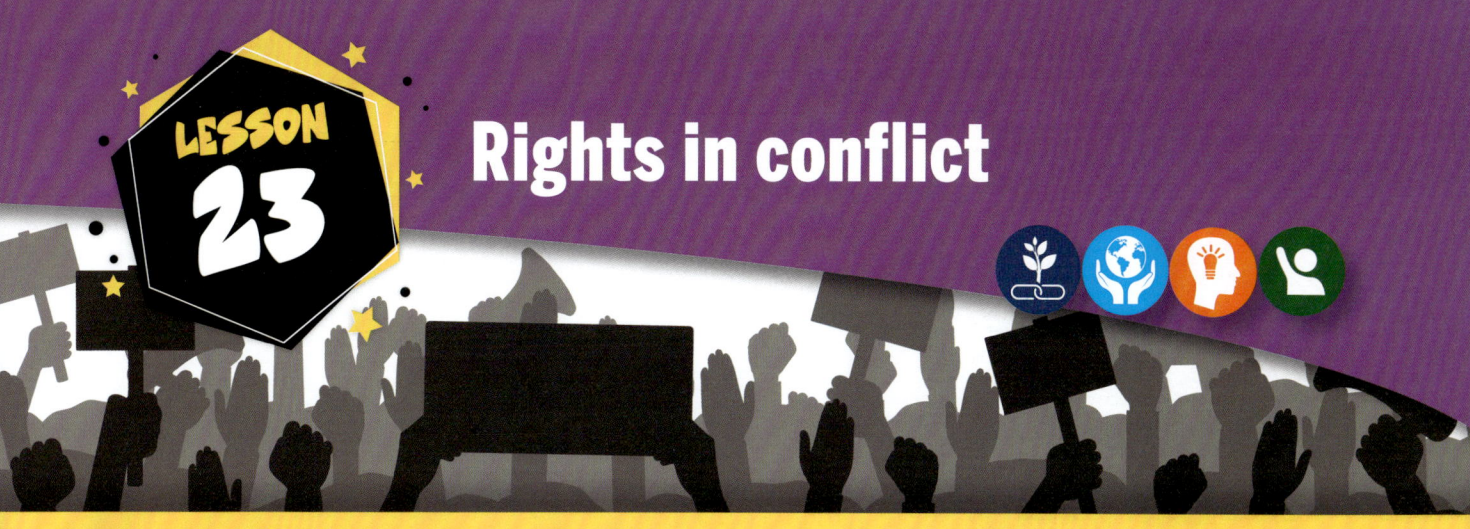

Learning outcome 1.9
Students should be able to outline different perspectives in situations where there is an apparent conflict of rights or an abuse of rights.

Exercise 23A Identifying how rights can come into conflict

Key Skills

Success criteria ☐ I can give reasons for rights being in conflict and suggest solutions.

Rights are sometimes in conflict. This happens when one person or group claims that they cannot enjoy their rights because they clash with the rights of another person or group. An example would be in a school where year groups have different breaktimes. Group 1 is not allowed to play football in the yard during the break because it would disturb group 2 who are in class at the time. Two rights are involved in this case: the right to leisure and the right to education. One group is prevented from enjoying their right whereas the other group is not. If one side in a conflict of rights is more powerful or is more likely to be listened to, their right usually gets priority over the other right.

1. Working in pairs, look at cartoon A and cartoon B in Q2 on the next page. Then discuss the questions and write your answers.

	Cartoon A	Cartoon B
(a) What conflicting rights are involved here?		
(b) How do you think this situation could be resolved?		
(c) Why do you think this situation has not been resolved?		
(d) What do you think is the most likely solution? Why?		

95

● CALL TO ACTION | *Chapter 2*

2. Now complete each cartoon to show the best possible solution.

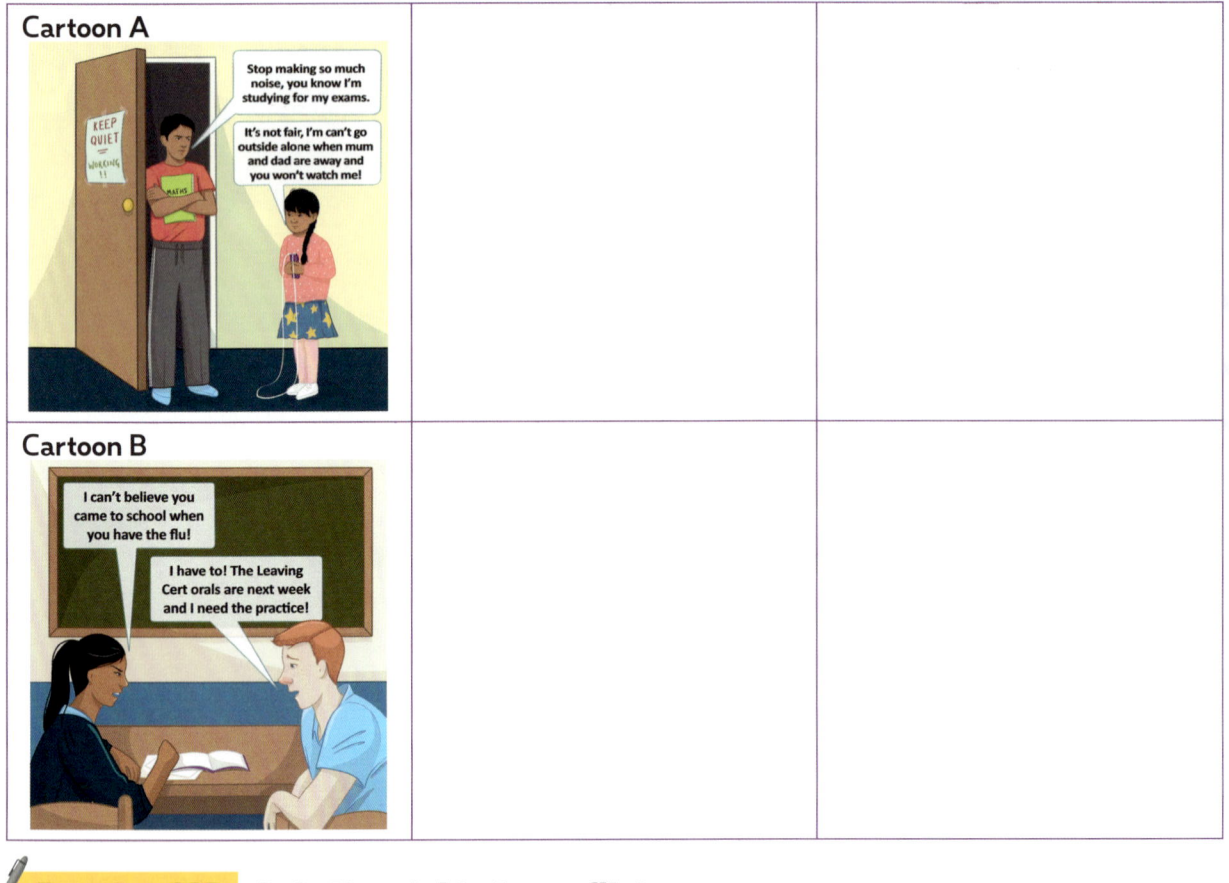

Cartoon A		
Cartoon B		

✎ Exercise 23B Debating rights in conflict

Key Skills   **Success criteria** ☐ I can give my opinion on a conflict of rights and explain my opinion.

When rights come into conflict, it is important to:

1. Understand why each side thinks as they do
2. Resolve the problem. This can be achieved by:
   - Trying to get each side to see the other side of the issue
   - Seeing if an agreement can be made in which each side compromises
   - Accepting that sometimes one side is more in the right than the other.

In many cases, people never get a chance to give their side of a story and the other side is the one everybody hears. Many people are unable to stand up for themselves and rely on others to make people aware of their side. These include people who cannot read or write or who are afraid of being persecuted when their rights are threatened.

You are going to take part in a walking debate based on the following motions:

1. It is ok to discriminate against someone because some rights are more important than others.
2. When the rights of adults and children come into conflict, adults' rights should get priority because adults know better.

You will need to think about how you can justify your position, listen to other students' viewpoints and reflect on others' responses. These factors can lead to you changing position.

Exercise 23C **Understanding different perspectives**

Key Skills Success criteria ☐ I can identify differences in stories based on perspective and explain why one perspective is sometimes the dominant one.

It is important to examine things from different perspectives (points of view). Read the following account of a familiar story, told from another perspective.

The Maligned Wolf, a story by Leif Fearn

The forest was my home. I lived there and I cared about it. I tried to keep it neat and clean. Then one sunny day, while I was cleaning up some garbage a camper had left behind, I heard some footsteps. I leaped behind a tree and saw a rather plain little girl coming down the trail carrying a basket. I was suspicious of this little girl right away because she was dressed funny all in red and her head covered up, so it seemed like she didn't want people to know who she was. Naturally, I stopped to check her out. I asked who she was, where she was going, where she had come from, and all that. She gave me a song and dance about going to her grandmother's house with a basket of lunch. She appeared to be a basically honest person, but she was in my forest and she certainly looked suspicious with that strange getup of hers. So I decided to teach her just how serious it is to prance through the forest unannounced and dressed funny.

I let her go on her way, but I ran ahead to her grandmother's house. When I saw that nice old woman, I explained my problem, and she agreed that her granddaughter needed to learn a lesson alright.

The old woman agreed to stay out of sight until I called her. Actually, she hid under the bed. When the girl arrived, I invited her into the bedroom where I was in the bed, dressed like the grandmother. The girl came in all rosy-cheeked and said something nasty about my big ears. I've been insulted before so I made the best of it by suggesting that my big ears would help me hear better. Now, what I meant was that I liked her and wanted to pay close attention to what she was saying. But she makes another insulting crack about my bulging eyes. Now you can see how I was beginning to feel about this girl who put on such a nice front, but was apparently a very nasty person. Still, I've made it a policy to turn the other cheek, so I told her that my big eyes helped me to see her better. Her next insult really got to me. I've got this problem with having big teeth. And that little girl made an insulting crack about them. I know that I should have had better control, but I leaped up from that bed and growled that my teeth would help me to eat her better. Now, let's face it, no wolf would ever eat a little girl, everyone knows that, but that crazy girl started running around the house screaming, with me chasing her to calm her down. I'd taken off the grandmother clothes, but that only seemed to make it worse.

And all of a sudden, the door came crashing open and a big lumberjack is standing there with his axe. I looked at him and it became clear that I was in trouble. There was an open window behind me and out I went. I'd like to say that was the end of it. But that grandmother character never did tell my side of the story. Before long the word got around that I was a mean, nasty guy. Everybody started avoiding me. I don't know about that little girl with the funny red outfit, but I didn't live happily ever after.

1. Can you think of any other stories where only one side of the events is commonly known?
   _____
   _____

■ CALL TO ACTION | *Chapter 2*

2. Give examples of how 'The Maligned Wolf' presents a different side of a well-known story.
   _____
   _____

3. Were any of the wolf's rights violated? If so, which ones?
   _____
   _____

4. Why do you think everybody believed Little Red Riding Hood's version of events?
   _____
   _____

5. How do you think the wolf could convince people to see his side of the story?
   _____
   _____

Exercise 23D Considering solutions to rights in conflict

Key Skills **Success criteria** ☐ I can give practical advice and suggest solutions in a situation where there is a conflict of rights.

Read the following scenario and consider the advice you would give to Daniel. Write your suggestions in the box that follows.

> Daniel and his family have recently moved to Limerick. Daniel has found it difficult settling in at his new school. He is a talented musician and a skilled soccer player. His class tutor also coaches the under-15 soccer team and has asked Daniel to join the squad. Daniel's parents do not want him to join the team because it would mean staying back after school twice a week. Because both his parents work late, Daniel must collect his younger sisters after school. He told his parents that being part of the team would give him the chance to make friends and help him settle in. But his parents said if they had to pay somebody to mind his sisters twice a week, they would not have enough money to pay for his music lessons. Daniel asks you for advice about what to do. What would you suggest?

Lesson 24: Human rights abuses

Learning outcome 1.9
Students should be able to outline different perspectives in situations where there is an apparent conflict of rights or an abuse of rights.

Exercise 24A Considering the impacts of human rights abuses

Key Skills   **Success criteria**   ☐ I can name consequences of an abuse of rights.

The UDHR lists the rights that all humans are entitled to. Sometimes countries deny their own people or other groups their human rights. When this happens, **human rights are abused**. These abuses can be planned, such as preventing people from voting, or can happen because a country does not intervene, such as not protecting minorities because the government wants the support of the majority. Examples of human rights abuses (and the rights that are denied) include:

- Discriminating in jobs against groups based on gender, religion, sexual orientation (the right to work)
- Not allowing girls to attend school (the right to education)
- Allowing air pollution from factories (the right to health)
- Taking property from people to give it to others (the right to property)
- Intelligence agencies spying on people's online activity (the right to privacy).

Working in pairs, discuss the following statements, and tick whether you think they are true or false.

	True	False
1. In 2017, 58 countries banned religious practice by one or more religious groups.		
2. 70% of the world's poor are male.		
3. Two-thirds of illiterate people in the world aged over 15 are female.		
4. In 2018, 9% of girls and 7% of boys worldwide were not attending primary school.		
5. In 2019, 50% of the countries rated best for freedom of expression were in Europe.		
6. 20,000 children die every day around the world due to poverty.		
7. The majority of people killed by landmines are men.		
8. South Sudan and Somalia were rated the most corrupt countries in the world in 2020.		

CALL TO ACTION | *Chapter 2*

Exercise 24B Analysing statistics on human rights abuses

Key Skills **Success criteria** ☐ I can name the type of abuses of rights that have occurred in Europe and where they took place.

Working in groups, look at the two pie charts below. The first one shows the number of judgements by the European Court of Human Rights against member states from 1959 to 2020. The second chart covers the same period but shows the articles of the ECHR under which the judgements were made. Study the figures and answer the following questions.

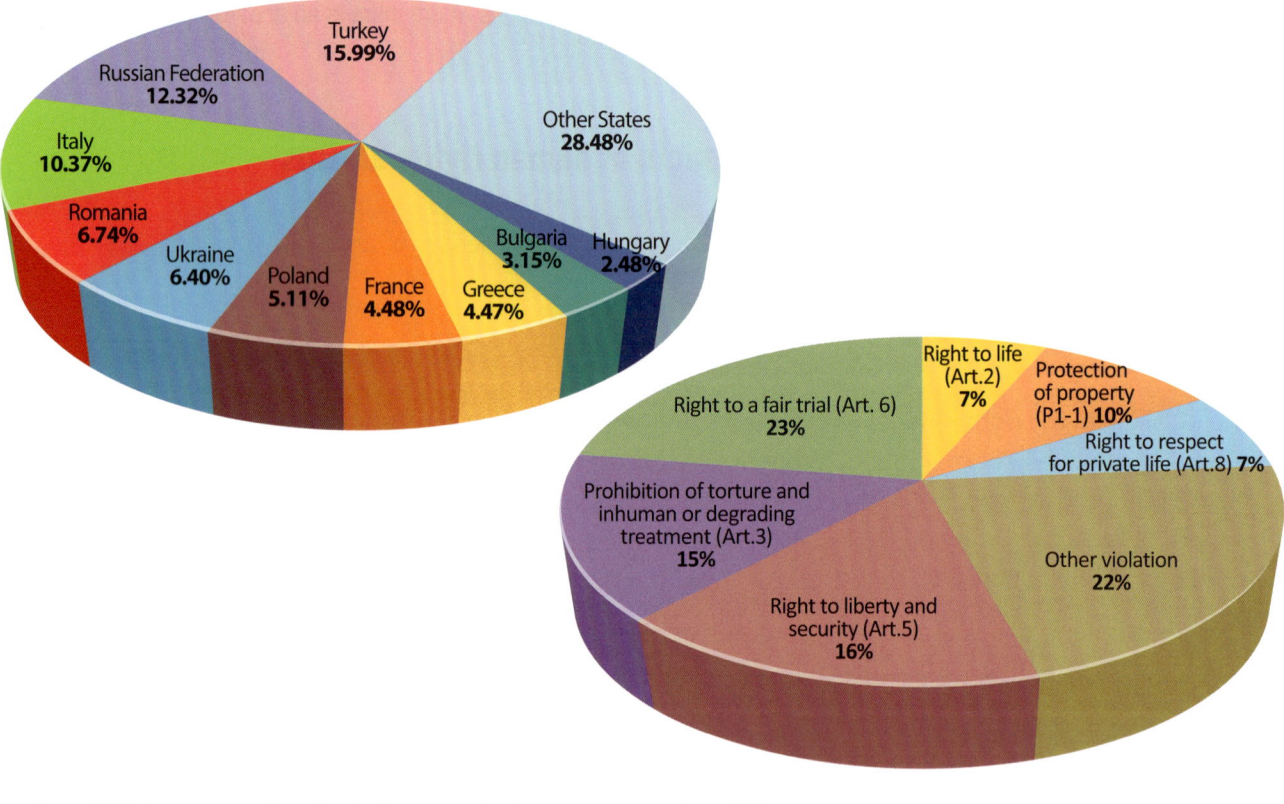

Chart 1 – Judgements by country:
- Turkey 15.99%
- Russian Federation 12.32%
- Italy 10.37%
- Romania 6.74%
- Ukraine 6.40%
- Poland 5.11%
- France 4.48%
- Greece 4.47%
- Bulgaria 3.15%
- Hungary 2.48%
- Other States 28.48%

Chart 2 – Judgements by article of ECHR:
- Right to a fair trial (Art. 6) 23%
- Right to life (Art. 2) 7%
- Protection of property (P1-1) 10%
- Right to respect for private life (Art. 8) 7%
- Prohibition of torture and inhuman or degrading treatment (Art. 3) 15%
- Right to liberty and security (Art. 5) 16%
- Other violation 22%

1. Which country has had the most judgements against it?
   _____

2. What does this tell you about the country?
   _____
   _____

3. Were you surprised by any figures? If so, what surprised you?
   _____
   _____

4. Under which article of the ECHR were most judgements made?
   _____

5. Why is the ECHR a better way of dealing with human rights abuses than the UDHR?
   _____
   _____

Lesson 24: Human rights abuses

Exercise 24C Analysing a situation where human rights are being abused

Key Skills

Success criteria ☐ I can identify my feelings when looking at a situation of rights abuse and suggest how the rights could be restored.

Watch the video about elder abuse and answer the following questions.

> **YouTube** Go to YouTube and search for 'Open Your Eyes – Margaret & Claire.flv' (4:46).

1. How does this video make you feel?

2. Why do you think Margaret accepted the situation?

3. What do you think she could do?

4. Do you think this type of situation is common?

5. Which rights have been taken from Margaret?

6. What could other people do to protect Margaret?

7. Why do you think elderly people are often at risk of being exploited by others?

8. How would you resolve this situation?

101

■ CALL TO ACTION | *Chapter 2*

Exercise 24D Identifying where LGBTI+ human rights are violated

Key Skills　　**Success criteria**　□　I can name countries where LGBTI+ human rights are violated.

Look at the map which shows the status of the rights of LGBTI+ people around the world and answer the questions that follow.

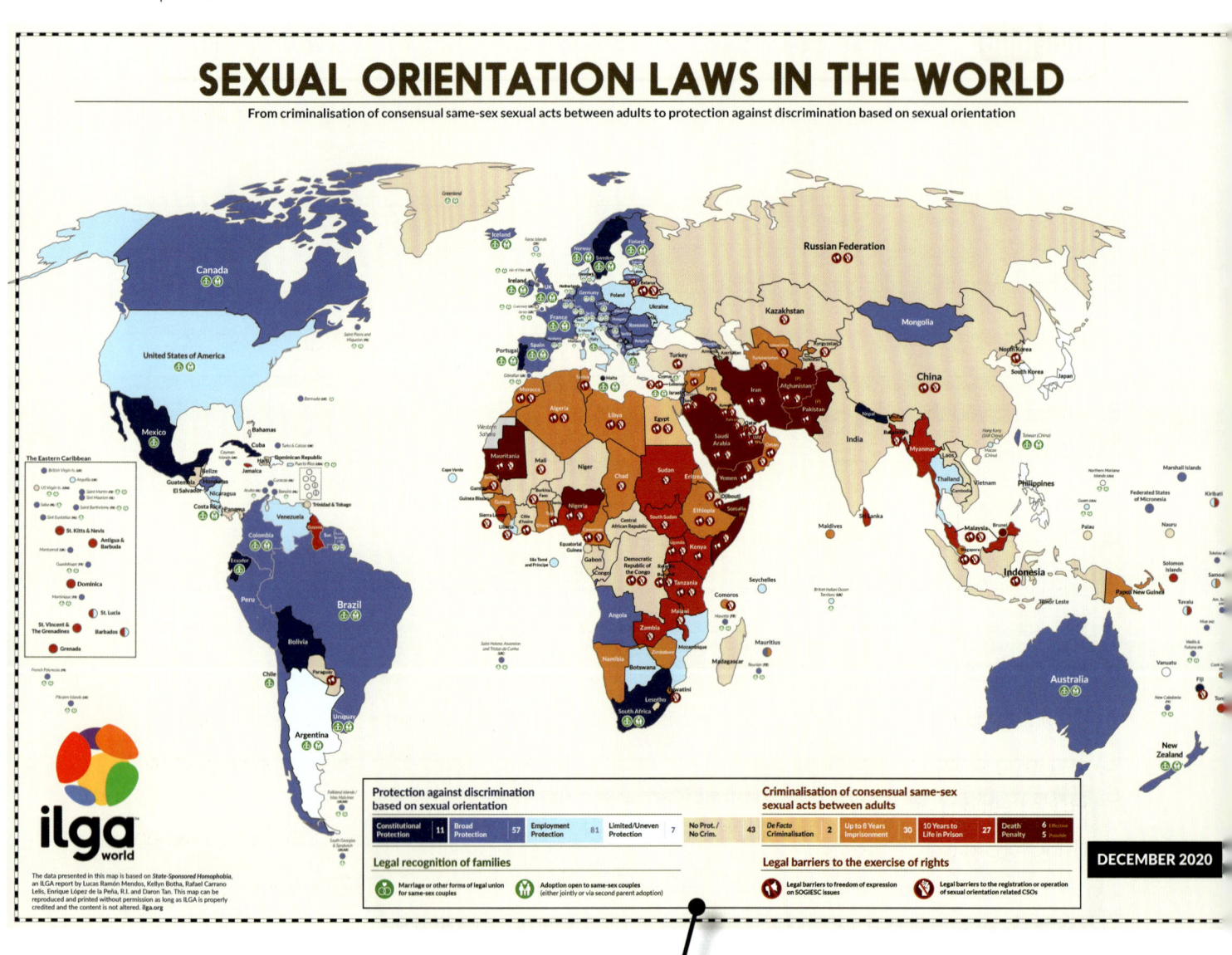

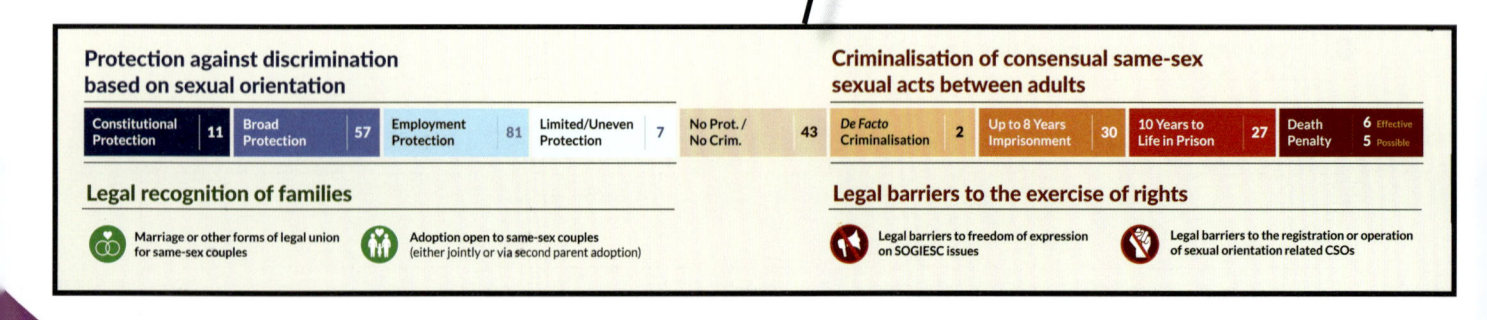

SEXUAL ORIENTATION LAWS IN THE WORLD
From criminalisation of consensual same-sex sexual acts between adults to protection against discrimination based on sexual orientation

Protection against discrimination based on sexual orientation
- Constitutional Protection: 11
- Broad Protection: 57
- Employment Protection: 81
- Limited/Uneven Protection: 7
- No Prot. / No Crim.: 43

Criminalisation of consensual same-sex sexual acts between adults
- De Facto Criminalisation: 2
- Up to 8 Years Imprisonment: 30
- 10 Years to Life in Prison: 27
- Death Penalty: 6 Effective, 5 Possible

Legal recognition of families
- Marriage or other forms of legal union for same-sex couples
- Adoption open to same-sex couples (either jointly or via second parent adoption)

Legal barriers to the exercise of rights
- Legal barriers to freedom of expression on SOGIESC issues
- Legal barriers to the registration or operation of sexual orientation related CSOs

DECEMBER 2020

ilga world

102

Lesson 24: Human rights abuses

1. In which continents are LGBTI+ rights less likely to be respected?
   _____
   _____

2. In which continents are LGBTI+ rights most likely to be respected?
   _____
   _____

3. Name a country where it is especially dangerous to be LGBTI+. Explain why.
   _____
   _____

4. LGBTI+ people have very different rights depending on where they live. Explain how an LGBTI+ person would have a different life in two different countries.
   _____
   _____
   _____

Exercise 24E Classifying violent and nonviolent actions and assessing their impact on human rights

Key Skills **Success criteria** ☐ I can identify how violent actions are often linked to a human rights abuse.

Working in groups, look at the following actions and classify them under the correct category.

- Shouting at somebody
- Blocking roads to protest against wage cuts
- Playing rugby
- Engaging in drone warfare
- Police beating protestors
- Being forced to join the army
- Making fun of somebody on social media
- Protesting against the government
- Pushing a person out of the way of a car
- Reading somebody's private messages and telling others about them
- Pulling off a person's religious head covering
- Being pushed in the crowd at a concert

1. Classify the actions under the following categories:

Violent	Rough	Peaceful

■ CALL TO ACTION | *Chapter 2*

2. Take three of the actions you classified as violent and note the effects these actions have on their victims.

Action 1	Action 2	Action 3

3. Pick one nonviolent action and say how it has an impact on a person's human rights.
_____
_____

4. Which human right is violated in each violent action?

Action 1	Action 2	Action 3

5. How could these rights be protected?

Action 1	Action 2	Action 3

6. Who is responsible for protecting these rights?

Action 1	Action 2	Action 3

Lesson 25: Simulated debate on disadvantage

Learning outcome 1.9
Students should be able to outline different perspectives in situations where there is an apparent conflict of rights or an abuse of rights.

Exercise 25A Identifying disadvantages faced by different people

Key Skills

Success criteria ☐ I can list the areas that I will speak about.

In Chapter 1, you learned about different groups of people in society that face disadvantage. These included people with disabilities, people without a home and asylum seekers. Since then, you have looked at the rights people are entitled to and the ways to protect these rights. You have also come across other cases of disadvantage in Irish society.

In this lesson, you are going to participate in a simulated debate. In a simulated debate, the whole class debates the issue of disadvantage, but everyone is taking on a role. The simulated debate will be presented as a TV programme.

Your teacher will allocate roles to you in advance of the debate. Once you have your role, consider the disadvantages your character faces in Irish society and note these below.

_____
_____
_____
_____
_____
_____
_____
_____
_____

■ CALL TO ACTION | *Chapter 2*

Exercise 25B — Taking part in a simulated debate on disadvantage

Key Skills

Success criteria ☐ I can speak on areas of disadvantage faced by one group in society.

In the simulated debate TV programme, one member of each disadvantaged group will speak on the difficulties facing them for one minute and then the TV presenter (the teacher) will open the debate to the floor. There will be some journalists and politicians present in the debate too. Audience members cannot speak until they have the microphone – given by the teacher.

Exercise 25C — Writing a report on the debate

Key Skills

Success criteria ☐ I can write about the debate mentioning the areas that were the most informative.

After the debate, consider what you learned from the process. If you played the role of one of the disadvantaged groups, write a diary entry on how the debate went, referring to how others responded to you and how you felt. If you were a journalist, write an account of the debate for your newspaper/website.

Lesson 26: My responsibilities

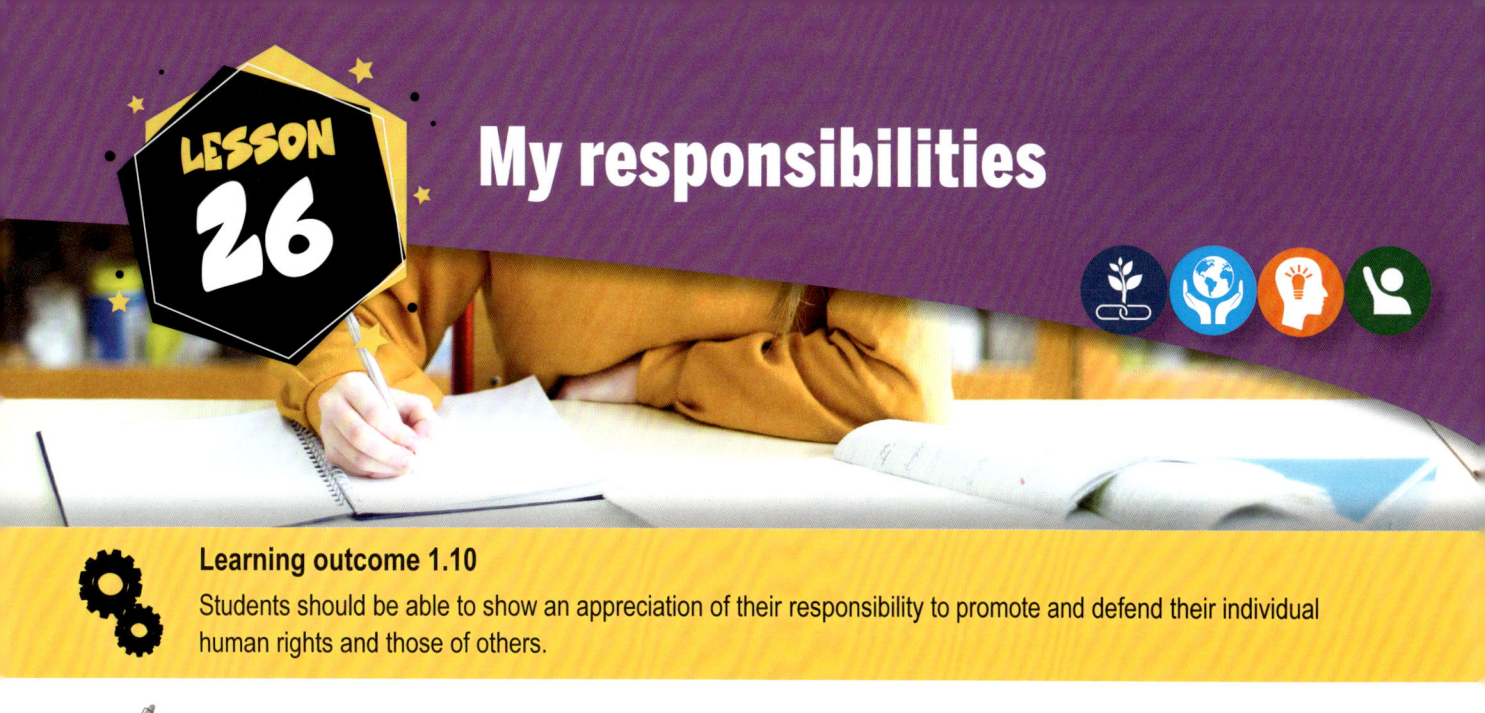

Learning outcome 1.10

Students should be able to show an appreciation of their responsibility to promote and defend their individual human rights and those of others.

Exercise 26A Identifying the responsibilities that correspond with my rights

Key Skills   **Success criteria**   ☐ I can name the different responsibilities linked to my rights.

You have already looked at rights and the importance of them. Each right comes with a **responsibility**.

Complete the box below by writing the responsibility linked to your rights. The first one has been done as an example.

I have the right to ...	Therefore, I have the responsibility to ...
1. education	try my best to learn and not prevent other students from learning
2. privacy	
3. religion	
4. my good name	
5. life	
6. a home	
7. healthcare	
8. to leisure	
9. to a nationality	
10. to have my own opinion	

■ CALL TO ACTION | *Chapter 2*

Exercise 26B — Identifying areas where I have responsibility and how this makes me feel

Key Skills **Success criteria** ☐ I can name the different areas for which I have responsibility and explain how I feel about it..

Answer the following questions.

1. What things do you have responsibility for at home?
   _____
   _____

2. What areas do you have responsibility for at school?
   _____
   _____

3. In what other areas do you have responsibility?
   _____
   _____

4. How do you feel about having responsibility?
   _____
   _____

5. What happens if you are not responsible?
   _____
   _____

6. Who is a good example of a responsible person? Explain your choice.
   _____
   _____

7. What responsibilities do you have for your country?
   _____
   _____

8. What responsibilities do you have for the world?
   _____
   _____

Lesson 26: My responsibilities

Exercise 26C — Identifying my rights and responsibilities in relation to the UNCRC

Key Skills **Success criteria** ☐ I can name situations where I have exercised rights and the responsibilities that I have as part of that right.

In Irish law, a person under the age of 18 is seen as a child. The **age of criminal responsibility** (the age at which a person can be convicted of a crime) is usually 12 but can be as young as 10 in very serious cases such as murder.

Look at some of the following articles from the UNCRC. Select two and answer the questions that follow.

- **Article 3**: Whenever an adult has anything to do with a child, he or she should do what is best for the child.
- **Article 10**: If you are living in a different country to your parents, you have the right to be reunited and live in the same place.
- **Article 12**: Whenever adults make a decision that will affect you, you have the right to give your opinion.
- **Article 16**: You have the right to a private life.
- **Article 30**: If you come from a minority group, you have the right to enjoy your own culture, practise your own religion and speak your own language.
- **Article 31**: The government should provide opportunities for you to enjoy cultural, artistic and recreational activities.
- **Article 32**: You should be protected from work that exploits you by paying very little, is dangerous and is likely to interfere with your education.
- **Article 37**: Even if you do something wrong, no one is allowed to punish you in a way that humiliates you or hurts you badly.

	Article	Article
1. Have you heard about any situations relating to this article in the media?		
2. What is your own experience with this article?		
3. What are your responsibilities under this article?		
4. If this article was denied to you, what could you do about it?		

■ CALL TO ACTION | *Chapter 2*

Exercise 26D **Identifying feelings associated with not acting responsibly and what I learned from this**

Key Skills	**Success criteria** ☐ I can write about a situation where I was irresponsible, noting my feelings and naming the things I learned from it.

Think about a situation where you did something irresponsible. Write a diary entry where you mention the incident, describe how you felt afterwards and what you learned from it.

LESSON 27

The importance of responsibility

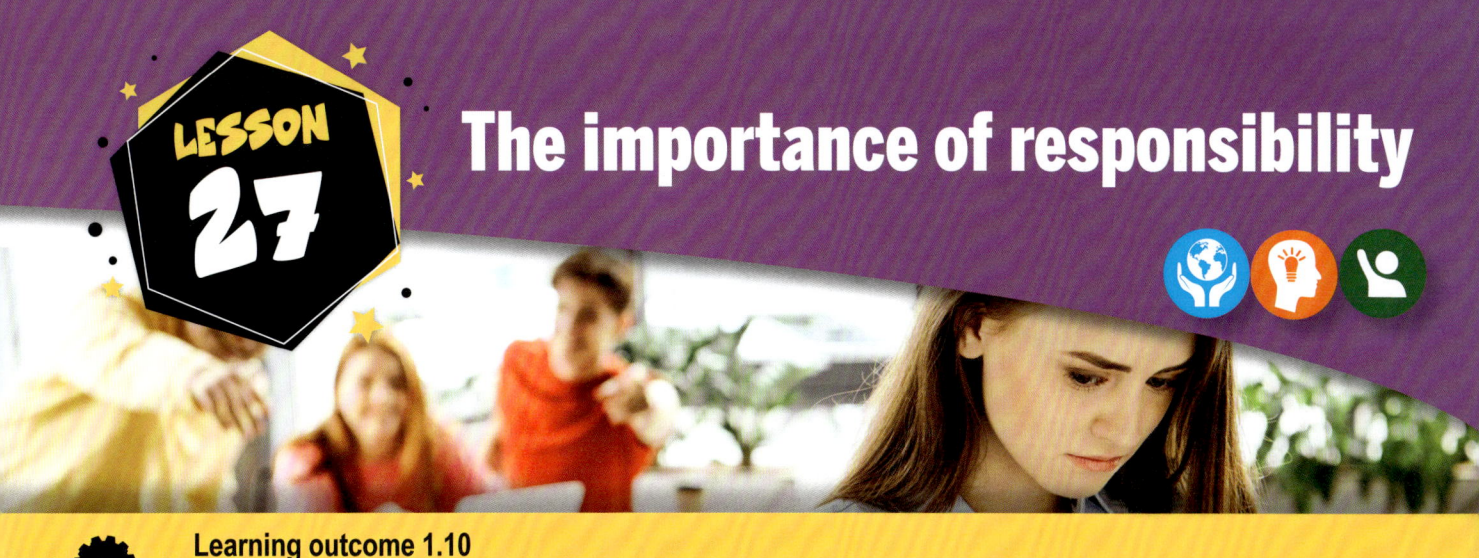

Learning outcome 1.10
Students should be able to show an appreciation of their responsibility to promote and defend their individual human rights and those of others.

Exercise 27A — Identifying the consequences of not acting responsibly

Key Skills

Success criteria ☐ I can identify responsibilities that are ignored and name the consequences of these.

When people fail to recognise and act on their responsibilities, it can have consequences. Sometimes the consequences are minor, such as forgetting to turn the light off at night. But sometimes they can be serious, for example, forgetting to put the spark guard in front of the fire can lead to a house fire.

Working in groups, look at the following situations. Identify the responsibilities being ignored and what the consequences are of not acting responsibly.

Situation	Responsibility being ignored	Consequence
1. Paul always makes noises when Nina speaks in class.		
2. Marcus forgot to bring his Maths book to school. While Jean is not looking, he takes her book and writes his name on it.		
3. Aoibh has asthma, but she smokes in the yard during breaktime.		
4. Ciara is always making nasty comments about her classmates on social media.		

■ CALL TO ACTION | *Chapter 2*

5. Dr O'Connor thinks that Martina is a hypochondriac. When Martina complains about having severe headaches at night, Dr O'Connor tells her to go home and sleep it off.		
6. Maninder is a Sikh, and wears a turban as part of his religion. Some of his classmates think it is funny to try to pull his turban off his head.		
7. Jack is eating crisps in the classroom. He throws the empty packet on the floor under his desk when he is finished.		
8. Joanne is renting a holiday home for the week. She invites all her friends for a huge party and the carpets get ruined.		

Exercise 27B Identifying who has responsibility

Key Skills

Success criteria ☐ I can name the people with responsibilities and suggest solutions to difficult circumstances.

Read the scenarios below and complete the questions on the next page.

1. Shane is 12 and has started mowing lawns for people in his town to save money for his school tour next year. His mother is worried that he is mowing lawns for people she does not know.	2. Liam is 15 and preparing for his exams at the end of the year. It is hard to get time to study as his dad expects him to spend every Saturday and Sunday working on the farm.
3. Sally is 22 and has been taking drugs for the past few years. She lives with a group of friends in the city. When she runs out of money, she goes home to her father. He gives her money because he is afraid of what will happen to her if he refuses.	4. Joseph and his family came to Ireland from the Republic of the Congo. Joseph's parents do not speak English. He cannot meet up with his friends on Saturdays as he has to help his parents with jobs they could do themselves if they spoke English. He is annoyed because they spend their time only with French-speaking friends.

Lesson 27: The importance of responsibility

5. Dylan's house had a small hole in the roof, but his parents ignored it. Now, the water is streaming in when it rains and the kitchen wall has mould growing on it. An engineer said the roof will need to be replaced, but Dylan's parents cannot afford to get it done.

6. Stephanie begged her parents to get her a pony when she was in primary school. She promised that she would look after it, but now she has no interest and her dad has to do all the work with the pony.

Story	Who is responsible for solving the problem?	How can the problem be solved?
1.		
2.		
3.		
4.		
5.		
6.		

Exercise 27C Writing about responsible actions and their impact

Key Skills

Success criteria ☐ I can write a report showing how somebody showed responsibility and the impact of their actions.

Watch the video about Patrick and Morgan Oliver. Then think of an incident when you were impressed by how a young person showed great responsibility. Write a news story about what this young person did and the consequences of their action.

YouTube
Go to YouTube and search for 'Missing paddleboarders found alive after 15 hours in water' (2:37).

_____
_____
_____
_____
_____

CALL TO ACTION | *Chapter 2*

Exercise 27D **Identifying the consequences when nobody takes responsibility for their action**

Key Skills

Success criteria ☐ I can name consequences of nobody taking responsibility for their actions.

Read this shortened version of Charles Osgood's 'Responsibility Poem'.

> There was an important job to be done and Everybody was sure that Somebody would do it. Anybody could have done it, but Nobody did it. Somebody got angry about that because it was Everybody's job. Everybody thought Anybody could do it, but Nobody realized that Everybody couldn't do it. It ended up that Everybody blamed Somebody when Nobody did what Anybody could have.

In the poem, we can see what happens when nobody takes responsibility for anything. Working in pairs, describe five changes that you think would happen in Irish society if nobody was responsible for their actions.

1. _____

2. _____

3. _____

4. _____

5. _____

LESSON 28
My human rights actions

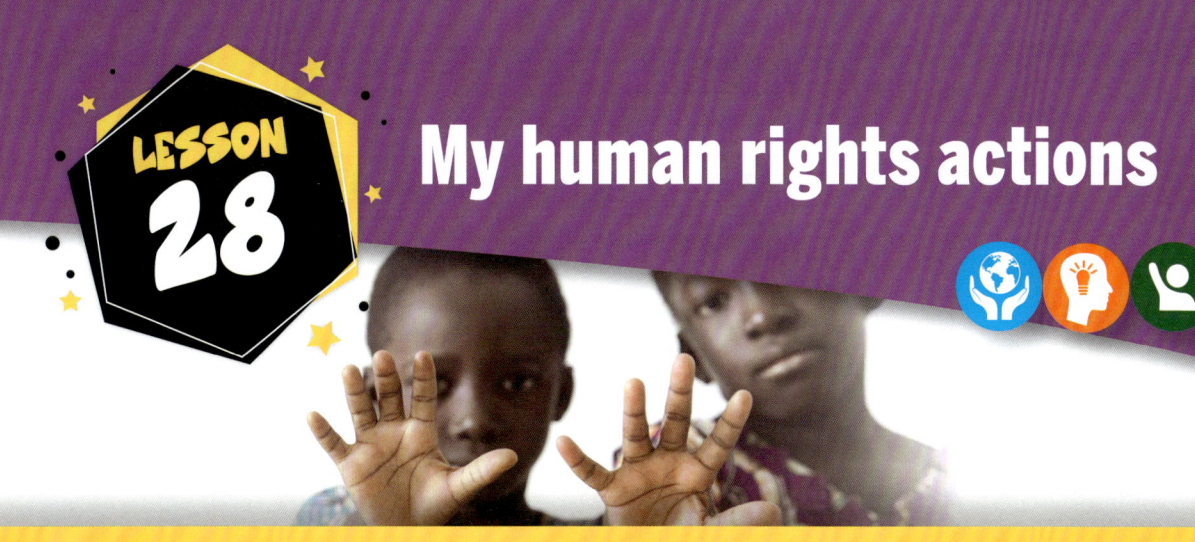

Learning outcome 1.10
Students should be able to show an appreciation of their responsibility to promote and defend their individual human rights and those of others.

Exercise 28A — Considering actions I could take to improve a situation in which human rights are violated

Key Skills

Success criteria
☐ I can explain what rights are violated and what actions I could take to improve the situation.

Read the three stories below and see if you can match the story to the location. Then answer the questions that follow.

1.	I am ten years old. We have no running water in our village, so we have to travel to a river to get water. As I am a girl, this is seen as a job for me. I spend many hours every day carrying heavy cans of dirty water and I cannot go to school.	A.	Brazil
2.	My family live in an isolated village, so we were never vaccinated against yellow fever. Now an outbreak has occurred in the village.	B.	Yemen
3.	My country has been at war for the past few years. My parents don't want me to go to school, because schools have been bombed.	C.	Angola

1	2	3

1. What actions would improve the human rights situation?
   _____
   _____

2. Who is responsible for these actions?
   _____
   _____

3. Do you think you could have any influence on these people/organisations?
   _____
   _____
   _____
   _____
   _____

■ CALL TO ACTION | *Chapter 2*

Exercise 28B Suggesting how I can intervene when rights are denied

Key Skills **Success criteria** ☐ I can give examples of actions I could take to improve a situation where rights are denied.

Conduct the following audit on your involvement in human rights actions.

1. What organisations are you a member of?
   _____
   _____

2. Are you a member of a human rights organisation?
   _____

3. Have you ever attended a demonstration? If so, which one(s)?
   _____
   _____

4. Have you ever signed a petition, written a letter or an email to protest against something or to advocate for something? If so, for what cause?
   _____
   _____

5. Have you followed a a human rights or a social justice campaign on social media? If so, which one(s)?
   _____
   _____

6. Have you liked a campaign on social media? If so, which one(s)?
   _____
   _____

7. Are there any social justice issues you feel strongly about? If so, what sparked your interest in the issue?
   _____
   _____

8. Would you speak up about this issue? Why/why not?
   _____
   _____

Exercise 28C Suggesting how I can intervene in a human rights issue

Key Skills **Success criteria** ☐ I can give examples of actions I could take to improve a human rights issue.

116

Lesson 28: My human rights actions

Look at the following three scenarios. What rights are being denied? What could you do in this situation?

Scenario	Right denied	What I can do
1. Lynne is being excluded by other girls in the class. They meet up after school, but never ask her to join them. The class have social media groups, but she is not included. She is never asked to parties and, if she tries to join in at breaktime, they either ignore her or walk away. Nobody wants to sit beside her.		
2. Jane returned to Ireland two years ago after spending most of her working life in London. She now lives in a nursing home. Jane has no children and her only nephew lives in New Zealand. She enjoys playing cards and chatting to people, but the other residents do not play cards and she never has visitors.		
3. Your local park has no facilities for young people. You love tennis and think there should be a tennis court built in it. Some of your friends like pitch and putt. But the park is boring at the moment – unless you play soccer, there is nothing to do there.		

■ CALL TO ACTION | *Chapter 2*

Exercise 28D — Raising awareness of a human rights issue

Key Skills

Success criteria ☐ I can design a poster that raises awareness of a specific human rights issue.

Working in pairs, look back over the stories in Exercises 28A and 28C. Choose one story, research the issue mentioned and design a poster to raise awareness of the issue. In your poster include a picture, heading and facts. Stick a photo of your poster here.

118

LESSON 29

Case study: Human rights in the West Bank

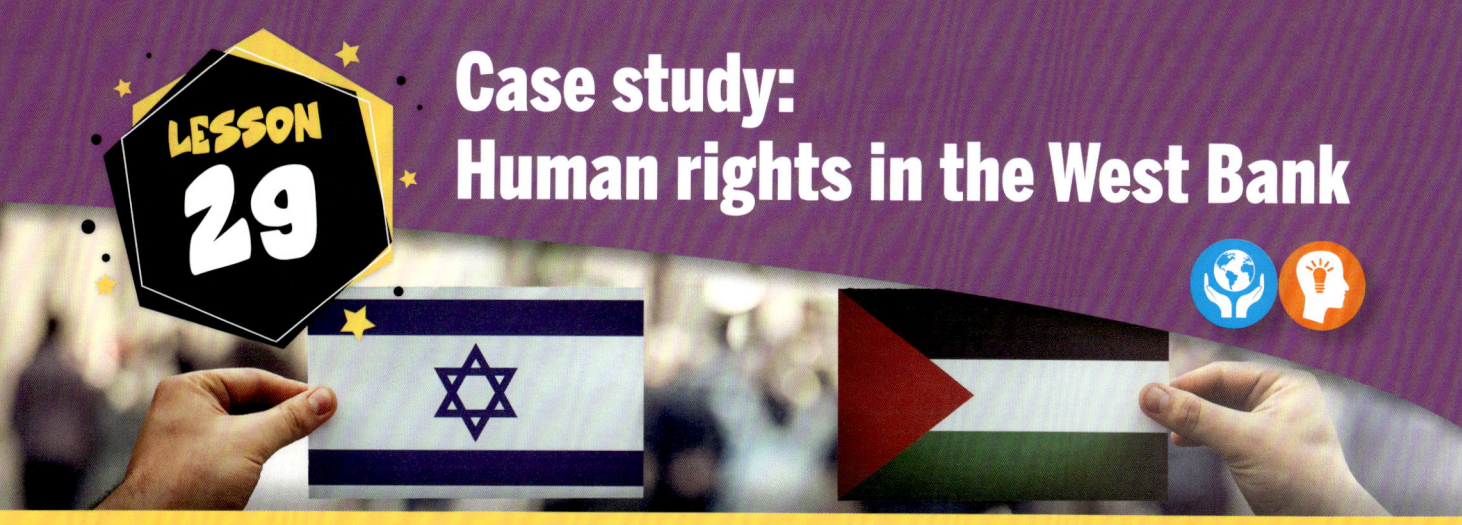

Learning outcome 1.9

Students should be able to outline different perspectives in situations where there is an apparent conflict of rights or an abuse of rights.

Exercise 29A Analysing maps to identify human rights concerns

Key Skills

Success criteria ☐ I can understand how the Israeli-Palestinian conflict is linked, in part, to who owns the land.

After World War I, Britain took over Palestine from the Turkish Ottoman Empire. At the time, Arab Palestinians were the majority and the Jewish population were in the minority. The Jewish population increased during the 1930s when many fled religious persecution in Europe and again in the 1940s after the Holocaust.

In 1947 as British rule was about to end, the UN suggested splitting Palestine into separate Arab and Jewish states. Jerusalem would become an international city and would not be the capital of either Israel or the Arab state. Jewish leaders accepted the plan, but it was rejected by Arab Palestinians. In 1948, Jewish Palestinians declared Israeli independence. This led to a war after which Israel controlled most of the territory. Jordan and Egypt took the Palestinian lands of the West Bank and Gaza and Jerusalem was divided between Israel and Jordan.

In the Six Day War in 1967, Israel took control of Gaza and the West Bank. These are known as the Occupied Territories. Many Palestinian refugees fled from the West Bank and Gaza to Jordan, Syria and Lebanon. Israel has never allowed these refugees to return home. Since 1967, Israeli settlers have taken over more and more land in the West Bank. The conflict between Palestine and Israel is still going on.

Shrinking Palestine

1946 | UN Plan 1947 | 1949-1967 | 2012

5 million Palestinians are classified as refugees by the UN

■ CALL TO ACTION | *Chapter 2*

Working in pairs, look at the map of Palestine and Israel and answer the questions that follow.

1. What does the map show?

   _____

   _____

2. Do you know if the number of Palestinians living in the Occupied Territories is reducing at the same rate as the land they own?

   _____

Exercise 29B Identifying human rights concerns using pictures

Key Skills

Success criteria ☐ I can explain how photos from the region show how the conflict is causing numerous human rights concerns.

Israel claims all the city of Jerusalem as its capital, even though the east of the city is in the Palestinian West Bank. Some 630,000 Israelis live in settlements built on land captured during the Six Day War despite this being against international law. In 2019, the European Court of Justice decided that food produced in Israeli West Bank settlements cannot be labelled as a product of Israel. Many Palestinians work in the settlements. However, their land continues to be taken for settlements, they are not allowed to use the roads linking the settlements to Israel and Palestinian civilians are tried in military courts instead of civil courts.

Working in pairs, look at the photos below from the region and explain what human rights are being denied or experienced by the people in each photo.

Picture	Describe the human rights experienced or denied.
1. *A Bedouin village*	
2. *A café in east Jerusalem*	
3. *An Israeli settlement on the West Bank*	
4. *Israeli soldiers and Palestinians*	

Lesson 29: Case Study: Human rights in the West Bank

5. *A beach on the Dead Sea*

6. *A protest in the West Bank*

Exercise 29C — Understanding the impact of discrimination on human rights issues

Key Skills

Success criteria ☐ I can understand statistics and what they represent.

The Israeli occupation of Palestinian Territory in facts and figures

- The Palestinian population in the Occupied Territories is 4.8 million.
- There were 5.6 million Palestinian refugees living outside Palestine as of December 2019.
- There are 630,000 Israeli settlers living in 278 settlements in the West Bank and East Jerusalem.
- Between 2011 and 2021, some 3,572 Palestinians (including 806 children) and 198 Israelis (including 14 children) died as a result of the conflict.
- The GDP per capita of the Occupied Palestinian Territory is US$3,463, compared with US$43,592 in Israel.
- The poverty rate is 36% in the West Bank and East Jerusalem, and 64% in Gaza.
- In the Occupied Territories, Palestinian access to water is below the internationally recommended level of 100 litres per capita. Israel controls 85% of Palestinian water sources.
- Some 2 million Palestinians are considered food insecure, including 600,000 in the West Bank and 1.4 million in Gaza.

(Source: United Nations)

Working in pairs, look at the facts and figures and answer the questions that follow.

1. How many Palestinian refugees are living outside Palestine?

2. Find four facts that show the inequality between the two sides.

CALL TO ACTION | Chapter 2

3. Why do you think such inequality exists?
   _____
   _____

4. Israel is wealthier than Palestine. How do you know this?
   _____
   _____

5. Show how Israel controls the Occupied Territories apart from using the army.
   _____
   _____

Exercise 29D Identifying how Israeli settlements impact on the Bedouin

Key Skills **Success criteria** ☐ I can name impacts on other people of human rights abuses.

Read the article and answer the questions that follow.

Kfar Adumim – Khan al-Ahmar

Kfar Adumim is an Israeli settlement 10 km east of Jerusalem where 400 settler families live in modern houses. The settlement was built in 1979, close to several tourist attractions, including the Ein Prat/Wadi Qelt Nature Reserve.

A short distance from Kfar Adumim is the Bedouin (nomadic Arab) village of Khan al-Ahmar, which is little more than a collection of tin shacks. The village is home to approximately 180 Bedouin, more than half of whom are children, and was established by refugees who were driven out of Israel in 1948. As the Bedouin are Indigenous Peoples (the ethnic group who are native to a place), they enjoy special rights over the land they occupy and the natural resources they use to sustain their traditional livelihoods and way of life.

For years, Israel has been trying to relocate the residents of Khan al-Ahmar against their wishes, to expand settlements in the region. Firstly, they created push factors to make the lives of the Bedouin as difficult as possible:

- By refusing to connect homes to the electricity network.
- By confiscating solar panels.
- By failing to give access to water.
- By rejecting applications for building permits.
- By demolishing homes and animal shelters and threatening further demolitions.
- By restricting access to roads.
- By restricting access to grazing lands.
- By denying people permits to work in settlements.
- By failing to protect the community from intimidation and attacks by Israeli settlers.

These push factors have led to violations of many human rights of the people of Khan al-Ahmar, including the rights to adequate housing and to an adequate standard of living. The Kfar Adumim settlement has taken almost all the land the Bedouin used to graze their animals. This has seriously affected their traditional source of livelihood. Villagers now rely on low-paid seasonal agricultural work elsewhere and humanitarian relief from the Palestinian authorities. This only just about covers essential household expenditure.

Lesson 29: Case Study: Human rights in the West Bank

The Israeli government ordered the demolition of Khan al-Ahmar on the grounds that villagers did not get relevant building permits. The Bedouin fought this through the Israeli courts. However, in 2018, the Supreme Court ruled that demolitions could go ahead. The village is now facing demolition and the forcible transfer of its residents to make way for further illegal settlements. The demolition order includes the village's school, which provides education for some 170 Bedouin children. If implemented, these actions will constitute war crimes, as well as violations of the human rights to adequate housing, education and non-interference with family and home.

Source: Amnesty International

1. What are the differences between Kfar Adumim and Khan al-Ahmar?

2. How have Israeli authorities attempted to remove the Bedouin from Khan al-Ahmar?

3. How did the Bedouin traditionally make their living?

4. How do the Bedouin make their living now?

5. What rights will the Bedouin lose following the Israeli Supreme Court decision in 2018?

6. Why are the Bedouin being forced off their land?

7. What actions do you think could be taken to protect the Bedouin village?

8. Why do you think these actions have not been taken?

9. Why do you think this article was written?

10. If a similar situation happened in Ireland, what could you do?

Lesson 30: Probable and possible futures

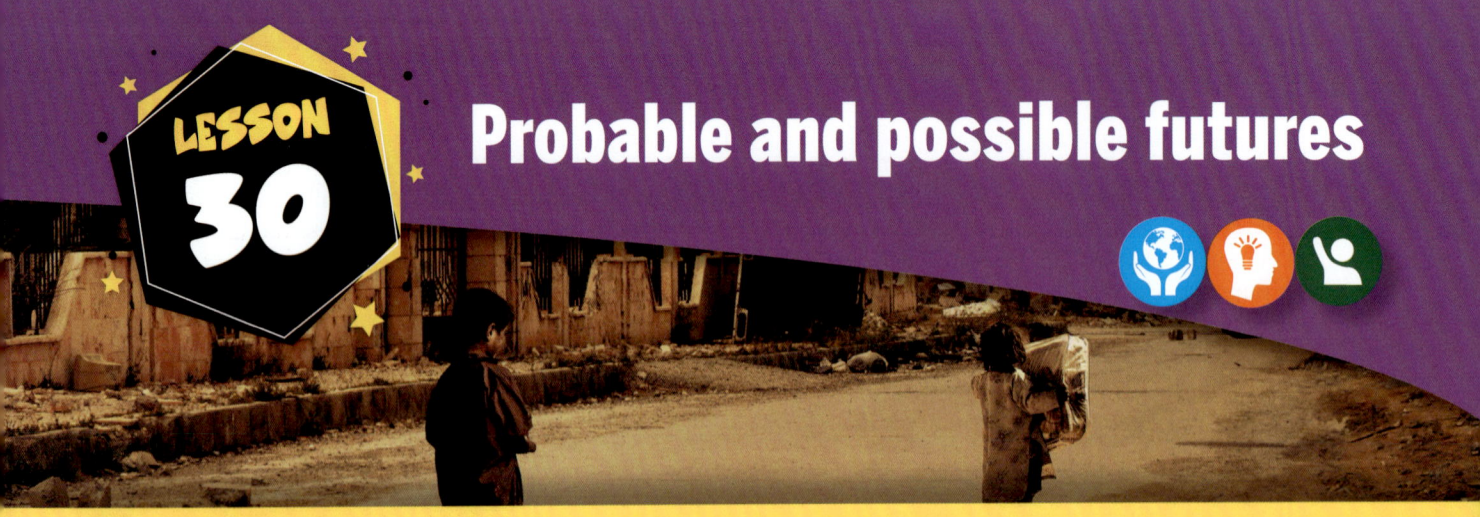

Learning outcomes 1.9
Students should be able to outline different perspectives in situations where there is an apparent conflict of rights or an abuse of rights.

Exercise 30A Identifying the likely futures of Palestinian children in the Occupied Territories

Key Skills

Success criteria ☐ I can name the likely future the children in these case studies face.

Read the articles and watch the video. Write what you think the probable futures of Palestinian children living in the Occupied Territories will be.

The following stories show the experience of Palestinians living in the West Bank.

At 2 a.m. on Nov. 14, 2013, Ruwaida Dar Khalil was warming a bottle for her baby son in her home in Sinjil in the occupied West Bank when four adult male Israeli settlers broke into the tiny house that she shares with her husband and five children. The men smashed windows with crowbars, before dousing the entrance in gasoline and setting it ablaze.

Ruwaida and her husband, Khaled, had no option but to hide on the roof until help arrived. Sinjil is surrounded on three sides by an Israeli military base and two settlements. Soldiers are a common sight in the neighbourhood, and Ruwaida finds it hard to understand why they didn't come to help her family on the night of the attack.

'That night, there were Israeli police officers on the corner … and soldiers usually come to our place every night,' she said. 'But … nobody showed up. Nobody cared. Why didn't anybody come to protect innocent children in this house?'

By the time Palestinian firefighters arrived and put out the fire, the roof had partially collapsed. All five of the children were treated for excessive smoke inhalation following the fire. The next day, Khaled found the words 'Regards from Eden, Revenge!' scrawled in spray paint on an outside wall. The message referred to Eden Attias, an Israeli soldier who had been killed by a Palestinian teenager a day earlier. Acts of violence like this are known as 'price tag' attacks and they are carried out by extremist Israeli settlers against Palestinians as revenge for any action taken against the settlements in the West Bank. This even includes actions by the Israeli government, like demolition orders against unauthorised settlements.

The Dar Khalil children continue to struggle with the after effects of the attack. Three-year-old Nisreen suffers from breathing difficulties and may have to have surgery. Eman struggles to sleep at night and refuses to go to the bathroom alone. She wakes up crying and thinks she hears settlers outside.

Lesson 30: Probable and possible futures

Childhood under siege

The Abu Shamsiya family lives in a modest two-room house in Hebron, the largest Palestinian city in the West Bank. Imad, his wife Faiza, and their three sons and two daughters are the frequent victims of both settler and military violence. In 2011, their daughter Marwa, then 7, was snatched by a group of settlers as she made her way home from school. They held her down and set her hair on fire. An Israeli soldier intervened and put out the fire, but it was more than a year before Marwa could sleep through the night without waking up and screaming.

In 2013, Imad's son Mohammad was on his way to the store to fetch bread when he was stopped by an Israeli soldier. The soldier asked him if he had recently thrown rocks, then he slapped Mohammad across the face twice and threatened to kill him.

'I went to tell my mom,' Mohammad said. 'When my mom came to ask the soldier why [he hit me], he slammed her against the wall. When my dad went later, the soldier told him he hit me because he felt like it.'

Source: Defense for Children International – Palestine

> **YouTube** Go to YouTube and search for 'Israeli-Palestinian conflict: The challenge of control over a Jerusalem neighbourhood' (3:00).

Probable futures

_____
_____
_____
_____
_____
_____
_____

Exercise 30B — Identifying the preferred future of Palestinian children in the Occupied Territories

Key Skills **Success criteria** ☐ I can name the preferred future these people face.

Having read the case studies and watched the video, write what your preferred future for the Palestinian children would be.

Preferred futures

_____
_____
_____
_____
_____
_____
_____

■ CALL TO ACTION | *Chapter 2*

Exercise 30C Identifying the factors needed to lead to the probable futures becoming preferred futures

Key Skills

Success criteria ☐ I can name the factors that need to change to move the probable futures to the preferred futures.

Look at the probable futures you chose in Exercise 30A. Write four of them along the diagonal line of the V marked 'Probable future'. Then look at the preferred futures you chose in Exercise 30B and write them along the other diagonal line. See if you can find four that are different to the probable future. Finally, consider what factors are needed to change the probable futures to the preferred futures. Write these factors in the centre of the V. See the sample below.

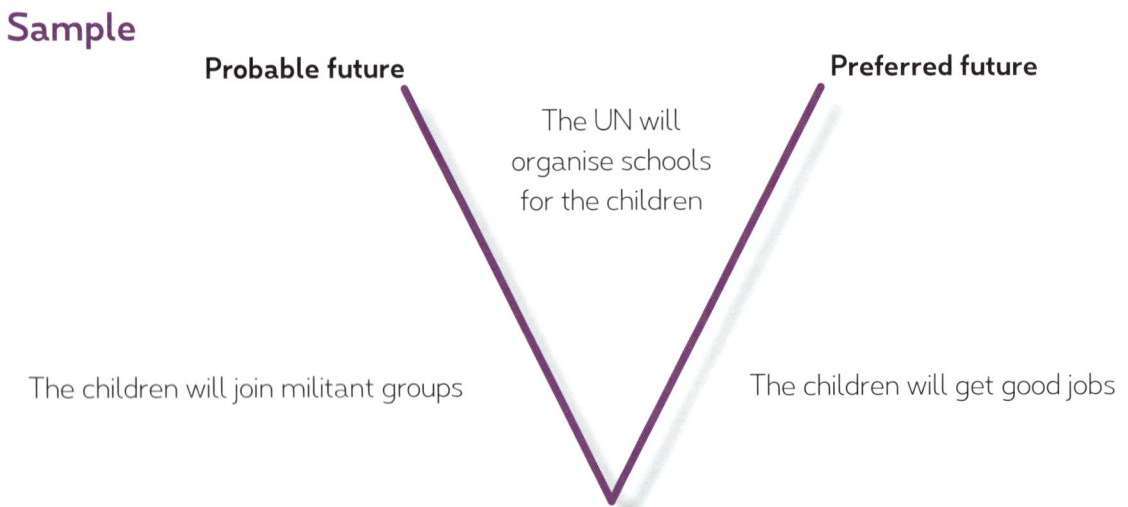

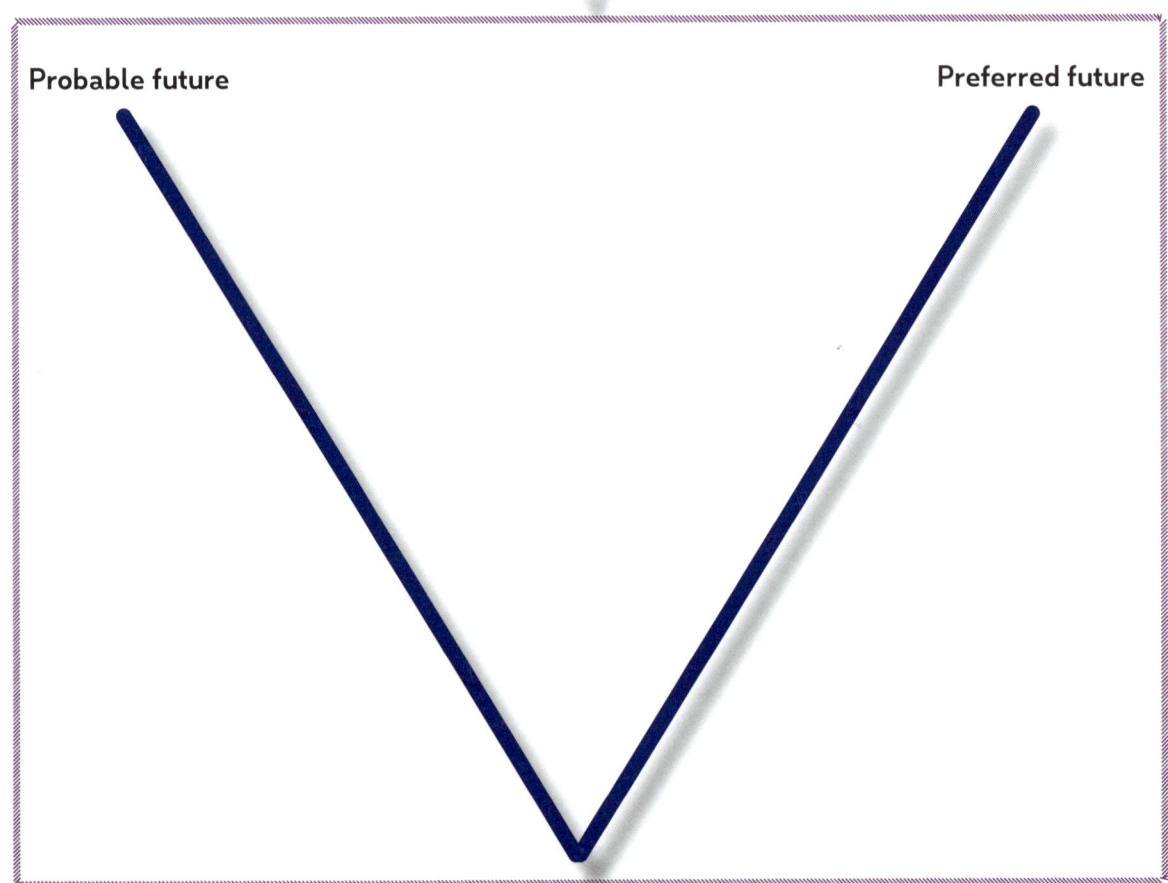

Sample

Probable future

Preferred future

The UN will organise schools for the children

The children will join militant groups

The children will get good jobs

Probable future

Preferred future

Reflection: Reflecting on my learning about human rights

Learning Outcome: 1.11
Students should be able to reflect on their ongoing learning and what it means for them.

Key Skills

Success criteria

☐ I can give examples of the skills I used to show how I understand issues such as rights, the UDHR, the ECHR, the UNCRC and responsibility.

☐ I can give examples of how my understanding of rights and responsibility has developed.

Look back at the skills and knowledge you have developed in this chapter. It is important to identify what you have learned and where you could learn more. Use the following worksheet to guide your reflection on human rights. Then working in groups, discuss your responses to each of the questions.

1. Before looking at human rights, I thought …	
2. Things I learned about human rights	
3. The area of human rights I found most interesting was …	
4. The reason I found this most interesting was …	
5. Where I got my information from	
6. How will the new information I have learned change what I do?	

127

Action: Organising a fundraiser

Having completed Strand 1, consider organisations you have studied or that you are aware of that work to promote human rights or human dignity such as Amnesty International, Focus Ireland or Trócaire. As a class decide which organisation you would like to support by organising a fundraiser. You can put forward proposals and explain why you would like to support the organisation and the class can vote on who to support. Then decide on the type of fundraiser you would like to organise, for example a bake sale, a raffle or a sponsored walk.

✓ Action 1 Deciding the tasks I can do

Key Skills **Success criteria** ☐ I can list the tasks I need to do to make the fundraiser a success.

Before you organise your fundraiser, it is important to decide the roles people will play. The class works as groups with different responsibilities:

Group 1	Getting permission for organising the fundraiser in school	Group 4	Sales
Group 2	Contacting the organisation you are fundraising for	Group 5	Finance
Group 3	Public relations	Group 6	Presenting the money

Once you have been assigned to a group, your group will meet up and decide what jobs it needs to do and who will do them. Write these jobs in the box below.

✓ Action 2 Outlining my role in the fundraiser

Key Skills **Success criteria** ☐ I can list the actions that I contributed to the fundraiser.

Write out the actions that you contributed to the fundraiser and explain how they were of benefit to the action.

_____

_____

Action: Organising a fundraiser

Action 3 — Reflecting on what I have learned from organising the fundraiser

Key Skills

Success criteria ☐ I can answer questions that describe what I did, what I learned from organising the fundraiser.

Answer the following questions.

1. What was my group's responsibility?

2. Who was in my group?

3. What jobs did I do?

4. What skills did I use?

5. What did I learn about the organisation I was fundraising for?

6. What did my group do well?

7. What would I do differently if I had to do it again?

8. What were the good things about working in a group?

9. What was hard about working in a group?

STRAND 2
Global Citizenship

Chapter 3 Sustainability   131

Chapter 4 Local and Global Development   199

Chapter 5 Effecting Global Change   235

Chapter 3 Sustainability

Global citizenship

LESSON 31

Learning outcome 2.1
Students should be able to communicate how they are connected to and dependent upon eco-systems, people and places, near and far.

Exercise 31A Assessing my awareness of what is happening in the world

Key Skills **Success criteria** ☐ I can identify the areas of global citizenship that I am aware of and the areas that I am not.

A **global citizen** is aware of and understands not just their own community or country but the wider world and their place in it. A global citizen aims to make the world a **fairer**, more **peaceful** and more **sustainable** place. They do this by:

- Their actions, for example, organising petitions
- Understanding that global citizenship refers to the whole world, not just parts of it
- Promoting fairness, peace and sustainability in the world
- Understanding that other people have different traditions and cultures.

Look at the questions below, consider your responses and write your answers.

1. Can you name three countries in each of these continents?	Europe
	Africa
	Asia
	Oceania
	North America
	South America

2. Can you name three world leaders who are democratically elected and three who are not?	Democratically elected	Not democratically elected

CALL TO ACTION | Chapter 3

3. Can you name three countries where there is an armed conflict going on at the moment?

4. Can you name three countries experiencing injustice at the moment? Name the injustice.

5. Can you name three environmental problems facing the world?

6. Can you name three organisations fighting injustice in the world?

7. Can you name three individuals fighting injustice in the world?

8. What were the three main news stories this week?

9. Were these stories local, national or global?

10. From your answers to the above questions, are you a globally aware citizen?

Lesson 31: Global citizenship

Exercise 31B Assessing my knowledge of a topical issue happening in the world

Key Skills **Success criteria** ☐ I can identify my knowledge of a topical issue.

Take one of the news stories you listed in Exercise 31A question 8 and answer the following questions.

1. What is the news story? _____
2. Give a brief description of the issue. _____
3. What are the causes of the problem? _____
4. Has the issue been resolved? _____
5. What are solutions to the problem? _____
6. Why do/might the solutions not work? _____

Exercise 31C Responding to a topical news item

Key Skills **Success criteria** ☐ I can explain how I can respond to an issue.

You have developed awareness and knowledge of a particular issue. What, if anything, could you do about this issue?

● CALL TO ACTION | *Chapter 3*

Exercise 31D Learning about other cultures

Key Skills   **Success criteria**   ☐ I can interview somebody about other countries and say what I have learned.

Working in pairs, interview your partner by asking the questions 1–8. When you have finished, answer questions 9 and 10.

1. How many countries have you been to?	In Europe
	In Africa
	In Asia
	In Oceania
	In North America
	In South America
2. Why did you go to these countries?	
3. In how many of the countries that you visited was English not the main language?	

134

Lesson 31: Global citizenship

4. Do you speak another language fluently apart from English or Irish?	
5. What do you know about the culture of one country outside Ireland?	
6. What do you like about this country outside Ireland?	
7. What countries would you like to visit?	
8. Where would you recommend visiting in Ireland? Why?	
9. What have I learned about my partner's view of the world?	
10. What other questions would I like to ask?	

Lesson 32: Interdependence

Learning outcome 2.1
Students should be able to communicate how they are connected to and dependent upon eco-systems, people and places, near and far.

Exercise 32A — Identifying the importance of interdependence

Key Skills

Success criteria ☐ I can explain how interdependence works.

Being **dependent** means relying on something or somebody. **Interdependence** means that two or more people or groups rely on each other for support and help. Everything in nature is connected, so people must be interdependent to survive and develop.

Producing bread shows how interdependent people are: one person plants the wheat seeds, takes care of the crop and harvests it. The wheat is then sent to the mill to produce flour. The flour is used by the baker to make bread. The bread is sold in the shop. This could not happen without interdependence as the farmer, miller, baker and shopkeeper are all needed in order to feed people.

Watch the video and answer the questions below.

> **YouTube** Go to YouTube and search for 'Birds on a Wire – For the Birds' (3:14).

1. What is the viewpoint of the small birds?

2. What is the large bird's viewpoint?

3. What does this story tell you about interdependence?

4. How might this have had a better outcome?

Lesson 32: Interdependence

Exercise 32B — Understanding how plants and animals are interdependent

Key Skills **Success criteria** ☐ I can identify ways in which plants and animals are interdependent.

People and animals rely on plants and trees to survive. Plants are important for human beings because:

- They take carbon dioxide out of the atmosphere to use in photosynthesis and give out oxygen, which animals and humans need to breathe.
- They are a source of food like fruit, vegetables, seeds, nuts and herbs.
- Plants hold water in the soil in areas that might otherwise flood.
- Paper, cotton and rubber are among the products produced from plants.
- They provide us with fuel, wood and other useful materials.
- Many medicines are made from plants.

For plants to grow, they need certain soil and climate conditions. Plants also depend on **pollinators**, which are insects like bees, to carry pollen from the male part of the flower to the female part. The pollinators are interdependent because they need the nectar from the flowers.

Pollinated flowers on many plants turn into berries and other fruits and become a source of food for animals. When an animal eats the berry, the seeds pass through its digestive system and, when deposited, a new plant grows.

Plants are eaten by insects, snails and slugs. Frogs eat insects, snails and slugs and dragonflies eat other insects. In this way, they protect plants. Plants that humans grow rely on us for fertilisers, water and disease control.

Choose the correct words from the word bank to complete the passage.

Bees are attracted to flowers because they require _____ for energy. This is then transformed into honey. Bees and other insects are _____, which means they carry pollen from the male part of the flower to the female part. On many plants, when the flower is pollinated, it produces berries and other fruits. The fruit is a source of _____ for animals. The plant benefits because the animal digests the seeds and, when they are deposited, it leads to a new plant growing. Plants use carbon dioxide in photosynthesis and give out _____ which animals and humans need to _____. Other insects such as _____ and animals such as _____ eat insects and slugs that could destroy plants. Some of the benefits of plants are that they can produce _____ for clothing, _____ for warmth and _____ for bread.

| oxygen | nectar | breathe | firewood | pollinators |
| dragonflies | food | wheat | cotton | frogs |

137

● CALL TO ACTION | *Chapter 3*

Exercise 32C — Examining a cycle of interdependence

Key Skills **Success criteria** ☐ I can identify consequences when the interdependence between plants and animals is disrupted.

Working in groups, look at the questions below, discuss them together and then write your answers.

1. What plants and animals live in your local area?

2. What do they need to survive?

3. What would happen if a plant or an animal died out?

4. What measures have been taken in your local area to help plant and animal life?

5. What threats do you see to plant and animal life in your local area?

6. Who is responsible for protecting plant and animal life?

Exercise 32D — Analysing interdependence in practice

Key Skills **Success criteria** ☐ I can give practical examples of interdependence.

Imports are goods and resources that are bought in by a country. **Exports** are goods and resources that a country sells to other countries.

Working in pairs, discuss whether each of the following statements is true or false.

	True	False
1. Ireland's main fruit imports are bananas and apples.		
2. Coffee is the second most traded commodity in the world.		
3. Ireland's main trading partners for bananas are Costa Rica and Belize.		
4. Potatoes are Ireland's biggest vegetable import.		

5. Pork is Ireland's largest meat export.		
6. More dairy produce is exported from Ireland than imported into it.		
7. Most Irish exports of infant formula go to China.		
8. The largest amount of wine imported into Ireland comes from Chile.		

Exercise 32E Examining the impact of incidents on interdependency

Key Skills   **Success criteria** ☐ I can explain how incidents impact on international trade.

Read the passage about the *Ever Given* container ship and answer the questions that follow.

The Suez Canal in Egypt connects the Mediterranean Sea with the Red Sea. It allows ships to travel from the Atlantic Ocean to the Indian Ocean without going around the southern tip of Africa, the Cape of Good Hope. This saves time and reduces the cost of travel. About 12% of all international trade passes through the canal. In March 2021, the container ship *Ever Given* was transporting a huge cargo that included fruit, electronic items and products used in summer like barbecues, sun loungers and lawnmowers from Malaysia to the Netherlands. High winds caused the ship to get stuck, blocking the canal to all users for six days. This caused a huge build-up of ships waiting at both sides of the canal to get through. The delay cost about €5 billion, as perishable items were lost and many items needed for manufacturing, such as microchips for cars, were delayed. Online orders were also affected.

1. Why is the Suez Canal so important for trade?

2. Name some of the goods the *Ever Given* was transporting.

3. Can you suggest any items that were being transported from Europe to Asia but could not get through because of the blockage?

4. What does this incident show about trade interdependence?

LESSON 33

International trade

Learning outcome 2.1
Students should be able to communicate how they are connected to and dependent upon eco-systems, people and places, near and far.

Exercise 33A Calculating how interdependence and trade relate to me

Key Skills **Success criteria** ☐ I can see how interdependence and trade are connected and affect me.

International trade happens when countries import to and export from other countries. The difference between a country's imports and exports is called its **balance of trade**. A positive balance means there are more exports than imports.

The following are some of the world's most traded items that Ireland imports. Tick how many of these you or your family purchase or use every day, and then answer the question below.

1. Oil		3. Natural gas		5. Wheat		7. Corn	
2. Coffee		4. Gold		6. Cotton		8. Sugar	

What does this tell you about interdependence?

_____

_____

Exercise 33B Understanding Ireland's international trade

Key Skills **Success criteria** ☐ I can name Ireland's main import and exports markets and name common goods imported and exported.

Working in pairs, examine the infographic on the next page and answer the following questions.

1. Where did most Irish exports go in 2017?

_____

2. From where did Ireland import the most goods in 2017?

_____

Lesson 33: International trade

Ireland's Trade in Goods 2017

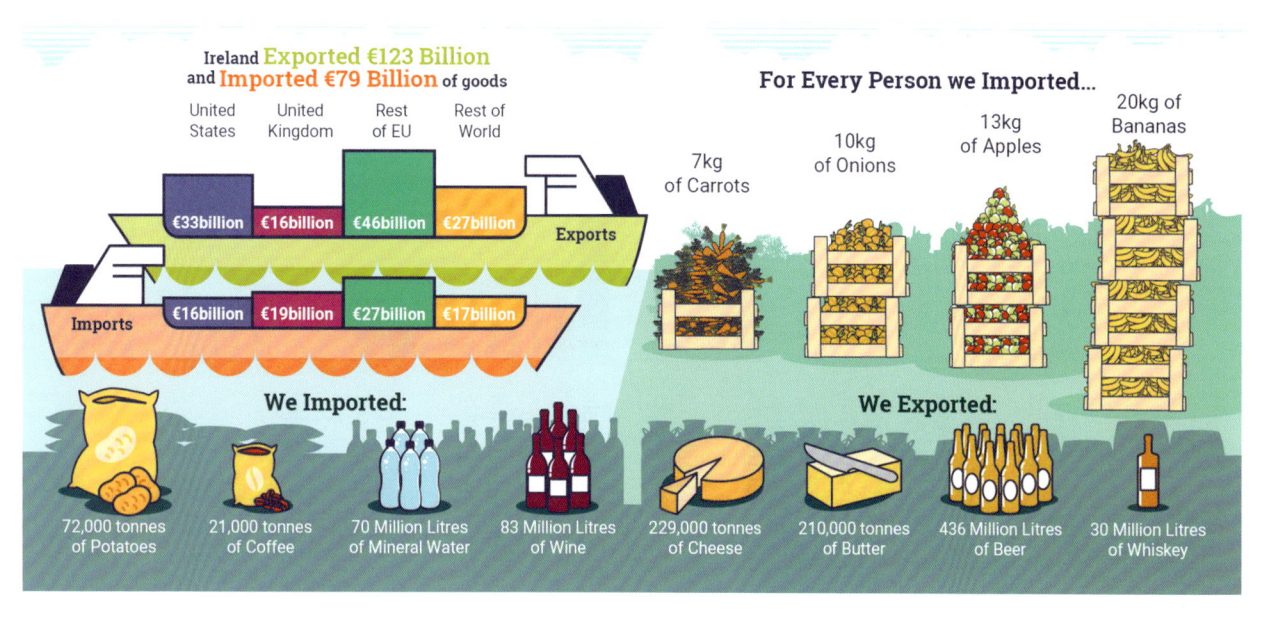

An Phríomh-Oifig Staidrimh — Central Statistics Office

Ireland **Exported €123 Billion** and **Imported €79 Billion** of goods

Exports:
- United States: €33 billion
- United Kingdom: €16 billion
- Rest of EU: €46 billion
- Rest of World: €27 billion

Imports:
- United States: €16 billion
- United Kingdom: €19 billion
- Rest of EU: €27 billion
- Rest of World: €17 billion

We Imported:
- 72,000 tonnes of Potatoes
- 21,000 tonnes of Coffee
- 70 Million Litres of Mineral Water
- 83 Million Litres of Wine

For Every Person we Imported...
- 7kg of Carrots
- 10kg of Onions
- 13kg of Apples
- 20kg of Bananas

We Exported:
- 229,000 tonnes of Cheese
- 210,000 tonnes of Butter
- 436 Million Litres of Beer
- 30 Million Litres of Whiskey

---

3. Did Ireland import or export more goods in 2017?

4. Name four items Ireland imported in 2017.

5. Could any of these have been produced in Ireland? If so, which ones?

6. Name four items Ireland exported in 2017.

7. What was Ireland's balance of trade in 2017?

8. Was it positive or negative?

Exercise 33C Identifying the products Ireland trades

Key Skills   Success criteria   ☐ I can explain what goods Ireland imports and exports.

1. Look at the bar chart on the next page of the Central Statistics Office (CSO) figures on Ireland's trade and answer the questions that follow.

141

CALL TO ACTION | Chapter 3

Irish imports and exports 2020

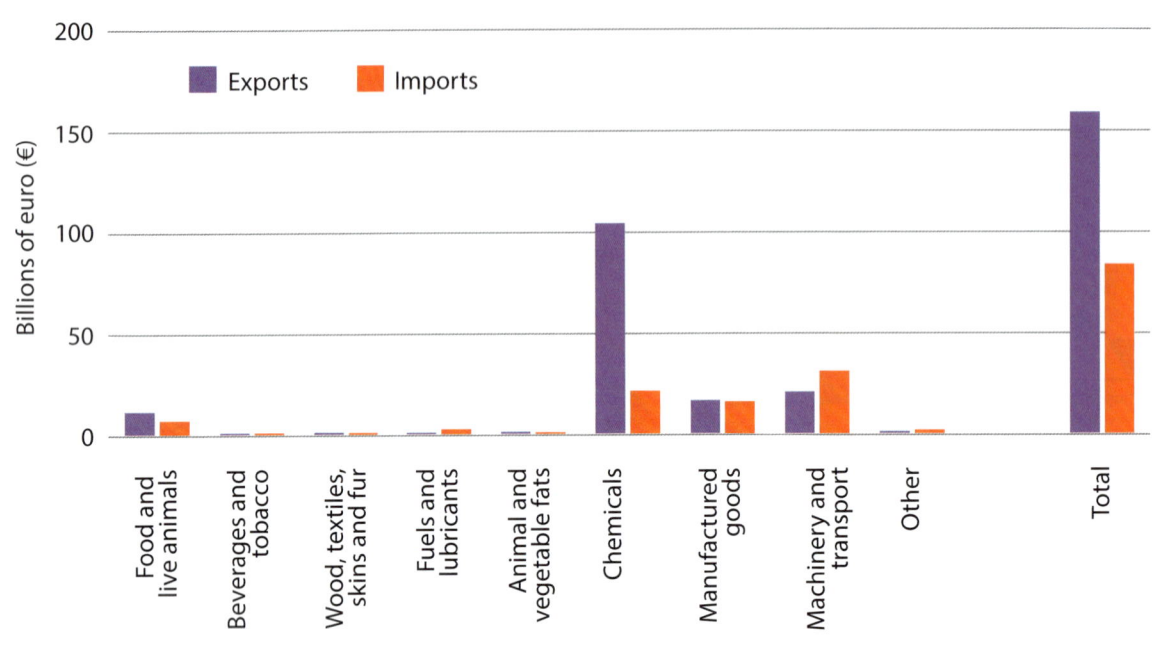

(a) Overall, does Ireland import or export more goods?

(b) Which category does Ireland export most of?

(c) How much of Ireland's total exports does this category account for?

(d) Which category is Ireland's main import?

(e) Can you suggest a product that would be in this category?

2. Look at the pie charts showing Ireland's food imports and exports and answer the following questions.

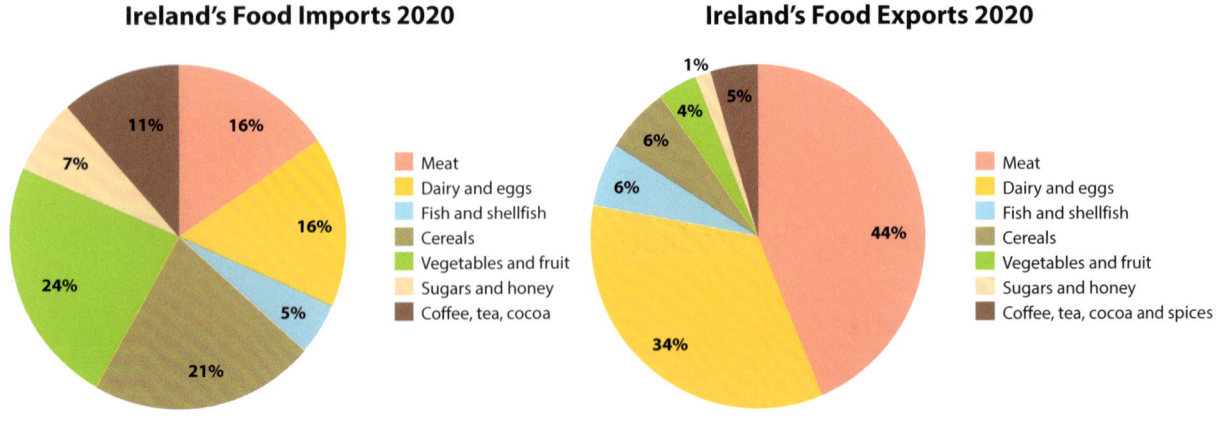

Ireland's Food Imports 2020

- Meat 16%
- Dairy and eggs 16%
- Fish and shellfish 5%
- Cereals 21%
- Vegetables and fruit 24%
- Sugars and honey 7%
- Coffee, tea, cocoa 11%

Ireland's Food Exports 2020

- Meat 44%
- Dairy and eggs 34%
- Fish and shellfish 6%
- Cereals 6%
- Vegetables and fruit 4%
- Sugars and honey 1%
- Coffee, tea, cocoa and spices 5%

(a) What food type does Ireland import most of?

(b) Can you suggest what any of these products are?

(c) Which is the least imported food type?

(d) Why do you think this may be?

(e) Which food type is most exported from Ireland?

(f) What are the second largest types of food exported?

(g) Do you notice any food type for which there are similar numbers of imports and exports?

(h) How would you explain this?

(i) Are there any food types for which there are much more imports than exports?

(j) Why do you think this is?

Exercise 33D Identifying the origins of products I use

Key Skills   **Success criteria** ☐ I can identify the countries from where the different items I use come.

1. Look at the following headings and list four items that you often use. Find where they come from.

	Food		School items	
	Item	Country	Item	Country
1.				
2.				
3.				
4.				

■ CALL TO ACTION | *Chapter 3*

	Clothes		Electronic items	
	Item	Country	Item	Country
1.				
2.				
3.				
4.				

2. On the map of the world below, colour in red the countries where your food items come from, colour in blue where your school items come from, colour in black where your clothes come from and colour in green where your electronics come from.

144

Lesson 34: Development

Learning outcome 2.2
Students should be able to consider a variety of definitions of development and devise their own definition of sustainable development.

Exercise 34A Identifying different types of development

Key Skills

Success criteria
- [ ] I can categorise developments under different categories.

Development is about improvement. For example, medical developments help to improve how we care for people who are sick. Many diseases have become rare because of vaccines, and physiotherapy has allowed people who suffered strokes or serious injuries to regain use of their bodies.

There are different types of development:

- **Personal development** is the activities that a person does to improve their skills, knowledge and quality of life. These include eating well and exercising, being aware of their skills and areas they need to develop.
- **Social development** involves helping people to reach their full potential because it is good for society, such as providing education.
- **Economic development** is when a country becomes wealthier. Its people can get better paid jobs and have higher standards of living.
- **Cultural development** is when activities such as music, drama, sporting events and celebrations of different cultures are promoted to benefit society. Cultural development improves people's standard of living because it is about enjoyment rather than just work.
- **Political development** is when politicians bring about improvements in the best interests of everyone in society.

Development can often be controversial because people have different views about how or whether a development should happen. For example, some people are opposed to a 34-storey development in Cork that has been given planning permission.

Look at the examples on the next page and identify what type of development is taking place. If you think there no development is taking place, tick none.

CALL TO ACTION | *Chapter 3*

	Type of development					
	Personal	Social	Economic	Cultural	Political	None
1. The government has decided to build a new theatre in Dublin to host operas, concerts and plays.						
2. Louisa is taking an assertiveness course to improve her ability to stand up to others.						
3. A new college is planned for your town as it has a large population of young people but has no third-level institution.						
4. The local county council will not provide finance for building public tennis courts in your town.						
5. People over the age of 17 are being given the right to vote in local elections.						
6. The Minister for Health has launched a healthy eating campaign.						
7. A new pharmaceutical factory is being built, which it is hoped will create 800 jobs.						
8. The old landfill dump is being turned into a public park.						

Exercise 34B Preparing a development proposal

Key Skills

Success criteria ☐ I can design and explain how to put a development in place in my school community.

Your class has decided to put a proposal to the student council to take to the school management about improving your year group's social area. Working in groups, prepare your proposal by filling in the following details.

1. What are the things you want changed?

_____

_____

2. What are the new things you want added?

_____

_____

Lesson 34: Development

3. What jobs can your year group contribute to reduce the costs?
   _____
   _____

4. How do you propose to finance the job?
   _____
   _____

5. How you will ensure that all students in the year group are allowed to give opinions and suggestions on the proposal?
   _____
   _____

6. Draw a brief sketch of the outline of the social area you propose to develop.

CALL TO ACTION | Chapter 3

Exercise 34C Appreciating the challenges of development

Key Skills

Success criteria ☐ I can identify disadvantages of development and consider other possibilities.

Read the case study and look at the photos below of Jamaica. Then answer the questions that follow.

Case Study

Jamaica

Development is usually an improvement, but it can have negative effects when not done properly. Jamaica is an island nation in the Caribbean, which is popular with tourists for its white sandy beaches and coral reefs. Some 9% of Jamaicans work in tourism. There are many all-inclusive resorts, where the accommodation, food, drink and activities are included in a package holiday. While this brings in many tourists, many do not leave the resort, so local businesses do not benefit. Many of these resorts are foreign-owned, with the profits sent out of Jamaica. Some environmental activists have suggested that the Jamaican government should promote small-scale community tourism instead.

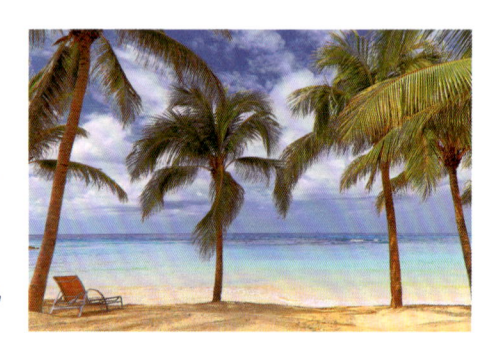

The mangrove forests that grow along Jamaica's coastline absorb CO_2, reduce erosion from the sea and protect the coast from storms. Mangrove trees are salt-tolerant, which means they can live on seawater and grow in low-oxygen soil. They also provide shelter for fish from other predators. Since 2000, over 770 hectares of Jamaica's mangrove forests have been cleared to make way for coastal developments. As a result, some areas of the coastline have had to be strengthened to prevent erosion and flooding. The government of Jamaica plans to restore the mangrove forests and to use more solar and wind power. However, it takes 20–30 years to restore a mangrove forest. In 2021, drone footage showed 5 hectares of mangrove forest and sea grasses had been cleared in Green Island to build a five-star luxury resort, which will create 3,500 jobs for locals and accommodate 4,000 tourists.

Lesson 34: Development

1. What do you think of when you see photos such as those on the previous page?

2. How do we know tourism is important in Jamaica?

3. What is the advantage of the all-inclusive resorts:

    (a) for the tourist?

    (b) for the locals?

4. What are the disadvantages of these resorts for the locals?

5. What are the benefits of mangrove forests?

6. How many hectares of mangrove forests have been cleared since 2000?

7. What types of development does the luxury resort being built on Green Island bring? (economic, social, etc.)

8. What types of development will this new resort not bring?

9. Are there alternatives to building the Green Island resort?

10. Why do you think these alternatives might be not as popular?

CALL TO ACTION | Chapter 3

Exercise 34D Analysing the benefits of mangrove forests

Key Skills   **Success criteria**   ☐ I can identify the benefits of mangrove forests.

Watch the video about mangrove forests and answer the following questions.

> **YouTube** Go to YouTube and search for 'Why mangrove forests are important – EU Jamaica' (2:20).

1. Why are mangroves like a wall?

2. What tourist opportunities do mangroves offer?

3. What is threatening mangrove forests?

4. What used to be a threat to mangrove forests in the past?

5. The EU supported the making of this video. Why might they have done so?

Lesson 35: Sustainability

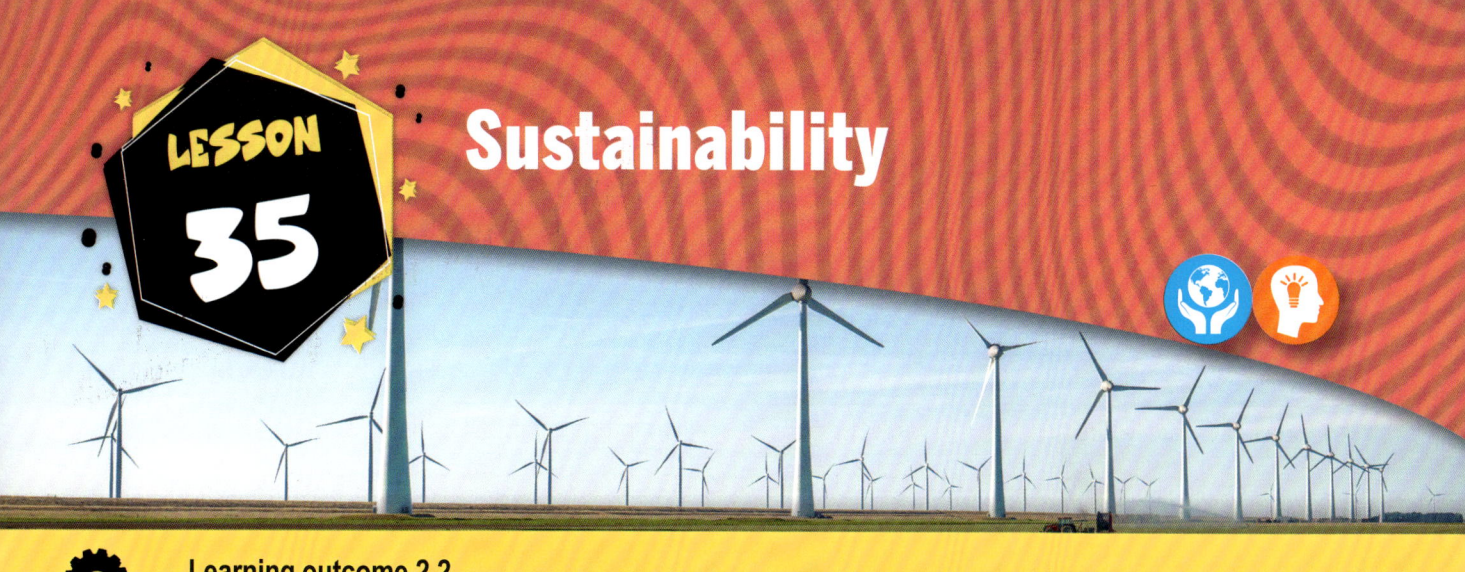

Learning outcome 2.2
Students should be able to consider a variety of definitions of development and devise their own definition of sustainable development.

Exercise 35A Distinguishing between different types of sustainability

Key Skills

Success criteria ☐ I can identify the different types of sustainability required for sustainable development.

Sustainability means making sure that the Earth can continue to provide food and water and allow everybody to have a high quality of life now and for future generations. In 1987, the **Brundtland Report** defined sustainable development as **development that meets the needs of the present without compromising the ability of future generations to meet their own needs**. This means that the Earth's limited resources need to be used carefully so that they are available for future generations.

There are three **pillars of sustainability**: social, environmental and economic. These are sometimes called people, planet and profits, which must be balanced to be sustainable.

1. **Social sustainability** is when communities, organisations and countries work well together. Socially unsustainable societies have high levels of poverty, poor access to healthcare or education and people have few rights.

2. **Environmental sustainability** is when the environment is protected and the resources are replaced at a similar rate to which they are being used. Environmentally unsustainable actions include not planting trees to replace those that have been cut down.

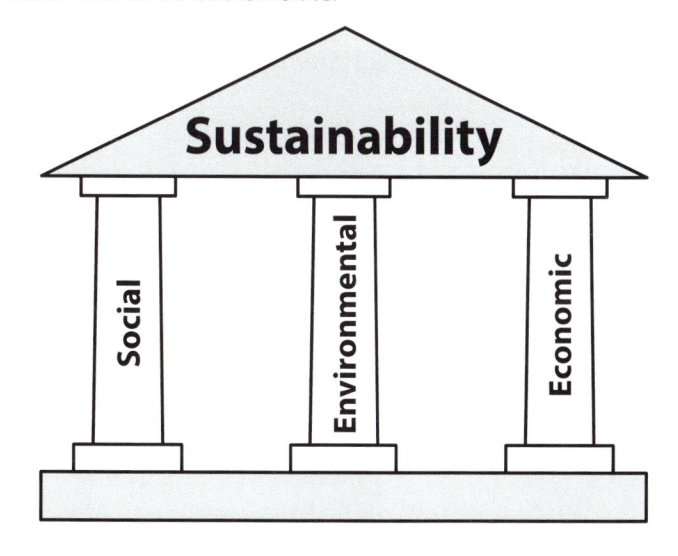

3. **Economic sustainability** is the ability of an economy to share wealth fairly in society and to do it in ways that are good for the environment.

Working in pairs, look at the factors on the following page and classify them as examples of social, environmental or economic sustainability.

CALL TO ACTION | *Chapter 3*

	Social	Environmental	Economic
Good medical care			
Healthy air			
Fair wages			
Planting trees			
Greenways for cycling			
Access to education for all			
Rule of law			
Tax on emissions			
Fair prices			
Clean water			

Did any factor cross a few categories? Why is this important?

_____

_____

Exercise 35B — Understanding how I can become more sustainable

Key Skills

Success criteria ☐ I can explain the sustainability actions I can do and understand what stops me being sustainable.

Working in pairs, answer the following questions.

1. The following are examples of sustainable actions. Can you explain why?

   (a) I do not leave the water running while brushing my teeth.

   _____

   (b) I turn off the lights when leaving a room.

   _____

   (c) I buy clothes that will last a long time.

   _____

   (d) I walk or cycle to school when I can.

   _____

2. Many people do not do these things. Can you explain why?

   (a) I do not leave the water running while brushing my teeth.

   _____

   (b) I turn off the lights when leaving a room.

   _____

   (c) I buy clothes that will last a long time.

   _____

   (d) I walk to school or cycle when I can.

   _____

Lesson 35: Sustainability

Exercise 35C — Understanding the impacts of unsustainability and how to counter them

Key Skills **Success criteria** ☐ I can match causes of unsustainability with actions that prevent these causes and explain likely outcomes of being unsustainable.

Dr Karl Henrik Robert, together with 50 scientists, identified **four causes of unsustainability**.

1. We extract so many natural resources like fuels and metals from the Earth that it cannot replace them.
2. We create things like plastics that take too long to break down.
3. We destroy the Earth's natural way of recovering, by clearing forests, draining wetlands, etc.
4. We make it impossible for people to meet their needs by not preventing poverty and other inequalities.

To be sustainable we must complete the following actions:

(a) Stop destroying nature at a rate that it cannot recover naturally.
(b) Reduce our dependence on fossil fuels (fuels formed over millions of years like oil, coal and gas).
(c) Stop producing products that take too long to break down naturally in the environment.
(d) Make sure we are not stopping people from meeting their needs.

Dr Karl Henrik Robert

1. Working in pairs, look at the causes of unsustainability and match them with the actions that we should take to solve this problem.

1	2	3	4

2. In pairs, discuss the problems that people will face in 2100 if no action is taken in the four areas of sustainability. Write them below.

   (a) Reducing dependence on fossil fuels:
   _____

   (b) Stopping manufacture of products that do not break down naturally:
   _____

   (c) Stopping the destruction of nature at a rate that it cannot replace itself:
   _____

   (d) Making sure we are not stopping people meeting their needs:
   _____

■ CALL TO ACTION | *Chapter 3*

Exercise 35D — Understanding how to reverse unsustainable developments

Key Skills **Success criteria**
☐ I can name the actions that improve unsustainable sites.
☐ I can summarise what sustainable development means to me.

Read the passage on Tramore Valley Park and answer the following questions.

The Kinsale Road Landfill was the main dump for the city of Cork until 2009. Almost 3 million tonnes of waste had been deposited at the site. Since it closed, Cork City Council has spent €40 million decontaminating the site and preventing it from causing environmental damage. It is still monitored by the Environmental Protection Agency and has gas collection and contaminated water pipes to remove harmful emissions. The gases collected are used to power houses in the city and the water is collected and treated. In 2019, Tramore Valley Park was opened on the site of the dump. The park includes a 2.5 km looped walkway, a BMX track, a rugby pitch, an outdoor gym and a wetlands area.

1. Why was this site unsustainable?

2. Is its current use sustainable?

3. Do you think this is a positive development? Explain why.

4. Who will benefit from this park?

5. Can you suggest any other sustainable activities that could take place in the park?

6. Do you know of any other sites where similar developments have happened? If so, what are they?

7. Write your own definition of what sustainable development means to you.

Lesson 35: Sustainability

Exercise 35E Identifying progress in the SDGs

Key Skills

Success criteria ☐ I can identify differences in achieving the SDGs by looking at maps and charts.

In 2015, the UN General Assembly set the **sustainable development goals** (SDGs). These are 17 interdependent aims to bring about a better and more sustainable future by 2030. The goals are based on the idea that improving areas like education, economic growth and climate change must be interlinked.

SUSTAINABLE DEVELOPMENT GOALS

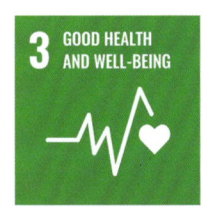

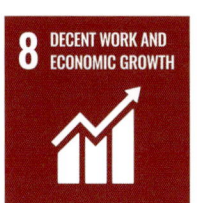

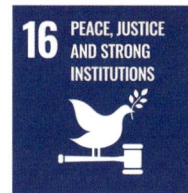

1. NO POVERTY
2. ZERO HUNGER
3. GOOD HEALTH AND WELL-BEING
4. QUALITY EDUCATION
5. GENDER EQUALITY
6. CLEAN WATER AND SANITATION
7. AFFORDABLE AND CLEAN ENERGY
8. DECENT WORK AND ECONOMIC GROWTH
9. INDUSTRY, INNOVATION AND INFRASTRUCTURE
10. REDUCED INEQUALITIES
11. SUSTAINABLE CITIES AND COMMUNITIES
12. RESPONSIBLE CONSUMPTION AND PRODUCTION
13. CLIMATE ACTION
14. LIFE BELOW WATER
15. LIFE ON LAND
16. PEACE, JUSTICE AND STRONG INSTITUTIONS
17. PARTNERSHIPS FOR THE GOALS

Each goal has several targets, which are monitored by the UN Division for Sustainable Development Goals (DSDG). All governments must implement these goals in their country. The following map from 2020 shows progress on climate action (Goal 13) in different countries.

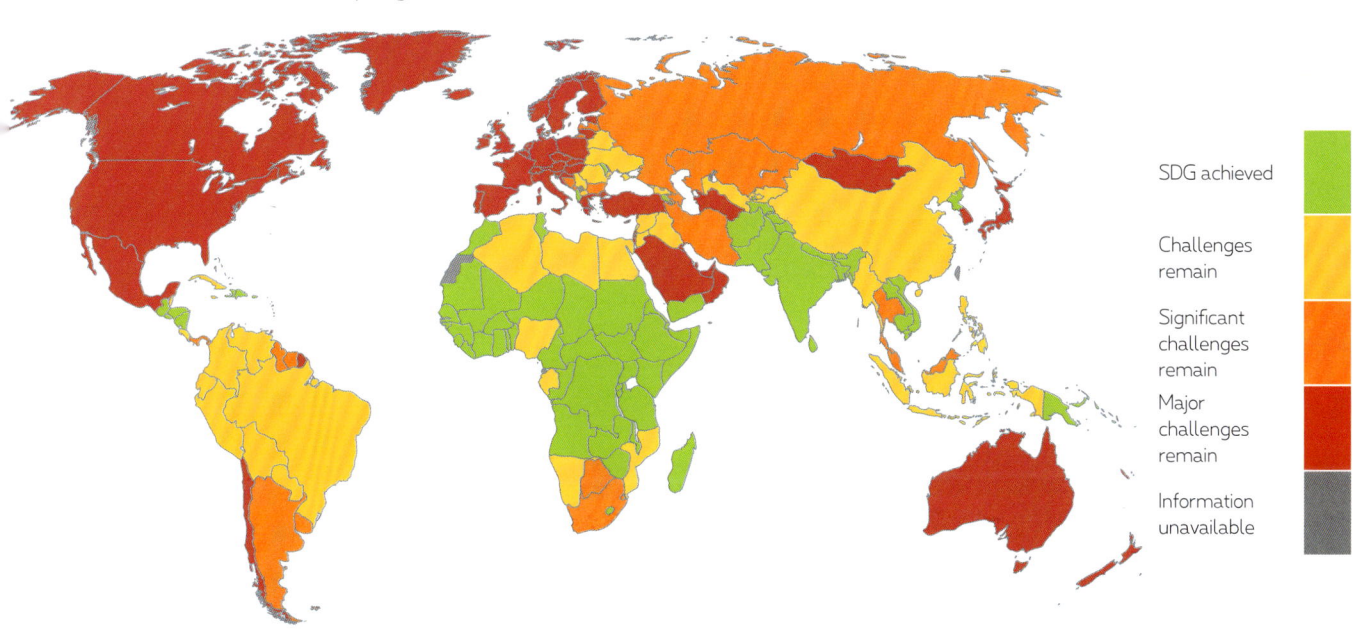

- SDG achieved
- Challenges remain
- Significant challenges remain
- Major challenges remain
- Information unavailable

■ CALL TO ACTION | *Chapter 3*

The following dashboard shows Somalia's progress on the SDGs:

On track or maintaining SDG achievement	↑	Moderately improving	↗
Stagnating	→	Major challenges remain	↓
Trend information unavailable	••		

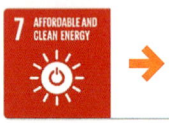

[Somalia SDG dashboard:
1 No Poverty ↓, 2 Zero Hunger →, 3 Good Health and Well-Being →, 4 Quality Education ••, 5 Gender Equality ↗, 6 Clean Water and Sanitation ↗,
7 Affordable and Clean Energy →, 8 Decent Work and Economic Growth ↗, 9 Industry, Innovation and Infrastructure →, 10 Reduced Inequalities ••, 11 Sustainable Cities and Communities ↗, 12 Responsible Consumption and Production ••,
13 Climate Action ↑, 14 Life Below Water ↗, 15 Life on Land →, 16 Peace, Justice and Strong Institutions ↗, 17 Partnerships for the Goals ↗]

The following dashboard shows Switzerland's progress on the SDGs:

[Switzerland SDG dashboard:
1 No Poverty ↑, 2 Zero Hunger ↗, 3 Good Health and Well-Being ↑, 4 Quality Education ↗, 5 Gender Equality ↗, 6 Clean Water and Sanitation ↗,
7 Affordable and Clean Energy ↑, 8 Decent Work and Economic Growth ↗, 9 Industry, Innovation and Infrastructure ↗, 10 Reduced Inequalities →, 11 Sustainable Cities and Communities ↗, 12 Responsible Consumption and Production ••,
13 Climate Action →, 14 Life Below Water ••, 15 Life on Land →, 16 Peace, Justice and Strong Institutions ↗, 17 Partnerships for the Goals →]

Working in pairs, look at the map on the previous page and Somalia's and Switzerland's progress and answer the questions.

1. Name two countries where the climate action goal has been achieved.

2. Name two countries where the climate action goal faces major challenges.

3. What does this tell you?

4. Look at the comparison between Somalia and Switzerland. Which country faces more challenges meeting the goals?

5. In which area is Somalia most successful?

6. In which areas is Switzerland most successful? Why do you think this is?

Lesson 36: My carbon footprint

Learning outcome 2.3
Students should be able to create a visual representation of data depicting their ecological footprint.

Exercise 36A Calculating my environmental impact

Key Skills

Success criteria ☐ I can identify the factors that add up to my impact on the environment.

Carbon footprint measures the amount of carbon dioxide and other greenhouse gases released because of a person's or an organisation's activities, such as travel. Burning fossil fuels releases carbon, which causes pollution and leads to the **greenhouse effect**. This causes the Earth to heat up. Reducing your carbon footprint can help to reduce global warming.

- **Direct carbon emissions** come directly from an activity. If you travel to school by car rather than walking, your direct carbon footprint will be higher.
- **Indirect carbon emissions** are not produced by an individual but generated because of decisions individuals make. For example, if you buy fresh flowers that have travelled from Kenya, the cost of the flight makes your indirect carbon footprint higher.

Greenpeace, Friends of the Earth and WWF are just some of the organisations fighting against climate change and raising awareness of how to do it. In Ireland, the **Environmental Protection Agency (EPA)** is a government agency responsible for protecting and improving the environment.

Answer the questions below to calculate how environmentally friendly you are.

Quiz

1. How do you get to school?
   - (a) Walk/cycle ☐
   - (b) Bus/train ☐
   - (c) Car ☐
2. How often does a member of your family fly in an aeroplane?
   - (a) Once a year or less ☐
   - (b) 2–3 times a year ☐
   - (c) At least once per month ☐
3. What type of vehicle(s) does your family have?
   - (a) None ☐
   - (b) Electric car ☐
   - (c) Diesel or petrol car ☐
4. Do you leave electrical items like laptops, TVs or games consoles on standby?
   - (a) Never ☐
   - (b) Sometimes ☐
   - (c) Often ☐

● **CALL TO ACTION | *Chapter 3***

5. Do you turn the lights off when you leave a room?
    (a) Always ☐   **(b)** Sometimes ☐   **(c)** Never ☐

6. Do you take part in a community clean-up?
    (a) Often ☐   **(b)** Sometimes ☐   **(c)** Never ☐

7. How often does your family do laundry?
    (a) Once per week ☐   **(b)** 2–3 times a week ☐   **(c)** Every day ☐

8. How often do you buy second-hand clothes?
    (a) Often ☐   **(b)** Sometimes ☐   **(c)** Never ☐

9. What kind of food does your family mostly eat?
    (a) Home-grown food ☐
    (b) Locally grown organic food ☐
    (c) Supermarket bought processed food ☐

10. What type of energy do you use in your home?
    (a) Wind/solar ☐   **(b)** Wood ☐   **(c)** Oil/gas ☐

Give yourself 1 point for each (a) answer, 2 points for each (b) answer and 3 points for each (c) answer. Add the points together to get your score.

Question	1	2	3	4	5	6	7	8	9	10	Total
Score											

10-15 points: You are very environmentally friendly, well done. 🙂

15-22 points: You are quite environmentally friendly, but you can make some changes. 😐

22-30 points: Many changes are needed. 🙁

Exercise 36B   Identifying actions to reduce my carbon footprint

Key Skills   **Success criteria** ☐ I can explain why actions I take will reduce my carbon footprint.

The following activities can help you to reduce your carbon footprint.
- Cycle or walk to school.
- Use public transport when you cannot walk or cycle.
- If you are travelling in a car, turn off the air conditioning.
- Turn off electrical devices at the mains and do not leave them on standby.
- Use low-energy light bulbs.
- Turn off lights when you leave a room and if they are not needed.
- Wash your clothes at a lower temperature.
- Have showers rather than baths. Keep showers short, especially if you have a power shower.
- Turn off the tap when brushing your teeth.
- Eat locally produced foods.
- Use a reusable water bottle.
- Reuse shopping bags.

Lesson 36: My carbon footprint

- Buy clothes made locally or buy second-hand clothes.
- Avoid buying items with too much wrapping.
- Recycle waste.
- Try to repair items that break.

Working in groups, look at the suggestions for reducing your carbon footprint. Choose five of them and discuss why they are good for reducing your carbon footprint. Rank them in order of importance. Then write your suggestions into the box.

	Action	Reason it reduces carbon footprint
1		
2		
3		
4		
5		

Exercise 36C **Explaining how to reduce carbon footprint**

Key Skills   **Success criteria**   ☐ I can explain, giving examples, how somebody can make changes in their lifestyle to reduce their carbon footprint.

Working in pairs, read about Oskar and decide five changes he needs to make to reduce his carbon footprint.

Oskar is 13 and lives 2 km from his school in Cork. His mother drops him off every morning, even though she works from home. Today, he wants to get in early to finish the homework he didn't do last night. His mother drops him off at the shop near the school where Oskar buys his lunch, a 1 litre bottle of water, a banana and a beef sandwich.

He arrives at school 40 minutes before class and starts his homework. He realises that he left his Maths copy at home, so he gets an empty hardback copy from his locker. After school, he is going to a soccer match against another school in town with some friends. They are going to cycle so he calls a taxi to get to the match. When he gets there, he has a burger from the take-away van. There are no bins, so he throws the wrappings on the ground. He's looking forward to a concert in Dublin next week. He will fly there with his family.

159

■ CALL TO ACTION | *Chapter 3*

What Oskar needs to change	How he can change it

Exercise 36D Calculating my carbon offset and representing it visually

Key Skills   **Success criteria**   ☐ I can calculate my carbon footprint, calculate how to offset my footprint and show that in a visual presentation.

Some carbon emissions cannot be reduced. For example, in school the heat is turned off at the weekend and only comes on during the winter months. To cut the carbon emissions further, the heating could be turned off in winter too and everybody could wear gloves and heavy coats, but that would not be very practical. **Carbon offsetting** is used when you cannot reduce your emissions any lower. A carbon offset is a reduction in carbon emissions or an increase in carbon storage by planting trees or restoring bogland, for example, to compensate for the emissions that cannot be reduced. Carbon offset credits are sold to companies who need to reduce their carbon footprint. Some environmentalists say that this is just 'greenwashing' as it does not lead to companies reducing their own carbon output.

How does carbon offsetting work?

Let's take a simple example – you go on a return flight to New York for a family wedding

1.44 tonnes CO_2
Return flight, Dublin to JFK, New York

One tree
One tree will absorb about 1 tonne of CO_2 over a life of 100 years

but ...
because the tree must be fully grown and because some will die it is best to plant 4 or 5 trees

6–8
So one return flight from Dublin to New York can be offset by planting 6–8 trees

Lesson 36: My carbon footprint

Search online for a carbon footprint calculator and calculate your carbon footprint under the following headings. Then, using the information in the infographic on the previous page, calculate how you could offset this footprint.

Activity	Carbon footprint	Carbon offset
Example – return flight Dublin to Faro	*0.52 tonnes of CO_2*	*Reforestation in Kenya €12*
1. Transport to and from my holiday last year		
2. Transport to and from school for a week		
3. Transport at the weekend for leisure activities		
4. My indirect or secondary carbon footprint		
Total		

Lesson 37

Tackling carbon footprint

Learning outcome 2.3
Students should be able to create a visual representation of data depicting their ecological footprint.

Exercise 37A Analysing how countries contribute to carbon footprint

Key Skills

Success criteria ☐ I can name countries responsible for greenhouse gas emissions and whether they are trying to reduce this.

Laws and fines encourage companies to act responsibly. They will also act responsibly if they believe it is what their consumers want. **Carbon Trust** works with businesses and governments to help them become more sustainable. The Trust's carbon footprint label shows that products have independently measured footprints. They have several different labels, including those on the right.

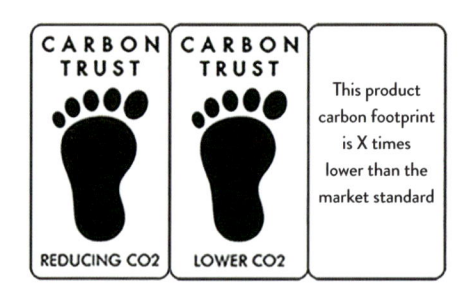

CARBON TRUST — REDUCING CO2
CARBON TRUST — LOWER CO2
This product carbon footprint is X times lower than the market standard

Countries can reduce greenhouse gas emissions by passing laws enforcing reductions, by supporting alternative energy sources like solar and wind energy and by raising taxes on emissions. The following types of taxes are commonly used:

- A **carbon tax** on the emissions produced
- An **ETS (Emissions Trading Scheme)** which sets a limit on the emissions produced. The producer must have enough permits to cover their emissions. Permits can be added to by carbon offsetting or buying permits from others.

Countries with a price on carbon

Note: Tokyo and several cities in China have their own emissions trading systems

Implemented/sheduled
- Emissions Trading System (ETS)
- Carbon tax
- ETS + carbon tax

Under consideration
- ETS or carbon tax
- Carbon tax implemented, ETS under consideration

The following bar chart shows that some countries are responsible for more emissions than others.

Largest producers of fossil fuel CO_2 emissions worldwide in 2019

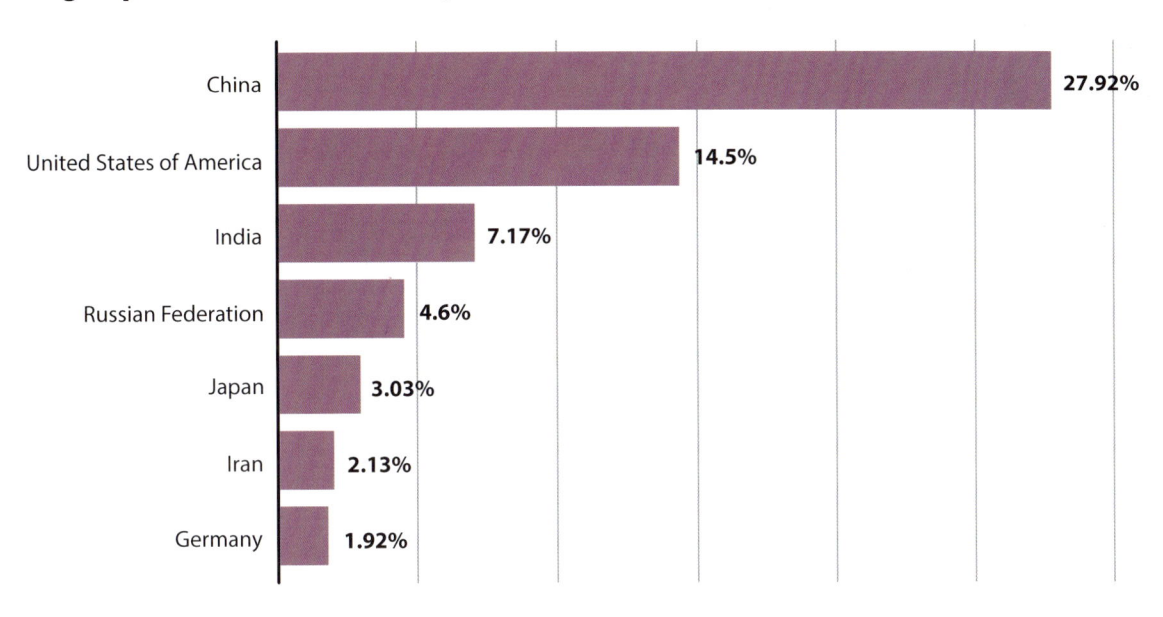

Country	Percentage
China	27.92%
United States of America	14.5%
India	7.17%
Russian Federation	4.6%
Japan	3.03%
Iran	2.13%
Germany	1.92%

Working in pairs, look at the map on the previous page and the bar chart above and answer the following questions.

1. Which continent has the most carbon taxes or ETS?

2. How many countries are considering a carbon tax or ETS?

3. On which continent are there few or no carbon taxes or ETS?

4. Which do you think is better, a carbon tax or ETS?

5. Which does Ireland have?

6. Which countries are the worst carbon emitters?

7. Which countries are the worst carbon emitters in Europe?

8. Looking at the two pieces of information together, are there any countries that should introduce a carbon tax or ETS? Name them.

■ CALL TO ACTION | *Chapter 3*

Exercise 37B — Explaining global warming and how I can work to prevent it

Key Skills **Success criteria** ☐ I can explain global warming and how I can work to prevent it.

In Ireland, a carbon tax is applied to fossil fuels. The aim is to encourage people to use renewable energies instead and to provide money to offset CO_2 emissions.

Climate change can be caused by human activities or by natural changes. **Global warming** is a type of climate change caused by humans releasing greenhouse gases into the atmosphere. These cause the Earth's surface, oceans and atmosphere to heat up.

Global warming has many negative effects.

- The polar ice-caps are melting, which has raised the sea levels, causing flooding in lower-lying land.
- The permafrost (permanently frozen soil) has reduced by 10%. This releases greenhouse gases, as well as bacteria and viruses that humans and animals may not have immunity to.
- Extreme weather conditions like very cold winters, heatwaves and more intense hurricanes have become more common.
- The seas and oceans are becoming more acidic as they absorb more CO_2.
- Birds, animals and insects are moving closer to the poles where the temperature is more comfortable.
- Insects like mosquitos are able to live further north and south. As a result, there has been an increase in diseases like malaria, which mosquitos transmit.

Watch the video on climate change and answer the following questions.

> **YouTube** Go to YouTube and search for 'Climate Change 101 with Bill Nye – National Geographic' (4:09).

1. How is global warming different from natural climate change?
   _____
   _____

2. Why have the amount of greenhouse gases increased?
   _____
   _____

3. According to the pie chart, what is the second most common greenhouse gas?
   _____

4. Do you know any source of this gas?
   _____
   _____

5. Where does 50% of the Earth's oxygen come from?
   _____

Lesson 37: Tackling carbon footprint

6. Why are sea levels rising?
   _____
   _____

7. What do scientists say we can do to reduce carbon emissions?
   _____
   _____

8. List which of these things you could do easily.
   _____
   _____

Exercise 37C Distinguishing between renewable and non-renewable energies

Key Skills Success criteria ☐ I can tell which are renewable energies and which are non-renewable.

The main greenhouse gas is carbon dioxide (CO_2), which is released when fossil fuels like oil or gas are burned. Methane (CH_4) and nitrous oxide (N_2O), which are released by agriculture, fossil fuels and even human sewage, are more dangerous than CO_2.

Renewable energy is sustainable because it can be replaced. The main types of renewable energy include:

- Solar energy – solar panels convert sunlight into electricity
- Wind energy – wind turbines convert wind into electricity
- Hydro energy – energy is created from the force of water
- Geothermal energy – pumps use the heat of the ground to heat water
- Tidal energy – converts the energy from tides into electricity

Look at the pictures below and indicate whether they are renewable or non-renewable energy sources.

An oil refinery *A hydroelectric dam* *Coal mining* *A wind farm* *Turf cutting*

	Renewable	Non-renewable
1.		
2.		
3.		
4.		
5.		

165

● CALL TO ACTION | *Chapter 3*

Exercise 37D Analysing the impact of global warming on the Maldives

Key Skills **Success criteria** ☐ I can explain how the Maldives are impacted by global warming and possible solutions to this.

The Republic of the Maldives is a collection of 1,190 coral islands in the Indian Ocean, 358 of which are inhabited. It has a population of about 550,000. Some 80% of the islands are less than 1 metre above sea level and regularly experience flooding. The highest point in the whole country is only 5.1 metres above sea level.

Tourists come to the Maldives for the white sandy beaches and coral reefs. With sea levels rising by 3-4 mm per year, most of the country risks being under water by the year 2100. The rising sea level is also a threat to fresh water supplies. The picture below shows the capital, Malé.

The government of the Maldives has increased rainwater harvesting and freshwater protection. It has bought territory from other countries to relocate its people to if sea levels continue to rise. The government has also constructed artificial islands like Hulhumalé, which was created by sucking millions of metres of sand from the seafloor and pumping it onto a coral platform. It is 2 metres above sea level and is expected to eventually house about 240,000 people. Hulhumalé uses solar energy and harvests rainwater. However, pumping sand causes sediment that damages coral reefs.

Read the case study of the Maldives and answer the following questions.

1. What dangers are the Maldives are facing?

2. Why is the impact of global warming unfair on the Maldives?

3. The government has proposed several solutions to the problem. Find an example of each of the following:

   (a) A short-term solution

   (b) A long-term solution

   (c) A solution that will be used if everything else fails

4. Hulhumalé is an example of both overcoming and creating environmental problems. Find an example of each.

   (a) Overcoming

   _____

   (b) Creating

   _____

5. The Maldives is not the only example of a country threatened by global warming. The Marshall Islands and Tuvalu are two other small island nations at risk. Choose one of these countries and research them by filling in the following details:

Country	
Location	
Threats they face	
Problems they are already facing	
Their planned solutions	
Similarities to the Maldives	
Differences to the Maldives	

Exercise 37E — Identifying effective methods of raising awareness

Key Skills

Success criteria ☐ I can explain whether or not raising awareness of carbon footprint is effective.

Working in groups, watch the video and study the poster and infographic on the next page about reducing carbon footprint. Discuss the questions that follow and then write your answers.

> **YouTube** — Go to YouTube and search for 'Carbon Footprint Advert' (1:00).

● CALL TO ACTION | *Chapter 3*

Reduce Your Carbon Footprint

facebook.com/carbonfootprintreduction
#ReduceCO2 #GoGreen

Carbon footprint of what you eat

Calculations of greenhouse gas emissions from the production, processing and transportation of specific food items.

● Main chart compares 110 g food against a journey in a midsized car
● Number shows kg of carbon dioxide equivalent produced per 1 kg of food

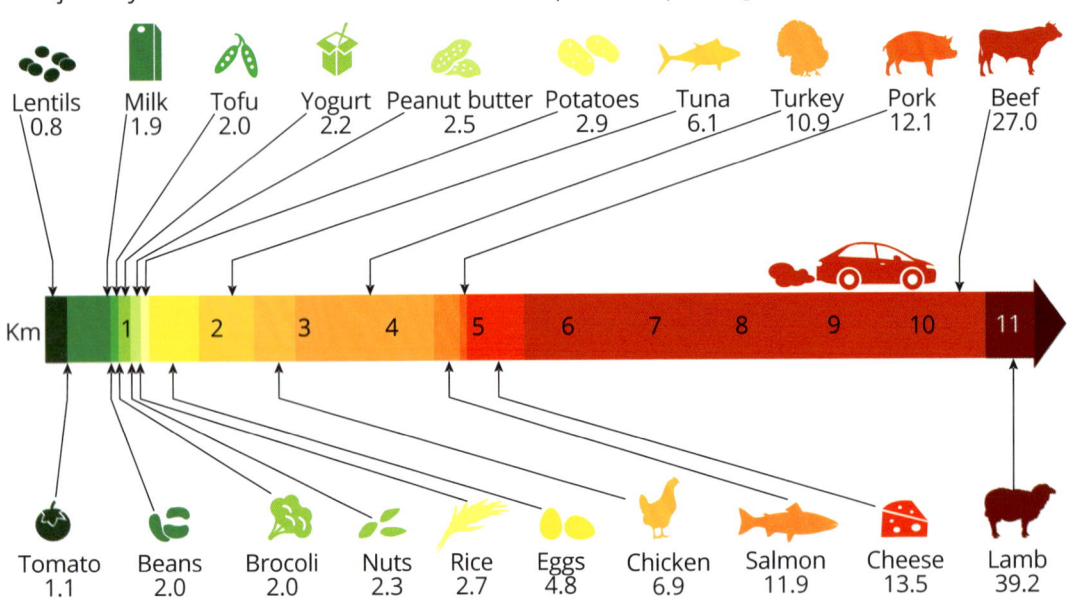

Lentils	0.8
Milk	1.9
Tofu	2.0
Yogurt	2.2
Peanut butter	2.5
Potatoes	2.9
Tuna	6.1
Turkey	10.9
Pork	12.1
Beef	27.0

Km scale: 1 – 11

Tomato	1.1
Beans	2.0
Brocoli	2.0
Nuts	2.3
Rice	2.7
Eggs	4.8
Chicken	6.9
Salmon	11.9
Cheese	13.5
Lamb	39.2

1. Which of the three methods of raising awareness was the most effective? Why?

2. Which do you think is more likely to get people to change their actions? Why?

3. Which is the easiest to share on social media?

4. Do you think sharing on social media is effective?

5. Would you share any of these on social media? Why/why not?

LESSON 38

Carbon footprint infographic

Carbon Footprint of the 2010 World Cup

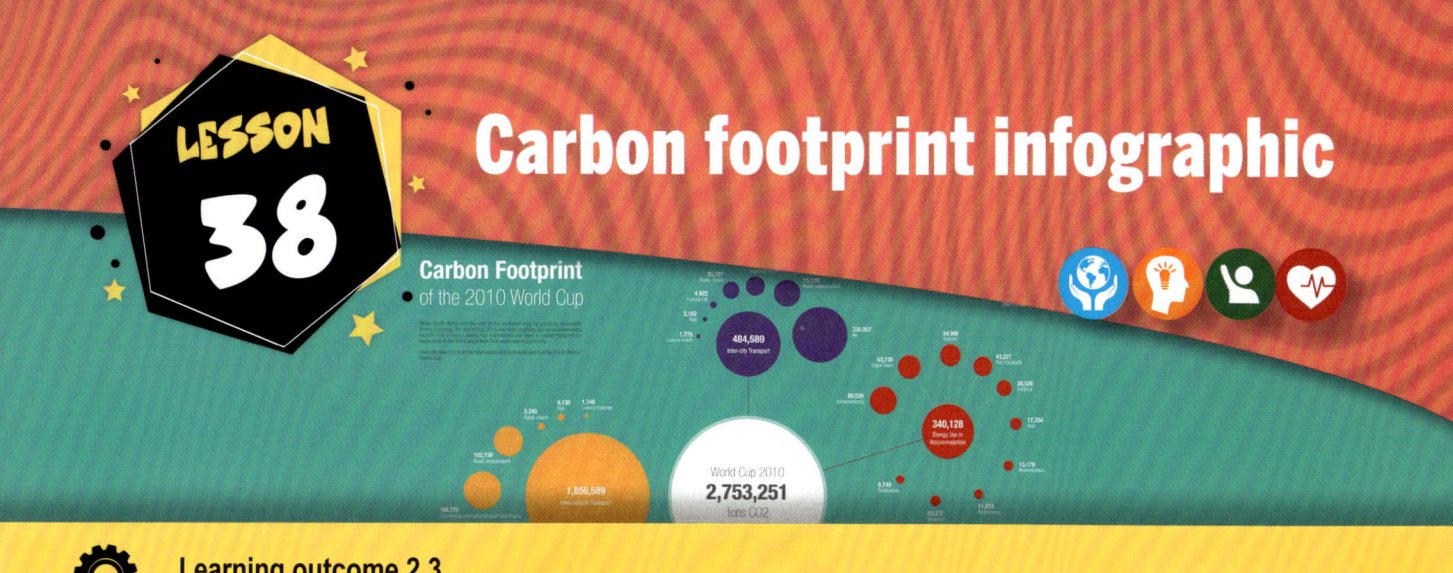

Learning outcome 2.3
Students should be able to create a visual representation of data depicting their ecological footprint.

Exercise 38A — Identifying the main points for my infographic

Key Skills **Success criteria** ☐ I can gather key points and summarise them for my infographic.

In Strand 1, Lesson 11, you learned how to make an infographic, why an infographic is useful and the different types of infographics. Look back at that section again.

You are going to produce an infographic to show your carbon footprint. Research the information you need to create your infographic. Use the skills and information you gained in Lessons 36 and 37. Below name the key pieces of information you want to put in your infographic.

_____
_____
_____
_____
_____
_____
_____

Exercise 38B — Selecting data to show the main points in my infographic

Key Skills **Success criteria** ☐ I can gather suitable data and show it using charts and pictures to support my points.

Create or select suitable charts and pictures to use in your infographic. Add them into the box on the next page.

169

■ CALL TO ACTION | *Chapter 3*

Exercise 38C Creating my infographic

Key Skills

Success criteria ☐ I can create an infographic that communicates my carbon footprint.

Create your infographic and put a copy of it in the box below.

170

LESSON 39 — The 4 Rs

Learning outcome 2.4
Students should be able to discuss sustainability strategies that individuals, communities, businesses, agriculture and governments can employ to address climate change.

Exercise 39A Contrasting the linear and circular economies

Key Skills   Success criteria   ☐ I can explain the differences between a linear and a circular economy and explain why the circular model is better.

Reduce, reuse, repair and recycle (the 4 Rs) are four sustainability strategies. They are sometimes called a hierarchy because the first one is the most important and the fourth should happen only when the others cannot be done.

1. Reduce means that we should limit what we buy and the amount of energy we waste.
2. Reuse means that we reuse items before getting rid of them or give them to somebody who will use them.
3. Repair means that we fix items that are damaged rather than dumping them and buying new ones.
4. Recycle only when it is not possible to reuse or repair the object.

Ireland has a **linear economy**, which means products are made, bought, used and disposed of. A **circular economy** is a more sustainable system because it involves reducing, reusing, repairing and recycling.

Watch the video about changing how the economy works and answer the questions below.

> **YouTube** Go to YouTube and search for 'Explaining the Circular Economy and How Society Can Re-think Progress – Animated Video Essay' (3:48).

1. What is the linear approach to an economy?

2. What is wrong with this approach?

● CALL TO ACTION | *Chapter 3*

3. How is the circular economy different?

_____

_____

4. What culture should we adopt?

_____

_____

5. What difference to the economy would licensing make?

_____

_____

6. What is needed in order for the circular economy to work?

_____

_____

Exercise 39B Analysing food waste

Key Skills   **Success criteria** ☐ I can give examples of food waste and how to avoid it.

You can use the following strategies to reduce food waste:

- Plan your meals for the week.
- Buy only the amount of perishable food that you need.
- Grow your own fruit and vegetables.
- Use leftover food for lunch the following day or as an ingredient in another meal, such as leftover roast chicken in a curry.
- Some foods can be frozen if they are near their use-by date and defrosted for eating later.

2020 National Food Waste Attitudes Survey — key insights

(epa — B&A Research & Insight)

About 3 in 5 people actively think about food waste, with highest attention amongst the 65+ age group and lowest amongst the 16-24 age cohort.

Food waste is the second most concerning 'food issue' after price. However, **only 1 in 10 people see food waste as the most concerning food issue.**

3 in 5 people believe they only waste a small amount of food - first step to good food management behaviours is to identify how much food and types they actually do waste.

People show high concern for all food waste issues, however, the **strongest response is towards financial loss (47%)** .i.e. the wasted money from throwing out uneaten food

Strong understanding exists that multiple stakeholders along the food supply chain have a role to play in preventing food waste. **89% of people feel that consumers have a responsibility in preventing food waste.**

+55 age group have predominately heard of food waste reduction through TV and newspaper. Younger age groups far more likely to have heard through social media and internet sites.

Empty nesters throw away the least amount of food overall with 22% saying they throw away no food at all. 25-34 age cohort throw out the most food in particular fruit, vegetables, dairy, potatoes and meat.

The 16-24 and 25-34 age cohorts appear to have a lack of knowledge of how to reduce their food waste. **2 in 5** of younger age groups say they would like to reduce food waste but they don't know how).

High numbers of people are checking their fridge (81%) and making a list (70%) before doing a shop. Those who actively think about **food waste are more likely to check their fridge and are more likely to make a shopping list.**

During national Covid lockdown restrictions, there **appears to be a reported decrease in food wasted at home**. Also increases in food planning behaviour – more people doing shopping lists, making a meal plan, checking and tracking of food in cupboards, fridges etc.

Bread, vegetables, fruit and salad are the most common types of food that are thrown out in households. In addition to price promotions, when shopping many people are buying additional food products due to impulse, pester power and poor planning.

Around 3 in 4 people understand what 'use by' means and about 9 in 10 understand what 'best before' means. However, **passing the 'use by' (68%) and 'best before' (55%) food dates are the main reasons why people throw out food in their household.**

Facts sourced from mywaste.ie

Lesson 39: The 4 Rs

Look at the EPA infographic on the previous page, then answer the questions.

1. Which age group wastes the least amount of food?

2. What percentage of people think they waste only a small amount of food?

3. What is the main reason people are concerned about food waste?

4. Who do people think has a responsibility to cut food waste?

5. If you were launching a campaign against food waste, where would you run the campaign for:
   (a) Older people?
   (b) Younger people?

6. Which group is responsible for the most food waste?

7. Why do you think these people bought the unneeded food in the first place?

8. What type of food is most likely to be wasted?

9. Why do you think this is?

10. What simple tips are suggested to reduce food waste?

11. Explain what is meant by 'best before' and 'use by'.

12. List other suggestions for avoiding food waste that are not included here.

13. Which of the 4 Rs is the best for dealing with the problem of food waste?

14. Could another one of the 4 Rs be used? If so, how?

CALL TO ACTION | *Chapter 3*

Exercise 39C — Taking action on food waste in school

Key Skills

Success criteria ☐ I can identify causes of food waste in my school, suggest strategies for dealing with this and communicate with my Student Council representative.

Facts on food waste

- Each year, enough food waste is produced in Ireland to fill Croke Park two and a half times.
- More than one-third of the food produced globally is dumped.
- The average household in Ireland wastes between €400 and €1000 on food each year.
- One billion hungry people could be fed on less than a quarter of the food that is wasted in the US, UK and Europe.
- An area larger than China is used to grow food that is never eaten.
- Some 25% of the world's freshwater supply is used to grow food that is never eaten.
- In most developed countries, over half of all food waste takes place in the home.

Facts sourced from mywaste.ie

Working in groups, consider how much food is dumped or left around the school or school yard after breaks. From the information in the facts above and in the infographic from Exercise 39B, consider the best way to convince your fellow students to reduce their food waste by answering the following questions.

1. Is food waste a problem in the school? If so when and where?

2. Why do you think this is?

3. What ideas do you have that could help to improve this problem?

4. Write a brief letter to your Student Council representative expressing your concern about the problem and suggesting changes that could be made.

Lesson 39: The 4 Rs

✎ Exercise 39D Understanding how to reuse items

Key Skills **Success criteria** ☐ I can identify how goods can be reused, what products are suitable for reuse and why people can be reluctant to buy second-hand products.

Reusing does not just mean you have to keep using a product yourself. It also includes buying and selling goods online, donating to charity shops and selling products in second-hand shops or car boot sales. These products are still in a useful condition, but you no longer need them.

Read the passage about Ella de Guzman and answer the questions that follow.

My name is Ella de Guzman and I'm the founder of Siopaella. When I first moved to Ireland from Canada in 2010, I noticed there were no shops that specialised in the resale of items, everything from high street to high-end. This is how Siopaella was born. Siopaella represents 'Ella's Shop', but the actual Irish translation of 'Siopaeile' is 'Another type of shop'. I felt this fitted in perfectly as we were a type of retail that was different from the rest. Since we started in 2011, we have kept over 140,000 items in circulation and we have also donated 100s of kilos of clothing to charity. One piece of advice I have for people who want to reuse, is to take care of your things when you first get them. When it comes to handbags for example, use make-up pouches inside so you avoid costly marks and spills. Clean and dust your bags often so they maintain their value. Items that are kept in great condition will be reused over and over again and passed down through several generations of owners, keeping them beautiful and more importantly, keeping them out of the landfill.

Source: www.mywaste.ie/Siopaella

1. Have you ever bought second-hand clothes? Why/why not?

_____

_____

2. What did Ella notice did not exist in Ireland?

_____

175

■ CALL TO ACTION | *Chapter 3*

3. Ella's business is sustainable but also successful. What does this tell us?

4. What other products could be reused in this way?

5. Why do you think people often do not consider buying second-hand goods?

6. What advice does Ella give to people who want to reuse?

7. Do you know any other sites that reuse goods? What are they?

Exercise 39E Understanding the life cycle of a mobile phone

Key Skills **Success criteria** ☐ I can explain the actions I would take with my phone in order to be more sustainable.

Many products are dumped when they break and are replaced by new items. However, furniture, clothes, electrical items and shoes can be fixed for much less than the cost of replacing them. People do not repair items because:

- They lack the skills needed to repair things, like sewing and woodwork.
- Replacements are often cheap to buy.
- The tools needed are often expensive.
- Manufacturers make products that will not last long so people must buy new ones.
- Some prefer to buy new products.

Most broken objects end up in landfill but there are many ways to prevent that:

- Free tutorials on YouTube explain how to repair broken objects.
- Repair businesses can fix goods at a fraction of the cost of a new item. A broken zip in a jacket that cost €150 could be repaired for €10.
- Items under warranty can be repaired free of charge by the manufacturer.
- Repair items at an early stage before the problem becomes too serious.
- Take care of items. For examples, bicycles kept indoors are less likely to rust than ones left out in the rain.

Ideally, recycling happens only when we cannot reduce, reuse or repair. Recycling products wastes fewer natural resources and less energy than making new products. Aluminium cans, glass bottles and jars, paper and plastic can all be recycled.

Lesson 39: The 4 Rs

Watch the video about the life cycle of a mobile phone. Then answer the following questions.

> **YouTube** — Go to YouTube and search for 'Carbon footprint – Life cycle of Mobile Phone' (1:30).

1. What model phone do you have?

2. How old is it?

3. How long do you plan on keeping your phone before replacing it?

4. What would make you change your phone?

5. If your phone were broken, what would you do with it: reuse, repair or recycle?

6. Give an advantage and a disadvantage of each method.

Reuse	
Repair	
Recycle	

177

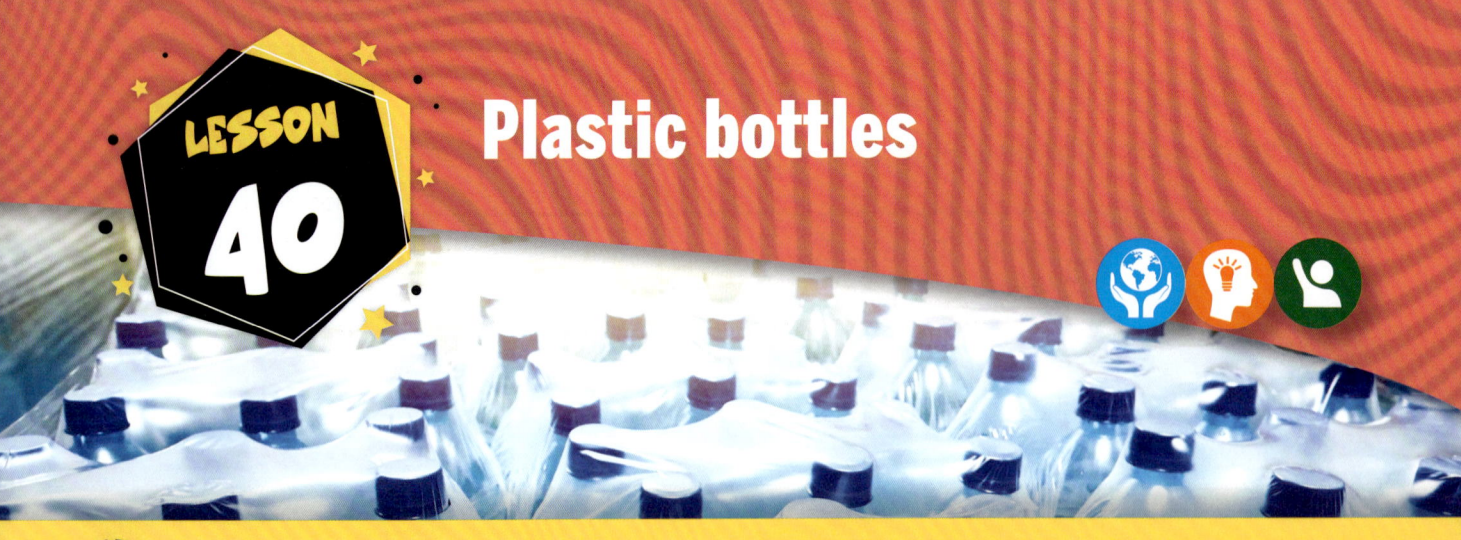

Lesson 40: Plastic bottles

Learning outcome 2.4
Students should be able to discuss sustainability strategies that individuals, communities, businesses, agriculture and governments can employ to address climate change.

Exercise 40A Assessing my knowledge about plastics

Key Skills

Success criteria ☐ I can answer questions about plastics.

Working in pairs, discuss whether each of the following statements is true or false.

		True	False
1.	Plastic bottles are made from oil.		
2.	Plastic is a problem only in developed countries.		
3.	Plastic bottles can be recycled into fleece.		
4.	Compostable plastics are made from corn.		
5.	Plastic bottles take 100 years to decompose.		
6.	Drinks companies started producing bottled water to promote a healthier lifestyle.		
7.	Plastic enters the human food chain when fish eat them.		
8.	Bottled water is better quality than tap water.		

Exercise 40B Understanding the stages of producing a plastic bottle

Key Skills

Success criteria ☐ I can explain how the production of plastic bottles is bad for the environment and is not sustainable.

Read the information on the life of a plastic bottle and answer the questions on the next page.
- Most plastic bottles are made from polyethylene terephthalate (PET) plastic, which is produced from crude oil.
- The oil is transported to oil refineries where the lighter elements from which plastics are made are separated from the heavier parts.
- The oil is shipped to a plastics factory where it is turned into plastic pellets.

Lesson 40: Plastic bottles

- The pellets are melted down into pre-forms which look like plastic test tubes.
- The pre-forms are sent to bottling companies where they are heated and expanded into bottles. They are sterilised, filled with water or other drinks and capped. They are labelled and packed into cases for shipping.
- The bottles are shipped to shops, restaurants and other businesses. This often means travelling very long distances.
- The bottles are bought and the water or other drink is consumed.
- The bottle is disposed either as litter, in landfill or recycled. You must wash a bottle really well before putting it in the recycling bin.
- Recycled bottles are brought to factories where, if they are clean enough, they are shredded and melted back into pellets.
- The pellets are used to make products such as fleece jackets or blankets, insulation or carpets.

1. Why does the manufacturer of a plastic bottle have a high carbon footprint?

2. Plastic bottles can be recycled into useful products. Why does this still have an impact on carbon footprint?

3. What happens to bottles that are not recycled?

4. Why are plastic water bottles unsustainable?

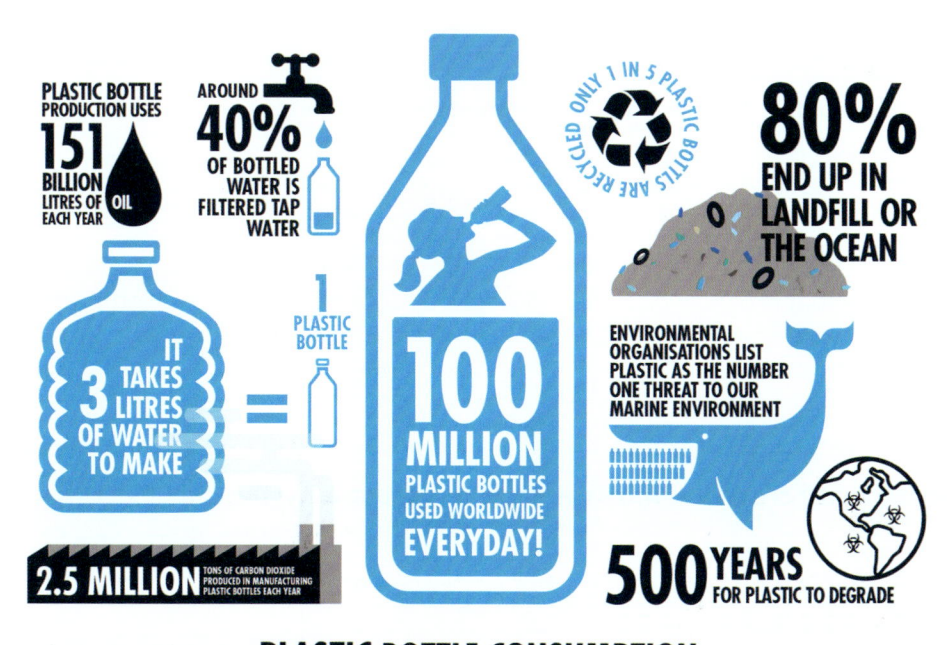

PLASTIC BOTTLE CONSUMPTION

- PLASTIC BOTTLE PRODUCTION USES 151 BILLION LITRES OF OIL EACH YEAR
- AROUND 40% OF BOTTLED WATER IS FILTERED TAP WATER
- IT TAKES 3 LITRES OF WATER TO MAKE 1 PLASTIC BOTTLE = 100 MILLION PLASTIC BOTTLES USED WORLDWIDE EVERYDAY!
- 2.5 MILLION TONS OF CARBON DIOXIDE PRODUCED IN MANUFACTURING PLASTIC BOTTLES EACH YEAR
- ONLY 1 IN 5 PLASTIC BOTTLES ARE RECYCLED
- 80% END UP IN LANDFILL OR THE OCEAN
- ENVIRONMENTAL ORGANISATIONS LIST PLASTIC AS THE NUMBER ONE THREAT TO OUR MARINE ENVIRONMENT
- 500 YEARS FOR PLASTIC TO DEGRADE

WWW.WATERLOVERS.COM

■ CALL TO ACTION | *Chapter 3*

5. Look at infographic on the previous page and find one example to support each of the following reasons not to buy bottled water:

Waste	
Environmental damage	
Bottled water is not needed	

Exercise 40C Analysing an opinion on sustainable water use

Key Skills   **Success criteria**   ☐ I can give examples of the impact of using bottled water on the environment.

Working in pairs, read the opinion piece from *The Irish Times*, discuss the questions that follow and then write your answers.

Let's make 2020 the year we give up bottled water

Mon, Jan 13, 2020 Sorcha Hamilton

This year it is estimated that more than half a trillion plastic bottles will be sold globally. The introduction of lightweight plastic transformed the retail sector in the 1970s – but its effect on the environment has been devastating, with a massive increase in plastic waste finding its way into the oceans and harming marine life. Despite efforts to reduce the presence of single-use plastics, progress is extremely slow. The EU voted to outlaw 10 single-use plastic items, including straws, forks and knives by 2021, and by 2029 at least 90 per cent of beverage bottles will have to be recycled. Imports of plastics to Ireland, however, show that there's still plenty of it coming into the country.

So what can we do about it? Drink more tap water, for a start. Buying bottled water when there is no alternative – or a boil water notice has been issued – is one thing; buying it as a lifestyle choice is a whole other issue. Bottled water requires up to 2,000 times the energy used to produce tap water. Consider its production, transportation and refrigeration – and it's easy to see how. If you're not a fan of the taste of your tap water, you can have a small filter tap installed at your sink or purchase a filter jug for your fridge. And don't forget your reusable water bottle. Check out *Refill Ireland's website* for a handy map of nearby water fountains.

Source: *The Irish Times*

1. The author says plastic transformed the retail sector (shopping). Can you give any examples of how shopping would be different without plastic?

2. The author says that progress on reducing single-use plastic is slow. Can you suggest any reasons why?

3. When does the author suggest it is acceptable to buy bottled water?

4. Why does using bottled water lead to a higher carbon footprint than tap water?

Lesson 40: Plastic bottles

5. Mention a solution the author suggests for the problem.

6. This is an opinion piece from a newspaper. Did you find it convincing? Why/why not?

7. Why would reducing your plastic consumption make you a better global citizen?

Exercise 40D Understanding why we use bottled water

Key Skills

Success criteria ☐ I can explain some reasons why people use bottled water.

Watch the video about bottled water. Working in groups, discuss the questions below and then answer them.

YouTube Go to YouTube and search for 'The Story of Bottled Water – The Story of Stuff Project' (8:04).

1. How does the video show that bottled water costs so much more than tap water?

2. What strategies do the bottled water companies use to convince people to buy bottled water?

3. Where does one-third of bottled water come from?

4. How does the video show that recycling bottles often does not work?

5. How many people in the world do not have access to clean water?

6. This is an American video. Is the situation in Ireland similar? Explain your answer.

7. What solutions would you suggest to this issue?

8. What solutions are suggested in the video?

Lesson 41: Plastic

Learning outcome 2.4
Students should be able to discuss sustainability strategies that individuals, communities, businesses, agriculture and governments can employ to address climate change.

Exercise 41A Understanding the negatives of plastic

Key Skills   **Success criteria**   ☐ I can explain the dangers of plastics.

Read the facts about plastic below and answer the questions that follow.

Some facts about plastic

- 17 million barrels of oil are needed to make a year's supply of plastic bottles in the US.
- A huge amount of fuel is used transporting plastic bottles. This contributes to air pollution.
- Bottled water often has not got enough fluoride, which is needed to prevent tooth decay.
- Plastic bottles can be used only once because they can release BPA, which has been linked to cancers.
- 80% of plastic bottles are not recycled.
- A plastic bottle made from PET takes 450 years to decompose.
- Plastic bottles can release toxic chemicals when they are decomposing.
- 10% of plastic ends up in the oceans where fish and seabirds swallow it.
- Products like toothpaste can contain tiny pieces of plastic called microbeads. These end up in the sea where they are eaten by fish. In 2020, Ireland outlawed microbeads.
- Over 40% of plastics are used for packaging.
- 500 billion plastic bags are used every year in the world.

1. Find two examples of how plastic can be wasteful.

   _____
   _____

2. Find two examples of how plastic can be harmful to health.

   _____
   _____

Lesson 41: Plastic

3. Find two examples of how plastic remains long after it is no longer used.

4. Why is some plastic used only once?

5. Suggest four ways that you could reduce your use of plastics.

6. Would the facts on the previous page change people's opinions on plastics? Why/why not?

7. Suggest another way to convince others to reduce their use of plastics.

Exercise 41B — Understanding the problem of single-use plastics

Key Skills

Success criteria ☐ I can explain, giving examples, why single-use plastics need to be reduced.

Biodegradable plastic is an alternative to plastic manufactured from oil. Biodegradable plastic is produced from corn and sugarcane. It can be broken down by bacteria and fungi. Some of these plastics can be turned into compost within 12 weeks. Most bioplastics, however, must be broken down by industrial composters. Many people do not know what to do with these plastics so they end up in landfill sites.

Watch both videos and answer the questions below.

Video 1: Go to YouTube and search for 'How does plastic end up in our oceans? Greenpeace UK' (1:20).

Video 2: Go to YouTube and search for 'Sick of plastic? You're not the only one ... It's time to ban single-use plastic' (0:58).

Video 1

1. Would this advertisement convince you? Why/why not?

2. How do simple household tasks lead to plastic getting into the sea?

183

■ CALL TO ACTION | *Chapter 3*

3. What does the plastic pollution in uninhabited islands and the Arctic tell you?

   _____
   _____

Video 2

1. What feeling do you have watching this video?

   _____
   _____

2. Why do you think the makers of this video wanted you to feel this way?

   _____
   _____

Both videos

1. Which of these videos is more convincing? Why?

   _____
   _____

2. Which do you think you learned the most from?

   _____

3. How would you improve either video?

   _____
   _____
   _____

Exercise 41C — Identifying how to reduce plastic waste production

Key Skills

Success criteria ☐ I can suggest how individuals, organisations and businesses and the country can respond to plastic waste.

In 2002, Ireland became the first country to introduce a levy on single-use plastic bags. This meant that people had to pay 15c for a single-use plastic bag or bring their own bag. Over the next 10 years, there was a drop in single-plastic bag use from 328 bags per person per year to 14 bags per person per year and there was less littering. The government also received €200 million in revenue from the levy.

EU annual plastic packaging waste per head of population 2018

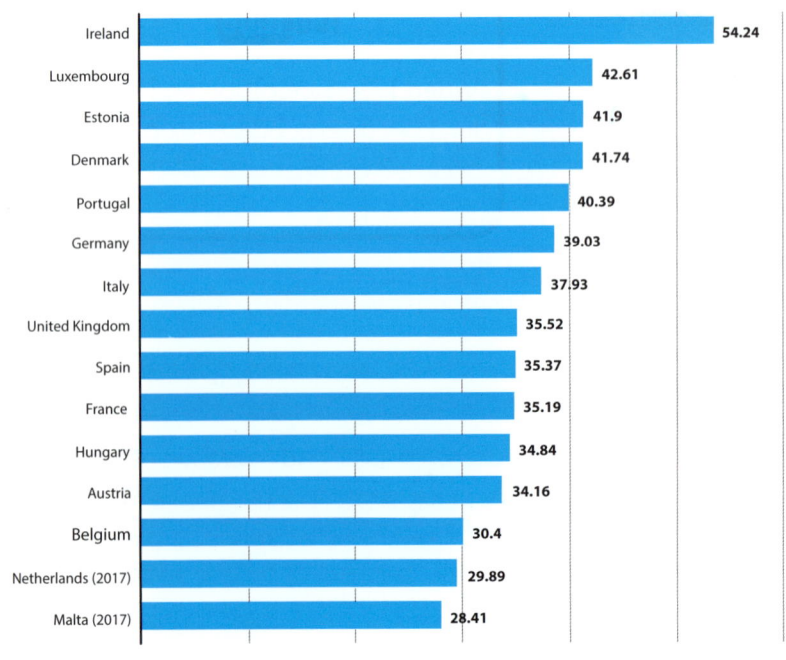

Country	kg
Ireland	54.24
Luxembourg	42.61
Estonia	41.9
Denmark	41.74
Portugal	40.39
Germany	39.03
Italy	37.93
United Kingdom	35.52
Spain	35.37
France	35.19
Hungary	34.84
Austria	34.16
Belgium	30.4
Netherlands (2017)	29.89
Malta (2017)	28.41

Lesson 41: Plastic

Working in pairs, read the information on the previous page about the plastic bag levy and examine the bar chart. Discuss the questions and then write your answers.

1. When this levy was introduced, there was very little opposition. Why do you think this was?

2. Do you think that made it easier to introduce? Why?

3. What shows its success?

4. What does the bar chart tell us about Ireland?

5. How does Ireland compare to Malta?

6. Give examples of things that you could do to lessen plastic waste in Ireland.

7. Give examples of things you see at school, in shops, in sports and leisure activities that could change the amount of plastic packaging waste.

8. Suggest two things the government could do to reduce the level of plastic waste produced in Ireland.

Exercise 41D **Identifying actions people, organisations and the government can take to reduce plastic waste**

Key Skills **Success criteria** ☐ I can design a public awareness advertisement.

You have been asked by an organisation to create a 20-second cartoon advert that can be shared on social media. In it, you must suggest three things that individuals, organisations and the government can do to tackle the problem of single-use plastic. Answer the questions on the next page first, and then sketch the elements you want in your advert.

■ CALL TO ACTION | *Chapter 3*

1. Which of the four Rs do you think is the best to use in this case? Explain why.
   _____
   _____

2. Note three actions to solve this problem that:
   (a) Each person could take
   _____
   _____
   _____

   (b) Organisations could take
   _____
   _____
   _____

   (c) The government could take
   _____
   _____
   _____

3. You will send the advert to a design company to create. Your advert will involve four scenes. Sketch and note the information you want each panel to include.

Lesson 42: Water

Learning outcome 2.4
Students should be able to discuss sustainability strategies that individuals, communities, businesses, agriculture and governments can employ to address climate change.

Exercise 42A Becoming aware of my household's water usage

Key Skills

Success criteria ☐ I can calculate my household's weekly water usage.

Water is needed for many things around the house:

- A standard toilet – 9 litres per flush
- A dual flush toilet – 5 litres per flush
- A dishwasher – 20 litres per full load
- Handwashing dishes – 49 litres per full load
- Standard electrical shower – 4 litres per minute
- Power shower – 8 litres per minute
- Bath – 80 litres per bath
- Running the tap when brushing teeth or shaving – 6 litres per minute
- Washing the car at home – 300 litres
- Washing the car at a carwash – 125 litres
- Watering plants – 135 litres per 15 minutes

Based on the figures above, calculate your household's weekly usage of water.

	One use	Number of times per week	Total volume
1. Flush the toilet			
2. Run the tap while I brush my teeth			
3. Have a shower (take into account the type and duration of shower)			
4. Have a bath			
5. Use the washing machine			
6. Use the dishwasher			
7. Handwash dishes			
8. Wash the car			
9. Water plants			
Overall total			

■ CALL TO ACTION | *Chapter 3*

Exercise 42B **Becoming aware of water wastage**

Key Skills **Success criteria** ☐ I can identify actions that reduce water wastage.

Facts about water

Watch the video and answer the questions below.

> **YouTube**
> Go to YouTube and search for 'Water Waste – Videos for Change' (1:10).

1. Identify the ways in which water is wasted.
   _____
   _____

2. How many of these do you do? List them.
   _____
   _____
   _____

3. What could you do differently to reduce water wastage?
   _____
   _____

Exercise 42C **Becoming aware of water in the developing world**

Key Skills **Success criteria** ☐ I can identify facts relating to water usage in the developing world.

Working in pairs, answer the following quiz on inequality (you will probably have to guess some of the answers).

Quiz

1. In 2019, how many people in the world lacked access to safe water?
   (a) 20 million ☐   **(b)** 84 million ☐   **(c)** 500 million ☐   **(d)** 884 million ☐

2. What is clean fresh drinking water?
   (a) Bottled water ☐
   (b) Water that does not contain salt or contaminants harmful to health ☐
   (c) Cooled water ☐   **(d)** Boiled water ☐

3. Which of these diseases is a diarrhoeal disease (a disease for which the common symptom is diarrhoea)?
   (a) Cancer ☐   **(b)** AIDS ☐   **(c)** Cholera ☐   **(d)** Lupus ☐

4. Which of the following is the second largest cause of deaths, after pneumonia, of children in developing countries?
   (a) Malaria ☐   **(b)** Meningitis ☐   **(c)** Diarrhoea ☐   **(d)** Measles ☐

5. Which sector uses the most water?
   (a) Domestic ☐   (b) Industry ☐   (c) Mining ☐   (d) Agriculture ☐

6. In many parts of the developing world, women must travel long distances collecting water which they carry:
   (a) On their back ☐   (b) In small trolleys ☐
   (c) On their head ☐   (d) On poles on their shoulders ☐

7. The average amount of water a person in the developing world uses per day for drinking, washing and cooking is the same as that used for:
   (a) A bath in Ireland ☐   (b) A car wash in Ireland ☐
   (c) A full load in the washing machine ☐   (d) A toilet flush ☐

8. Access to drinking water in the developing world is worst in:
   (a) Cities ☐   (b) Towns ☐   (c) Villages ☐   (d) Rural areas ☐

Exercise 42D Becoming aware of water scarcity

Key Skills

Success criteria ☐ I can identify different types of water scarcity (shortages) and where is mostly likely to be affected by it.

Water insecurity is when people do not have access to a safe, constant and adequate supply of water. Water insecurity can have two causes:

1. There is a physical shortage of water, such as in areas hit by drought or desert areas. This is known as **physical scarcity**.
2. There is water but there are no wells, pumps or ways of transporting the water. This is known as **economic scarcity**.

Water is needed for drinking, cooking, washing, feeding animals and watering plants. Around 1.42 billion people live in areas of high or extremely high water scarcity.

Global physical and economic water scarcity

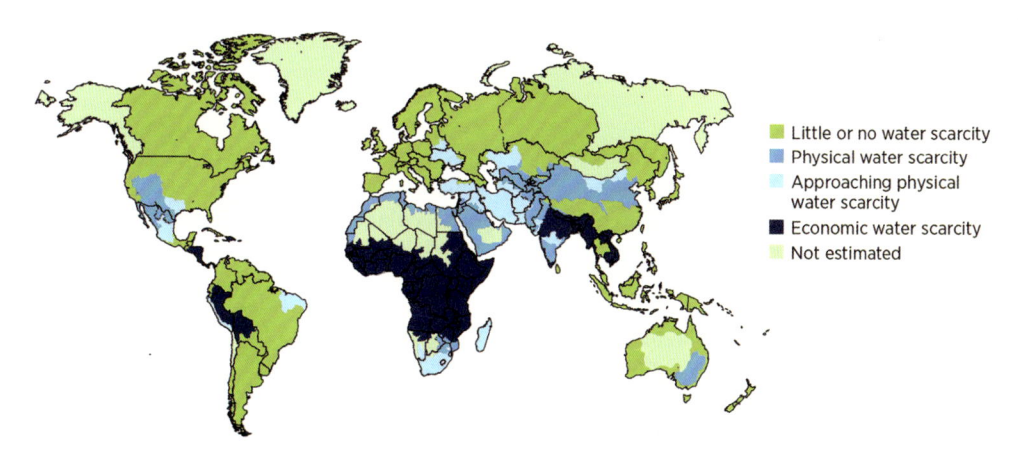

- Little or no water scarcity
- Physical water scarcity
- Approaching physical water scarcity
- Economic water scarcity
- Not estimated

Working in pairs, look at the map above and answer the following questions.

1. What parts of the world have little or no water scarcity?

CALL TO ACTION | Chapter 3

2. Why do you think this is?

3. Name a part of the world with physical water scarcity.

4. Name a part of the world facing economic water scarcity.

5. Which of these types of scarcity is easier to solve?

6. How could it be solved?

7. Can you give any reasons as to why it is not solved?

Exercise 42E — Identifying the impacts of access to clean water on people's lives

Key Skills **Success criteria** ☐ I can name the negative consequences of not having access to safe clean water and name the positive impacts of having a ready supply of water.

There are three types of drinking water:
- **Unimproved** drinking water does not protect the source from outside contamination, especially sewage. It comes from unprotected wells, springs or surface water.
- **Improved** drinking water is protected from outside contamination. It comes from protected wells, springs, rainwater or public taps.
- Water that is **piped** into a dwelling, plot or yard. This water is also improved, as it is treated to make it safe to drink.

Read 'Grace's Story' and then answer the questions on the next page.

Grace's Story

My name is Grace and I am nine years old. My family lives on a maize and rice farm in the south of Malawi. The women in our village do the farming as it is considered women's work. Girls often get married young so they may need to leave school. In the morning, I get up early with my mother to light the fire and collect water for the house. I used to hate this job. I had to walk for an hour, then climb down a bank to the river to gather water in a big bucket. It was difficult to get back up the bank. I had to watch out for wild animals too! There can be snakes in the grass near to the water, and I've heard stories of children getting snatched by crocodiles in the river! My father says that isn't true though … still, during the rainy season we would go in pairs to keep watch. My brother doesn't have to help with the chores. He just gets up and goes to school.

One day, there was a big meeting in our village. A group called Concern Worldwide wanted to put in boreholes – deep holes that bring up water in our own village so we don't have to travel. We also had talks about how we should use the water to stay healthy. Sometimes small children would die because the river water wasn't clean. Now we have the borehole I don't have to spend as much time collecting water or helping in the fields so I can go to school. When I'm older I want to be a community health worker and help people to stay healthy.

Source: 'Someone Like Me', Concern Worldwide

Lesson 42: Water

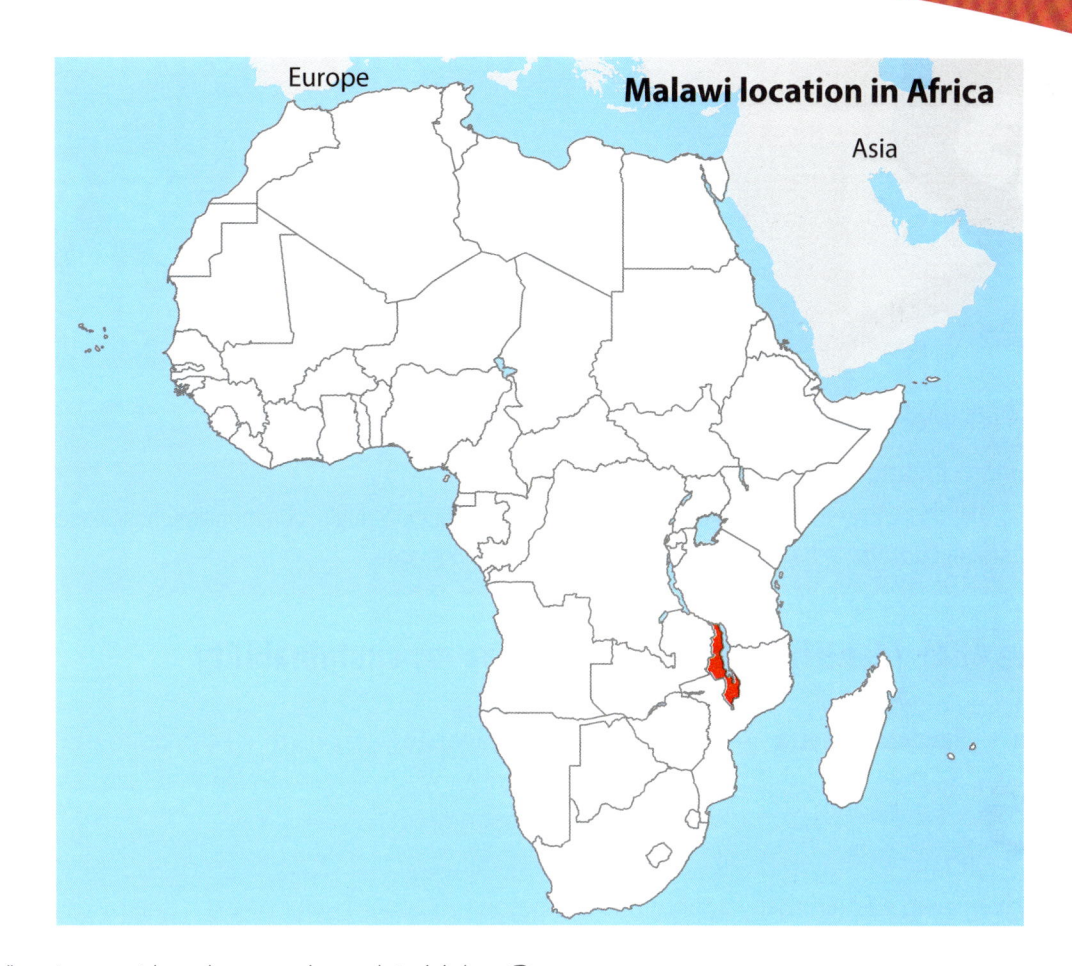

Malawi location in Africa

1. What is considered women's work in Malawi?

2. Why do girls often leave school early?

3. What are the dangers of getting water from the river?

4. Why does Grace's brother not have to collect water?

5. What have been the results of the borehole for Grace and her family?

6. Can you think of any other benefits of the borehole not mentioned here?

7. What type of water supply did Grace originally have?

8. What type does she have access to now?

Lesson 43: My sustainability actions

Learning outcome 2.4
Students should be able to discuss sustainability strategies that individuals, communities, businesses, agriculture and governments can employ to address climate change.

Exercise 43A Identifying how I can improve my sustainability

Key Skills **Success criteria** ☐ I can name sustainability actions that I can do myself, those I can promote with my family and those that I can ask for government action on.

Look at the following sustainability actions. Note whether you could achieve each one by doing it yourself, with your family's help or with action from the government.

Action	Myself	My family	Government action
1. Replace all bulbs with energy-saving bulbs			
2. Buy locally produced foods			
3. Buy food in season			
4. Create a compost heap			
5. Rewild part of my garden			
6. Donate my old clothes and books to charity			
7. Recycle leftover cooked foods			
8. Heat only the rooms that are being used			
9. Wear warmer clothes indoors when it is cold			
10. Use public transport, walk or cycle			
11. Turn off lights when a room is empty			
12. Do not drink bottled water			
13. Grow my own fruit and vegetables			
14. Take shorter showers			
15. Use only environmentally friendly cleaning products			
16. Turn off and plug out electrical appliances rather than leaving them on standby			
17. Replace our home's boiler with a more energy-efficient one			
18. Install a wind turbine and solar panels			
19. Avoid air travel when going on holidays			
20. Reduce the number of products I buy with plastic wrapping			

Lesson 43: My sustainability actions

Exercise 43B — Identifying actions I must take to improve my sustainability

Key Skills **Success criteria** ☐ I can identify reasons for my inaction and suggest how to overcome these.

Considering the sustainable actions you have already identified, focus on the ones you could improve. Identify why you do not do it as well and suggest how you could do it better.

1. What actions could you take to improve your sustainability?

2. Why do you not do these?

3. What do you need to do to improve this?

Exercise 43C — Creating a blog post explaining what sustainability means to me

Key Skills **Success criteria** ☐ I can identify what sustainability is to me and how to promote it.

You have looked at reasons for sustainability over these lessons. Below write a blog post where you say:

- What sustainability means to you
- How you practise it
- How you can improve it
- Why you think it is important
- Why others should think so too.

193

CALL TO ACTION | *Chapter 3*

Exercise 43D Evaluating solutions to water shortages

Key Skills **Success criteria** ☐ I can name solutions to water scarcity in Ireland and in the developing world.

The following are some solutions to water shortages. Decide which of these would be helpful in Ireland and which are helpful in the developing world. Tick both if both apply. Then explain why they are suitable solutions.

Solution	Ireland	Developing world	Reason
1. Launch a campaign to educate people about their behaviour			
2. Collect rainwater			
3. Build desalination plants – these take the salt from seawater			
4. Increase the cost of water			
5. Bore wells in villages			
6. Use drip irrigation, which delivers water directly to plants' roots			
7. Grow drought-resistant crops			
8. Ban flushing raw sewage into the seas			
9. Pipe safe and clean water to areas with physical shortages			
10. Repair leaks in pipes			

Reflection: Reflecting on my learning about sustainability

Learning outcome 2.12
Students should be able to reflect on their ongoing learning and what it means for them.

Key Skills

Success criteria
- [ ] I can give examples of how my thinking about sustainability has developed.
- [ ] I can give examples of what I do differently to protect the environment.

Look back at the skills and knowledge you have developed in this chapter. It is important to identify what you have learned and where you could learn more. Use the following worksheet to guide your reflection on sustainability. Then, working in groups, discuss your responses for each of the sections below.

1.	Before looking at sustainability, I thought …	
2.	Things I learned about sustainability	
3.	Where I got my information from	
4.	How I know the information was reliable	
5.	The different types of sources I got my information from	
6.	The most interesting thing I learned was …	
7.	How the new information I have learned will change what I do	

195

Action: Organising a guest speaker

A helpful way of learning more about a topic is by inviting a guest speaker with expert knowledge on the topic to speak to the class. You can ask the speaker specific questions and they can give an account of their personal involvement in the area.

✓ Action 1 — Identifying the tasks I need to do to complete the action

Key Skills

Success criteria ☐ I will identify the specific tasks my committee must do.

Begin your action by assigning different roles for everybody. Each person works in a group and each group has specific responsibilities for carrying out the action. Once each group has been formed, its members meet and decide their roles, share the roles with the class and note them here.

Group	Members	Responsibilities
1. Invitation		
2. Publicity		
3. Room		
4. Welcoming		
5. Speakers		

At this point, the class decides on the area you wish to learn more about.

Action: Organising a guest speaker

✓ Action 2   Identifying a suitable guest speaker

Key Skills   **Success criteria**   ☐ I will identify a suitable organisation and contact it to send a guest speaker.

Research an organisation that works in the area and see what it does. Check whether it sends speakers to schools.

1. Which organisation/person would help us to learn more?
   _____

2. How could they help us?
   _____
   _____

✓ Action 3   Compiling a list of my group's actions

Key Skills   **Success criteria**   ☐ I will identify the specific actions my group did.

Then work in your groups to conduct your actions and note them here.

What actions did we do in my group?
_____
_____
_____
_____
_____
_____

✓ Action 4   Noting questions for the speaker and the responses I received

Key Skills   **Success criteria**   ☐ I can identify areas I want further information on and how to ask questions to get these answers. I will be able to show my understanding by noting the answers I have received.

Write out the questions that you would like to ask the guest speaker. As the presentation is made, see whether the questions have been answered or note other questions that you think of. Note the answers you receive to your questions.

CALL TO ACTION | *Chapter 3*

1. My questions	
2. Questions that come up as I listen to the presentation	
3. Answers	

✓ **Action 5** **Summarising my learning**

Key Skills **Success criteria** ☐ I can write an account of the information I learned from the guest speaker.

Thinking back over the guest speaker's presentation, note the points that you learned below.

Chapter 4 Local and Global Development

Case study: Kenya

LESSON 44

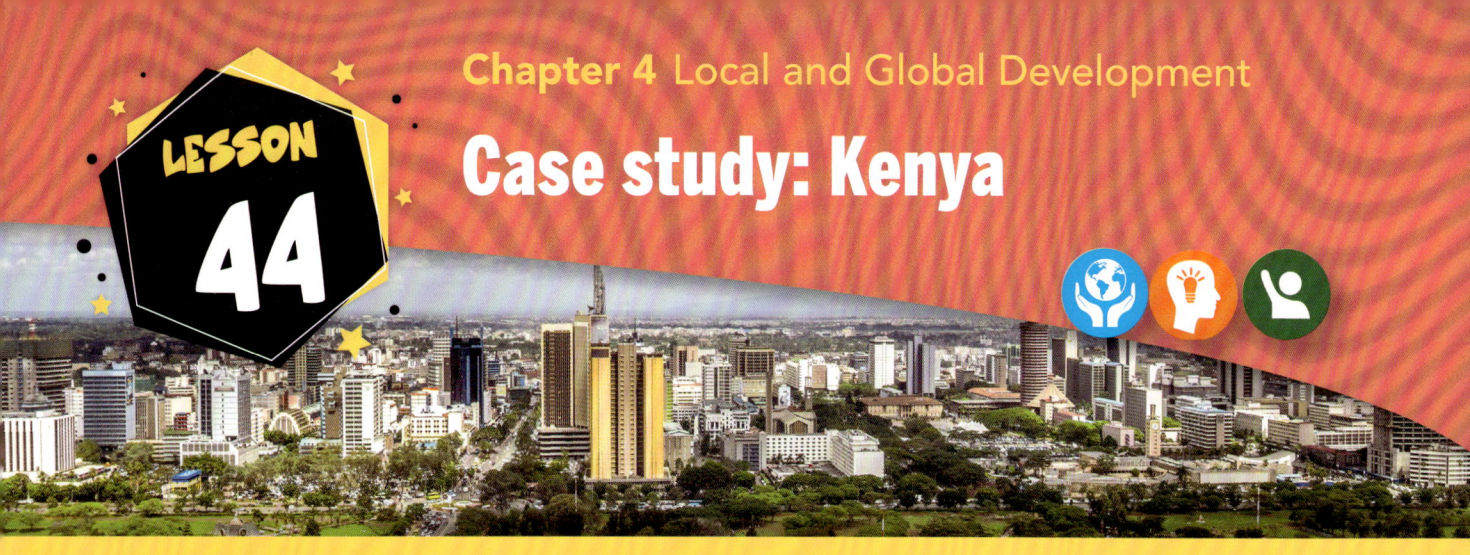

Learning outcome 2.5
Students should be able to examine case studies or personal testimonies of people experiencing poverty or inequality from different contexts and countries and how they are working to overcome this.

Exercise 44A Identifying symptoms of poverty

Key Skills

Success criteria ☐ I can give examples of poverty and how it differs from being wealthy.

Kenya is a country of 48 million people in the east of Africa. In 2020, it was the sixth largest economy in Africa. Kenya has a coast on the Indian Ocean, but most Kenyans live inland in the highlands. The capital Nairobi has a population of over 4 million.

There is a lot of poverty in Kenya. Symptoms of poverty include poor housing, homelessness, poor healthcare, lack of access to food, lack of access to water, lack of access to education, underfunded schools and hospitals and unsafe neighbourhoods.

Working in pairs, read the facts about Kenya and look at the photos. Discuss the questions on the next page and then write your answers.

Kenya facts
- Agriculture, tea, coffee and flowers are major industries.
- Tourism is another major industry, with many people coming to visit the reserves set up to protect animals like lions, cheetahs and hippos.
- School is free in Kenya, but poor and rural children often do not attend because they have to help their parents at home.
- Drought is common in many parts of Kenya.
- Most of Kenya's poor live in the rural north-east.
- 72% of Kenyans have access to improved water.
- 84% of the population can read and write, 58% complete primary school and 14% complete secondary school.
- 36% of the population lives below the international poverty line (*see* page 210).
- 69.7% of the population has access to electricity.
- Life expectancy in Kenya is 66.7, compared to 82.3 in Ireland.
- Child mortality (deaths of children under five years of age) is 43.2 per 1,000 live births. In Ireland, the figure is 3.3.

■ CALL TO ACTION | *Chapter 4*

1. What symptoms of poverty can you identify from this information?
   _____
   _____

2. If you were to travel to a rural village in north-east Kenya, what symptoms of poverty do you think you might find?
   _____

3. Describe three differences you would expect to find between the village and your own area.
   _____
   _____
   _____

Exercise 44B Linking symptoms of poverty to causes of poverty

Key Skills   **Success criteria** ☐ I can trace symptoms of poverty to their causes.

The causes of poverty in Kenya include the following:

- More than 80% of the population rely on agriculture for income and food security. However, plots of land are becoming smaller as parents pass their land on to more than one child.
- More than 80% of the land is arid (dry) or semi-arid.
- There are 12,800 tractors in Kenya, this compares with 175,000 in Ireland, which has a much smaller population.
- More than 25% of the population live in areas where there are often droughts.
- Just over 8,000 people (0.018% of the population) in Kenya own more wealth than the other over 44 million (99.9%) combined.
- Nearly 60% of young women do not attend secondary school and few Kenyan women own property.
- Corruption is common at all levels of government and police are often willing to take bribes from criminals.
- In 2019, the three main causes of death were HIV/AIDS, respiratory infections and diarrhoeal diseases.
- Rivers are the main source of water for **millions of Kenyans**. Mosquitoes breed in stagnant water and malaria is spread by mosquito bites.

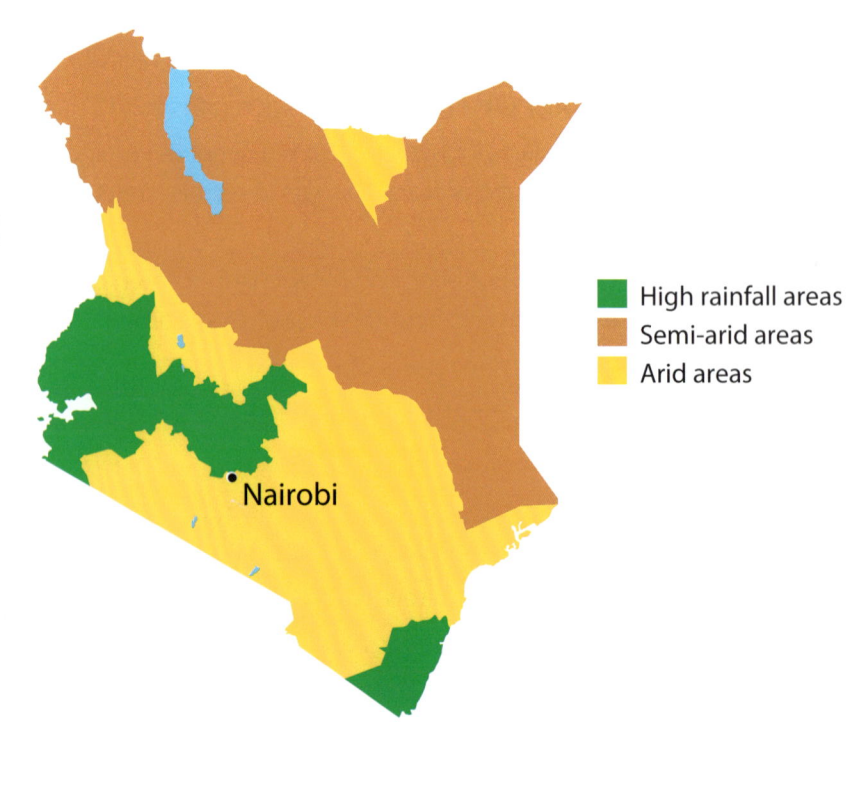

■ High rainfall areas
■ Semi-arid areas
■ Arid areas

200

Working in pairs, read about the causes of poverty in Kenya. Discuss the following question and write your answers. Take two of the symptoms of poverty you identified in Exercise 44A and link it to a cause.

Symptom	Cause
For example: More than 25% of the population live in areas where there are often droughts.	Lack of access to water
1.	
2.	

Exercise 44C Identifying how people fight poverty

Key Skills

Success criteria ☐ I can give examples of how the Green Belt Movement has helped to tackle poverty.

Working in pairs, read Wangari Maathai's story and answer the questions.

Wangari Maathai (1940–2011) was the first African woman to win the Nobel Peace Prize for her work as the founder of the Green Belt Movement. In 1971, Wangari became the first East African woman to get a doctorate.

Through her work with women's volunteer associations, she saw that many of the problems in Kenya were due to environmental damage. Rural Kenyan women told her how their streams were drying up, so they had to walk further for firewood for fuel. When she was a child, Wangari collected water from springs which were protected by tree roots. The springs dried up after the trees were gone. Trees bind the soil, store rainwater and provide food and firewood.

Wangari believed bad government caused poverty and saw the planting of trees as a way out of this. She was arrested and beaten for criticising President Daniel arap Moi. In 1976, Wangari introduced community tree planting and, after getting UN funding, began a programme that paid women to plant trees in their community. She set up the Green Belt Movement, which plants trees to preserve the environment.

In 2002, Wangari was elected to the Kenyan parliament and became Assistant Minister for Environment and Natural Resources. In 2004, she was awarded the Nobel Peace Prize for her contribution to sustainable development, democracy and peace. Wangari Maathai died aged 71 in 2011. Her movement has planted more than 30 million trees in Kenya.

> *We tend to put the environment last because we think the first thing we have to do is eliminate poverty. But you can't reduce poverty in a vacuum. You are doing it in an environment.*
> – Wangari Maathai

1. What two things was Wangari Maathai the first to achieve?

2. What is the benefit of trees for water supply?

3. What did she see as the cause of poverty in Kenya?

■ CALL TO ACTION | *Chapter 4*

4. How has her movement benefited the environment?
   _____
   _____

5. What point is she making in the quote?
   _____
   _____

Exercise 44D Identifying the benefits of electrification

Key Skills **Success criteria** ☐ I can give examples of how electrification can lead to sustainable development and raise people's incomes.

Watch the video on solar power in Kenya and answer the questions that follow.

> **YouTube** Go to YouTube and search for 'How Kenyan Farmers are preserving food through solar power' (4:33).

1. How much farm produce is wasted?
   _____
   _____

2. Why do these farmers not use the generators?
   _____
   _____

3. What are the benefits of this facility?
   _____
   _____

4. Why is this an example of sustainable development?
   _____
   _____

5. How does it differ from the US and China?
   _____
   _____

6. There is a double benefit to sustainability in this story. What are the benefits?
   _____
   _____

Lesson 45: Fairtrade

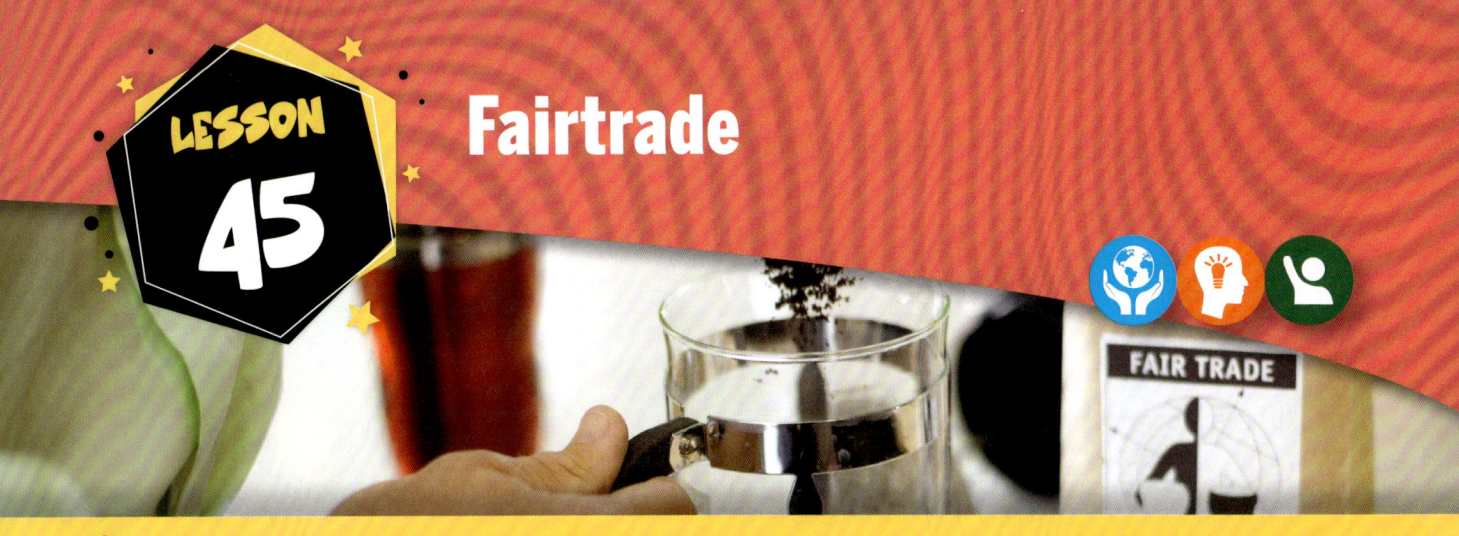

Learning outcome 2.5
Students should be able to examine case studies or personal testimonies of people experiencing poverty or inequality from different contexts and countries and how they are working to overcome this.

Exercise 45A Testing my knowledge of Fairtrade

Key Skills

Success criteria ☐ I can understand the benefits of Fairtrade.

Small producers, especially those in the developing world, are often exploited by big companies forcing them to accept less money for their product. **Fairtrade** is a movement that ensures producers of products like coffee, cocoa, wine, fruit and cotton receive a fair payment. Fairtrade helps people to earn a **living income**, which is enough money for healthy food, clean water, education, clothes and medicine. Fair payment also provides enough money to cover the cost of sustainably producing their crop or product. The producers also receive a **Fairtrade premium**, which is extra money to invest in their business.

Fairtrade also gives producers interest-free loans before harvest time when their costs are highest, but before they have received any payment. To achieve the Fairtrade mark, producers must meet certain standards, like no child labour, fair working conditions and fair payment. All businesses selling products meeting these standards can carry the **Fairtrade mark**. This mark tells consumers that the product has been produced fairly.

Look for this mark when shopping

Working in pairs, answer the quiz below (you will probably have to guess some of the answers).

Quiz

1. In 2020, Lidl and Aldi between them sold what percentage of Fairtrade bananas in Ireland?
   (a) 11% ☐   (b) 21% ☐   (c) 41% ☐   (d) 51% ☐
2. How many people worldwide depend on coffee for their livelihood?
   (a) 5 million ☐   (b) 15 million ☐   (c) 25 million ☐   (d) 125 million ☐
3. What percentage of producers in the Fairtrade system are small farmers?
   (a) 10% ☐   (b) 40% ☐   (c) 62% ☐   (d) 82% ☐

■ CALL TO ACTION | *Chapter 4*

4. Most cocoa comes from Côte d'Ivoire. What is the average daily income of a cocoa farmer in Côte d'Ivoire?

   (a) €1.62 ☐   (b) €2.12 ☐   (c) €12.12 ☐   (d) €50.12 ☐

5. The carbon footprint of Fairtrade cotton is five times less than conventional cotton farming because:

   (a) It uses less energy. ☐
   (b) It is grown in areas near large markets. ☐
   (c) Fewer insecticides are used in producing it. ☐
   (d) It can only be used raw and not processed. ☐

6. The first Irish product to receive a Fairtrade mark was:

   (a) Bewley's Coffee ☐   (b) Barry's Tea ☐   (c) Fyffes Bananas ☐   (d) Lyons Tea ☐

7. What country is the largest producer of Fairtrade wines in the world?

   (a) France ☐   (b) South Africa ☐   (c) Chile ☐   (d) Argentina ☐

8. Which Fairtrade product is at risk because of climate change?

   (a) Coffee ☐   (b) Cocoa beans ☐   (c) Bananas ☐   (d) All of them ☐

Exercise 45B **Understanding how Fairtrade improves the lives of small producers**

Key Skills   **Success criteria** ☐   I can name the benefits of Fairtrade to small producers.

Watch the video about Fairtrade bananas and answer the questions that follow.

> **YouTube** — Go to YouTube and search for 'The Story Behind Your Fairtrade Banana' (1:40).

1. Misalia's plantation is 0.7 hectares. Do you think this is a large plantation?
   _____

2. What has Fairtrade allowed Misalia to do for her business?
   _____
   _____

3. How many banana workers have benefited from Fairtrade?
   _____

4. What will Fairtrade allow Misalia to benefit from in her personal life?
   _____
   _____

5. Is Fairtrade a type of charity? Explain your answer.
   _____
   _____

Lesson 45: Fairtrade

Exercise 45C Understanding how Fairtrade benefits families

Key Skills   **Success criteria**   ☐ I can name the benefits of Fairtrade to individuals and families.

Read the case study about Manuel and answer the questions that follow.

Case study: Manuel – cocoa producer

Manuel built his house in 1970, out of wooden planks and zinc roof panels. But when Hurricane George swept through the Dominican Republic in 1998, Manuel's roof panels were scattered round the countryside. If he had more money, he would rebuild his house with concrete walls. But that depends on sales of Fairtrade cocoa. Cocoa is the main ingredient of chocolate.

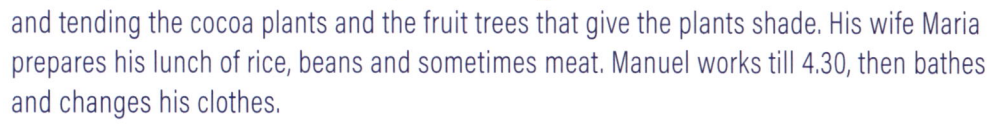

Manuel's day starts at 6 a.m. with a breakfast of bananas and a cup of cocoa. Two hours later, he is clearing weeds and tending the cocoa plants and the fruit trees that give the plants shade. His wife Maria prepares his lunch of rice, beans and sometimes meat. Manuel works till 4.30, then bathes and changes his clothes.

He especially likes sowing the cocoa, because the new plants are his security for the future. Manuel and Maria have six children, three of whom have emigrated. One works with Manuel on the farm.

Manuel's had to work in the fields from a young age and did not go to school. He inherited his land from Maria's family. He now belongs to a group of 42 farmers who are part of the Conacado cooperative. Conacado sells part of its crop to the Fairtrade market. For this, the farmers receive a guaranteed minimum price and the Fairtrade premium, a bonus to be spent on community projects. Amongst the benefits of belonging to the group, Manuel singles out the interest-free loans farms can get to tide them over till harvest time. Conacado also helps hard-up farmers with fertiliser and new young cocoa plants.

Source: Fairtrade Ireland, fairtrade.ie

1. How was Manuel's home damaged by Hurricane George?

2. If Manuel had more money, what improvements would he make to his home?

3. What is cocoa used for?

■ CALL TO ACTION | *Chapter 4*

4. Where does Manuel live? Do you know where it is?

5. Describe a typical day in Manuel's life.

6. Describe Manuel's family.

7. List two things that the farmers in the Conacado cooperative get from being part of the Fairtrade system.

8. Can you suggest one community project the farmers might spend their Fairtrade premium on?

9. Three of Manuel's children have emigrated. Does this remind you of anything in Irish history? Explain.

10. What could you do to help improve Manuel's life?

Exercise 45D — Looking at how Fairtrade benefits communities, sustainability and overcoming poverty

Key Skills   **Success criteria**   ☐   I can name the benefits of Fairtrade to communities, sustainability and overcoming poverty.

Watch the video about cocoa farmers protecting the rainforest and answer the questions that follow.

▶ Go to schools.fairtrade.org.uk and search for 'Guardians of the Rainforest (shorter version)' (3:54).

1. What are the risks to the rainforest?

2. Why is secondary school so expensive?

Lesson 45: Fairtrade

3. What is forest-friendly farming?
   _____
   _____

4. How are the cocoa beans prepared to sell?
   _____
   _____

5. How does the community decide how to spend the Fairtrade premium?
   _____
   _____

6. Having watched how this community practises forest-friendly farming, how do you think this type of farming benefits the environment?
   _____
   _____

Exercise 45E Identifying and promoting Fairtrade

Key Skills   **Success criteria** ☐ I can name Fairtrade products and make others aware of these.

1. Working in groups, make a list of six products bought every day by members of your group. Research whether these products are Fairtrade and, if not, whether a Fairtrade option exists. Write your answers below.

Product	Fairtrade or not?	Fairtrade alternative

2. Then make a list of Fairtrade products for sale in your school/local shop and circulate it in your school community.
   _____
   _____
   _____
   _____
   _____
   _____
   _____

Lesson 46: Causes of poverty

Learning outcome 2.6
Students should be able to express an informed opinion about the root causes of poverty, both locally and globally.

Poverty is when people do not have enough resources or income to provide an acceptable standard of living. This includes things considered as normal for other people in society, such as enough food, clothing, shelter, healthcare and education.

Exercise 46A: Identifying groups most likely to be impacted by poverty in Ireland

Key Skills

Success criteria ☐ I can explain which groups are affected by the different levels of poverty and suggest why.

Poverty in Ireland

There are three ways of measuring poverty in Ireland:

1. People whose disposable income is below 60% of the median (midpoint of all incomes) are **at risk of poverty**. In 2019, the median disposable income in Ireland was €23,979 so the at-risk-of-poverty figure was anyone earning less than €14,387 (60% of €23,979).

2. People are considered **materially deprived** when they are unable to afford two or more basic necessities from the following list:
   - Two pairs of strong shoes
   - A warm waterproof overcoat
   - New clothes when needed
   - A meal with meat, chicken, fish or a vegetarian equivalent every second day
   - A roast joint meal or its equivalent once a week
   - Being able to keep the home adequately warm
   - Presents for family or friends at least once a year
   - Replacing worn-out furniture
   - Having family or friends for a drink or meal once a month
   - A morning, afternoon or evening out in the last fortnight for entertainment.

3. **Consistent poverty** is when people have an income below 60% of the median and experience material deprivation.

Lesson 46: Causes of poverty

In Ireland, the Central Statistics Office (CSO) carries out the Survey on Income and Living Conditions (**SILC**) each year to calculate poverty data. Look at the statistics in the bar chart on poverty in Ireland and answer the questions that follow.

Poverty and deprivation by primary economic status, 2019

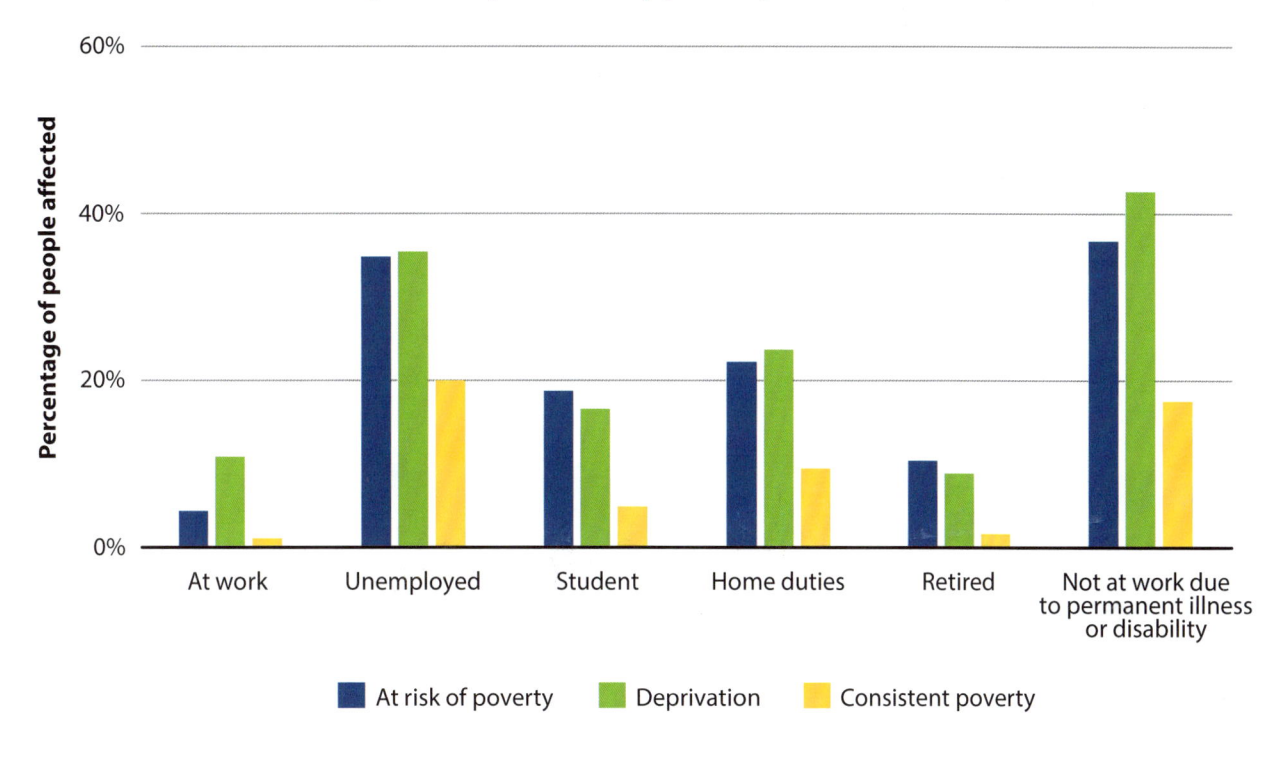

■ At risk of poverty   ■ Deprivation   ■ Consistent poverty

1. Which categories of poverty are the highest for the different groups?
   _____
   _____

2. Which is the lowest for all groups?
   _____

3. Which group is most affected?
   _____

4. Which groups have lower levels of poverty?
   _____

5. Do you know any measures to help people who are experiencing poverty?
   _____
   _____

6. Do you think these measures are working? Why/why not?
   _____
   _____

CALL TO ACTION | Chapter 4

Exercise 46B Understanding the challenge of living in poverty

Key Skills **Success criteria** ☐ I can explain how poverty could limit how I live my life.

The World Bank sets the **international poverty line** at US$1.90 (€1.60) per day for low-income countries (such as Afghanistan, Liberia and Haiti), US$3.20 (€2.70) for lower to middle-income countries (such as India, Egypt and Ukraine) and US$5.50 (€4.64) for upper to middle-income countries (such as Brazil, Mexico and China). Ireland is classed as a high-income country with a rate of US$21.70 (€18.33) per day. Anybody living below these rates is classed as living in extreme poverty. In 2020, just under 10% of the world's population lived on less than US$1.90 per day and more than 40% – 3.3 billion people – lived on less than US$5.50.

Percentage of people in each country living below the international poverty line

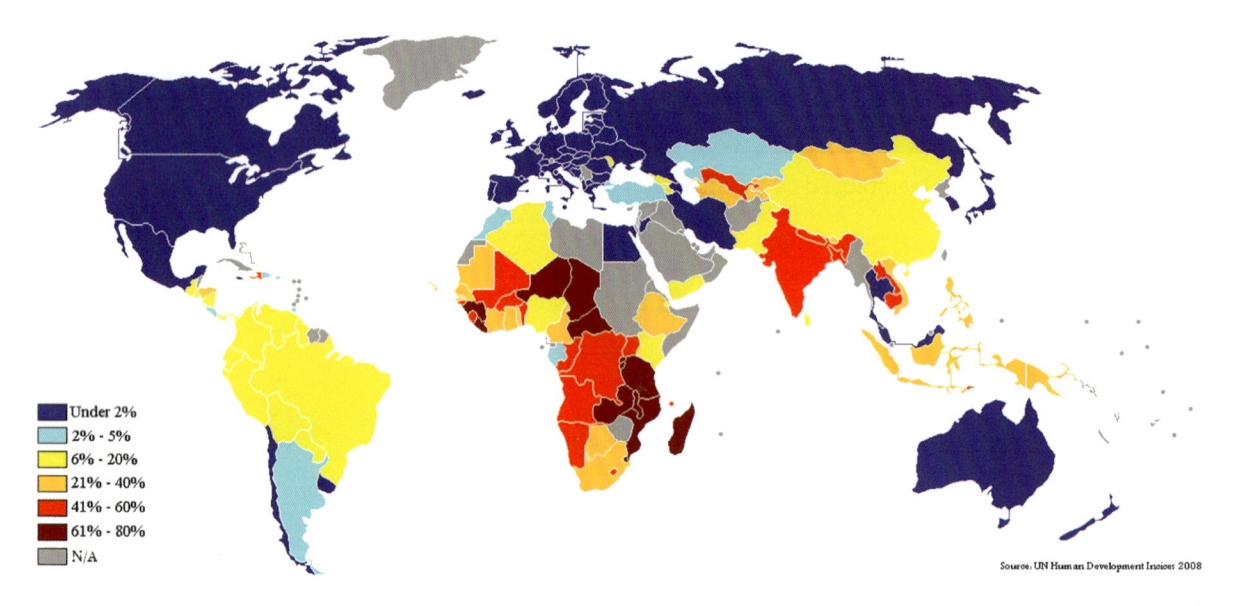

Legend:
- Under 2%
- 2% - 5%
- 6% - 20%
- 21% - 40%
- 41% - 60%
- 61% - 80%
- N/A

Source: UN Human Development Indices 2008

1. Make a list of how you could carry out your weekly activities on €18.33 per day, which comes to €128.31 per week, if you had to pay for all the costs yourself. Remember to include the cost of accommodation, food, transport, electricity and fuel and purchases such as medicine if needed, plus pens, pencils, etc.

Monday	Tuesday	Wednesday	Thursday

Friday	Saturday	Sunday	Total

Lesson 46: Causes of poverty

2. How much would you have left for leisure activities?

3. What spending do you have to limit to meet the target?

4. Could you live on this amount per week? Why/why not?

5. What would happen if there were an emergency, for example, the boiler breaking or somebody in the household getting sick?

Exercise 46C — Identifying situations of poverty and their causes

Key Skills

Success criteria ☐ I can classify different types of poverty and name their causes.

Working in pairs, identify whether the following people are living in poverty and if so which category. Then identify the cause of their poverty.

Situation	Is this person living in poverty?					Cause of poverty
	No	Yes			
		What category of poverty?		
		At risk	Deprivation	Consistent	
1. Laura's father works in the UK. He makes good money, but most of it goes to paying back a debt from when her parents' small business collapsed. Her mother can only work mornings, because she looks after the children. She never has any time off because there is nobody to mind them.					
2. Leanne has two children, Alice is six and Tom is five. Tom has special needs and Leanne needs to stay at home to take care of him. She tried working part-time last year, but it cost more to pay someone to care for Tom than she was earning.					

CALL TO ACTION | Chapter 4

3. Denis is 61. He worked in a hardware shop until it closed last year. He got a job in a supermarket, but the pay is poor, and he has no fixed hours. His children are in college in Dublin. Every cent he earns is gone at the end of the week.					
4. Paul and Sharon live in a rented flat with their two small children. There is mould growing on their bedroom wall, but they are afraid that if they complain to the landlord he will ask them to move or raise their rent. They could not afford to pay a higher rent.					
5. All Callum's friends are going skiing with the school this year, but he is not going. Neither his mam or dad is working. His mam says that they cannot afford the cost of the tour and the equipment he would need to go.					
6. Noreen is retired and lives alone. She has savings but is worried about spending them. She does not light a fire in winter. Instead she puts on warmer clothes and goes to bed early. Her son is always arguing with her saying that she should give herself some comfort and she cannot take her money with her, but Noreen will not listen.					
7. Andrea bought a new house five years ago. Since then she has had chronic back pain, which means she needs physiotherapy every week. Most of her income goes on the mortgage and bills, leaving her little for food or clothes.					
8. Michaela's friends always have new clothes and new phones. Her parents give her €20 per week and tell her that she must get everything she needs with that. They say they are teaching her to manage her money.					

Exercise 46D **Appreciating the impact of poverty**

Key Skills **Success criteria** ☐ I can name the consequences of poverty on families and explain the difficulty escaping it.

Read 'Faye's Story' and answer the questions below.

Faye's Story

John and I had a small company selling gym equipment. We did okay at first, but that changed and we were left with more costs than profits every month. The bank refused to give us a further loan unless we gave a personal guarantee that we would cover the cost of the loan even if we went out of business. We didn't realise the danger we were getting into. We kept going for a few months before we went out of business. The bank called us in and arranged for us to begin paying back the loan. We had to get jobs. Then I had our son, Simon, and I couldn't work, because the cost of childcare would have been huge.

John decided to go to the UAE. We thought if he worked there for a year it would give us a start on paying back the loan but it hasn't been enough. My car broke down and I cannot afford to fix it. John's parents gave me his dad's car and they share his mam's car now.

It's a never-ending nightmare. We're looking for jobs all the time for John, but there is nothing that pays even close to what he gets in the UAE. It's awful to see so much of the money John is earning going to the bank. I feel so lonely, I can't afford to go out, the only family we have are John's parents and they're getting on. Minding Simon is too much for them. I wish at times we could walk away from it all, go to Australia or Canada, start a new life, but this is going to follow us forever. We'll never get a loan to buy a house or a car if this isn't cleared. I've said to John to just come back, sign on and hope he picks something up, but he says we must be able to give Simon a start in life. He's right, but God it's hard.

1. What has caused this family's problems?

2. How have they tried to resolve this situation?

3. Why does Faye say it is a never-ending nightmare?

4. What are the consequences of this on her family?

5. Why are there no obvious solutions?

Lesson 47: Global poverty

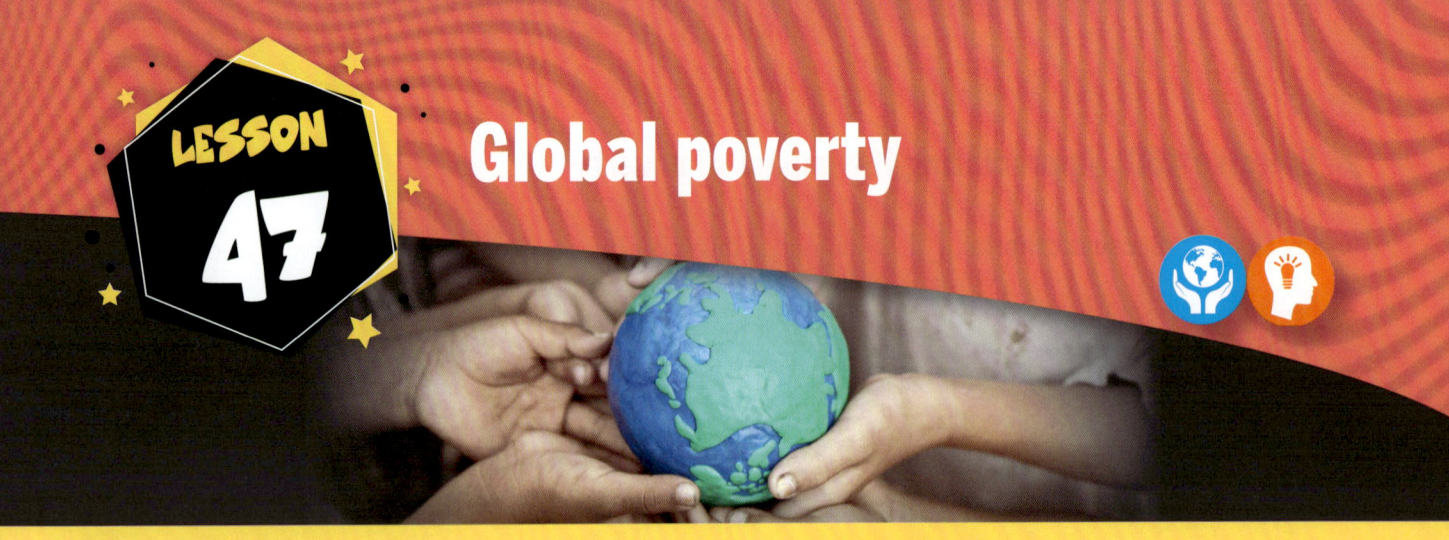

Learning outcome 2.6
Students should be able to express an informed opinion about the root causes of poverty, both locally and globally.

Exercise 47A Understanding MPI

Key Skills

Success criteria ☐ I can name countries where the MPI is low and explain what that means.

The global **Multidimensional Poverty Index** (MPI) measures how poor people are deprived in health, education and living standards. The MPI is mostly applied to Global South countries. A person who is deprived in one-third or more of the indicators is classed as poor.

- Health accounts for one-third of the index and includes:
  - nutrition – if a person in the household is undernourished
  - child mortality – if a child in the household under 18 has died in the previous five years.
- Education accounts for another third and includes:
  - years of schooling – no member of the household has completed five years of school
  - school attendance – a school-age child is not attending years 1–8 in school.
- Standard of living accounts for the final third and includes:
  - cooking fuel – the household cooks food with wood, charcoal or dung
  - sanitation – the toilet is shared with another household
  - drinking water – the household does not have access to clean drinking water within a 30-minute round trip from the home
  - electricity – the household has no electricity
  - housing – the floor, roof or walls is of inadequate materials, for example, a dirt floor
  - assets – the household does not own more than one of the following: radio, television, telephone, computer, animal cart, bicycle, motorbike, fridge, car or truck.

Lesson 47: Global poverty

Look at the map showing MPI rates in the world and answer the following questions.

Share of population living in multidimensional poverty, 2014

Proportion of people who are poor according to the Multidimensional Poverty Index (MPI). The MPI weights ten indicators of deprivation in the context of education, health and living standards. Individuals are considered poor if deprived in at least one third of the weighted indicators (see source for more details).

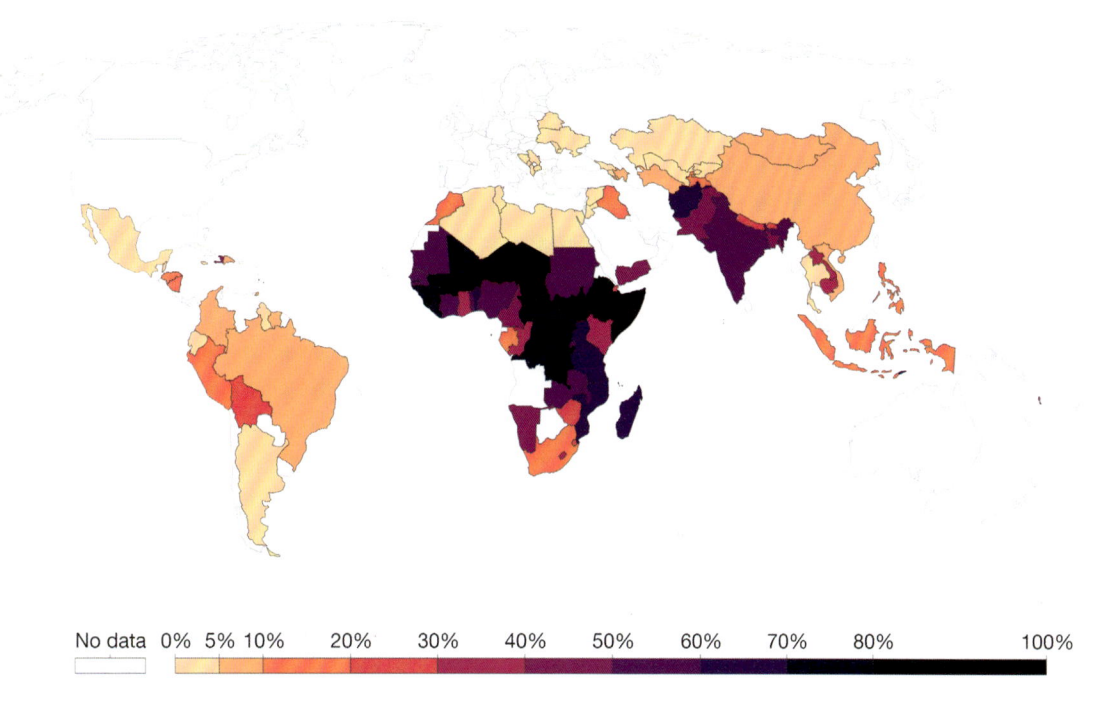

Source: OPHI Multidimensional Poverty Index - Alkire and Robles (2016)   OurWorldInData.org/extreme-poverty/ • CC BY

1. Name a country where more than 80% of the population live in multidimensional poverty.

2. Which continent is most affected by multidimensional poverty?

3. In which Asian countries are more than half the population living in multidimensional poverty?

4. Research one of the countries with high rates of poverty. Can you find reasons for the high levels of poverty?

215

● CALL TO ACTION | *Chapter 4*

Exercise 47B Identifying global poverty and its effects

Key Skills **Success criteria** ☐ I can give examples showing how extreme poverty is concentrated in certain places and some effects of it.

Working in pairs, discuss the statements and tick whether you think they are true or false.

	True	False
1. India has the greatest number of people living in extreme poverty.		
2. Nearly 356 million children in the world live in extreme poverty.		
3. Half a billion children live in multidimensional poverty.		
4. A person earning €29,000 is among the world's richest people.		
5. 30% of the population of Sub-Saharan Africa (south of the Sahara) lives in extreme poverty.		
6. Children are more than twice as likely as adults to be living in extreme poverty.		
7. Almost three-fifths of the world's extreme poor live in just five countries.		
8. Approximately 297,000 children under five die every year from diarrhoeal diseases due to poor sanitation, poor hygiene or unsafe drinking water.		
9. Malnutrition is the second most common cause of poor health and death around the world.		
10. Only 40% of adults in Niger can read and write, because they had little or no education as they had to work to provide extra income for the family.		

Exercise 47C Identifying symptoms of poverty

Key Skills **Success criteria** ☐ I can name symptoms of poverty.

Working in pairs, discuss the following and tick the ones that are symptoms of poverty.

1. Children begging on the street	
2. Adults hanging around the streets in groups talking for long periods in the day	
3. A Christmas party in a nice restaurant	
4. Toilets shared by a number of households	
5. Unsafe neighbourhoods	
6. People with sores and unhealthy-looking skin	
7. Nail bars	
8. People sleeping in railway stations	
9. No clean drinking water	
10. Children not going to school from the age of 14	

Lesson 47: Global poverty

Exercise 47D — Identifying causes of poverty in developing countries

Key Skills   **Success criteria**   ☐ I can name the causes of poverty in developing countries.

1. Working in pairs, look at the following stories and identify the cause of poverty in each case.

	Cause
(a) Abida is a mother of five children. She is struggling to provide for her family after her husband was killed and the family were forced to leave their home in Yemen.	
(b) Maya is 13 and works washing dishes in a restaurant in Kathmandu in Nepal. She cannot go to school because her family needs the money she earns.	
(c) Mariam lives in Bamako in Mali. Like many of her friends, she spent only a short time in primary school, but her brothers went for longer.	
(d) Emmanuel is a maize farmer in Malawi. In the past few years, he has lost his crop twice due to drought and flooding caused by global warming.	
(e) Diego lives in a rural village in Guatemala with no tap water. He and the other villagers get water from a pipe, but the family get diarrhoeal illnesses.	
(f) La Win was a farmer in Myanmar until the army seized his land. He now works as an agricultural labourer for only €2.70 per day.	
(g) Mercy lives in Kenya and must walk 8 km twice a day to collect water for her family. She carries the water on her head, while carrying her baby on her back and minding her two other young children.	
(h) Emilio and his family live in Honduras. His brother lives in the US and sends him some money when he can. Criminal gangs know Emilio receives this money, and force him to pay them a fee, leaving him with very little money.	
(i) Joao is a farmer in Mozambique. He is struggling to survive because drought and flooding destroyed his crop last year and he had no savings to buy seeds to replant.	
(j) Fatouma is 14 and lives in Niger. Her family have decided that she must get married because they will be paid a dowry (money from the groom to the bride's family).	

■ CALL TO ACTION | *Chapter 4*

2. Which of these causes could be prevented?
   _____
   _____

3. Who could help to prevent them?
   _____
   _____

4. Why do you think they are not being prevented?
   _____
   _____

Exercise 47E — Understanding how poverty affects indigenous people

Key Skills

Success criteria ☐ I can name the causes and effects of poverty on indigenous people.

Watch the video about palm oil production. Then, working in pairs, discuss the following questions and write your answers below.

> **YouTube**: Go to YouTube and search for 'Living in Fear: Guatemala Trócaire Lent 2019' (2:31).

1. Why are the indigenous people being driven off their lands?
   _____
   _____

2. How are they driven away?
   _____
   _____

3. Why are they not protected?
   _____
   _____

4. What improvement has occurred?
   _____
   _____

5. Do you think this improvement will last? Why/why not?
   _____
   _____

6. What causes of poverty are obvious here?
   _____
   _____

Lesson 48

Case study: Kiribati

Learning outcome 2.6
Students should be able to express an informed opinion about the root causes of poverty, both locally and globally.

Exercise 48A Identifying causes, indicators and impacts of poverty in Kiribati

Key Skills

Success criteria ☐ I can name the causes, indicators and effects of poverty by researching charts and literature.

Kiribati (pronounced *Ki-ree-bas*) is a remote republic made up of a group of islands in the Pacific Ocean. It has a population of nearly 120,000 people. Kiribati's main exports are copra, from which coconut oil is extracted, sea cucumber, tuna and shark meat.

Kiribati's islands are on average only 2 m above sea level. As a result, they are threatened by problems linked to climate change, such as coastal erosion, flooding and damage to freshwater. In 2012, Kiribati purchased land in Fiji in case its population had to be resettled because of climate change. The government plans to use this land to provide nutritious food for Kiribati, as currently almost all vegetables are imported. Rising sea levels have contaminated some wells with seawater. Even during the rainy season, there have been droughts which have meant less rainwater is collected. The capital, South Tarawa, has only enough groundwater to provide for 50% of the population.

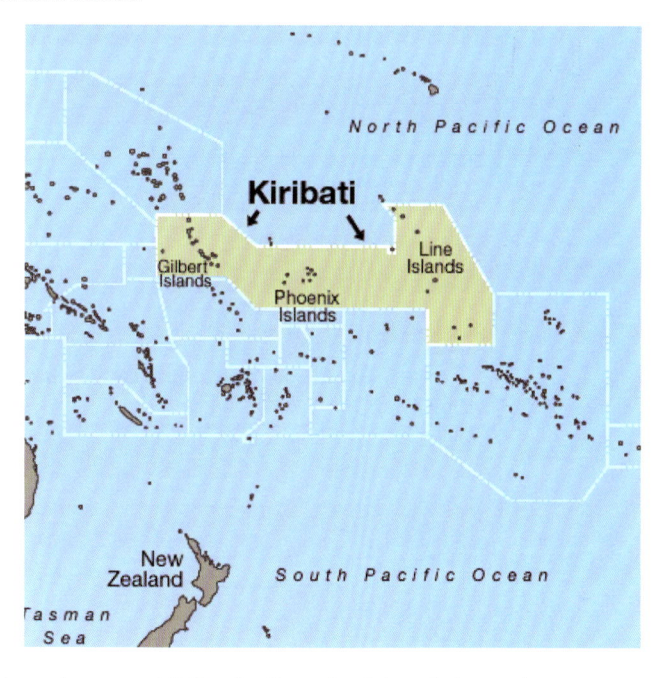

Australian and New Zealand companies mined phosphate on Kiribati's Banaba Island throughout the twentieth century. This contaminated the island's natural caves, which stored rainwater. The 300 people living on Banaba Island now rely on a desalination (removing salt from seawater) plant for water. When the desalination plant broke down, the crops died and people were forced to drink contaminated water while waiting for water to come from South Tarawa. The islanders are now asking Australia and New Zealand to pay for the restoration of the caves as a means of collecting water.

CALL TO ACTION | *Chapter 4*

Facts about Kiribati

- Child mortality is 33.66 deaths per 1,000 live births.
- Life expectancy is 67.59 years.
- 28.4% of the population use unimproved water.
- Kiribati has 0.2 doctors per 1,000 people. Ireland has 2.7 per 1,000.
- Unemployment is at 31%.
- There is no recycling of water.
- There is 100% access to electricity.
- Copra farmers earn low incomes.
- 46% of the population are classed as obese.
- In South Tarawa the only dumps are located by the sea and waste is often dumped in the ocean.
- Many people use the ocean or the lagoon as a toilet.
- Internet access is among the lowest in the world.

The charts below compare Kiribati with Ireland and a range of other countries, including Fiji and Tonga, two of Kiribati's neighbours in Oceania.

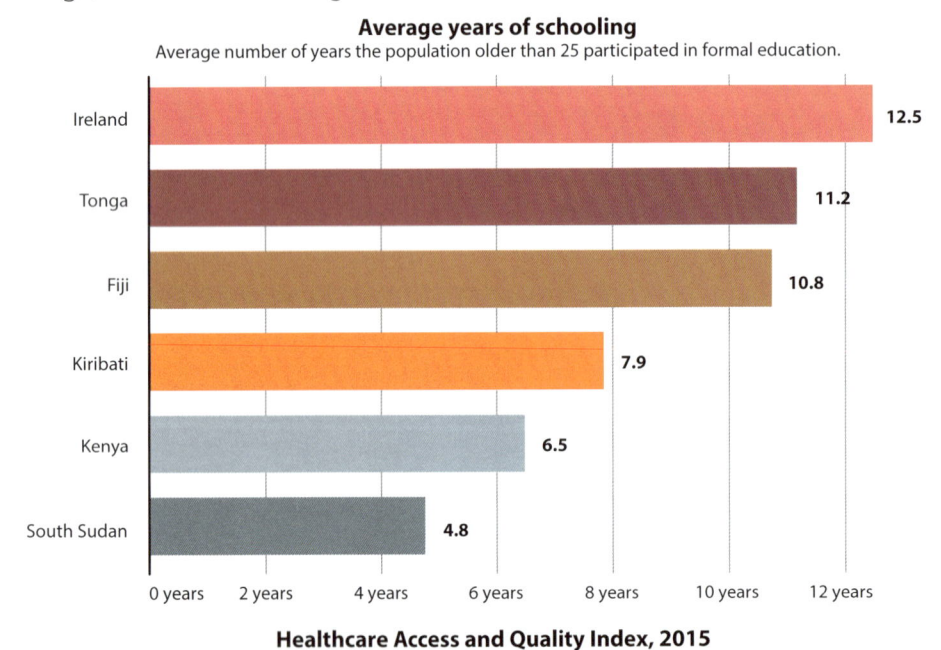

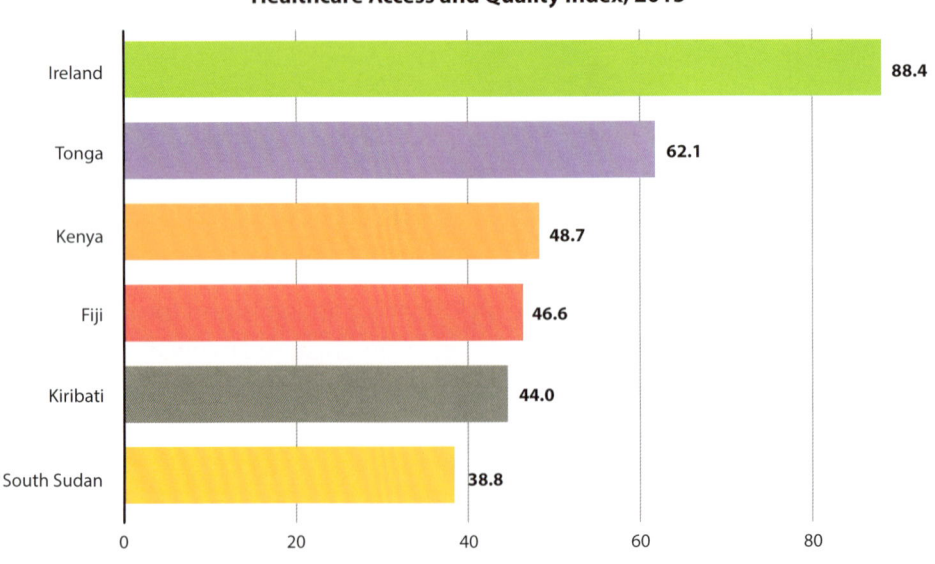

Average years of schooling
Average number of years the population older than 25 participated in formal education.

Country	Years
Ireland	12.5
Tonga	11.2
Fiji	10.8
Kiribati	7.9
Kenya	6.5
South Sudan	4.8

Healthcare Access and Quality Index, 2015

Country	Index
Ireland	88.4
Tonga	62.1
Kenya	48.7
Fiji	46.6
Kiribati	44.0
South Sudan	38.8

Lesson 48: Kiribati

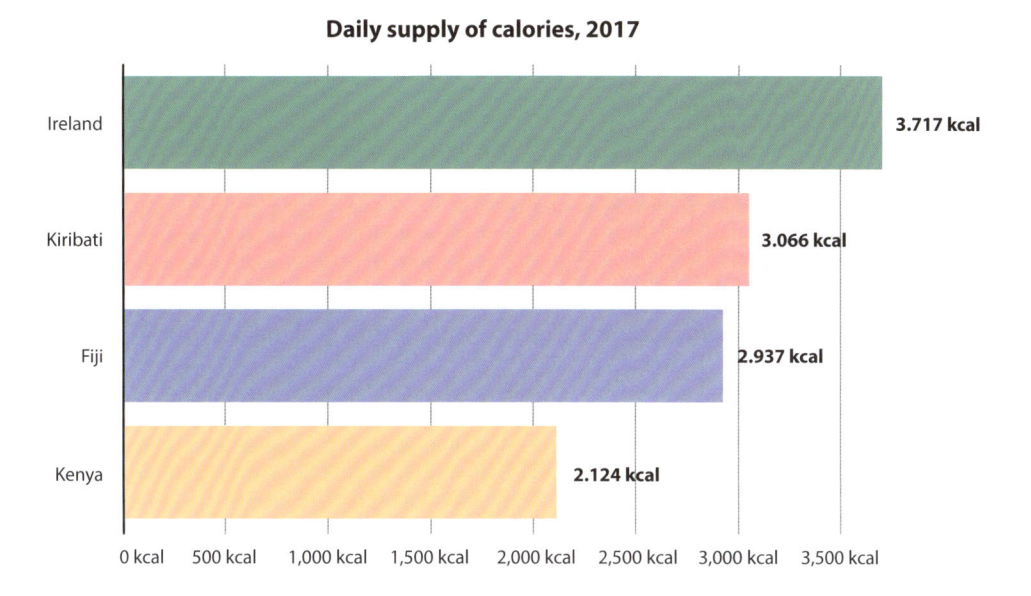

Daily supply of calories, 2017

Ireland	3,717 kcal
Kiribati	3,066 kcal
Fiji	2,937 kcal
Kenya	2,124 kcal

Working in groups, look at the information on Kiribati. Then try to identify the problems the country faces. Begin by writing the issue (poverty and inequality) in the centre of the tree. Then look for the causes of poverty and inequality, putting these at the roots, and the effects, putting these at the top of the tree.

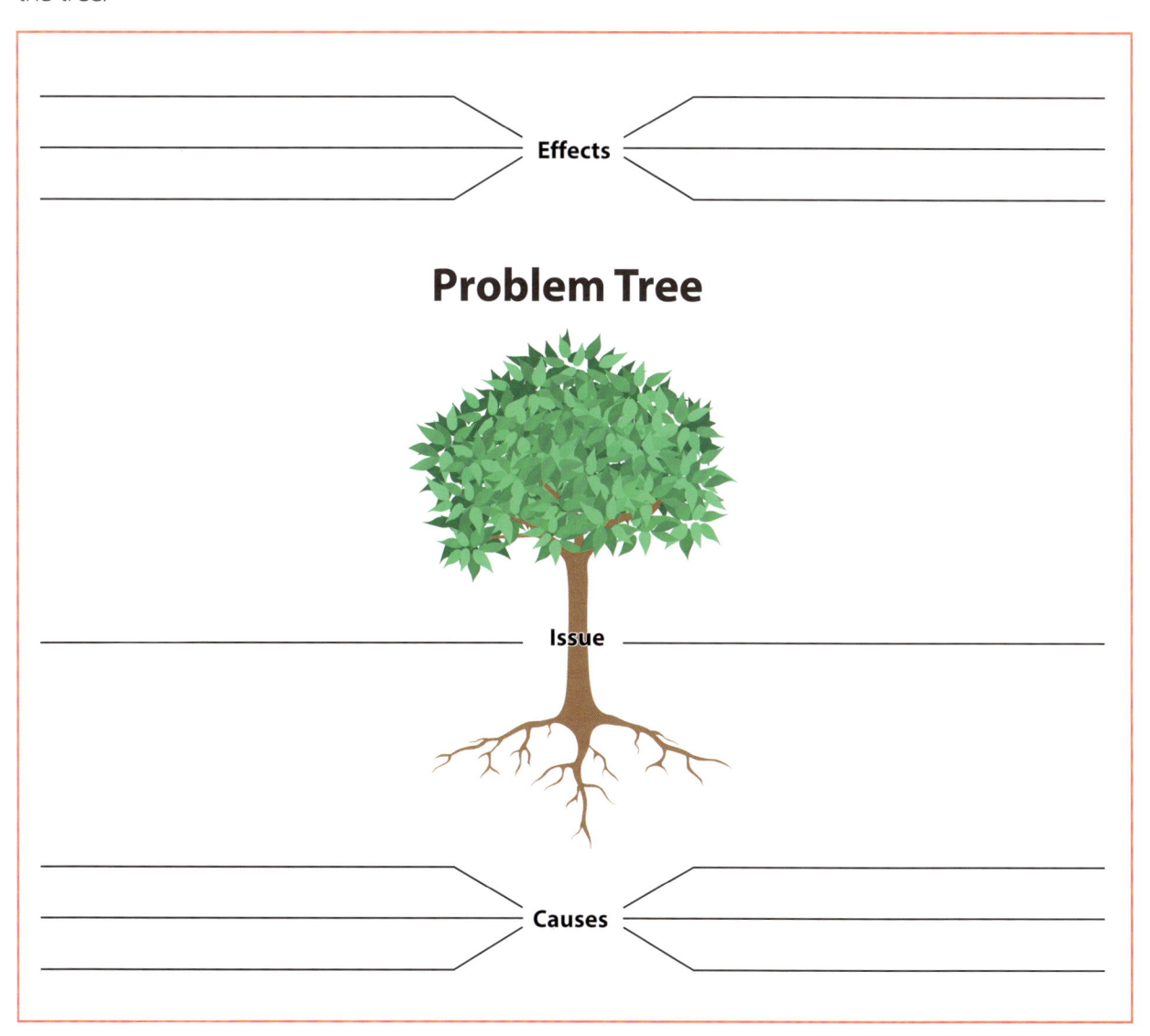

Problem Tree

Effects _____ _____

Issue _____

Causes _____ _____

● CALL TO ACTION | *Chapter 4*

✏️ **Exercise 48B** **Identifying solutions to poverty in Kiribati and their impacts**

Key Skills **Success criteria** ☐ I can name the solutions to poverty and their impacts.

Working in groups, look at the problems you identified in Kiribati. Then try to identify solutions to the problems. Put these at the roots of the tree. Then look for the impacts of these solutions, putting these at the top of the tree.

Impacts

Solution Tree

Issue

Solution

✏️ **Exercise 48C** **Researching further about problems and solutions to poverty in Kiribati**

Key Skills **Success criteria** ☐ I can research more about causes of and solutions to poverty in Kiribati.

Looking at the problems and solutions you have identified, research Kiribati to find out more about the problems and what solutions have already been suggested. Then add this new information to the problems and solutions you have already suggested and complete the grid on the next page.

222

Lesson 48: Kiribati

Problems		Solutions	
Causes	Effects	Solutions	Impacts

Problems		Solutions	
Causes	Effects	Solutions	Impacts

LESSON 49

Local development

Learning outcome 2.7
Students should be able to discuss, with evidence, positive and negative effects of development in their local area.

Exercise 49A Identifying the positives and negatives of development

Key Skills **Success criteria** ☐ I can list positives and negatives of developments.

When a new development in the community is positive, there are more activities for residents, better jobs are available, and more people come into the area with skills. Positive development can bring new life to an area that had been disadvantaged or underdeveloped. On the other hand, development that is not sustainable can ignore the residents, destroy the landscape and cause environmental damage. Some developments can have both positive and negative outcomes.

Look at the following examples of development and identify the positive and negative effects of each.

	Positives	Negatives
1. A new greenway for walkers and cyclists is being built alongside the road. As a result, the road is being narrowed and the speed limit reduced.		
2. In an effort to move away from relying on fossil fuels, a new wind park is being built off the coast of a popular tourist area.		
3. A new sewage treatment plant is being built on the site of an old factory near a town.		
4. An exclusive new golf club is being built on a scenic site where locals go walking.		

5. A new 20-storey building is being built in the city centre where the highest building is currently five storeys tall.		
6. An old hospital that was once a famine workhouse is being demolished to make way for a new hospital building.		
7. A shopping centre on the outskirts of the town is to be doubled in size.		
8. A motorway is to be constructed through a natural oak forest. Some of the trees being cleared are over 200 years old.		

Exercise 49B Designing a sustainable development

Key Skills

Success criteria ☐ I can produce a report that is sustainable, profitable and supported.

Read the information about a development proposal.

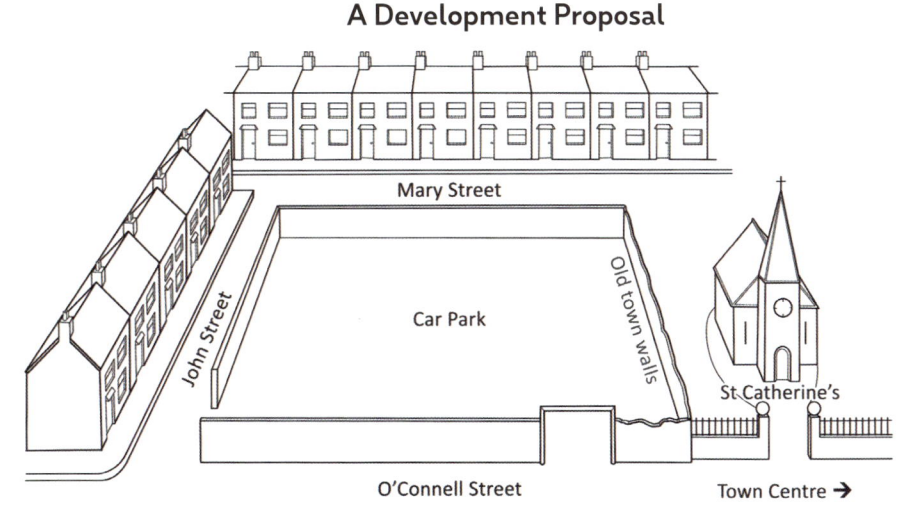

A Development Proposal

(Diagram showing: Mary Street with houses along it, John Street, O'Connell Street, a Car Park in the middle, Old town walls, St Catherine's church, and Town Centre →)

The site is one acre in size and is in the heart of the town. At the moment, it is used as a car park. The houses of local people run along two sides. Many older people live here, but some houses have recently been bought by people working in the centre of the town and completely renovated. A third side faces onto a busy road, taking traffic into the town square. The final side is taken up by what may be a part of the old town walls and part of the old Church of Ireland church, St Catherine's.

Enhanced Developments, a large development company, bought the site for €1 million and applied to the county council to build a five-storey building on the site and to widen the streets. The proposed building included a supermarket, an off licence, offices and apartments. However, several objections were raised concerning the development of the site and planning permission was refused.

■ CALL TO ACTION | *Chapter 4*

The following views were expressed:
1. The older residents do not want the site developed or the road widened.
2. Some residents think the supermarket will bring new facilities and increase the values of their homes.
3. People with children say the site should be used for leisure activities instead.
4. Historians and archaeologists do not want the old town walls damaged.
5. A group of architects believe that the proposed building is too high and would be an eyesore.
6. Politicians must listen to the views of the people and decide what they believe is in the best interests of the town.

The developers want to make money from the site. They have failed to get planning permission for their original plans. Your class is a company that specialises in sustainable development. Enhanced Developments have hired you to design a new plan for developing the site that will be sustainable, profitable and likely to encourage people to accept the proposal. Working in groups, you will each be allocated one of the following tasks:

- Architecture – your job is to design a building that appeals to people living in the area. You must ensure that it contains enough units to make it profitable.
- Costing – your job is to design a building that makes money. You must calculate how much it would cost to build and how much you could sell units for.
- Public relations (PR) – your job is to promote the development and say what is positive about it and how it will be better than what is currently there.
- Historians – you must look at how the concerns of historians and archaeologists can be satisfied.
- Sustainable development (SD) – you must look at how this project can be sustainable.
- Community liaison (CL) – you must look at how you can encourage the local community to support this project.

In your group, discuss how you could amend this design to make it sustainable, profitable and something that will be supported by the people.

My team task	
Members	
How will we develop this site?	

LESSON 50: A development proposal

Learning outcome 2.7
Students should be able to discuss, with evidence, positive and negative effects of development in their local area.

Exercise 50A — Communicating with others to design a sustainable development

Key Skills

Success criteria ☐ I can coordinate a proposal between the different sectors.

In your group for Exercise 49B, you came up with a solution for one area of a proposal. You will now work in a new group which will be composed of one member from each of the original groups. Note the suggestions your new group members came up with for Exercise 49B. Discuss any areas of difference. Write your findings in the box.

Architecture	Costing	PR

Historians	SD	CL

CALL TO ACTION | *Chapter 4*

Exercise 50B Writing a report

Key Skills **Success criteria** ☐ I can synthesise the different elements of the development.

Having reviewed the work you did together, write out the proposal that the group from Exercise 50A will make to Enhanced Developments.

INSERT COMPANY NAME AND LOGO HERE

Summary of objections:
_____
_____
_____

Suggested changes to original plan and why these changes are needed:
_____
_____
_____

New proposals on how to develop the site:
_____
_____
_____

How will this affect the expected profit:
_____
_____
_____

Why we think these suggestions will be practical:
_____
_____
_____

Exercise 50C Presenting the proposal

Key Skills **Success criteria** ☐ I can reflect on my learning.

You will now each make a presentation on the different designs and discuss each on completion. Then answer the following questions.

1. What points were common across all presentations?
   _____
   _____

2. What new points emerged?
   _____
   _____

3. What have I learned from this task?
   _____
   _____

Lesson 51: Simulated debate on a development proposal

Learning outcome 2.7
Students should be able to discuss, with evidence, positive and negative effects of development in their local area.

Exercise 51A Identifying different viewpoints in a development

Key Skills

Success criteria ☐ I can list the viewpoints I have and why.

In Lesson 50, you worked in a group to design a development proposal. In this lesson, you are going to participate in a simulated debate. The whole class will debate the proposal, but everyone is in role. The simulated debate will be presented as a TV programme.

Your teacher will allocate roles to you in advance of the debate. These could include being for or against the development, an audience member, the TV presenter or a journalist. Once you have your role, consider the arguments your character would make in favour or against the development. Write them here.

CALL TO ACTION | *Chapter 4*

Exercise 51B — Participating in a simulated debate

Key Skills

Success criteria ☐ I can participate by making arguments for or against a development and explain why I hold those views.

In the simulated debate TV programme, one member of each group (for and against) will speak about their perspective for one minute and then the TV presenter will open the debate to the floor. There will be some journalists and politicians present in the debate too. Audience members cannot speak until they have the microphone – given by your teacher.

Exercise 51C — Writing a report about the debate

Key Skills

Success criteria ☐ I can write about the debate, mentioning the areas that were the most informative.

After the debate consider what you have learned from the process. Write your character's diary entry on how the debate went, referring to how others responded to you and how you felt. If you were a journalist, write an account of the debate for your newspaper/website.

Reflection: Reflecting on my learning about local and global development

Learning outcome 2.12
Students should be able to reflect on their ongoing learning and what it means for them.

Key Skills

Success criteria ☐ I can give examples of how my thinking about local and global development has developed.

Look back at the skills and knowledge you have developed in this chapter. It is important to identify what you have learned and where you could learn more. Use the following worksheet to guide your reflection on local and global development. Then working in groups, discuss your responses to each of these questions.

1. Before looking at local and global development, I thought …	
2. Things I learned about local and global development	
3. Where I got my information from	
4. How I know the information was reliable	
5. The different types of sources I got my information from	
6. The most interesting thing I learned was …	
7. How the new information I have learned will change what I do	

Action: Organising a visit to a successful sustainable development

A helpful way of learning more about a topic is by organising a visit to a site where you can learn more about the topic and see it in action.

✓ Action 1 — Identifying the tasks I need to do to complete the action

Key Skills

Success criteria ☐ I will identify the specific tasks my committee must do.

Begin your action by allocating different roles to everybody. Each person works in a group and each group has specific responsibilities for carrying out the action. Once your teacher has formed the groups, its members meet and decide their roles. These roles are shared with the class and noted here.

Group	Members	Responsibilities
1. Organisation		
2. Contact		
3. Transport		
4. Publicity		

Action: Organising a visit to a successful sustainable development

✓ Action 2 — Identifying a suitable sustainability project

Key Skills **Success criteria** ☐ I will identify a suitable sustainability project.

Research a sustainability project, such as Cloughjordan Ecovillage, and see what it does. Check whether it accepts visits from schools.

1. Which project would help us to learn more?

   _____

2. How could it help us?

   _____
   _____
   _____

✓ Action 3 — Identifying the actions my group contributed

Key Skills **Success criteria** ☐ I will identify the specific actions my group did.

Then work in your groups to conduct your actions and note them here.

What actions did we do in my group?

_____
_____
_____
_____
_____
_____
_____
_____
_____
_____
_____
_____
_____

■ CALL TO ACTION | *Chapter 4*

✓ **Action 4** **Noting my questions and the responses to them**

Key Skills **Success criteria** ☐ I can identify areas I want further information on and how to ask questions to get these answers. I will be able to show my understanding by noting the answers I have received.

Write out the questions that you would like to ask when visiting the project. Note the answers to your questions after visiting the project.

1. My questions	
2. Answers	

✓ **Action 5** **Summarising my learning**

Key Skills **Success criteria** ☐ I can write an account of the information I learned from the visit.

Thinking back over the visit, note the points that you learned below.

_____
_____
_____
_____
_____
_____
_____
_____

Chapter 5 Effecting Global Change

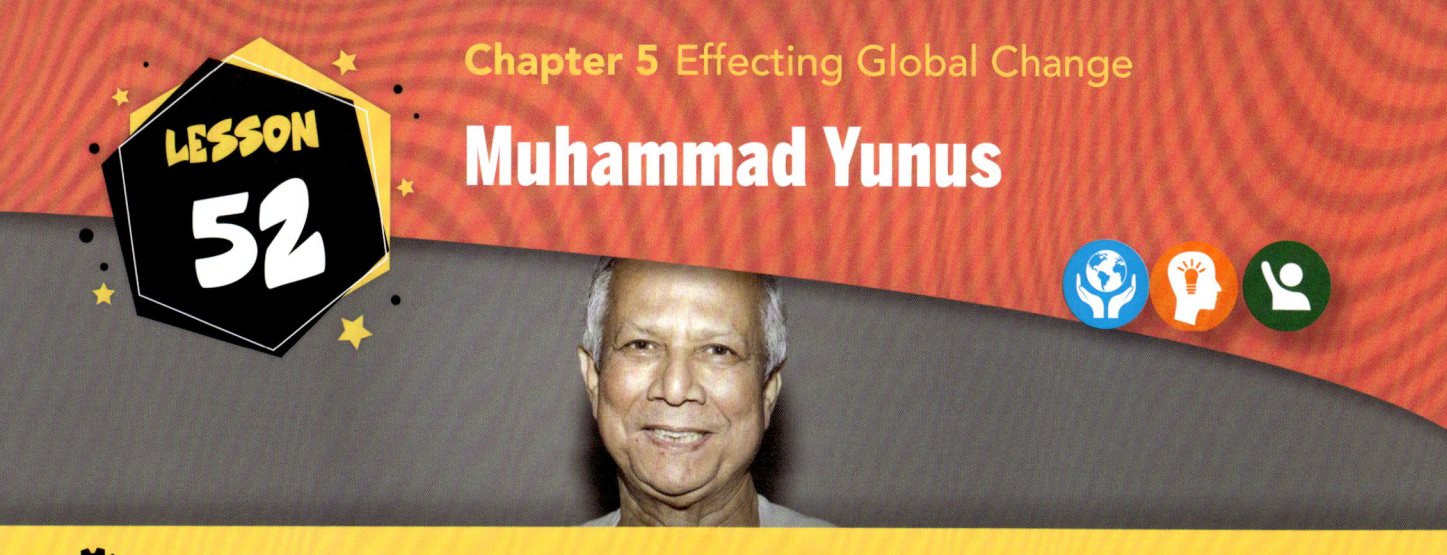

Lesson 52: Muhammad Yunus

Learning outcome 2.8
Students should be able to identify one person and one institution with power and influence in the world today, explaining the role of each.

Exercise 52A — Understanding how to make a profit

Key Skills

Success criteria ☐ I can identify business potential.

Power means having control or influence over others. There are several types of power:

- **Economic power** involves money and wealth. For example, people in charge of companies control a lot of wealth, which gives them power.
- **The power of celebrity:** celebrities or sports stars are well known, so their opinions can influence others.
- **Political power** allows a person or an organisation to make laws, raise taxes or give grants and money.
- **Military power** gives a person or organisation the power to use soldiers and weapons.

Powerful people can use their power for good or for bad.

Work in pairs to complete the following exercise:

The school canteen sells cheese sandwiches for €2.50 and they always sell out quickly. You are considering setting up a rival cheese-sandwich business. You are aiming to sell 100 sandwiches per week.

The school canteen has the following costs:

- A 20-slice loaf of sliced bread costs €1.50
- A tub with enough butter for 100 sandwiches costs €3.50
- A 10-slice packet of cheese costs €3.00.

Your financial situation is as follows:

- You need to replace your shoes. A new pair of shoes costs €15.
- You also want to visit the doctor about back pain. A doctor's consultation costs €40.

1. Do you think you could create a business selling sandwiches?

2. How could you compete with the school canteen?

■ CALL TO ACTION | *Chapter 5*

3. Could you make a profit?

4. How much would you need to pay to buy the materials to make 100 sandwiches?

5. How long would it take you to have enough money to buy the shoes you need?

6. How long would it take you to have enough money to visit the doctor?

Exercise 52B **Understanding the difficulty in making money when you are poor**

Key Skills   **Success criteria**   ☐ I can calculate how moneylenders keep people poor.

Many people have skills such as sewing, woodworking or baking which they could develop into a business, but they lack the money to get started. They cannot borrow money from their families because they are also poor and banks will not lend them money. Many poor people work in poorly paid jobs and if they need extra money they have to borrow from lenders who charge huge interest rates.

Continue looking at the sandwich proposal and consider the following:

> You decide to set up a business preparing and selling sandwiches, but you have no money to buy the bread, cheese and butter. The bank will not lend you money because the manager said you will not pay it back. The manager said that if you could make money you would not be poor. Your only option is to borrow the money from a moneylender. He offers you all the money you need to make 100 sandwiches but you must pay back the full amount plus 100% interest every month.

1. How much money would you have to pay back at the end of one month?

2. How much profit would you make now?

3. Have you any other options for borrowing the money? What are they?

4. How long would it take you to have enough money to buy the shoes?

5. How long would it take you to have enough money to visit the doctor?

6. What does this example show about being poor?

Lesson 52: Muhammad Yunus

Exercise 52C Understanding the reason for microcredit

Key Skills

Success criteria ☐ I can identify advantages and disadvantages of microcredit.

In 1976, Muhammad Yunus, an economics professor in Bangladesh, loaned $27 to 42 village craftswomen. The women paid back the loan, with each of them making a profit. This showed that it was possible for poor people to both make profits and repay loans. Yunus established the Grameen Bank in 1983 to provide **microcredit**, or small loans, to people who were too poor to get a loan from banks. Microcredit charges a low interest rate that allows the bank to make a profit but is at a level that the borrower can afford. The bank was such a success that it spread to many other countries. Yunus and the Grameen Bank were awarded the 2006 Nobel Peace Prize

The following extract from his book *Banker to the Poor* describes Yunus and his students' meeting with Sufia, a young mother living in poverty. Working in pairs, read the extract and answer the questions on the next page.

'How old are you?'

'21.'

I did not use a pen and notepad for that would have scared her off, I let my students do that on return visits.

'Do you own this bamboo?' I asked her.

'Yes.'

'How do you get it?'

'I buy it.'

'How much does the bamboo cost you?'

'Five taka.' That was 22 US cents.

'Do you have five taka?'

'No, I borrowed from the paikars.'

'The middleman? What is your arrangement with them?'

'I must sell my bamboo stools back to them at the end of the day, to repay my loan. That way what is leftover to me is my profit.'

'How much do you sell for?'

'Five taka and 50 paisa.'

'So you make 50 paisa profit?'

She nodded. That came to a profit of just 2 US cents.

'And could you borrow the cash and buy your own raw material?'

'Yes, but the money-lender would demand a lot. And people who start with them only get poorer.'

CALL TO ACTION | Chapter 5

'How much do the money-lenders charge?'

'It depends. Sometimes they charge 10 per cent per week. I even have a neighbour who is paying 10 per cent per day!'

'And is that all you earn from making these beautiful bamboo tools, 50 paisa?'

'Yes.'

Right now, her labour was almost free. It was a form of bonded labour, or slavery. The trader always made certain that he paid Sufia a price that only covered the cost of the materials and just enough so that she would not die but would need to keep on borrowing from him.

1. Why do you think that Sufia would have been scared by Muhammad Yunus taking notes?

2. Why did Sufia borrow from the middlemen rather than from the moneylenders?

3. Why does Yunus say that Sufia was like a slave?

4. What did people like Sufia need to escape poverty?

5. Later in his book, Yunus says in an ideal world there would be no poverty and no need for social welfare payments. Do you think this is right? Why/why not?

6. What are the advantages of microcredit to the poor?

7. What are the advantages of microcredit to society?

8. Can you see any disadvantages?

Exercise 52D **Understanding the benefits of microcredit**

Key Skills   **Success criteria** ☐ I can identify the differences microcredit make for the poor.

Watch the video and answer the questions below.

> **YouTube** — Go to YouTube and search for 'Muhammad Yunus – Banker to the Poor – Infinite Fire' (7:26).

1. How was Yunus different to the people he was helping?

2. What did he realise was the cause of poverty?

3. What were the benefits of loans?

4. Why did the poor not get loans?

5. What did Yunus realise when he loaned $27?

6. What did the borrowers of the Grameen Bank do with the money they borrowed?

7. What changes did Yunus make to ensure the poor could borrow from the bank?

8. What is especially unusual about the payback rate?

9. How do we know this system works?

■ CALL TO ACTION | *Chapter 5*

Exercise 52E Identifying the changes microcredit makes to people's lives

Key Skills **Success criteria** ☐ I can identify the changes microcredit brings to individuals and their communities.

Read the case study on this page about Ervehe, who benefited from a microcredit programme, and answer the questions that follow.

Case Study

Case study: Ervehe

Ervehe and her husband own a small plot of land in an Albanian village. They used to work in the village agricultural cooperative, but they were made redundant. Their eldest son emigrated to Italy to find work to help his family, but as an illegal emigrant in Italy, he finds it very difficult to earn a living. Not very long ago, some friends told Ervehe that a group of women in the neighbourhood village had created a credit union named 'TEUTA'. Ervehe got involved in expanding the credit union in her own village and took out a loan which helped her to build a 600 m^2 greenhouse and plant different vegetables. Since then, she and her husband work long hours every day in their greenhouse. She also helps as an assistant treasurer in her own village, travels to other villages for credit union meetings and has made a lot of friends.

Source: 'Give Credit to the Poor', Development Education Department, Concern Worldwide

1. What indications do we get that Ervehe's family are poor?

2. How has Ervehe developed because of microcredit?

3. What is TEUTA?

4. Find an example of how Ervehe is giving something back to her community.

Lesson 53: The United Nations

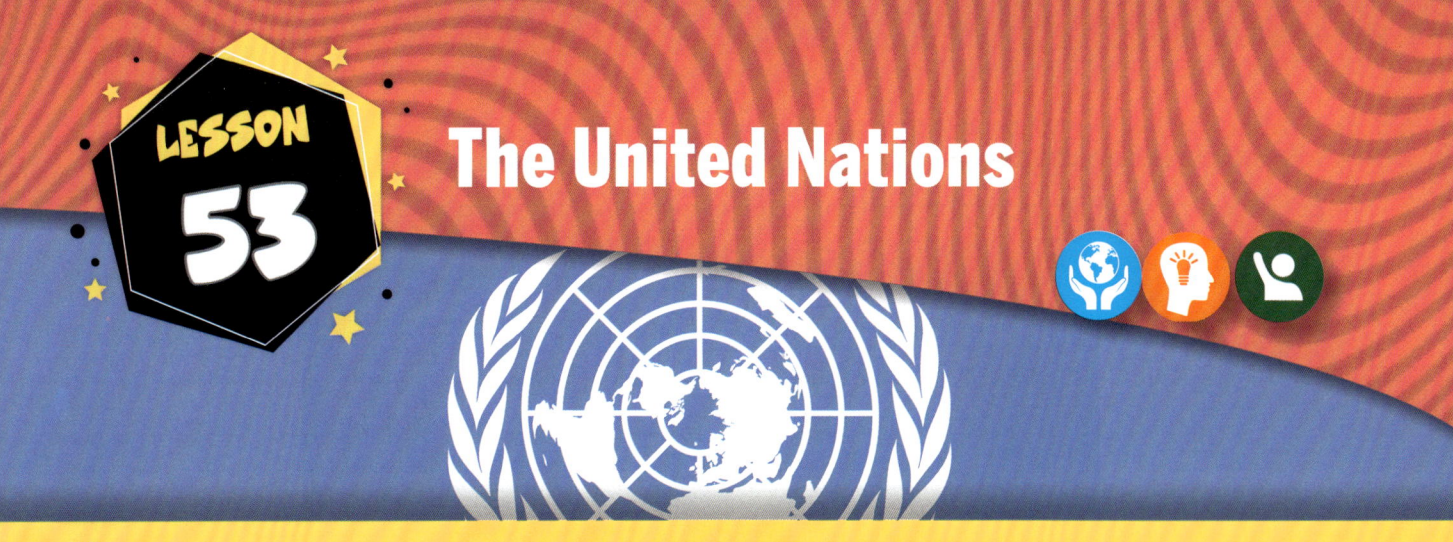

Learning outcome 2.8
Students should be able to identify one person and one institution with power and influence in the world today, explaining the role of each.

Exercise 53A Understanding the roles of UN institutions

Key Skills

Success criteria ☐ I can identify the powers of the UN and its agencies.

Institutions (or organisations) often have economic or political power because they have access to money and politicians. As with people, institutions can use their power for good or for bad.

The **United Nations** was founded on 24 October 1945 in San Francisco, California, following World War II. The aims of the UN are to:

1. Prevent wars breaking out
2. Eliminate poverty
3. Protect human rights.

There are currently 193 member states of the UN. The organisation uses six official languages: Arabic, Chinese, English, French, Russian and Spanish.

- The **General Assembly** is made up of member countries.
- The **Security Council** aims to resolve conflicts and keep peace. It has 15 members, five are permanent: China, France, Russia, the UK and the US. Permanent members can veto (block) any decisions. The Security Council can set up peacekeeping missions.
- The **Secretary-General** is the person in charge of running the UN.

The UN also has specialised agencies carrying out specific tasks for the UN. These include:

- The World Health Organization (**WHO**) deals with global public health.
- **UNESCO** promotes international cooperation through education, science and culture.
- The **World Bank** aims to fight poverty and provide technical assistance for developing countries.
- The Food and Agriculture Organization (**FAO**) aims to prevent world hunger.
- The International Monetary Fund (**IMF**) provides financial stability and promotes high employment, sustainable economic growth and the reduction of poverty around the world.
- **UNICEF** provides development and humanitarian aid for children.

CALL TO ACTION | Chapter 5

Working in pairs, discuss the questions below and write your answers.

1. Do you know of any actions the UN has taken to achieve its three aims? What are they?

    (a) Preventing wars: _____
    _____

    (b) Eliminating poverty: _____
    _____

    (c) Protecting human rights: _____
    _____

2. Why do you think the six languages that are official UN languages were chosen?
   _____

3. Are there other languages that you think should be on this list?
   _____

4. Why do you think that there are five permanent Security Council members?
   _____
   _____

5. Why do you think there are specialised UN agencies?
   _____
   _____

Exercise 53B — Understanding how UN peacekeeping missions work

Key Skills **Success criteria** ☐ I can explain the work of UN peacekeeping missions.

Watch the video about UN peacekeeping. Working in pairs, discuss the questions and then write your answers.

> **YouTube**: Go to YouTube and search for 'Explainer – What is UN Peacekeeping' (1:05).

1. How widespread are UN peacekeeping missions?
   _____

2. How much do they cost?
   _____

3. Why must UN missions work in these difficult places?
   _____

242

Lesson 53: The United Nations

4. What expert skills do they bring to these areas?

5. Name any examples of their successes.

6. Mention anything that struck you watching the video.

Exercise 53C Being aware of conflict zones

Key Skills

Success criteria ☐ I can identify the areas of the world where conflict is taking place.

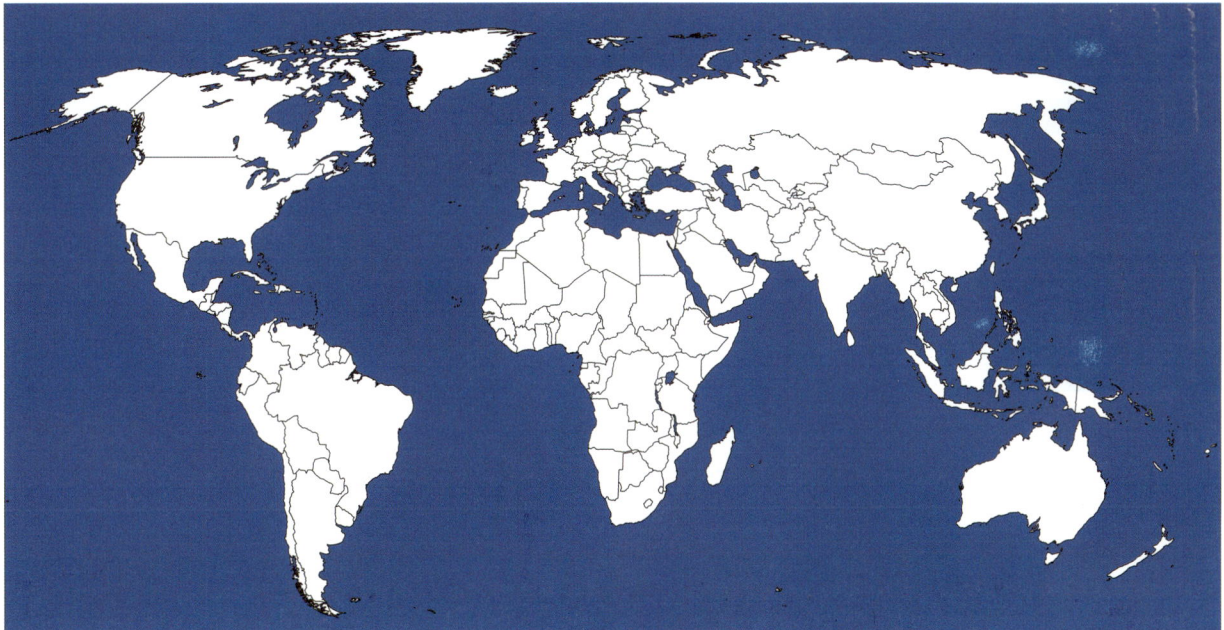

Working in pairs, look at the map above. Research online three areas where conflict is taking place and colour these areas on the map. Discuss what you know about the conflicts and then fill in the table below.

Area	What I know about it

243

■ CALL TO ACTION | *Chapter 5*

Exercise 53D Understanding how the UN Security Council works

Key Skills **Success criteria** ☐ I can identify the actions the UN Security Council can and would take.

The Security Council is in charge of **peacekeeping**. Its jobs include:
- Attempting to prevent conflict by discussion
- Sending peacekeepers to enforce peace settlements
- Helping to rebuild countries damaged by war
- Setting up international tribunals to bring war criminals to justice.

The Secretary General appoints a Head of Mission who is in charge of the peacekeeping mission. The soldiers, who wear blue helmets and use white vehicles with UN clearly marked on them, are supplied by the member states. Police and human rights monitors also participate in peacekeeping missions. Ireland has participated in over 20 missions, including in Lebanon, the DRC and Liberia.

Total size of United Nations peacekeeping forces

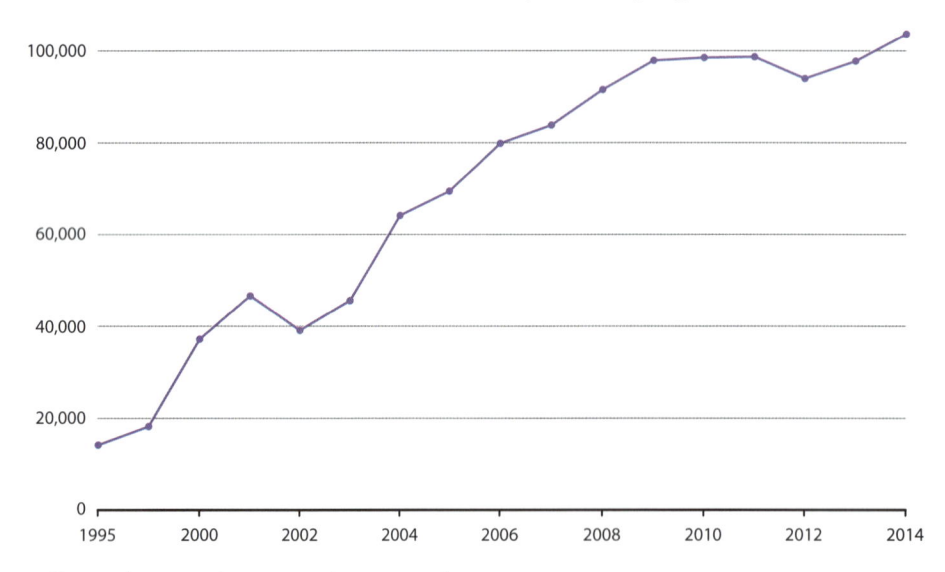

The Security Council can take several actions. It can:
- Impose economic sanctions which limit imports and exports to a country
- Impose arms embargos which ban the export of ammunition and weapons to a country
- Use force such as in East Timor to establish a temporary government to lead the country to independence.

Working in pairs, answer the following questions.

1. Why do you think the UN peacekeepers wear blue and use white vehicles?

2. What does the graph above tell us?

3. Can you name any country where Ireland has sent a peacekeeping mission?

Lesson 53: The United Nations

4. What do you think the best UN response would be in the following situations? Explain why. What do you think would actually happen?

Situation	What should happen?	Why?	What do you think would really happen?
(a) Russia invades eastern Ukraine.			
(b) The President of Mali is using his army to put down a democracy protest.			

Exercise 53E Researching a UN peacekeeping mission

Key Skills **Success criteria** ☐ I can research a peacekeeping mission and evaluate its effectiveness.

Since 1945, the UN has run over 70 peacekeeping missions. Successful missions included the Liberian and East Timor missions. On the other hand, the UN failed to prevent the 1994 Rwandan genocide in which up to 1 million people were killed.

Research one UN peacekeeping mission using the following headings.

Where the mission is/was: _____

The different sides: _____

The background: _____

_____

_____

UN involvement: _____

_____

_____

Solution: _____

_____

Was the mission a success? _____

Sources of my information:

1. _____
2. _____
3. _____

LESSON 54: Causes of deforestation

Learning outcome 2.9
Students should be able to analyse one global issue or challenge, under the following headings: causes, consequences, impact on people's lives and possible solutions.

Exercise 54A Understanding the benefits of tropical rainforests

Key Skills   **Success criteria**   ☐ I can identify the benefits of the Amazon Rainforest.

About 30% of the Earth is covered with forest. Trees help to reduce the impact of climate change by absorbing carbon dioxide and reducing greenhouse gases. **Deforestation** happens when forests are cleared to make way for the land to be used for another purpose. The causes of deforestation differ – in Brazil it is for agriculture, whereas in Indonesia it is palm tree plantations.

Forest degradation occurs when the forest can no longer work properly by absorbing carbon or producing food and shelter for animals, birds, insects and people. This forces animals, birds and insects to leave the forest, which degrades the forest even more. Forest fires and unsustainable logging are major causes of forest degradation. Many forests being cleared are the hot and humid tropical rainforests found on the equator. This has a major impact on the environment.

Watch the video on the Amazon Rainforest and answer the questions below.

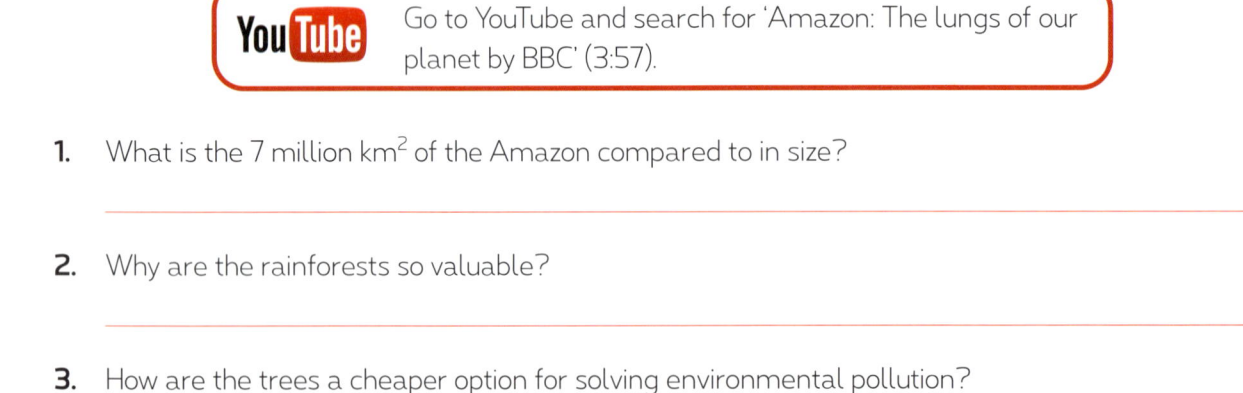

> **YouTube** Go to YouTube and search for 'Amazon: The lungs of our planet by BBC' (3:57).

1. What is the 7 million km^2 of the Amazon compared to in size?

2. Why are the rainforests so valuable?

3. How are the trees a cheaper option for solving environmental pollution?

4. Why must we consider the rainforests as not just something far away?

Lesson 54: Causes of deforestation

Exercise 54B Understanding the negative effects of deforestation

Key Skills **Success criteria** ☐ I can identify consequences of deforestation.

The benefits of trees and forests include:

- They soak up carbon dioxide and release oxygen.
- They maintain the water cycle and generate rainfall.
- They protect against storm damage.
- They are a source of food, timber and fuel for humans.
- They prevent soil erosion by soaking up water and holding the soil in place with their roots.
- They prevent landslides as they absorb water running down hills.
- Many plants growing in forests are used in medicine.
- Forests provide food, homes and protection to animals.
- Forests support indigenous tribes.

Working in pairs, look at the benefits of trees and forests. Choose three of these benefits. What do you imagine the result of deforestation could be on these?

Benefit	Result of deforestation

● CALL TO ACTION | *Chapter 5*

Exercise 54C **Explaining how forest cover is changing and why**

Key Skills   **Success criteria**   ☐ I can explain how forestry is evolving and why.

Share of land covered by forest

- Brazil
- Malaysia
- Indonesia
- France
- Nigeria
- China
- Ireland

Look at the graph above and answer the questions.

1. Which countries have the largest share of forest area?

   _____

2. What does the graph show us has been happening since 1994?

   _____

3. Is this trend the same for all countries?

   _____

4. Why do you think this might be?

   _____

Exercise 54D **Identifying causes of deforestation**

Key Skills   **Success criteria**   ☐ I can explain why different types of deforestation occur and their impact.

There are many reasons why deforestation occurs, including:
- Natural causes such as flooding, hurricanes or fires
- To provide land for agriculture
- To allow mining for minerals and drilling for oil
- To provide land for people to live on

248

Lesson 54: Causes of deforestation

- To grow other tree plantations, which can produce food or be used as fuel or timber
- Roads in forests making illegal logging easier
- Corruption allowing companies to get around environmental regulations.

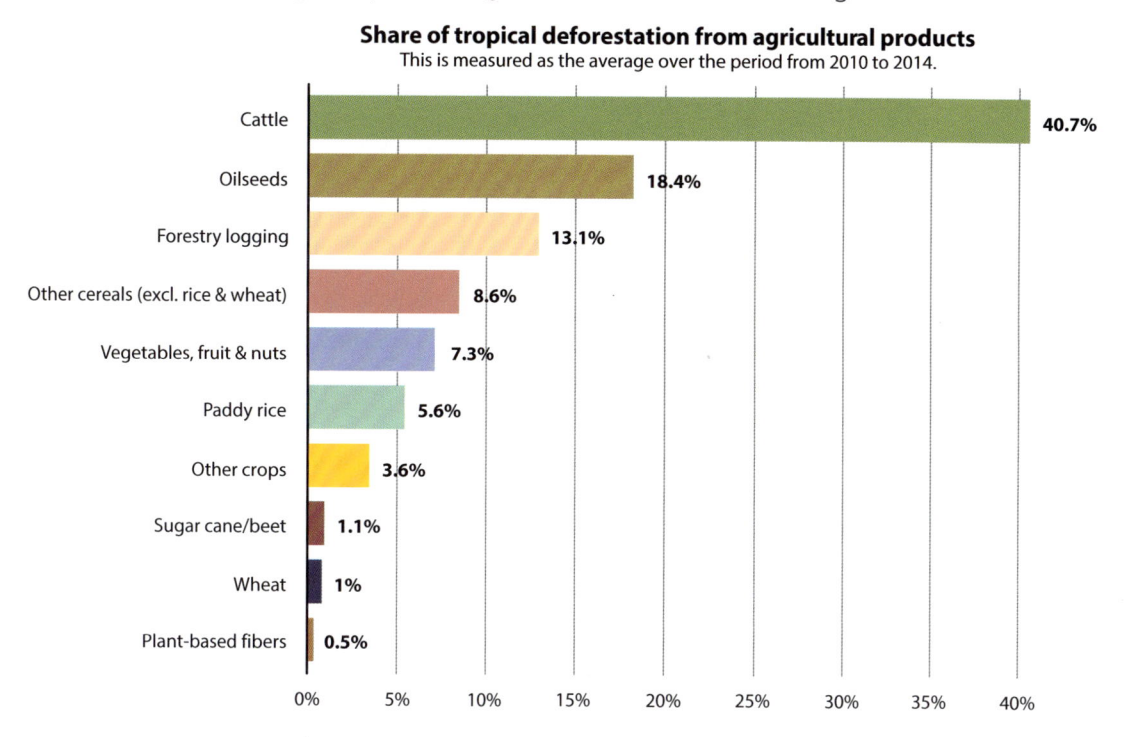

Share of tropical deforestation from agricultural products
This is measured as the average over the period from 2010 to 2014.

Cattle	40.7%
Oilseeds	18.4%
Forestry logging	13.1%
Other cereals (excl. rice & wheat)	8.6%
Vegetables, fruit & nuts	7.3%
Paddy rice	5.6%
Other crops	3.6%
Sugar cane/beet	1.1%
Wheat	1%
Plant-based fibers	0.5%

Working in pairs, look at the causes of deforestation and the chart above and answer the questions.

	How does this cause deforestation?	Rank the causes from most (1) to least serious (6)
Natural causes		
Individual farmers		
Ranches/ plantations		
Mining		
Commercial timber (logging)		
Population growth		

How could the industries in the graph be successful without cutting down forests?

249

Lesson 55: Consequences of deforestation and its impacts on humans

Learning outcome 2.9
Students should be able to analyse one global issue or challenge, under the following headings: causes, consequences, impact on people's lives and possible solutions.

Exercise 55A Identifying the impacts of losing endangered species

Key Skills

Success criteria ☐ I can explain how the loss of endangered species affects the rainforests.

There are many different consequences of deforestation, including the following:
- Deforestation means fewer trees to soak up carbon dioxide. This increases the greenhouse gases in the atmosphere and causes global warming.
- Many plants, animals and insects are lost because their homes and food sources are destroyed and they become easier targets for hunting.
- Deforestation disrupts rainfall patterns, which causes drought.
- It increases the damage caused by storms and floods as the water is held in the ground by tree roots.
- Deforestation removes or damages the forest canopy, which blocks the sun during the day and keeps the heat at night. This is important for maintaining the water cycle.

Working in pairs, read the facts about species endangered by deforestation and try to match the species with the description. Then identify the benefit this species brings to the rainforest and the impact their removal would have on the forest.

Species

tapir   African forest elephant   jaguar   gorilla   hornbill

Lesson 55: Consequences of deforestation and its impacts on humans

	Species	Benefits to rainforest	Impact of its loss
1. This animal is the largest of the great apes. Their biggest threat is deforestation as humans clear the forest for agriculture. As they are fruit eaters, they spread seeds in their dung and they clear space for seedlings to grow.			
2. These large fruit-eating birds spread seeds around Asia's tropical forests which helps new plants to grow. They also travel over cleared areas of forests spreading seeds. Deforestation causes them to lose their sources of food and nesting sites.			
3. This animal is the largest cat in the Americas. It preys on herbivores, which controls their population. Otherwise, the herbivores would destroy the forest. Deforestation has provided easier access to these cats for poachers.			
4. These large animals have seen their population fall by over 86%. When they eat vegetation in the forest, they create gaps for new plants to grow. They leave dung full of seeds, which causes new trees, bushes and grasses to grow.			
5. This animal, which resembles a large pig, is native to the Amazon Rainforest. Its main threats are deforestation and hunting. They spend more time in degraded forests and because they spread so many seeds in their dung, they are regenerating these areas.			

● CALL TO ACTION | *Chapter 5*

Exercise 55B Creating a meme

Key Skills

Success criteria ☐ I can create a meme warning of the dangers of deforestation that inspires people to think.

Look at the meme on the right. It warns that by buying products that cause deforestation, such as palm oil, we are causing orangutans to lose their natural habitat. Create your own meme that warns about the impact of deforestation on one endangered species that convinces people to take action. Print out your meme and stick it below, along with the information you found in your research. You can use PowerPoint or www.canva.com to create the meme.

Once the forests are gone there is no way back

It's time to think of the consequences when we do our weekly shopping

Facts about the endangered species	Meme

Exercise 55C Identifying how indigenous people are affected by deforestation

Key Skills

Success criteria ☐ I can explain how deforestation affects indigenous people.

Impact of deforestation for indigenous people

- Deforestation destroys the food sources of indigenous people who live in the forests. They are often pushed off the land before the deforestation begins. Those who stand up to protect their rights suffer intimidation, physical abuse and even death.
- Deforestation causes degradation of the soil, which reduces the amount of food produced from the land and the money people earn.

Lesson 55: Consequences of deforestation and its impacts on humans

- It increases the likelihood of flooding, as water is not soaked up by trees.
- Deforestation affects small-scale farming, hunting and collecting plants for medicine.
- It causes drier weather and drought.
- Illnesses that existed only among forest wildlife spread in deforested areas as insects, rodents and other animals are driven out of their natural habitat. They then come into contact with people.

Working in pairs read the passage on the Orang Rimba and answer the questions that follow.

> The Orang Rimba are a nomadic hunter-gatherer tribe who have lived in the forests of Sumatra for generations. The Indonesian government has signed over most of their ancestral lands to palm oil plantation companies. As a result, many Orang Rimba are forced to live in plantations, collecting palm oil seeds and hunting wild boar. For collecting the seeds, the tribe have been accused of theft by the company operating in the area, even though the palm oil is on Orang Rimba ancestral land. One Orang Rimba man said: 'That is our ancestral land. It's forbidden for children to take the seeds which have fallen from the palm oil trees. How can it be forbidden? They planted palm oil trees all over our land.'
>
> The palm oil company, BKS, ordered the Orang Rimba to leave. Members of the tribe reported that they were preparing to go when they were attacked, beaten and stabbed by security staff from BKS, who then set fire to their shelters, vehicles and hundreds of loin cloths. According to custom, loin cloths are the tribespeople's most precious possessions. They represent wealth and prestige and are used to pay fines in Orang Rimba customary law.
>
> Source: Survival International

1. How have the Orang Rimba lost their homes?

2. How do they survive?

3. How are they forced off their land?

4. Do you think the palm oil company is unaware of the Orang Rimba's way of living?

5. Why do you think we hear more about the impact of deforestation on animals such as the orangutan than about the Orang Rimba?

■ CALL TO ACTION | *Chapter 5*

Exercise 55D **Understanding the difference between a monoculture and a forest**

Key Skills **Success criteria** ☐ I can name differences between a monoculture and a forest.

Ecosia is a search engine that donates 80% of its profits to non-profit organisations that work on reforestation. Watch the following Ecosia video, which explains why reforestation is important. In agriculture, monoculture involves growing one type of crop only.

> **YouTube** Go to YouTube and search for 'The Importance of Forests – How to protect Forests' (6:24).

1. What are the benefits of forests?

2. What percentage of forests have been cleared?

3. How many rural people depend on forests to survive?

4. Why can animals not thrive in a monoculture?

5. How does the soil between a monoculture and a forest differ?

6. Why are soybeans grown?

7. How can we guarantee forest protection?

8. In this video you see the differences between a forest and plantations. What differences surprised you?

Lesson 56: Solutions to deforestation

Learning outcome 2.9
Students should be able to analyse one global issue or challenge, under the following headings: causes, consequences, impact on people's lives and possible solutions.

Exercise 56A Understanding how individual actions can make a difference to deforestation

Key Skills   **Success criteria**   ☐ I can identify the difference one person can make to reforestation.

The solutions to deforestation can be led by people, governments and companies.

People can make differences by:

1. Using less paper, as more than 40% of timber logging is used to make paper
2. Using recycled paper and cardboard or paper from managed forests
3. Repairing and reusing furniture and other products made of timber
4. Reducing the amount of firewood burned
5. Using **RSPO labelled products**, which show that the palm oil comes from a sustainable source
6. Supporting organisations such as Greenpeace and the World Wildlife Fund
7. Educating family and friends about the consequences of deforestation and the benefits of the forests
8. Voting for politicians who support protection of the tropical rainforests
9. Planting trees
10. Making people aware of companies who benefit from deforestation and exploit indigenous people.

CALL TO ACTION | *Chapter 5*

Read the case study of Jadav Payeng and answer the questions that follow.

Case Study

Reforestation Hero

At 16, Jadav 'Molai' Payeng, the son of a buffalo trader from a marginalised tribal community in India, saw hundreds of dead snakes. The snakes were the victims of a major drought occurring on Molai Forest Reserve on Majuli Island in India. The Molai Reserve was once a place of wonder with an area of approximately 2,500 acres. But every year during the monsoon season, the river floods everything in sight, destroying homes and farms. Because of extensive soil erosion, there are concerns the reserve will be fully submerged within 20 years causing the 150,000 inhabitants to lose their homes and livelihoods.

Jadav realised that someone had to do something, so he started planting a tree sapling a day in the barren soil. He left behind his formal education to give all his attention to the forest. Now over 40 years later, his forest covers 1,390 acres—approximately the size of 15 football stadiums.

At first, planting trees was time consuming until the trees started providing the seed themselves. As his forest grew dense, so did the number of inhabitants. Soon, the forest was filled with hundreds of species of birds, with deers, rhinos and tigers, with even a herd of elephants straying into his forest for three months of the year.

Jadav's life changed in 2007, when a photojournalist discovered him seeding his forest and wrote an article about him. He soon gained the attention of the Indian government and then the entire country – winning multiple awards for his incredible achievements and giving TED talks. He believes Majuli Island can be saved from erosion by planting coconut trees that grow straight and, when planted together in close proximity, protect the soil. This would not only help India's economy but help fight climate change. His worst fear for his forest is deforestation for financial gain.

Source: Chezza Zoeller, One Earth

1. What inspired Jadav to begin planting trees?

2. How large is the forest he planted?

3. What makes this achievement especially impressive?

4. What environmental problems are affecting the area?

5. Why was planting trees difficult in the beginning?

Lesson 56: Solutions to deforestation

6. What changed Jadav's life?

7. Jadav has an idea that could make a difference. What is it?

8. What is his worst fear?

9. What has Jadav proven by his tree-planting story?

Exercise 56B **Considering the actions an individual can take to reduce the harmful impacts of deforestation**

Key Skills   **Success criteria**   ☐ I can name the benefits of reforestation.

Working in pairs, watch Antonio Vicente's story and answer the questions below.

> **YouTube** Go to YouTube and search for 'Restoring the Rainforest – 60 Second Docs' (1:08).

1. What started Antonio's interest in reforestation?

2. How do you know he was committed to doing this?

3. What difference has it made?

4. Name any features of the tropical rainforest you see in the video.

Exercise 56C **Identifying the positive role governments can play in reforestation**

Key Skills   **Success criteria**   ☐ I can name the impacts of government actions for reforestation.

257

CALL TO ACTION | Chapter 5

Governments play an important role in fighting deforestation, such as:

- Protecting indigenous people's rights to the land by making laws and punishing those who do not obey them
- Educating people on the dangers of clearing tropical rainforests and the benefits of the forest ecosystem
- Putting limits on the number of trees that can be logged and fining companies that do not respect the limits
- Making logging companies replace the trees that are cut down
- Preventing logging companies replacing trees with monocultural plantations
- Providing an alternative way of making a living for the local people, such as working as tour guides
- Supporting restoration of degraded forests
- Punishing corruption
- Making it easy to report illegal logging
- Banning the importation of illegally logged timber, as the US, the EU and Australia have
- Providing grants and tax incentives for companies to engage in sustainable forestry.

Working in pairs, read the passage on South Korea's reforestation programme, and answer the questions that follow.

Turning bare land into a green nation: How South Korea recovered its degraded forests

A government-led reforestation programme in South Korea has produced a substantial increase in forest since the mid-1950s, with 60 per cent of the country now covered in forests. In the late 1960s, the South Korean government launched strong forest protection policies and declared illegal logging a serious crime. Several years later, the national police enforced government policies to prevent illegal logging, with about 1.4 million hectares of forest planted to help the recovery of growing forest stocks. The increased use of coal in the 1970s also contributed to forest recovery efforts by reducing the demand for firewood, which had until then been the biggest cause of deforestation in South Korea. At the same time economic growth and the migration of rural populations into cities resulted in a drop in firewood consumption and an increase in the amount of growing forest stock. Local governments led tree-planting efforts and villagers were encouraged to build tree nurseries and sell seedlings for the reforestation programme. In the 1980s, President Park Chung-hee declared reforestation the first national priority and called on the public to contribute to the goal of 'turning bare land into a green nation'.

Source: Rachel Rivera, Forest News

1. How do we know that this plan was a success?

2. What government decisions made it a success?

Lesson 56: Solutions to deforestation

3. What other factors helped the programme to succeed?
   _____
   _____

4. Do you think this programme was ahead of its time? Why/why not?
   _____
   _____

5. What does the success of Korea's reforestation show about government involvement in this issue?
   _____
   _____

Exercise 56D Examining how industries are responding to sustainability in palm oil production

Key Skills

Success criteria ☐ I can explain how companies are responding to palm oil sustainability.

The World Wildlife Fund has a palm oil scorecard for consumer brands. You can use this to check where your local shops and companies get their palm oil from. The infographic below shows some of their findings.

Look at the infographic and answer the questions on the next page.

WWF PALM OIL BUYERS SCORECARD 2019: KEY FINDINGS

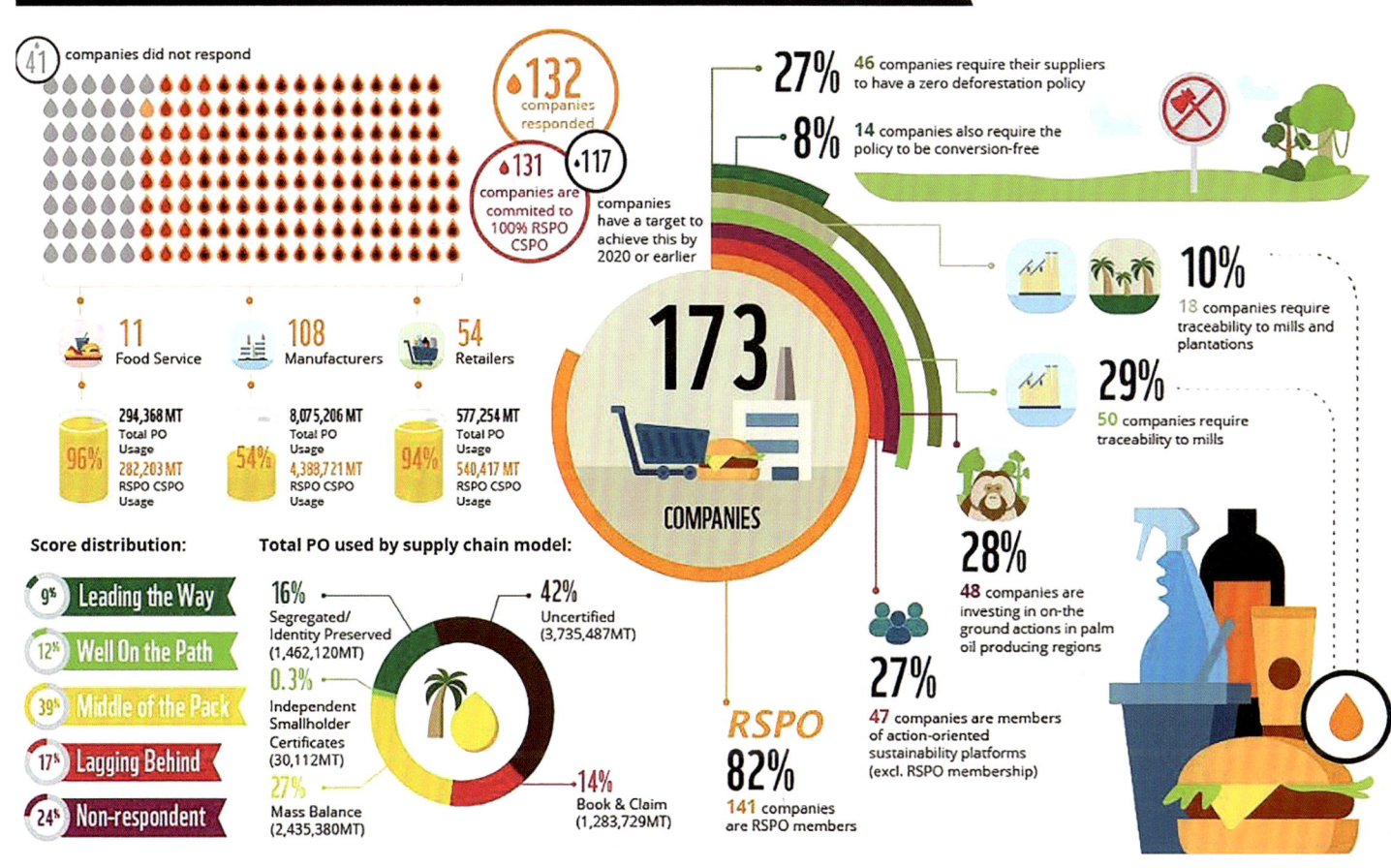

- 41 companies did not respond
- 132 companies responded
- 131 companies are committed to 100% RSPO CSPO
- 117 companies have a target to achieve this by 2020 or earlier

- 27% — 46 companies require their suppliers to have a zero deforestation policy
- 8% — 14 companies also require the policy to be conversion-free
- 10% — 18 companies require traceability to mills and plantations
- 29% — 50 companies require traceability to mills
- 28% — 48 companies are investing in on-the ground actions in palm oil producing regions
- 27% — 47 companies are members of action-oriented sustainability platforms (excl. RSPO membership)
- RSPO 82% — 141 companies are RSPO members

173 COMPANIES

- 11 Food Service — 294,368 MT Total PO Usage — 96% 282,203 MT RSPO CSPO Usage
- 108 Manufacturers — 8,075,206 MT Total PO Usage — 54% 4,388,721 MT RSPO CSPO Usage
- 54 Retailers — 577,254 MT Total PO Usage — 94% 540,417 MT RSPO CSPO Usage

Score distribution:
- 9% Leading the Way
- 12% Well On the Path
- 39% Middle of the Pack
- 17% Lagging Behind
- 24% Non-respondent

Total PO used by supply chain model:
- 16% Segregated/Identity Preserved (1,462,120MT)
- 0.3% Independent Smallholder Certificates (30,112MT)
- 27% Mass Balance (2,435,380MT)
- 14% Book & Claim (1,283,729MT)
- 42% Uncertified (3,735,487MT)

259

CALL TO ACTION | Chapter 5

1. Why do you think 41 companies did not respond?

2. What percentage of companies are RSPO members?

3. What percentage of companies are judged to be leading and well on the way to improving palm oil sustainability?

4. What percentage are lagging behind?

5. What actions could:

    (a) You take to put pressure on the companies that are lagging behind?

    (b) Other companies take?

    (c) The government take?

6. Name two actions that these companies are taking that will lead to more sustainably produced palm oil.

7. Find how many products in your home are RSPO certified. List them here.

Lesson 57

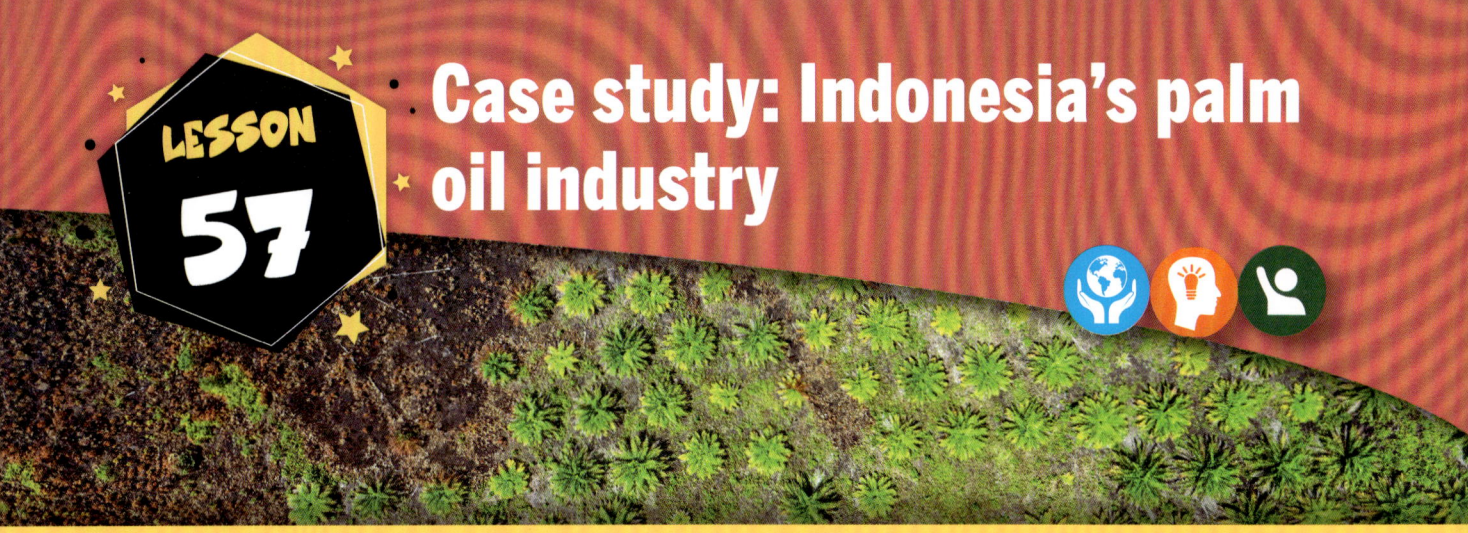

Case study: Indonesia's palm oil industry

Learning outcome 2.9
Students should be able to analyse one global issue or challenge, under the following headings: causes, consequences, impact on people's lives and possible solutions.

Exercise 57A Analysing the impact of deforestation on orangutans

Key Skills   **Success criteria**   ☐ I can analyse an advert about stopping deforestation.

Indonesia is a large country in south-east Asia with a population of almost 275 million people. It contains the largest rainforest in Asia, which is home to many indigenous people and over 3,000 animal species, including the orangutan and Sumatran tiger.

Some 85% of the world production of **palm oil** comes from Indonesia and Malaysia. Palm oil comes from the pulp of the fruit and is used in foods. Palm kernel oil, which comes from crushing the kernel of the fruit, is used in cosmetics and cleaning products. Palm oil is even used in biofuels. It has a much higher yield than any other oil, producing 35% of the world's vegetable oil on only 10% of the land. Because the trees produce huge crops and palm oil can be used in so many different products, it is very profitable. Many people work in the palm oil industry.

Palm oil has caused huge deforestation rates in the tropical rainforests of Indonesia and Malaysia. The area under forest in Indonesia has dropped from 80% in the 1960s to 50% to make way for palm oil trees. This has:

- Driven indigenous people from their lands and homes and endangered many species
- Caused less CO_2 to be absorbed as the trees are cut down
- Degraded the soil
- Released methane in the wastewater at palm oil refineries
- Caused huge fires as the trees and peat they grow on are burned to clear them, releasing CO_2 into the atmosphere
- Caused air pollution from smoke and fumes.

Watch the story about the orangutan and answer the questions that follow.

> **YouTube** Go to YouTube and search for 'There's a Rang-Tan in my bedroom – Bradley J' (2:08).

■ CALL TO ACTION | *Chapter 5*

1. Why do you think the orangutan is upset by the chocolate and the shampoo?
   _____
   _____

2. How is this story told?
   _____
   _____

3. What is the aim of the video?
   _____

4. What is good about the video?
   _____
   _____

Exercise 57B Analysing palm oil statistics

Key Skills   **Success criteria**   ☐ I can analyse charts and explain what they mean.

Look at the chart and answer the questions.

Oil palm production
Oil palm crop production is measured in tonnes.

Country	Production
Indonesia	40.57 million t
Malaysia	19.52 million t
Thailand	2.78 million t
Colombia	1.63 million t
Nigeria	1.05 million t
Guatemala	875,000 t
Honduras	650,000 t
Papua New Guinea	630,000 t
Ecuador	560,000 t

0 t   5 million t   15 million t   25 million t   35 million t

1. What does this chart tell you about Indonesia and Malaysia?
   _____
   _____

262

Lesson 57: Case study: Indonesia's palm oil industry

2. Where in the world are the other countries shown on the chart located?

3. What does this tell you about palm oil production?

Exercise 57C Analysing statistics on oil production and land use

Key Skills   **Success criteria**   ☐ I can explain, using statistics, why the palm oil industry is so profitable.

Despite the negative impact on the environment, the palm oil industry is very successful because of how profitable it is. Palm trees are easy to grow, produce a large crop, do not need pesticides and have lots of uses.

Look at the chart and answer the questions below.

Share of vegetable oil land use and production by crop

Global land use for vegetable oils | Global vegetable oil production

Crop	Land	Production
Palm	8.6% of land	36% of production
Soybean	39% of land	25.5% of production
Rape and Mustard	12% of land	11.3% of production
Sunflower	8.3% of land	9% of production
Groundnut	9% of land	2.5% of production
Cottonseed	10% of land	2.1% of production
Olive	3.3% of land	1.6% of production
Coconut	3.6% of land	1.4% of production
Sesameseed	3.6% of land	0.6% of production

Very high yields means palm produces 36% of oil but needs less than 9% of land

Low yields means these crops use a much larger share of land than they produce in oil

1. The production of which oil uses the most land?

2. The production of which oil uses the least land?

3. What oil is the most widely produced?

4. What does this chart tell us about palm oil?

5. What problems do you see with banning palm oil?

263

■ CALL TO ACTION | *Chapter 5*

Exercise 57D **Identifying the challenges of the palm oil industry**

Key Skills   **Success criteria** ☐ I can explain why the palm oil industry needs to be reformed.

The simple solution to the problem would be to ban palm oil, but this would see many people lose their livelihoods. It could also be replaced by another industry that could be even more harmful. Some oils are not suited to replacing palm oil, especially in cosmetics. A more sustainable solution would involve some of the following actions:

- Using RSPO-certified palm oil
- Stopping using palm oil and vegetable oils in fuels, as these oils are more suited to the food and cosmetics industries which cause less environmental damage than burning the oils as fuel
- Ensuring better tree management, which can increase the yields by 75%
- Fining companies involved in deforestation and in forest fires
- Converting the methane produced by the palm oil refineries into electricity
- Raising public awareness of palm oil. EU food companies must state if they use palm oil in their products. However, cosmetics and cleaning products use chemical names like palmitate, palmate, stearic acid and sodium lauryl sulphate to hide the fact that palm oil is used.
- Using other oils instead of palm oil in foods
- Commercially producing oil from algae, yeast or fungi to replace palm oil.

Look at the video about palm oil and answer the questions.

> **YouTube** Go to YouTube and search for 'Why boycotting palm oil is not a solution – Ecosia' (5:38).

1. What was Nayla taught about the forest?

2. Why is palm oil such an important industry in Indonesia?

3. What are the disadvantages of palm oil plantations?

4. How do these plantations affect the orangutan?

5. What solutions to deforestation by palm oil plantations are suggested?

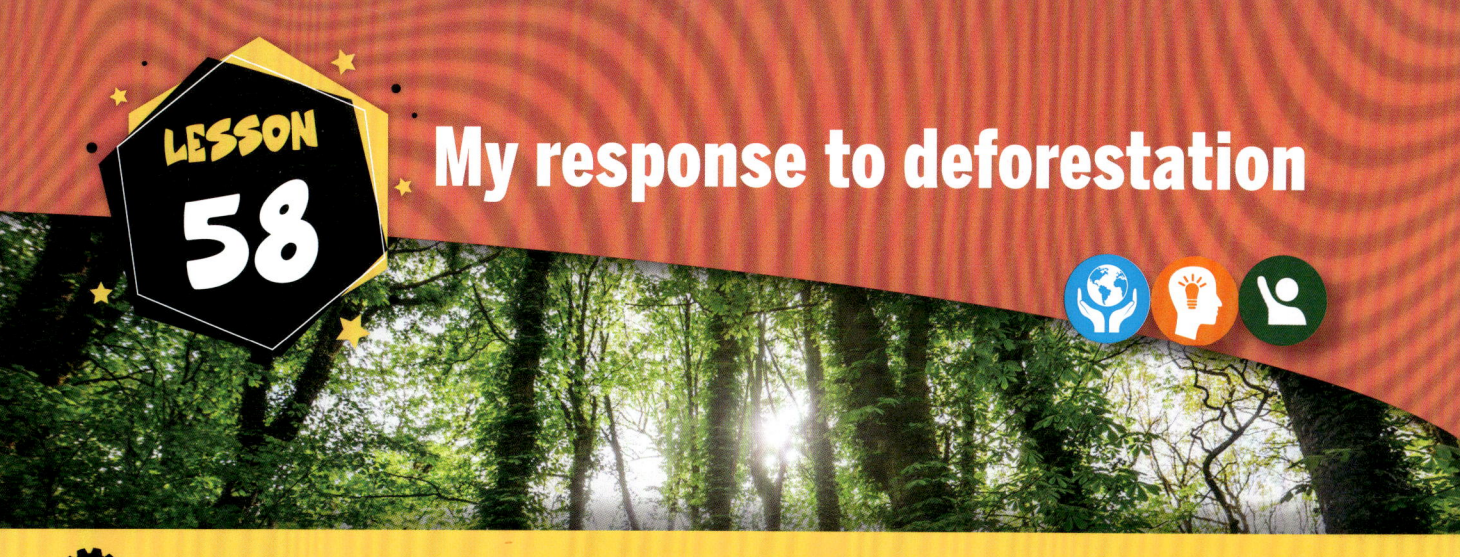

Lesson 58: My response to deforestation

Learning outcome 2.10
Students should be able to evaluate how they can contribute in responding to one challenge facing the world.

Exercise 58A Evaluating the benefits of contacting a politician

Key Skills

Success criteria ☐ I will identify the advantages and disadvantages of contacting politicians to prevent deforestation.

Over the past few lessons, you have looked at the impact of deforestation and at people and organisations effecting global change. In this lesson, you will identify what *you* could do to respond to this challenge. Your actions could include:

- Contacting politicians
- Raising public awareness
- Fundraising for an NGO working against deforestation
- Joining an organisation that works in the area
- Organising a petition.

There are many other ways that you could contribute. In deciding how to respond to the challenge, it is important to consider what works best for the cause. Key things to consider include:

- Why you are doing it
- What you want others to do
- How your response will make a difference.

Work in groups to discuss the following questions and write your answers below.

1. What are the advantages of contacting politicians?

2. Are there any disadvantages?

265

■ CALL TO ACTION | *Chapter 5*

3. Who should we contact? How should we contact them?

4. How do we measure the success of this action?

Exercise 58B Evaluating the benefits of a public awareness campaign

Key Skills **Success criteria** ☐ I will identify the advantages and disadvantages of a public awareness campaign.

Work in groups to discuss the following questions and write your answers below.

1. What are the advantages of raising public awareness?

2. Are there any disadvantages?

3. Who do we want to reach and how will we do it?

4. What do we want them to do?

5. How do we measure the success of this action?

Exercise 58C Evaluating the benefits of fundraising for an NGO working against deforestation

Key Skills **Success criteria** ☐ I will identify the advantages and disadvantages of fundraising for an NGO working against deforestation.

Work in groups to discuss the following questions and write your answers below.

1. What are the advantages and disadvantages of fundraising for an NGO?

Lesson 58: My response to deforestation

2. Who should we contact to organise raising money?

3. What should we do to raise money?

4. How do we measure the success of this action?

5. Can you name an NGO that is working to stop deforestation?

6. Name a benefit of becoming a member of an organisation that works to prevent deforestation.

Exercise 58D Evaluating the benefits of organising a petition

Key Skills   **Success criteria**   ☐   I will identify the advantages and disadvantages of organising a petition.

Work in groups to discuss the following questions and write your answers below.

1. What are the advantages of organising a petition?

2. What are the disadvantages?

3. Who do we promote it with?

4. How do we do it?

5. Who do we want to act on it?

6. What do we want them to do?

7. How do we measure the success of this action?

267

Lesson 59

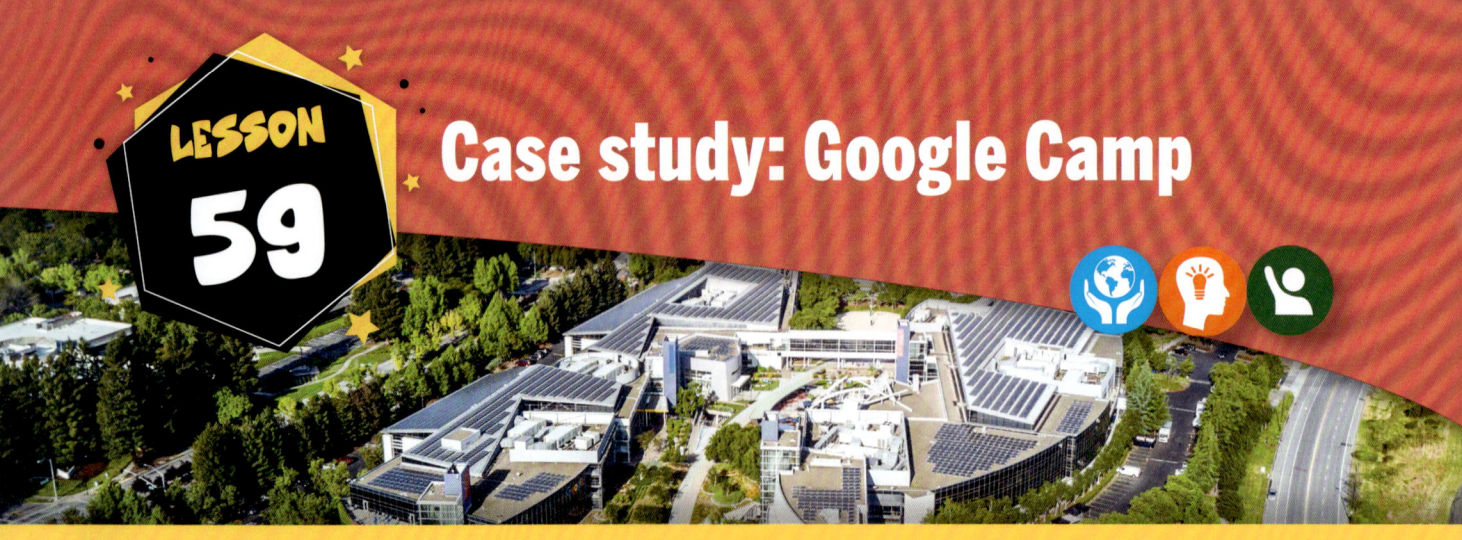

Case study: Google Camp

Learning outcome 2.11
Students should be able to examine a campaign for change in the area of sustainability and assess reasons why it has or has not been successful.

Exercise 59A Identifying positives and negatives of climate change conferences

Key Skills **Success criteria** ☐ I can identify positives and negatives of climate change conferences.

Google Camp is a private meeting of business leaders, IT specialists and celebrities. It takes place every year near the town of Sciacca on the Italian island of Sicily. The camp was the idea of Google founders Larry Page and Sergey Brin and takes place over three days. It has discussed issues such as human rights, education and, in 2019, climate change.

The following EcoWatch report by Jordan Davidson describes what was known about the 2019 camp on climate change. Read the report and answer the questions.

> Google's seventh annual meeting of the minds, dubbed Google Camp, is happening at a seaside resort in Sicily and this year, it is dedicated to the climate crisis. Luminaries [*people who influence others*] from tech, business, entertainment and politics descended upon the Italian island to discuss ideas and solutions for tackling the climate crisis at the three-day event that costs Google upwards of $20 million, according to *Business Insider*. The highly secretive event at the Verdura Resort near a UNESCO World Heritage ruins prevents attendees from posting on social media while in attendance. On the first night, Chris Martin of Coldplay performed a private concert for attendees, with the Valley of the Temples ruins in nearby Agrigento as a backdrop.

1. Why do you think these people were invited to Google Camp?
   _____
   _____

2. Why do you think the camp is secretive?
   _____
   _____

Lesson 59: Case study: Google Camp

3. Can you think of any actions that might happen because of the camp?
   _____
   _____

4. How is involving celebrities problematic?
   _____
   _____

Exercise 59B — Identifying the positives and negatives of using celebrities in campaigns

Key Skills

Success criteria ☐ I can identify positives and negatives of celebrity involvement in campaigns.

The benefits of using celebrities to promote campaigns include:
- People are more likely to be aware of the campaign when a celebrity is involved
- Journalists and the media will be more interested in the campaign
- Celebrities are used to dealing with the media and can sell causes to other people.

The disadvantages include:
- The celebrity may do something that damages the campaign, like a movie star travelling around the world on private jets while campaigning for climate justice
- The celebrity may receive more attention than the campaign
- The celebrity might not appear sincere and may seem to be doing it to help their career or public image
- The celebrity might expect first-class travel, hotels, etc.

Working in pairs, discuss two campaigns you know of that are fronted by celebrities. In what ways are these campaigns helped by celebrity involvement and in what ways are they damaged? Write your answers below.

Campaign	Celebrity	Helped by celebrity involvement	Damaged by celebrity involvement

■ CALL TO ACTION | *Chapter 5*

Exercise 59C — Understanding the importance of public perception in a campaign

Key Skills **Success criteria** ☐ I can identify how perception influences whether or not something succeeds.

Read more of the EcoWatch report about Google Camp and answer the questions.

The Verdura Resort is a short distance from the airport in Palermo, though many guests arrive via private helicopter or on private yachts, according to *Forbes*. In fact, the Palermo airport had made preparations for the expected arrival of 114 private jets, according to *Giornale Di Sicilia*. The influx of private jets, private yachts, helicopters, sports cars and limousines seems in stark contrast to the theme of the conference. By contrast, Greta Thunberg, the teenage activist, avoids meat, dairy and air travel, to reduce her carbon footprint. She will sail to New York from Europe to attend the UN Climate Summit next month.

The transportation of the various Google Camp guests, including Leonardo DiCaprio, Harry Styles, Prince Harry and Meghan Markle and Mark Zuckerberg amongst many others have drawn condemnation on social media and in the press. After all, a flight from New York to Palermo, Sicily, generates around 4.24 metric tons of CO_2, or the equivalent of 540,652 smart phones being charged at one time, according to *Euronews*. That's a lot of carbon for just a few people. That doesn't include the greenhouse gases emitted by the 2,300 horsepower diesel-engine private yachts.

After Prince Harry gave an impassioned speech about saving nature in his bare-feet at the conference, one *New York Post* columnist wrote, 'It doesn't get much sillier than being lectured on carbon footprints by a prince whose family rattles around in multiple palaces.'

1. Why do you think people were interested in the camp?

2. Do you think Google Camp had public support? Explain your answer, giving reasons from the passage.

3. How might this conference have been different if Jadav Payeng was speaking about the climate crisis rather than Prince Harry?

4. If you were to run a campaign on climate change, what would you do differently?

Lesson 59: Case study: Google Camp

5. What do you think the organisers were hoping to achieve by organising the event?

   _____

   _____

6. What have people learned about climate change because of this event?

   _____

   _____

Exercise 59D   Analysing media coverage of Google Camp 2019

Key Skills   **Success criteria**   ☐ I can identify how the presentation of an event in the media is important for its success.

Look at how the 2019 Google Camp was covered by an infographic in a popular newspaper and by an article in *Euronews*. Answer the questions that follow.

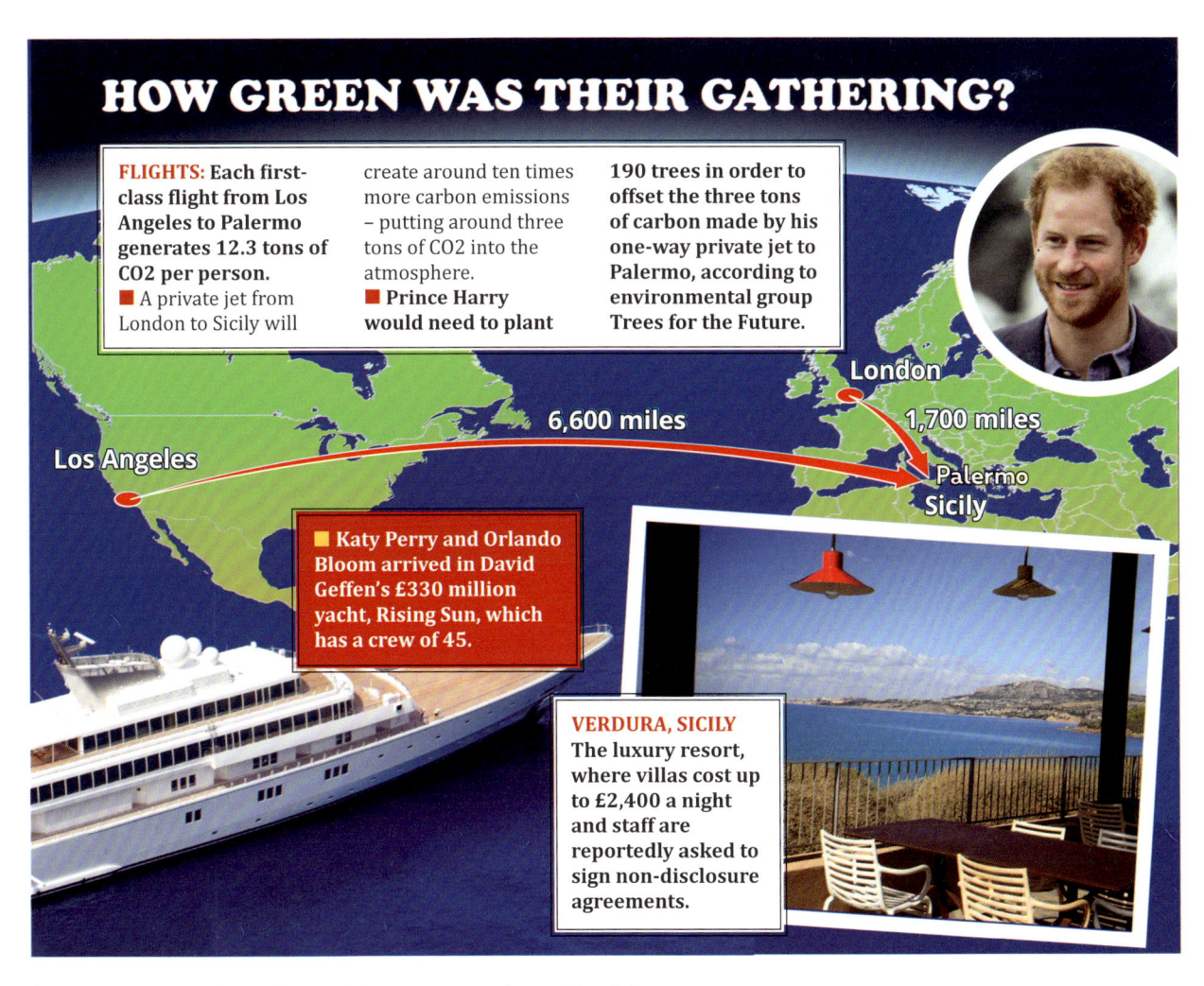

HOW GREEN WAS THEIR GATHERING?

FLIGHTS: Each first-class flight from Los Angeles to Palermo generates 12.3 tons of CO2 per person.

■ A private jet from London to Sicily will create around ten times more carbon emissions – putting around three tons of CO2 into the atmosphere.

■ Prince Harry would need to plant 190 trees in order to offset the three tons of carbon made by his one-way private jet to Palermo, according to environmental group Trees for the Future.

Los Angeles — 6,600 miles → Palermo, Sicily
London — 1,700 miles → Palermo, Sicily

■ Katy Perry and Orlando Bloom arrived in David Geffen's £330 million yacht, Rising Sun, which has a crew of 45.

VERDURA, SICILY
The luxury resort, where villas cost up to £2,400 a night and staff are reportedly asked to sign non-disclosure agreements.

Source: Infographic adapted from an article in *The Metro* newspaper

■ CALL TO ACTION | *Chapter 5*

Deputy Editor of *Euronews Green*, Maeve Campbell, wrote:

> While the facts remain, following the influx of private vehicles to Google's Italian retreat, there is an argument to be made that both the coverage generated (at least 20 articles by major outlets) and the environmental awareness resulting from it, makes it all worth it. To centre such an important event around climate change in this day and age is a positive step in the right direction – particularly given the amount of influential figures in attendance, all with staggering platforms to effect change all around the world. To have them all in one place, working together to achieve a common goal that could really make a difference along the road to becoming carbon neutral before 2050 – perhaps the positives outweigh the negatives. And even if you disagree, at least the very fact they all arrived in such sheer extravagance has brought all the more attention to the event and the eco themes surrounding it.

1. What view of the event does the infographic present?

2. What impression do you have of the event having examined in the infographic?

3. How is the coverage of Google Camp similar in the infographic and in the article?

4. How does their coverage differ?

5. What point does Maeve Campbell make?

6. Do you agree with her? Why/why not?

Lesson 60

Case study: Fridays for Future

Learning outcome 2.11
Students should be able to examine a campaign for change in the area of sustainability and assess reasons why it has or has not been successful.

Exercise 60A Identifying how a campaign grows

Key Skills   **Success criteria**   ☐ I can identify reasons for a campaign being successful.

In 2018, 15-year-old **Greta Thunberg** began protesting against climate change outside the Swedish Parliament on Fridays instead of going to school. Greta vowed to continue until the Swedish government met the carbon emissions reduction they had agreed to at the Paris Climate Treaty. Pictures of her holding a sign went viral on social media and other students began similar protests. This led to the school climate strike under the hashtag #FridaysForFuture, which saw students protesting outside parliaments and city halls in many other places, such as European countries, the US, Australia and Japan.

Greta's protest developed into a worldwide campaign calling for change. In March 2019, the first Global Strike for Climate was held where over 1 million people demonstrated in 125 countries. There were three other international strikes held in 2019. Greta attended the 2019 UN Climate Action Summit in New York. She travelled there by a solar-and-wind-powered racing yacht, to avoid flying by plane because of the carbon emissions of aircraft. Her speech to the conference became famous for criticising politicians for doing nothing and leaving it to young people to demand change. As she left the US to sail back to Europe, she said: 'My message to the Americans is the same as to everyone – that is to unite behind the science and to act on the science'.

The following are some quotes from Greta Thunberg's speeches:

> I don't want you to be hopeful. I want you to panic. I want you to feel the fear I feel every day. And then I want you to act. I want you to act as you would in a crisis. I want you to act as if the house was on fire – because it is.
>
> *Addressing the World Economic Forum in Davos, 2019*

> This is all wrong. I shouldn't be up here. I should be back in school on the other side of the ocean. Yet you all come to us young people for hope. How dare you! You have stolen my dreams and my childhood with your empty words.
>
> *Addressing the UN Climate Action Summit 2019*

CALL TO ACTION | *Chapter 5*

> The fact we are still having this discussion, and even more that we are still subsidising fossil fuels directly or indirectly using taxpayer money, is a disgrace. It is a clear proof that we have not understood the climate emergency at all.
> *Addressing a US House of Representatives Committee, 2021*

> Leaders are happy to set targets for decades into the future, but flinch when immediate action to cut emissions is needed.
> *Interview with The Guardian, 2020*

Look at Greta Thunberg's quotes and the two photos below and answer the following questions.

The photo on the left was taken in August 2018, the one on the right in September 2019.

1. What is the difference between the two photos?

2. What does this show?

3. Have you heard of Greta Thunberg and if so, how?

4. Why do you think Greta's ideas spread so quickly?

5. Do you think her age was a positive or a negative in her campaign? Why?

6. Write the key points from each of Greta's quotes.

274

Lesson 60: Case study: Fridays for Future

7. Why do you think her speeches are often quoted by others?
   _____

8. Do you think her speeches are effective? Explain your answer.
   _____
   _____

Exercise 60B   Analysing a video campaign

Key Skills   **Success criteria**   ☐ I can identify the effective elements of a video campaign.

Watch the video of Greta Thunberg. Working in pairs discuss the following questions, then write your answers.

> **YouTube** Go to YouTube and search for 'A #NatureNow message from Greta Thunberg' (3:39).

1. What must be done to combat climate change?
   _____
   _____

2. What tools in nature take the carbon out of the air?
   _____
   _____

3. How do we know that more needs to be done about climate change?
   _____

4. What three things must we do?
   _____
   _____
   _____

5. What makes this an effective video for raising awareness?
   _____
   _____

6. The video is about doing more than raising awareness. What else should people do?
   _____
   _____

CALL TO ACTION | *Chapter 5*

Exercise 60C Examining negative reactions to campaigns

Key Skills **Success criteria** ☐ I can identify the impact of negative reactions to campaigns.

The response to Greta Thunberg has not always been positive but Greta has used criticisms to poke fun at those making them. Russian President Vladimir Putin described her as a 'kind and very sincere but poorly informed teenager'. In response, Greta changed her Twitter bio to 'a kind but poorly informed teenager'. When the Brazilian President Jair Bolsonaro described Greta as a brat, she again changed her Twitter bio to *pirrahla*, the Portuguese word for 'brat'. When Boris Johnson spoke about 'the politically correct green action of bunny hugging', she changed her bio to 'bunny hugger'.

When she was named *Time Magazine* Person of the Year for 2019, then US President Donald Trump tweeted:

> **Donald J. Trump** @realDonaldTrump • 2019
> So ridiculous. Greta must work on her Anger Management problem, then go to a good old fashioned movie with a friend! Chill Greta, Chill!
> 💬 123   🔁 345   ♡ 234

The following year, when Donald Trump tried to stop the counting of votes in the 2020 US presidential election as he was losing, Greta used his tweet against him.

> **Greta Thunberg** @GretaThunberg • 2020
> So ridiculous. Donald must work on his Anger Management problem, then go to a good old fashioned movie with a friend! Chill Donald, Chill!
> 💬 123   🔁 345   ♡ 234

Working in pairs discuss the following questions and write your answers below.

1. Why do you think the politicians criticised Greta?

2. What do you think of her response?

3. What impact do you think these criticisms would have on her campaign?

Lesson 60: Case study: Fridays for Future

Exercise 60D Understanding people's view of climate change

Key Skills   **Success criteria**   ☐ I can analyse statistics on public attitudes to climate change.

Working in pairs, look at the bar chart of attitudes to global problems among the Irish public and the average of other EU citizens. Discuss the questions and then write your answers.

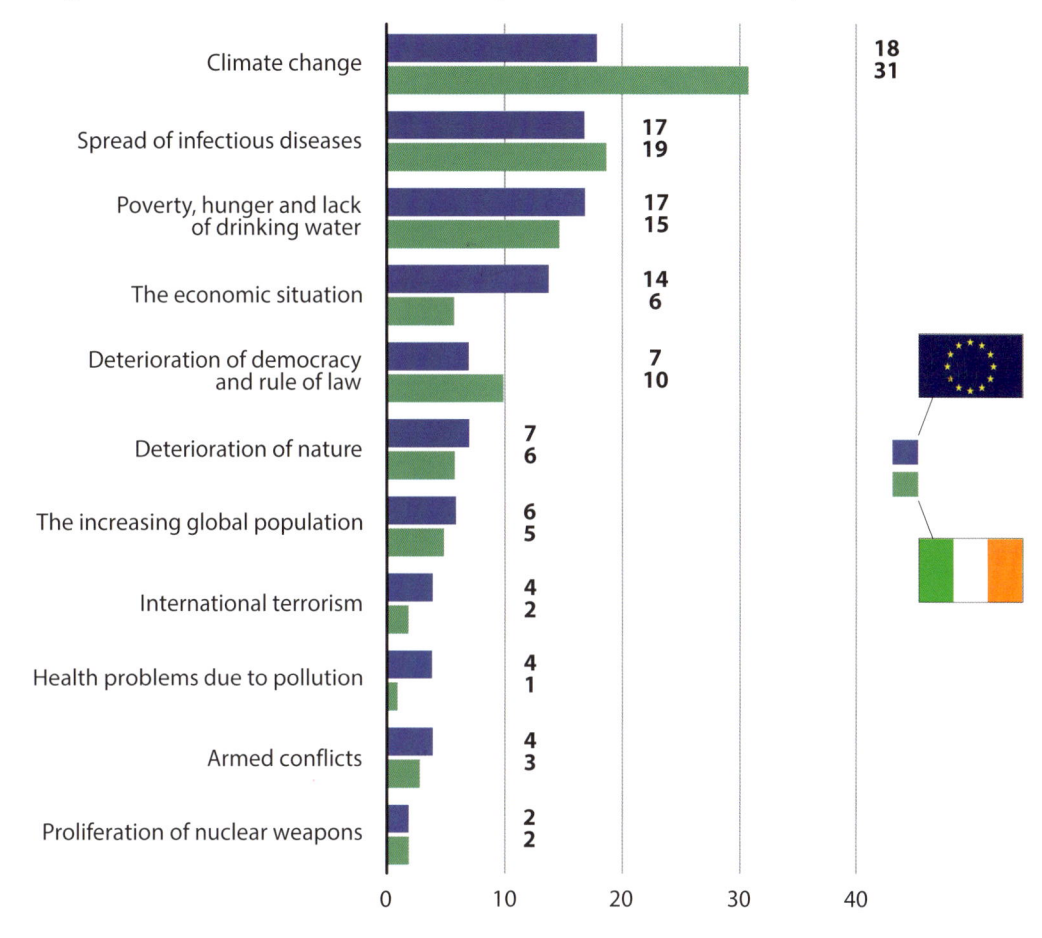

Problem	EU	Ireland
Climate change	18	31
Spread of infectious diseases	17	19
Poverty, hunger and lack of drinking water	17	15
The economic situation	14	6
Deterioration of democracy and rule of law	7	10
Deterioration of nature	7	6
The increasing global population	6	5
International terrorism	4	2
Health problems due to pollution	4	1
Armed conflicts	4	3
Proliferation of nuclear weapons	2	2

1. What do Irish people believe is the biggest problem facing the world?

2. How does this compare to the EU average?

3. What problems are viewed more seriously by other EU citizens than people in Ireland?

4. Do you agree with the Irish people on what is the biggest issue? Why/why not?

5. Do you think Greta Thunberg's campaign had an impact on these findings? Why/why not?

277

Reflection: Reflecting on my learning about effecting global change

Learning outcome 2.12
Students should be able to reflect on their ongoing learning and what it means for them.

Key Skills

Success criteria
- [ ] I can give examples of how my thinking about effecting global change has developed.
- [ ] I can give examples of how I think differently about effecting global change.

Look back at the skills and knowledge you have developed in this chapter. Use the following questions to guide your reflection on effecting global change. Then working in groups discuss your responses to each of these questions.

1. Before looking at effecting global change, I thought ...	
2. Things I learned about effecting global change	
3. Where I got my information from	
4. How I know the information was reliable	
5. The different types of sources I got my information from	
6. The most interesting thing I learned was ...	
7. How the new information I have learned will change what I do	

Action: Creating an awareness campaign

An awareness campaign is one in which you aim to make people aware of a particular issue. The campaign explains why the issue is important, what can be done and how people can help. Some campaigns have national or international awareness days or weeks. These can be useful times to launch an awareness campaign, but you do not have to stick to these days.

✓ Action 1 — Identifying a suitable area to raise awareness of

Key Skills   **Success criteria**   ☐ I will identify a suitable area to raise awareness of.

Consider any of the topics you have covered in this chapter on effecting global change. Would you like to raise awareness about any of these? Who do you want to make aware of it and why?

1. Which area would we like to raise awareness of?

2. Who will we raise awareness with? Why?

✓ Action 2 — Exploring the benefits of different actions

Key Skills   **Success criteria**   ☐ I will identify the advantages and disadvantages of each method of raising awareness.

There are many different strategies you can use to raise awareness. These include social media campaigns, infographics, posters or videos.

Work in groups to discuss the advantages and disadvantages of each awareness-raising method and note them here. Consider questions like:

- What is the best method for the group we are aiming to reach?
- What methods are practical/impractical?

	Advantages	Disadvantages
1. Social media campaign		

279

CALL TO ACTION | *Chapter 5*

	Advantages	Disadvantages
2. Infographic		
3. Poster		
4. Video		

✓ Action 3 — Identifying the actions my group completed and summarising my learning

Key Skills

Success criteria
- ☐ I can identify the actions my group did.
- ☐ I can explain what I learned from organising the campaign.

To do your action, each person should work in a group with specific responsibilities for carrying out the action. Once your group has completed your action answer the questions below.

1. Note the actions that your group conducted.

_____
_____
_____
_____
_____

2. Thinking back over the campaign, note what you learned.

_____
_____
_____
_____
_____

STRAND 3
Exploring Democracy

Chapter 6   The Meaning of Democracy   282

Chapter 7   The Law and the Citizen   340

Chapter 8   The Role of Media in a Democracy   387

LESSON 61

Chapter 6 The Meaning of Democracy
Power and influence

Learning outcome 3.1
Students should be able to create a visual representation of the day-to-day contexts and institutions to which they belong, highlighting where they have power and influence

Exercise 61A Analysing young people's power

Key Skills   **Success criteria**   ☐ I can identify situations where young people have power.

Power is the ability to get something done or to get people to do something. Power can involve strength. **Influence** is when you get people to do something by convincing them that it is the right thing to do rather than by using strength.

Watch the video about the power of young people and answer the questions below.

> Go to YouTube and search for 'The Power of Young People – National Youth Council of Ireland' (2:53).

1. How many of the five powerful people mentioned were politicians?
   _____

2. Pick one of the protests and say what the protesters wanted to be improved.
   _____
   _____

3. According to the video, what are the negatives of having power?
   _____
   _____

4. What are the positives of power?
   _____
   _____

5. What may determine the future of all life on this planet?
   _____
   _____

Lesson 61: Power and influence

Exercise 61B — Identifying who has power and influence

Key Skills **Success criteria** ☐ I can identify who has power and influence in the world and in my life.

Answer questions 1-2 individually, then in pairs discuss questions 3-4. Write your answers below.

1. Who has power in my life? Why do they have this power?
   _____
   _____

2. Who has influence in my life? Why do they have this influence?
   _____
   _____

3. Who has power in the world? Why do they have this power?
   _____
   _____

4. Who has influence in the world? Why do they have this influence?
   _____
   _____

Exercise 61C — Identifying situations where I have power and influence

Key Skills **Success criteria** ☐ I can identify situations where I have power and influence and explain how I have power and influence.

Consider situations where you have power and influence. Write your answers to the questions below.

1. What power do you have in your family? Why do you have this power?
   _____
   _____

2. What influence do you have in your family? Why do you have this influence?
   _____
   _____

3. What power do you have in your school? Why do you have this power?
   _____
   _____

4. What influence do you have in your school? Why do you have this influence?
   _____
   _____

5. Are there other situations where you have power?
   _____

CALL TO ACTION | *Chapter 6*

6. Why do you have this power?

7. Are there other situations where you have influence?

8. Why do you have this influence?

Exercise 61D — Analysing young people's influence

Key Skills **Success criteria** ☐ I can identify situations where young people have influence.

Having power and influence can make you feel good about yourself and respected by others. Powerful and influential people can make decisions that are for the good of everyone. However, power and influence can also lead to people making the wrong decision.

Sometimes we assume that young people have no power or influence, because they do not have the right to vote until they reach the age of 18. This is not always the case. You have already identified situations where you have power and what gives you that power. You have also looked at young people who have power and influence, such as Greta Thunberg and Malala Yousafzai.

Watch the video about types of influencers and answer the questions below.

YouTube: Go to YouTube and search for 'SEL Video for Students: Influencer Types' (2:07).

1. What is a reinforcer? Why are they called that?

2. Explain the difference between a neutraliser, a shaper and a follower.

3. How is a follower also an influencer?

4. The type of influencer a person is can change. Why is that?

5. Which type of influencer do you think you are? Why?

6. Which is the best type of influencer? Why?

284

LESSON 62

Creating a visual image of power and influence

Learning outcome 3.1
Students should be able to create a visual representation of the day-to-day contexts and institutions to which they belong, highlighting where they have power and influence

In the Lesson 61, you identified areas where you have power and influence in your own life. In this lesson, you will present these areas of power and influence as a visual image. Your image should show the areas where you have most power and influence and those where you have least.

Exercise 62A — Creating a visual representation of the areas where I have power and influence

Key Skills

Success criteria ☐ I can rank the areas where I have power and influence from the most to the least and represent these areas visually.

Rank five areas where you have power and influence from 1 to 5, with 1 being most and 5 being least.

Most power and influence   **Least power and influence**

1 _____ 2 _____ 3 _____ 4 _____ 5 _____

Draw a ladder in the box. Place the areas of power and influence that you identified on it by drawing a picture to represent them. Place the areas where you have least power and influence at the bottom and the areas where you have most at the top.

LESSON 63

Democracy

Learning outcome 3.2
Students should be able to describe decision-making processes and the roles of different groups in their class/school.

Exercise 63A   Identifying the origins of democracy

Key Skills   Success criteria   ☐ I can explain the origins of democracy.

Democracy is when people have the power to choose who represents them in government. They have a role in decision-making by voting. Generally, the people who have the power to vote are adults over the age of 18. '**Suffrage**' and '**franchise**' are terms that mean the right to vote in elections.

Watch the video about democracy and answer the questions that follow.

> **YouTube** Go to YouTube and search for 'Democracy – A short introduction' (3:09).

1. What was democracy like in Ancient Greece?

2. Who were not considered citizens in Ancient Greece?

3. What did the Magna Carta do?

4. What are indirect, or representative, democracies?

5. What does the legislative do in a democracy?

6. What does the executive do in a democracy?

7. What does the judiciary do in a democracy?

Exercise 63B Analysing a poem on democracy

Key Skills **Success criteria** ☐ I can explain a poem on democracy.

Langston Hughes (1901–1967) was a black American poet and novelist. In 1870, the 15th Amendment to the US Constitution gave black men the right to vote. However, they had to pay poll taxes and pass literacy tests before they could actually vote. Until the Voting Rights Act of 1965, some states exploited these unfair rules to deny people the right to vote. This poem by Hughes was published in 1949.

Read Langston Hughes's poem on democracy and answer the questions below.

Democracy

Democracy will not come
Today, this year
Nor ever
Through compromise and fear.

I have as much right
As the other fellow has
To stand
On my two feet
And own the land.

I tire so of hearing people say,
Let things take their course.
Tomorrow is another day.
I do not need my freedom when I'm dead.
I cannot live on tomorrow's bread.

Freedom
Is a strong seed
Planted
In a great need.

I live here, too.
I want freedom
Just as you.

1. What does Hughes say will prevent democracy?

2. In your opinion, is this poem about: war, equality or money and property? Explain your answer.

3. Do you think that the poet is making a strong argument? Explain your answer.

4. What does Hughes mean when he says 'people say let things take their course'?

5. Why do you think a poem like this is important?

CALL TO ACTION | Chapter 6

Exercise 63C — Identifying firsts in Irish representation

Key Skills

Success criteria ☐ I can identify when significant historical developments in Irish representation took place.

Timeline of Irish democracy

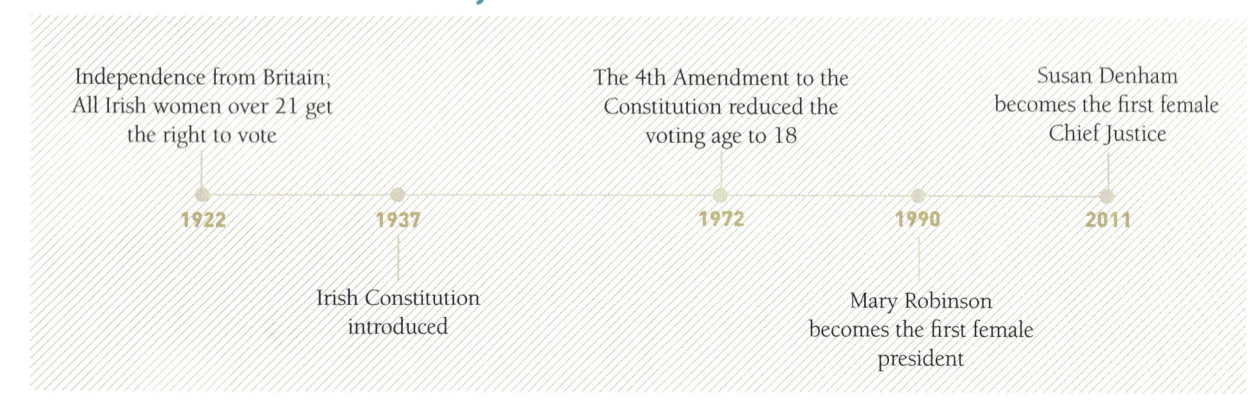

- **1922** — Independence from Britain; All Irish women over 21 get the right to vote
- **1937** — Irish Constitution introduced
- **1972** — The 4th Amendment to the Constitution reduced the voting age to 18
- **1990** — Mary Robinson becomes the first female president
- **2011** — Susan Denham becomes the first female Chief Justice

The timeline above shows some key dates for democracy in Ireland.

- In 1922, Ireland got independence from Britain and all citizens (men and women) over the age of 21 got the right to vote.
- In 1937, the Constitution was passed. An article in the Constitution could be changed only by a vote of the people.
- One such change was the fourth amendment in 1972, which saw the voting age reduced from 21 to 18.
- In 1990, Mary Robinson was elected the first female President of Ireland.
- In 2011, Susan Denham became the first female Chief Justice.

Working in pairs, look at the following firsts in Irish democracy, then see if you can match them to the years in which they happened. Check whether you were correct by researching online.

1. Mary Harney became the first female Tánaiste.	2. When Brian Crowley became a senator there were no facilities for wheelchair users in the Oireachtas.	3. Dr Moosajee Bhamjee was elected as a Labour Party TD for Clare. He was Ireland's first Muslim TD.	4. Leo Varadkar became Ireland's first openly gay Taoiseach.
5. Eileen Flynn became the first Traveller to be a member of the Oireachtas when she became a senator.	6. Máire Geoghegan-Quinn became Ireland's first female EU commissioner.	7. Robert Briscoe became Dublin's first Jewish Lord Mayor.	8. Councillor Uruemu Adejinmi became the first black county mayor in Ireland when she became Mayor of Longford.

1992	1956	1997	1993	2010	2020	2021	2017

Lesson 63: Democracy

Exercise 63D — Analysing the impact of reducing the voting age to 12

Key Skills

Success criteria ☐ I can explain the advantages and disadvantages of reducing the voting age to 12.

Working in pairs, watch the video about the impact of reducing the voting age to 12 and answer the questions below.

> **YouTube** — Go to YouTube and search for 'Should We Let 12-Year-Olds Vote?' (8:07).

1. Who could not vote when the US became independent?
   _____

2. What sounded like a silly question in 1776?
   _____

3. Why did Phyllis Kahn suggest that 12-year-olds should have the right to vote?
   _____

4. To what did she compare the arguments made to not give 12-year-olds the right to vote?
   _____
   _____

5. Why is the question of voting rights for 12-year-olds topical again?
   _____
   _____

6. What do all the young people in the video believe would be different if they had the right to vote?
   _____
   _____

289

LESSON 64 — Decision-making

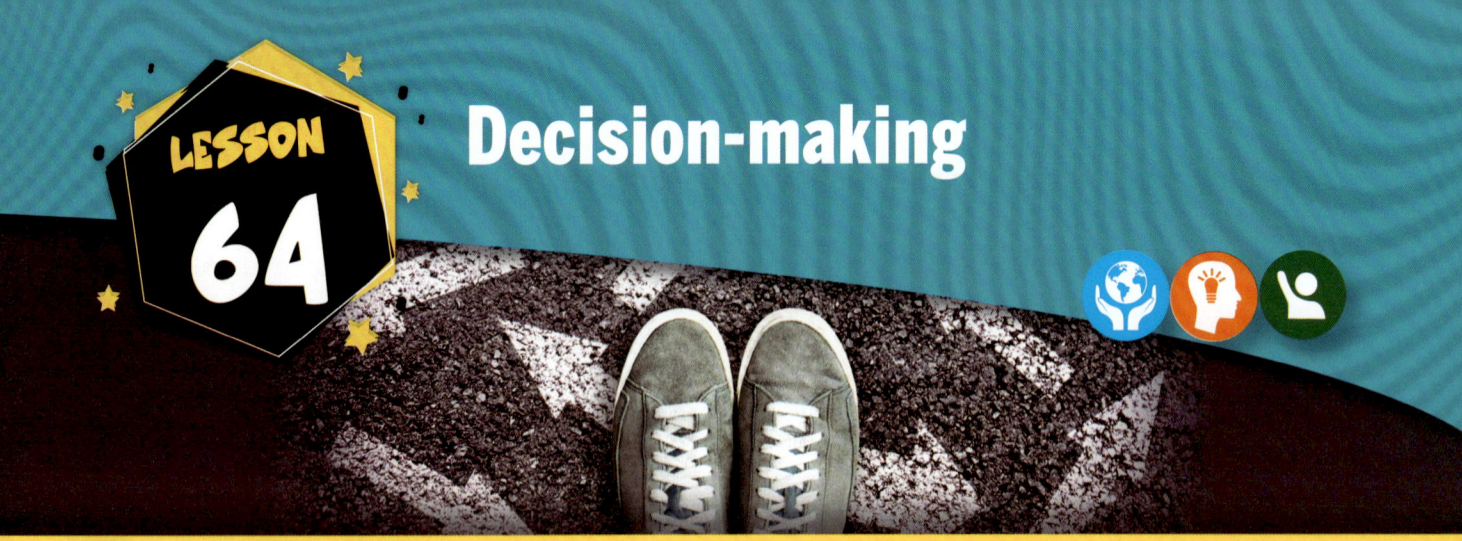

Learning outcome 3.2
Students should be able to describe decision-making processes and the roles of different groups in their class/school.

Exercise 64A — Analysing decision-making in class

Key Skills

Success criteria ☐ I can name situations where I have or do not have a role in decision-making in classes, why I have or do not have a role and what I would do differently if I had a role.

People make decisions all the time: in the morning you decide whether to eat your breakfast before showering. When you come to school, you decide who to speak to, when to enter the school building, whether to put your phone in your pocket or to leave it in your locker. Many decisions are made quickly: you buy a bar because you are hungry or you go inside because it is raining. These are easy decisions to make because the reason for making them is clear. You can decide without having to get the agreement of everyone.

Working in pairs, consider the following areas in your classes at school and decide your level of input in making decisions.

In my classes	Do you have a role in making decisions in this area?	Why/why not?	What would you do differently if you had a role in making the decision?
Where you sit			
Homework			
The books and copies you use			
Tests			

Lesson 64: Decision-making

Exercise 64B Analysing decision-making in school

Key Skills

Success criteria ☐ I can name situations where I have or do not have a role in decision-making in school, why I have or do not have a role and what I would do differently if I had a role.

Working in pairs, consider the following areas of school life and decide your level of input in making decisions.

In my school	Do you have a role in making decisions in this area?	Why/why not?	What would you do differently if you had a role in making the decision?
Uniform			
Timetable			
School rules			
Other areas (name them)			

Exercise 64C Auditing my student council

Key Skills

Success criteria ☐ I can identify the strengths and weaknesses of my student council.

Student councils are meant to allow students have a voice on what is happening in schools. Student councils are consulted on decisions and raise areas of concern with school management.

If your student council representative is part of your class, interview them on their work by asking the questions that are relevant to them and writing their answers below. If your student council representative is not part of your class, discuss the relevant questions in pairs and answer them below.

1. What were the student council representative's/your policies?

   _____
   _____

2. How many candidates ran in the election?

   _____

● CALL TO ACTION | *Chapter 6*

3. How often do you hear from your student council representative?/How often do you tell your class what you are doing in the student council?
   _____

4. What areas does the representative/do you discuss?
   _____

5. How does the student council tell students about its work?
   _____

6. What has the student council delivered for students?
   _____
   _____

7. What has it not delivered?
   _____
   _____

Exercise 64D Evaluating different models of decision-making in schools

Key Skills

Success criteria ☐ I can evaluate the effectiveness of democratic schools by identifying their advantages and disadvantages.

Sometimes decisions are more difficult to make. In these cases, you need to consider the following:
- Do I get to decide?
- What are the options?
- Can I list the positives and negatives of the different options?
- Can I now decide?
- When I think about a decision afterwards, was it correct or what could I have done differently?

Watch the video about democratic education in schools.

> **YouTube**: Go to YouTube and search for 'Democratic School Education – Sprouts' (3:23).

Imagine that the principal has asked your class to make changes in your school so it will be like the democratic schools shown in the video. In groups, discuss the following questions and write the answers.

1. Would you like to go to one of these democratic schools?
   _____

2. What changes would have to be made to your school to make it a democratic school?
   _____
   _____
   _____

Lesson 64: Decision-making

3. What are the advantages of your proposed changes?
   _____
   _____

4. What are the disadvantages?
   _____
   _____

5. Design a brief notice for the school notice board, explaining what the proposed changes are and the reasons why you are making these suggestions.

Lesson 65: Voting

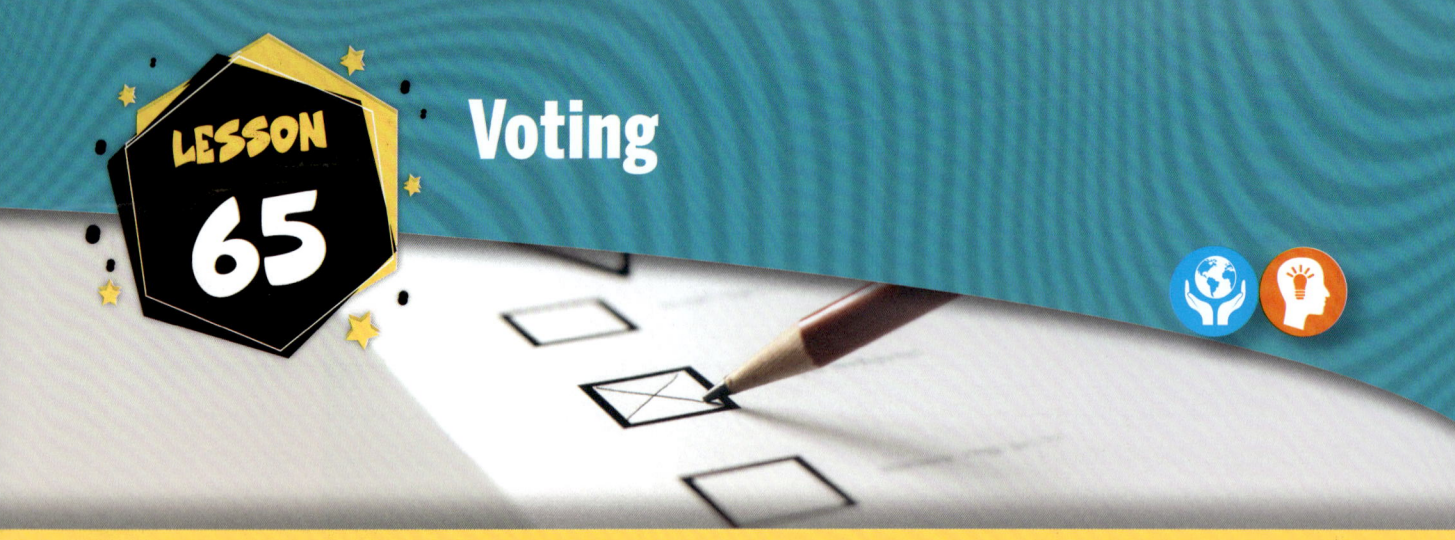

Learning outcome 3.3
Students should be able to describe democratic structures for decision-making at local and national government levels.

Exercise 65A Examining democracy around the world

Key Skills

Success criteria ☐ I can explain differences in the democracies in different countries.

Bhutan is a small kingdom in the Himalayas. In 2005, King Jigme Singye Wangchuck announced that Bhutan would become a democracy and that his son would become king. In 2008, the first elections were held. Many people in Bhutan were nervous about democracy because there had been problems with democracy in other countries in the region. Democratic elections have been held in Bhutan since. However, the constitution remains vague about the king's powers and there is no independent judiciary as the king appoints judges. There is some independent media as there are three private newspapers in the capital.

Australian elections take place every three years and voting is compulsory. The turnout has not fallen below 90% since compulsory voting was introduced. People can vote by postal vote, at overseas voting centres, in hospitals or in nursing homes. People who do not vote are fined $20 unless they provide a valid reason for not voting such as illness, being involved in a car crash or natural disasters. Those who do not pay the fine are referred to court.

Voter turnout: Australia vs Ireland		
Year	Australia	Ireland
2011		70%
2013	93%	
2016	91%	65%
2019	91%	
2020		63%

Lesson 65: Voting

In 2007, Austria became the first European country to lower its voting age to 16 hoping to get young people interested in politics and democracy. Many people criticised this decision saying that 16- and 17-year-olds were too immature to vote. In the 2007 election, 88% of eligible first-time voters voted. While the level of voter participation has since dropped, more young people in Austria turn out to vote than in other European countries.

Elections are rare in Saudi Arabia. Local elections were held in the 1950s and 1960s, but there were no further elections until 2005. Elections were due in 2009, but were not held until 2011. In 2015, women finally received the right to vote and to stand in elections. As Saudi Arabia is an absolute monarchy it has a consultative assembly, rather than a parliament. This means it can only suggest laws, not make them. Political parties are not allowed.

After reading about the different types of government, answer the questions below.

1. Why were people uneasy about democracy coming to Bhutan?

2. In what ways has democracy in Bhutan still got progress to make?

3. What is the penalty in Australia for not voting?

4. Does compulsory voting make people more likely to vote?

5. What made Austria unique in Europe?

6. Do you think Austria's decision was a good one?

7. What progress has Saudi Arabia made towards democracy?

8. Which of the countries do you think is the most democratic? Why?

9. Which is the least democratic? Why?

■ CALL TO ACTION | *Chapter 6*

Exercise 65B Understanding the voting process

Key Skills   **Success criteria**   ☐ I can explain why voting happens in Ireland and the process involved.

At 18, an Irish citizen is eligible to vote but must add their name to the **register** in order to do so. You can check the register online at www.checktheregister.ie, a Garda station or a local library.

Irish citizens can vote in every election and referendum, but some elections are open to people living in Ireland who are not citizens.

- British citizens can vote in Dáil and local elections.
- EU citizens can vote in European and local elections.
- Non-EU citizens can vote in local elections.

Watch the video and answer the questions that follow.

▶ Search online for 'Oireachtas CSPE video' and then click on 'Why vote?' (1:43).

1. For what two reasons may Irish citizens need to vote?

2. Name five types of election.

3. How often must a general election take place?

4. What is a referendum?

5. What do you receive in the post before an election?

6. What is a ballot paper used for?

Exercise 65C Putting the voting process in chronological order

Key Skills   **Success criteria**   ☐ I can explain the order in which the voting process happens.

On the next page, the steps involved in voting have been mixed up. Working in pairs, put them in the correct order. The first one has been done for you.

Lesson 65: Voting

A. You go to the polling booth where you receive a ballot paper.	B. A few days before the election, you receive a polling card in the post.	C. The following day the votes are counted.
D. When you have finished, you fold the ballot paper and put it in the ballot box.	E. The ballot boxes are taken to a counting centre.	F. You vote 1, 2, 3, 4, etc. in order of your preference.
G. You check that your name is on the register of electors.	H. You take the ballot paper to an area where nobody can see what you write on the paper.	I. The clerk checks your ID and crosses your name off the register.

Step 1	Step 2	Step 3	Step 4	Step 5	Step 6	Step 7	Step 8	Step 9
G								

Exercise 65D Analysing an election count

Key Skills   **Success criteria** ☐ I can identify the candidates elected in a constituency.

A candidate must get the same or more votes than the quota to be elected, unless there are no more candidates left. In that case the highest vote left wins.

Look at the results of the 2020 general election for Limerick County and answer the questions.

Limerick County: 3 Seats
Quota: 11,523

Candidate	Party	Count 1	Count 2	Count 3	Count 4	Count 5	Count 6
Patrick O'Donovan	FG	9228	9458	9952	10893	15552	
Niall Collins	FF	8436	8631	8885	11870		
Séighin Ó Ceallaigh	SF	6916	7204	7814	8125	8579	8955
Richard O'Donoghue	Ind	6021	6599	7050	7647	8587	10320
Tom Neville	FG	5810	5970	6358	6765		
Michael Collins	FF	5150	5320	5532			
Claire Keating	GP	2503	2688				
Conor O'Donoghue	Aon	714					
Robert O'Donnell	Ind	402					
Con Cremin	Ind	373					
John Dalton	R	313					
Cristín Ní Mhaoldhomhnaigh	NP	224					

1. What is the quota?

2. Was any candidate elected on the first count? If so, name them.

3. How many candidates were eliminated on the second count?

4. Was any candidate elected on the fourth count? If so, name them.

5. Which three candidates were elected?

Lesson 66: Local government

Learning outcome 3.3
Students should be able to describe democratic structures for decision-making at local and national government levels.

Exercise 66A Reviewing the role of the local authorities

Key Skills | **Success criteria** ☐ I can identify the functions of local authorities.

There are 31 local authorities in Ireland. These are made up of:
- Cork, Dublin and Galway **city councils**
- Limerick and Waterford **city and county councils**
- 26 **county councils**, including three in Dublin (Dún Laoghaire-Rathdown, South Dublin and Fingal).

Dublin City Council represents over half a million people and Leitrim County Council represents the smallest population with just over 30,000 people. Cork County Council covers the largest area and Cork City Council covers the smallest area.

Local authorities are elected every **five** years and are responsible for:
- Roads, trimming hedges, street lights, speed limits, etc.
- Housing
- Libraries
- Planning permission
- Fire services
- Register of electors
- Environmental protection
- Recreational amenities and parks
- Animal control.

The councillors make policy decisions at council meetings, which take place in city or county halls. Local authorities can make **bye-laws**, which include laws on littering or parking. Every year, each council elects a councillor as either **cathaoirleach** or **mayor**. The mayor's/cathaoirleach's role is mostly to act as the public face of the council for the year. The **chief executive** is an employee and is not elected. They are in charge of the day-to-day running of the council, such as employing staff and organising contracts.

Kilkenny County Hall

Lesson 66: Local government

Working in pairs, read the passage below and fill in the blanks by adding the correct words from the box below.

There are _____ councils in Ireland. Local _____ are in charge of many of the _____ in cities and _____. Councils are elected every _____ years. People want to live in _____, quiet areas where there are lots of services such as _____, parks and public _____ being regularly collected. The _____ runs the council and the _____ (known as cathaoirleach in some places) is the public representative of the council. The councils pass _____ to control areas such as parking and _____.

| bins | mayor | bye-laws | services | five | clean | libraries |
| counties | authorities | thirty-one | littering | chief executive |

Exercise 66B Researching my local authority

Key Skills   **Success criteria** ☐ I can research my local authority.

Research your local council and answer the following questions. You will get most of the answers on your local authority's website.

1. Is your local authority a county council, a city council or a city and county council?

2. Name some of your local councillors.

3. Who is the mayor/cathaoirleach?

4. Where does the council meet?

5. How many of the councillors are:
   (a) men? _____
   (b) women? _____

6. List three areas that your local council is in charge of.

299

■ CALL TO ACTION | *Chapter 6*

Exercise 66C — Identifying the role of local authorities in the daily life of local citizens

Key Skills   **Success criteria**   ☐ I can identify the tasks my local council does on a daily basis that are of benefit to local citizens.

YouTube: Go to YouTube and search for 'Your Council, Working for You. Around the Clock' (1:49).

Watch the video and answer the questions.

1. What leisure areas do local councils provide and look after?
   _____
   _____

2. In what areas are local authorities of benefit to tourism?
   _____
   _____

3. What environmentally friendly services do they provide?
   _____

4. In what ways do they keep their area safe?
   _____

5. What cultural activities do they provide?
   _____

Exercise 66D — Creating a poster to raise awareness about the positive work the council does

Key Skills   **Success criteria**   ☐ I can identify the positive work my local council does and create a poster representing this work.

Working in groups, discuss things that make you proud of your local community, for example, the sports and leisure and recycling facilities. How many of these are provided or funded by your local council? Create a poster promoting your community highlighting these positives. You could draw it on the next page or create it using software and print it and stick it on the next page.

What makes you proud of your community?
_____
_____

How many of these are provided by the council?
_____

Lesson 66: Local government

LESSON 67

The government

Learning outcome 3.3
Students should be able to describe democratic structures for decision-making at local and national government levels.

Exercise 67A Classifying the jobs of local, national and European governments

Key Skills **Success criteria** ☐ I can classify different tasks according to the government that has responsibility for them.

Working in pairs, classify the following jobs according to whether they are the responsibility of the local, national or EU governments.

- Manages the libraries
- Decides the rates of income taxes
- Negotiates trade deals with other countries
- Decides on health spending
- In charge of defence
- Cleaning up litter
- Deciding how the education system works
- Providing parks and leisure facilities

Local	National	EU

Exercise 67B Analysing the work of the government

Key Skills **Success criteria** ☐ I can answer questions on the election and composition of a government.

After a general election, the Dáil meets at Leinster House to elect a new head of government, the **Taoiseach**. The main parties nominate their leaders as Taoiseach. The vote is carried out for one person at a time and if a candidate gets more votes in favour than against, they are elected. After receiving their seal of office from the president, the new Taoiseach appoints their **ministers** (the cabinet). Generally, a government needs to have a majority of seats in the Dáil, but sometimes they do not. This is called a **minority government**. In Ireland, one party rarely has enough votes to form

Lesson 67: The government

a government on their own so two or more parties come together in government. This is called a **coalition government**.

The government serves for five years, but if it loses a confidence vote in the Dáil, the Taoiseach must ask the President to dissolve the Dáil. This means that a general election must take place.

The government is made up of the **Taoiseach** and the **cabinet**. The **Tánaiste** is the deputy Taoiseach and is also a minister. They also stand in for the Taoiseach when the Taoiseach is not available. Other people who attend cabinet meetings include the **Attorney General**, who is the government's lawyer and the **Chief Whip** who must ensure that there are enough votes in the Dáil to pass government bills.

Ministers are in charge of making policy decisions, for example, the Minister for Health may decide to ban smoking. The day-to-day running of each government department is carried out by a secretary-general. The secretary-general is the manager of the department and does not change from government to government. Most government departments also have ministers of state, who are sometimes called junior ministers. An example is the Minister of State for European Affairs in the Department of Foreign Affairs. Ministers of state help senior ministers and are often in charge of particular areas within a department or across a few departments.

Leinster House

Read the information given above and answer the questions that follow.

1. How often must an election take place?

2. What is a coalition government?

3. What happens if a government loses a confidence vote?

4. What is the Tánaiste's role in government?

5. What is the Attorney General's role?

6. What does the Chief Whip do?

7. What is a secretary-general's role in a government department?

8. What is a minister of state?

■ CALL TO ACTION | *Chapter 6*

Exercise 67C Identifying members of government and their roles

Key Skills

Success criteria ☐ I can research the government ministers and the government departments.

Research the following current members of cabinet. Look at websites such as gov.ie or Wikipedia and fill in the missing details below.

Position	Person	Political party they represent
1. Taoiseach		
2. Tánaiste		
3. Minister for Finance		
4. Minister for Health		
5. Minister for Education		
6. Minister for Foreign Affairs		
7. Minister for Justice		

Exercise 67D Assessing my knowledge of the government

Key Skills

Success criteria ☐ I can identify the words that best explain how the government works.

Working in pairs, fill in the blanks in the following exercise:

The head of government in Ireland is the _____. The current head of government is called _____ and is the leader of _____. In order to become head of government in Ireland, a person must be elected by a majority in the _____.
Then this person goes to Áras an Uachtaráin to receive their seal of office from the _____. Governments in Ireland are mostly made up of two or more political parties. This is called a _____ government. The deputy head of government is called the _____. The current deputy head of government is _____.
_____ is a political party that is in the government. The head of government and the ministers are also referred to as the _____.

304

Lesson 68: The Oireachtas

Learning outcome 3.4
Students should be able to use the correct terminology to describe Irish and European democratic institutions, structures, political parties and roles.

Exercise 68A Identifying key people and parties in the Dáil

Key Skills

Success criteria ☐ I can identify the key positions and main parties in the Dáil.

The **Oireachtas** is the Irish parliament. It consists of two houses, the **Dáil** and the **Seanad** and meets in **Leinster House** in Dublin. It is responsible for electing a government, holding them to account and passing laws.

The Dáil's main role is passing laws. A member of the Dáil is called a **Teachta Dála** (**TD**) or a **Deputy**. The number of TDs depends on the size of the population. Since the 2020 general election there are 160 TDs. Only Irish citizens aged 21 and over can become a TD.

The Dáil chamber

The **Ceann Comhairle** is the chairperson of the Dáil. They are elected by TDs in a secret ballot in the first meeting after a general election. The Ceann Comhairle does not take part in votes unless there is an equal number of votes in favour and against. In this case, the Ceann Comhairle can use a casting vote and generally votes with the government. A Ceann Comhairle is automatically re-elected in a general election. The Ceann Comhairle:

- Makes sure the Dáil follows the rules for conducting business
- Calls on TDs to speak
- Keeps order in the Dáil
- Organises votes.

Sometimes a confidence vote is held on a minster or a government. If the Dáil votes in favour of no confidence, the minister or government must resign.

There are several political parties in the Dáil, as well as independent TDs who do not belong to any party. The leader of the largest political party not in government is the **leader of the opposition**.

Working in pairs, look at www.oireachtas.ie to find the following information.

1. What constituency do you live in?

2. Name the TDs that represent your constituency.

305

■ CALL TO ACTION | *Chapter 6*

3. Who is the current Ceann Comhairle?

4. Who is the leader of the opposition?

5. Identify the following information about the political parties in the Dáil.

Political party	Party leader	Number of TDs

Exercise 68B Identifying people who can serve as TDs

Key Skills   **Success criteria** ☐ I can identify whether people are eligible to be TDs.

If a councillor is elected as a TD, they must resign their council seat, and if an MEP is elected to the Dáil they must resign as an MEP or vice versa. Serving Gardaí, serving members of the defence forces, serving judges and most serving civil servants (people who work in a government office) cannot be TDs. If a TD is sentenced to a prison sentence of over six months, they can no longer be a TD.

Working in pairs, decide whether the following can be TDs. Answer by saying Yes if … or No unless … and explain what needs to happen in order for them to be a TD.

	Can this person be a TD?	
	Yes/No	No unless …
1. Barbara Smith (19) wants to stand in next year's general election.		
2. The Lord Mayor of Dublin was elected to the Dáil.		
3. Rachel Lewis, a 28-year-old Garda sergeant, wants to run for the Dáil.		
4. Clinton Moore, a US national, wants to stand for the Dáil to protest against Ireland's tax system.		
5. An MEP was elected to the Dáil in a by-election.		

Lesson 68: The Oireachtas

Exercise 68C Examining the work of a TD

Key Skills

Success criteria ☐ I can distinguish between a TD's local and national roles.

TDs work **locally** and **nationally**. Their local work might involve asking questions of ministers in the Dáil for their constituents (people living in their constituency), such as what the government are doing for workers in a factory that is going to close. TDs' national job means they pass laws and the budget every year, they elect a government and they sit on committees that advise the Dáil on specialist areas, such as finance and health. A TD cannot be arrested going to or from the Oireachtas. They cannot be sued for defamation (damaging someone's good reputation) for any allegations they make in the Dáil.

Working in pairs, look at the work of a fictional TD and decide whether the tasks she does are related to her local work or her national work.

Miriam Jones is a TD for Mayo and is a member of the opposition party in the Dáil. These are just some of the jobs she did this week. For each, decide whether it is national or local work.

	Local or national?	Reason for your choice
1. She asked the Minister for Education about the closure of a one-teacher school in Mayo.		
2. She suggested an amendment to the Employment Equality Acts in a Dáil Committee meeting.		
3. She voted against the budget because it does nothing for pensioners.		
4. She organised a meeting in Ballina to generate tourism in the area.		
5. She met a representative of an organisation campaigning to pass a new law on patients' rights.		

● CALL TO ACTION | *Chapter 6*

Exercise 68D Understanding the role of the Seanad

Key Skills   **Success criteria**   ☐ I can explain the role of the Seanad and how its members are elected.

All bills must pass through the **Seanad** before they can be signed into law by the President. The Seanad can delay bills rather than blocking them from becoming law. Members of the Seanad can suggest changes to all bills, except finance bills.

The Seanad chamber

A member of the Seanad is called a senator. The **Cathaoirleach** of the Seanad chairs meetings and is a member of the **Council of State**, which advises the President. Elections to the Seanad are indirect, which means that voters do not choose between candidates for an office, but elect people who then choose. They are elected in the following way:

- Some members are elected to panels by TDs, outgoing senators and county and city councillors.
- Graduates of UCD, UCC, NUIG, Maynooth University and Trinity College elect members.
- The Taoiseach selects the final senators, which can help the government to have a majority in the Seanad.

Sometimes the Taoiseach's appointments or university senators are experts in areas such as law, medicine and economics. Up to two senators can be ministers in government, but they cannot be Taoiseach, Tánaiste or Minister for Finance. It is very rare that senators become ministers. In 2020, Senator Pippa Hackett became Minister of State for Agriculture with responsibility for land use and biodiversity.

Senator Pippa Hackett

After the 2020 election, there were 24 female senators (40%) and 36 female TDs (22.5%).

> **YouTube** Go to YouTube and search for 'Seanad Éireann Tour – English Version' (2:27).

Watch the video and read the text about the Seanad. Answer the questions that follow (questions 1–4 are based on the video).

1. How many senators are in Seanad Éireann?

2. How many panels are senators elected from?

3. How many senators represent the universities?

4. When must an election to Seanad Éireann take place?

5. Can you think of any advantage of having experts in the Seanad?

6. Why does the Taoiseach get to choose the final 11 senators?

7. Can a senator become a minister?

8. Why do you think women are better represented in the Seanad than in the Dáil?

Lesson 69: The Constitution and the President

Learning outcome 3.4
Students should be able to use the correct terminology to describe Irish and European democratic institutions, structures, political parties and roles.

Exercise 69A — Analysing an advertisement from the Referendum Commission

Key Skills

Success criteria ☐ I can explain the role of the Referendum Commission by analysing an advertisement.

The Irish Constitution, also known as **Bunreacht na hÉireann**, was passed by the people in 1937 and is the most important source of law in the State.

- Articles 1–39 of the Constitution explain how the government, Oireachtas, presidency and the courts operate.
- Articles 40–44 explain the rights that every person is entitled to.

Any changes to the Constitution must be passed by a **referendum** of the people. A referendum is held only when a bill proposing the changes is passed by both the Dáil and the Seanad. An independent **Referendum Commission** is responsible for:

- Providing information about what the proposed changes will mean and what they will not mean. They do this by placing adverts online and in the media and by posting a guide to homes.
- Making people aware that the referendum is taking place
- Encouraging people to vote.

In 2015, a referendum was held on whether to reduce the age at which a person could become president from 35 to 21. In the referendum, 73% of voters voted against reducing the age.

Some amendments to the Constitution change the law, others change the institutions responsible for law. In 2013, two referendums were put to the people: one to introduce the Court of Appeal was accepted, but the other to abolish the Seanad was rejected.

> **YouTube**: Go to YouTube and search for 'The Court of Appeal Referendum – Main Changes – Referendum 2013' (1:50).

Working in pairs, watch the Referendum Commission advert for the 2013 Court of Appeal Referendum and answer the questions on the next page (questions 1–4 are based on the video).

● CALL TO ACTION | *Chapter 6*

1. What does the announcement tell us about what is in the advert?

2. What does the first speaker tell you about the referendums?

3. What do you learn about the Court of Appeal?

4. If you want to find out more detail, what can you do?

5. What are the Referendum Commission's responsibilities?

6. Would this advert have any effect on how you would vote? Explain why.

Exercise 69B   Assessing my knowledge of the Constitution

Key Skills   **Success criteria** ☐ I can identify correct and incorrect statements relating to the Constitution.

Only Irish citizens aged 18 and over who are registered to vote can vote in a referendum.

The ballot paper on the right was used for the referendum on removing blasphemy as an offence. In referendums, you either vote yes or no. If the majority of votes are in favour of changing the Constitution, the President signs the bill into law and the Constitution is changed.

Working in pairs, discuss whether each of the statements about the Constitution on the next page is true or false (you will probably have to guess some of the answers).

An bhfuil tú ag toiliú leis an togra chun an Bunreacht a leasú atá sa Bhille thíosluaite?

Do you approve of the proposal to amend the Constitution contained in the undermentioned Bill?

An Bille um an Seachtú Leasú is Tríocha ar an mBunreacht (Cion a aisghairm arb éard é ní diamhaslach a fhoilsiú nó a aithris), 2018

Thirty-seventh Amendment of the Consitution (Repeal of offence of publication or utterance of blasphemous matter) Bill 2018

Ná cuir marc **ach san aon chearnóg amháin**
Place a mark in **one square only**

Má thoilíonn tú, cuir X sa chearnóg seo ....
If you **approve**, mark X in this square ....   **Tá / Yes**

Mura dtoilíonn tú, cuir X sa chearnóg seo ....
If you do **not approve**, mark X in this square ....   **Níl / No**

310

		True	False
1.	The first national language is Irish.		
2.	A person can be tried only in a criminal case by a court of law or an Oireachtas committee.		
3.	A president can be removed from office if five Supreme Court judges declare them to be incapacitated.		
4.	Where only one candidate is nominated to be president, no election takes place.		
5.	The president cannot leave the country without the government's approval.		
6.	The Oireachtas can impose any penalty, including the death penalty, for a crime.		
7.	A majority of senators and a third of TDs can ask the president not to sign a bill into law and instead call a referendum of the people.		
8.	The government has the power to declare war without the consent of the Oireachtas.		

Exercise 69C — Examining my knowledge of the presidency

Key Skills

Success criteria ☐ I can assess my knowledge of the presidency.

The **president** is the head of state in Ireland and is elected by the people. To run for president, a person must be 35 or older and must get:

- The nomination of 20 members of the Oireachtas

  OR

- A nomination from four local authorities.

An outgoing president can nominate themselves.

If only one candidate is nominated, they become president without an election. The presidential term of office is seven years, and the president can run for a second term. The two main powers the president has are:

1. If the government loses a vote of confidence in the Dáil, the president can decide whether to allow an election to take place or to see if it is possible to form an alternative government.

2. Following consultation with the Council of State, the president can decide to refer a bill to the Supreme Court to check if it is constitutional.

Every bill must be signed by the president before it becomes a law. However, the president cannot refuse to sign a bill unless they think it is unconstitutional.

Working in pairs, tick the correct answers in the quiz below:

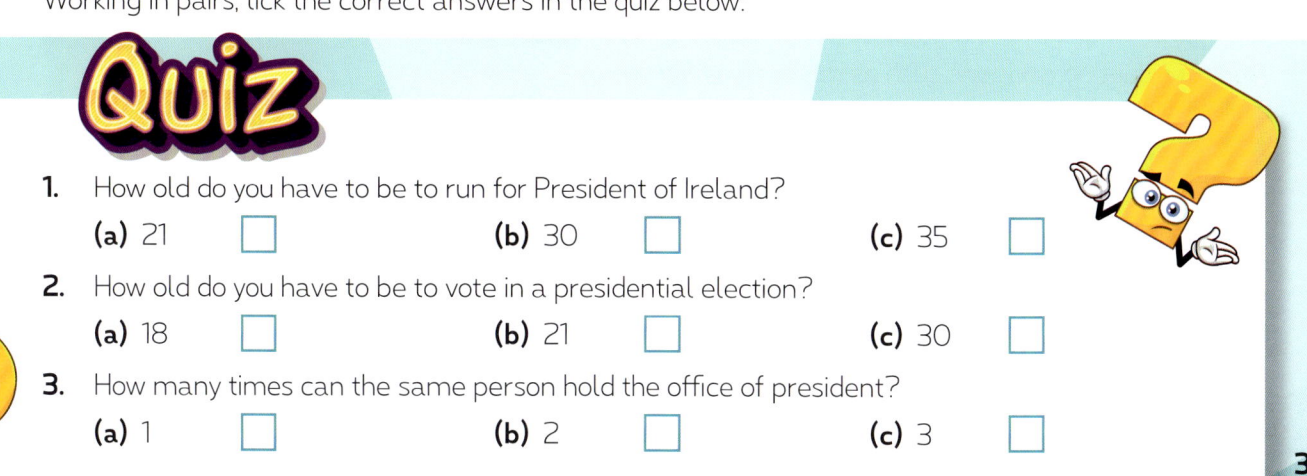

Quiz

1. How old do you have to be to run for President of Ireland?
   (a) 21 ☐ (b) 30 ☐ (c) 35 ☐

2. How old do you have to be to vote in a presidential election?
   (a) 18 ☐ (b) 21 ☐ (c) 30 ☐

3. How many times can the same person hold the office of president?
   (a) 1 ☐ (b) 2 ☐ (c) 3 ☐

■ CALL TO ACTION | *Chapter 6*

4. How long is the president's term of office?

   (a) 4 years   (b) 5 years   (c) 7 years

5. Where does the president live?

   (a) Áras an Uachtaráin   (b) Farmleigh House   (c) Leinster House

6. What is the name of the group of people who advise the president?

   (a) The OPW
   (b) The Council of State
   (c) The Council of Presidential Advisers

7. The president has two main powers. Which of the following is **not** one of those powers?

   (a) The power to dissolve the Dáil
   (b) The power to refer bills to the Supreme Court
   (c) The power to refuse to sign a bill into law

8. There are three ways in which a person can receive a nomination to run in a presidential election. Which of the following is **not** one of these ways?

   (a) A petition of 20,000 citizens
   (b) A nomination from 20 members of the Oireachtas
   (c) A nomination from four local authorities

Exercise 69D Analysing the composition of the Council of State

Key Skills   **Success criteria**   ☐ I can analyse the composition of the Council of State.

The president's residence is **Áras an Uachtaráin** in the Phoenix Park in Dublin.

If the president is absent, resigns, is removed from office or dies, a **Presidential Commission** carries out the president's functions. This is made up of the Chief Justice, the Ceann Comhairle of the Dáil and the Cathaoirleach of the Seanad.

The **Council of State** is a group of people who advise the president on decisions such as referring a bill to the Supreme Court. The Council is made up of:

Áras an Uachtaráin

- The Taoiseach, the Tánaiste, the Chief Justice, the Presidents of the Court of Appeal and the High Court, the Ceann Comhairle, the Cathaoirleach of the Seanad and the Attorney General
- Former Taoisigh, former presidents and former Chief Justices
- Up to seven members appointed by the president. In 2019, President Higgins nominated the following seven members:

1. Dr Cara Augustenborg: environmental scientist
2. Sinéad Burke: writer and disability activist
3. Dr Sindy Joyce: sociologist and the first Traveller to earn a PhD in Ireland
4. Maurice Malone: Birmingham Irish Association CEO
5. Dr Johnston McMaster: former co-ordinator of Education for Reconciliation in Northern Ireland
6. Dr Mary Murphy: lecturer in Irish Politics and Society
7. Seán Ó Cuirreáin: former Irish Language Commissioner

Look at the list of members of the Council of State appointed in 2019. Then answer the questions that follow.

1. In what ways are the Council members qualified to advise the president on whether to refer a bill to the Supreme Court?

2. What are the advantages of having former politicians and judges on the Council of State?

3. What is the advantage of the president being able to make their own appointments?

4. Is there any major group of people not represented on the Council of State?

5. Are there any areas of expertise that you would add to the Council of State if you were president?

6. Name the seven people you would appoint to the Council of State.

Lesson 70: EU institutions

Learning outcome 3.4
Students should be able to use the correct terminology to describe Irish and European democratic institutions, structures, political parties and roles.

Exercise 70A — Examining my knowledge of the EU

Key Skills **Success criteria** ☐ I can assess my knowledge of the EU.

The European Economic Community (EEC) was set up by the Treaty of Rome in 1957 and by 1993 a single market had been formed. This allowed free movement of goods, money, services and people within the member states of the EEC. It brought cooperation between countries in Europe to prevent any more devastating wars like World Wars I and II.

The EEC established a common agricultural policy to guarantee farmers a good price for their products. Under the 1993 Treaty of Maastricht, the EEC became the EU to show that it involved more than just economic union.

Working in pairs, tick the correct answers in the quiz below (you will probably have to guess some of the answers).

Quiz

1. What treaty created the European Economic Community (the original name for the EU)?
   - (a) the Treaty of Dublin ☐
   - (b) the Treaty of Versailles ☐
   - (c) the Treaty of Rome ☐
2. When is Europe Day celebrated each year?
   - (a) 17 March ☐
   - (b) 9 May ☐
   - (c) 24 October ☐
3. What are the ministers in the EU government called?
   - (a) Commissioners ☐
   - (b) MEPs ☐
   - (c) Ministers ☐
4. How many original members were in the EEC?
   - (a) 6 ☐
   - (b) 8 ☐
   - (c) 12 ☐
5. When did Ireland join the EEC?
   - (a) 1957 ☐
   - (b) 1973 ☐
   - (c) 1993 ☐

Lesson 70: EU institutions

6. What is the government of the EU?

    (a) the European Commission ☐ (b) the European Parliament ☐ (c) the Court of Auditors ☐

7. Which of the following is the correct EU flag?

    (a) ☐   (b) ☐   (c) ☐

8. Where does the European Parliament meet?

    (a) Strasbourg and Lisbon ☐ (b) Paris and Berlin ☐ (c) Brussels and Strasbourg ☐

Exercise 70B — Analysing the role of EU Institutions

Key Skills

Success criteria ☐ I can analyse information and explain the role of EU institutions.

Any country applying to join the EU must be democratic, obey the rule of law, have a functioning market economy and be able to implement EU laws. Since 1957, the EU has grown on six occasions with 10 members joining in 2004. Only one member, the UK, has left the EU.

There are three main decision-making bodies in the EU: the **EU Commission**, the **Council of Ministers** and the **European Parliament**.

1. The EU Commission is the government of the EU and proposes and enforces laws. Each member state appoints a **commissioner** who serves a five-year term and their appointment must be approved by the European Parliament. One of the 27 commissioners serves as **President of the Commission**. The Commission is based in the Berlaymont building in Brussels.

The Berlaymont Building

2. The **Council of the European Union**, generally known as the **Council of Ministers**, and the European Parliament must jointly agree the EU budget and any new laws before they can become law. The Council is a meeting of ministers of the 27 member states. The ministers attending depends on the topic being discussed. For example, environment ministers meet when environmental policies are being discussed. Some topics, such as tax and foreign policy, require a **unanimous** vote (every member votes to accept), but most decisions are taken by a qualified majority vote. This means that any decisions passed by the Council must be agreed by at least 55% of the member states and these states must represent at least 65% of the population of the EU. The President of the European Council organises and chairs meetings to find agreement between member states and reports back to the European Parliament after each meeting.

3. The **European Parliament** is made up of **MEPs** from each member country, who are directly elected by the people every five years. The number of MEPs a country has depends on population but no country can have fewer than six or more than 96.

● CALL TO ACTION | *Chapter 6*

In Ireland, European Parliament and local elections are held on the same day. The parliament meets in Strasbourg and Brussels. The head of the parliament is the President of the European Parliament. Unlike national parliaments, the European Parliament cannot suggest new laws, it can only debate laws introduced by the Commission and cannot reject the EU budget.

Read the information on the three main decision-making bodies of the EU and answer the questions below.

The European Parliament Building

1. What is the role of the Commission?
   _____
   _____

2. Find out who Ireland's commissioner is.
   _____

3. Who is the President of the European Commission?
   _____

4. What type of ministers would meet in the Council of Ministers if the topic under discussion was the EU budget?
   _____

5. If there was a proposal on tax that 26 members agreed with, but one member did not, what would happen?
   _____
   _____

6. In what way is the European Parliament different to national parliaments?
   _____

7. What advantage do countries with large populations like Germany and France have in the parliament?
   _____

Exercise 70C   Reviewing my knowledge of the EU

Key Skills   **Success criteria**   ☐ I can answer questions that test my understanding of the EU.

Nineteen EU member states are part of the **eurozone** which means they use the euro as their currency. The euro came into circulation in 2002 and is the second most traded currency in the world. The **European Central Bank** is one of the key European institutions and works independently of governments to ensure price stability, control money supply, decide interest rates and ensure that banks are functioning properly.

Eurozone members are shown in blue.

Lesson 70: EU institutions

The **EU Court of Auditors** is in charge of ensuring that EU funds are spent properly and can audit any person or organisation dealing with EU funds. The **EU Court of Justice** rules on how to interpret EU law and ensures that member states apply EU laws in the same way.

Working in pairs, complete the crossword below using information learned in this lesson.

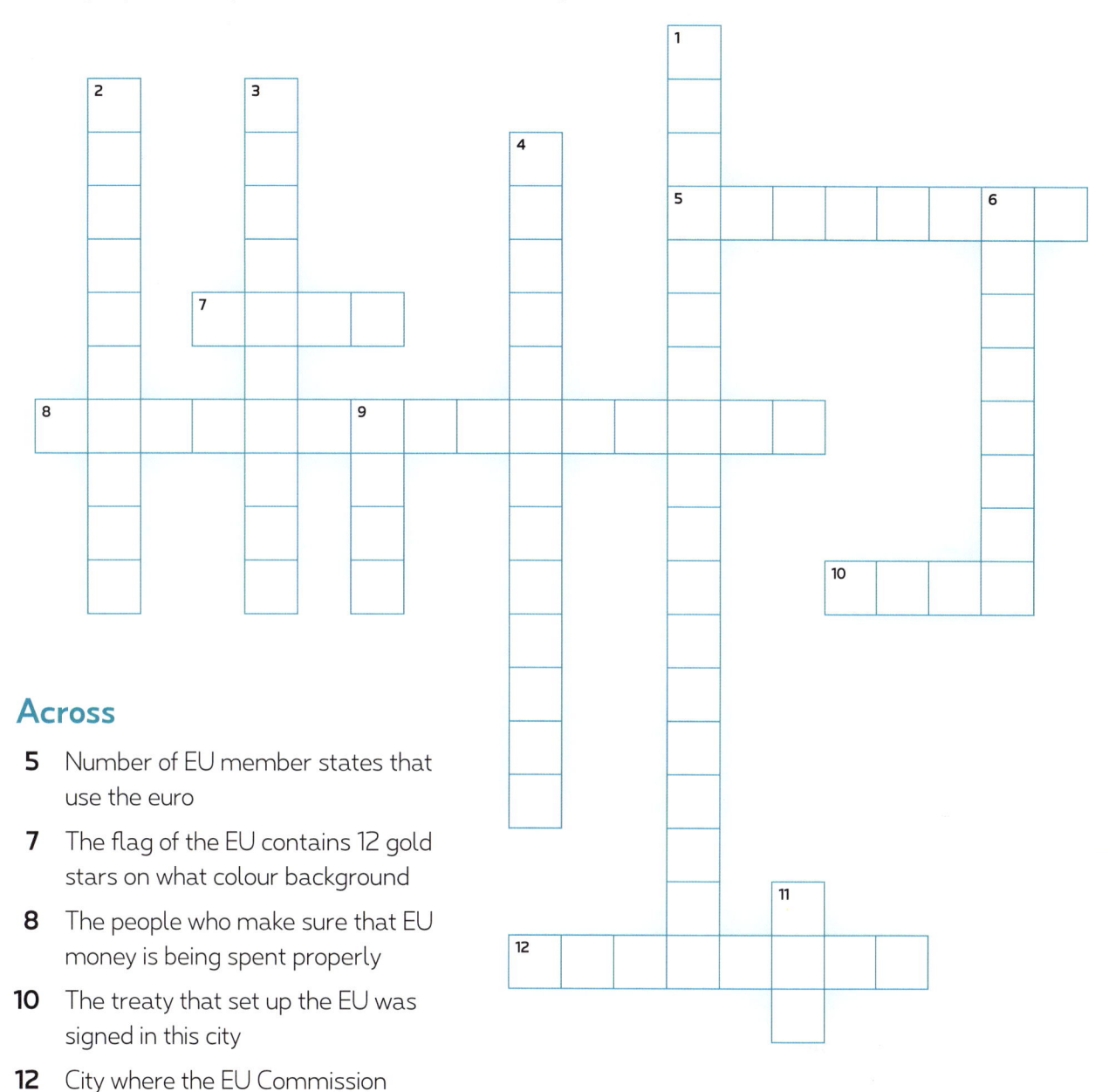

Across

5   Number of EU member states that use the euro

7   The flag of the EU contains 12 gold stars on what colour background

8   The people who make sure that EU money is being spent properly

10 The treaty that set up the EU was signed in this city

12 City where the EU Commission is based

Down

1   Laws must be agreed by the European Parliament and the …

2   The European Parliament meets in Brussels and what other city?

3   The number of seats a country has in the European Parliament is based on …

4   The only country to have left the EU is the …

6   Term given to the countries that use the euro as their currency

9   The number of years an EU Commissioner serves

11 Person elected to the European Parliament

■ CALL TO ACTION | *Chapter 6*

Exercise 70D **Identifying the advantages and disadvantages of the EU**

Key Skills **Success criteria** ☐ I can categorise the advantages and disadvantages of EU membership.

Working in pairs, read the statements below and categorise them as advantages or disadvantages. For the disadvantages discuss and note what could be done to improve these.

1. Since the EU was founded there have been no wars between member states.
2. Many people have moved to Ireland from other EU member states and work in essential jobs.
3. With over 400 million people living in the EU, Irish businesses have a huge market for their goods.
4. The European Commission is not democratically elected.
5. The EU promotes environmental protection and has led to cleaner beaches, etc.
6. EU citizens can live and travel anywhere in the EU without a visa.
7. Ireland is the only English-speaking member of the EU.
8. Smaller countries are poorly represented in the European Parliament.
9. The EU takes a long time to make decisions because it must get agreement from so many groups.
10. Nineteen EU members use the euro, which makes trade and travel easier in the EU.

Advantages of EU membership	Disadvantages of EU membership: How could this disadvantage be improved?

Lesson 71

Systems of democratic government

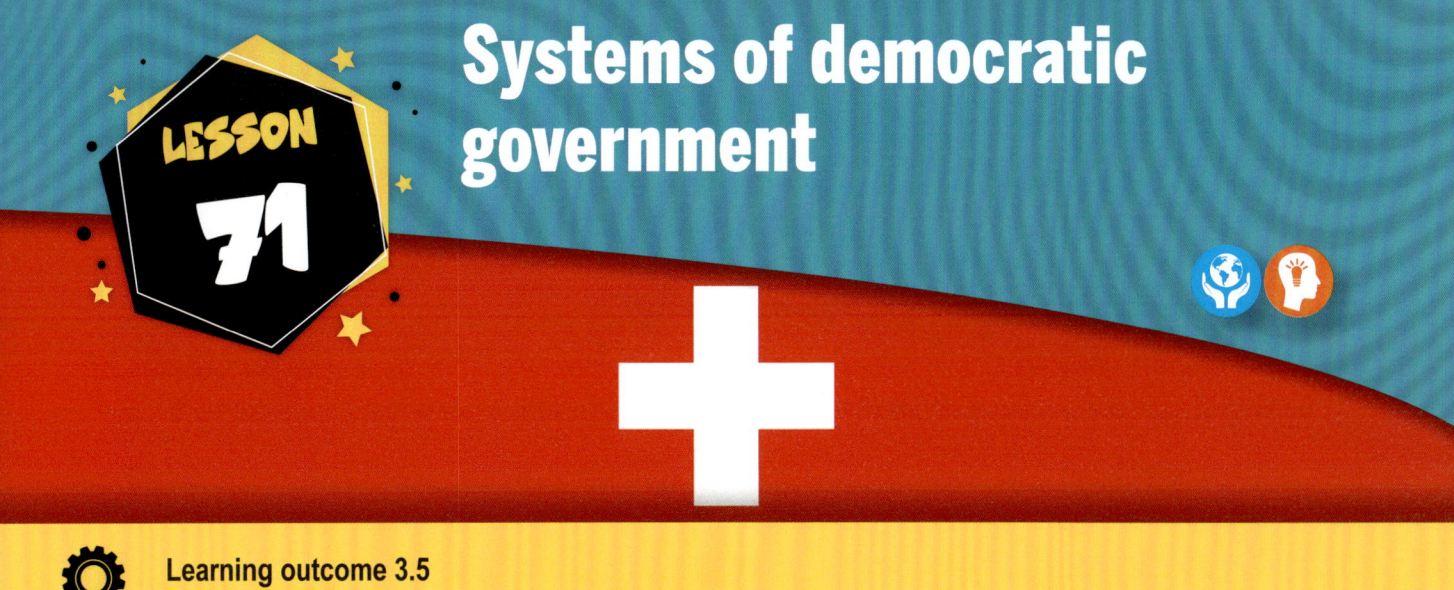

Learning outcome 3.5

Students should be able to compare two or more systems of government, taking particular note of the ways in which the state interacts with its citizens, and citizens can shape their state.

Exercise 71A Understanding direct democracy and federalism

Key Skills

Success criteria ☐ I can explain how direct democracy and federalism work in Switzerland.

Switzerland is a wealthy country known for banking, watchmaking, being a tax haven and neutrality. The population is 8.7 million. Switzerland only granted women the right to vote in 1971 and only joined the UN in 2002. It has not joined the EU.

Switzerland is a **federal** republic with 26 cantons. Decisions are taken at three levels:

1. **Federal** (national) – The two houses of parliament make laws. The Federal Council is a seven-member cabinet elected by the parliament. The President of the Confederation is elected from the seven members and rotates each year. The Federal Court is the judiciary.
2. **Canton** (state) – Each canton has a parliament, government and court system.
3. **Municipality** (community) – There are 2,222 municipalities in Switzerland.

Switzerland is a **direct democracy** which means that people may challenge laws made by parliament in a referendum if they raise 50,000 signatures. A **people's initiative** is when 100,000 people propose an amendment to the Swiss Constitution. Freedom of the press is guaranteed in the Swiss Constitution.

Working in pairs, read the information above, watch the video on Switzerland and answer the questions that follow.

> **YouTube** Go to YouTube and search for 'Switzerland's direct democracy' (5:54).

1. At what three levels do Swiss people make decisions?

2. What is a *landsgemeinde*?

■ CALL TO ACTION | *Chapter 6*

3. Mention two of the things the Swiss people can vote on.
   _____
   _____

4. How often is the national (federal) parliament elected?
   _____

5. How is a people's initiative different to a referendum to overturn a law passed by parliament?
   _____
   _____

6. What advantages of direct democracy are mentioned?
   _____
   _____

7. What disadvantages are mentioned?
   _____
   _____

8. Name a controversial people's initiative that was passed.
   _____

9. What must the parliament do when a people's initiative has been passed?
   _____

10. Why is Switzerland not higher on the democracy barometer?
    _____

Exercise 71B — Analysing democracy and its impact on wealth

Key Skills   **Success criteria** ☐ I can explain how democracy impacts wealth.

Working in pairs, look at the graph, which shows GDP per capita (the wealth per resident) in a range of countries. Then answer the questions that follow.

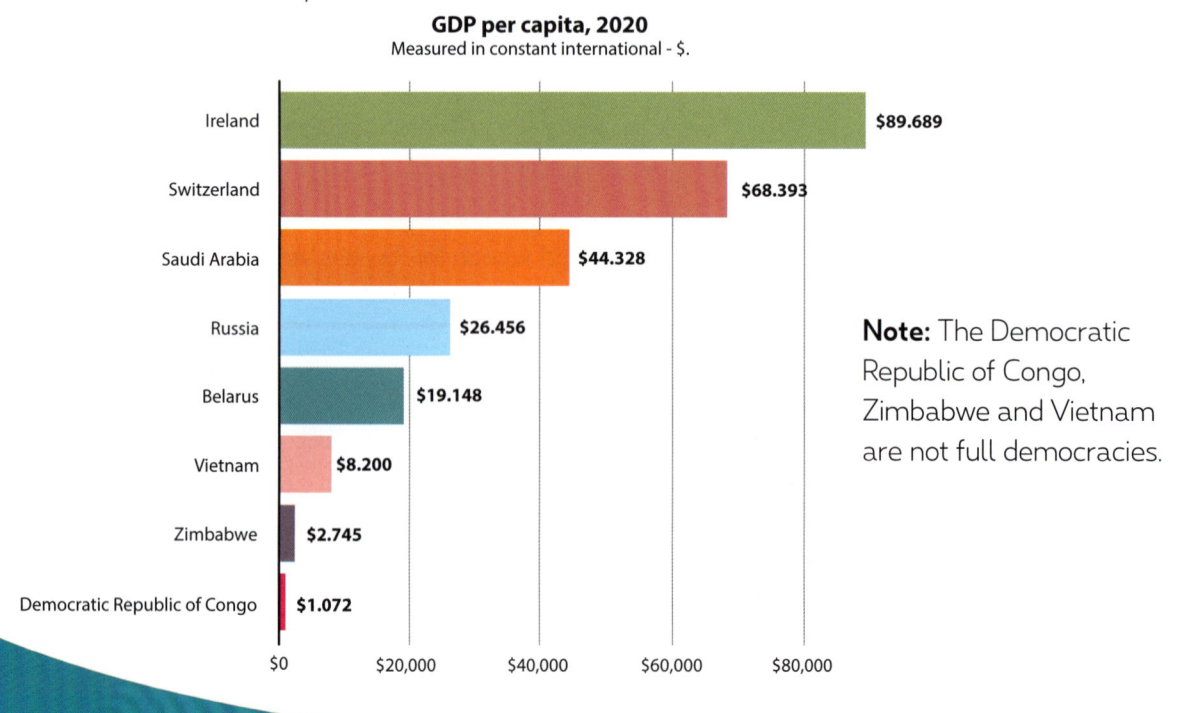

GDP per capita, 2020
Measured in constant international - $.

Country	GDP per capita
Ireland	$89.689
Switzerland	$68.393
Saudi Arabia	$44.328
Russia	$26.456
Belarus	$19.148
Vietnam	$8.200
Zimbabwe	$2.745
Democratic Republic of Congo	$1.072

Note: The Democratic Republic of Congo, Zimbabwe and Vietnam are not full democracies.

320

Lesson 71: Systems of democratic government

1. Which of these countries are most democratic?
   _____

2. Which are least democratic?
   _____

3. What does the GDP per capita chart tell you about:
   (a) Switzerland? _____
   (b) Ireland? _____
   (c) Zimbabwe? _____

4. Why do you think that the GDP per capita tends to be lower in countries with authoritarian governments?
   _____

Exercise 71C Identifying forms of government

Key Skills **Success criteria** ☐ I can match types of governments with countries.

There are several different types of government, which include:

- **Totalitarianism** – the government controls everything, even people's private lives
- **Authoritarianism** – the government rules by fear, often backed up by the police and army
- **Absolute monarchy** – a king or queen rules without consulting anybody else
- **Constitutional monarchy** – there is a king or queen but the decisions are made by the parliament
- **Constitutional republic** – the government, parliament and president are elected and there is a written constitution to prevent any one person or group from holding all the power. In a **presidential republic**, the president is the most powerful person; in a **parliamentary republic** the prime minister is the most powerful person.
- **Direct democracy** – citizens are consulted directly about decisions by voting in referendums and may overturn laws made by parliament
- **Anarchy** – there is no government structure, no order and no rules.

Write the type of government each of the following countries has.

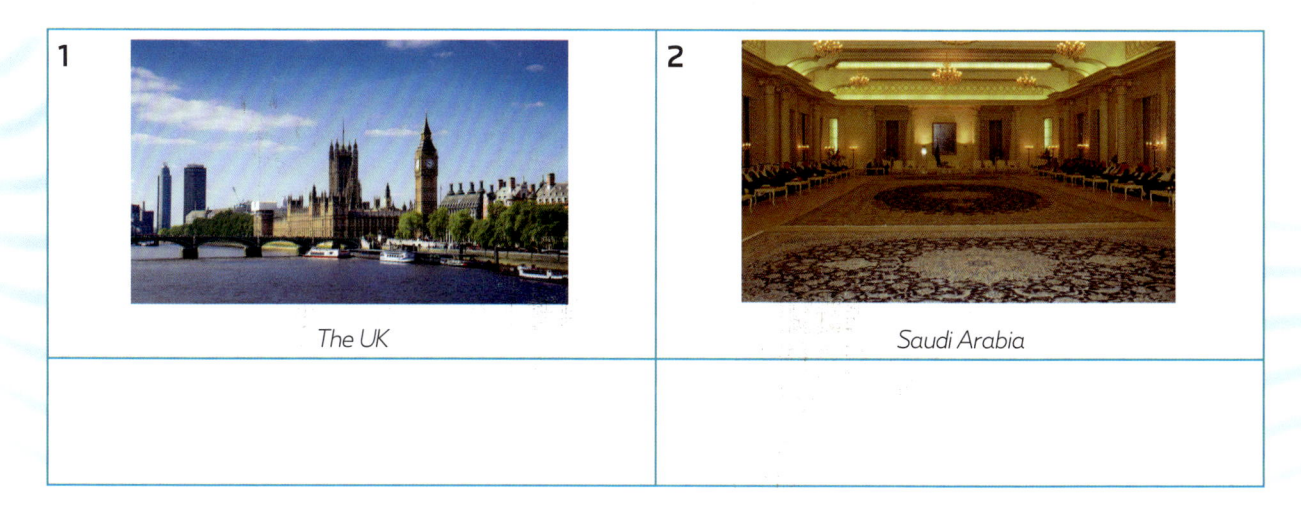

1	2
The UK	Saudi Arabia

321

● CALL TO ACTION | *Chapter 6*

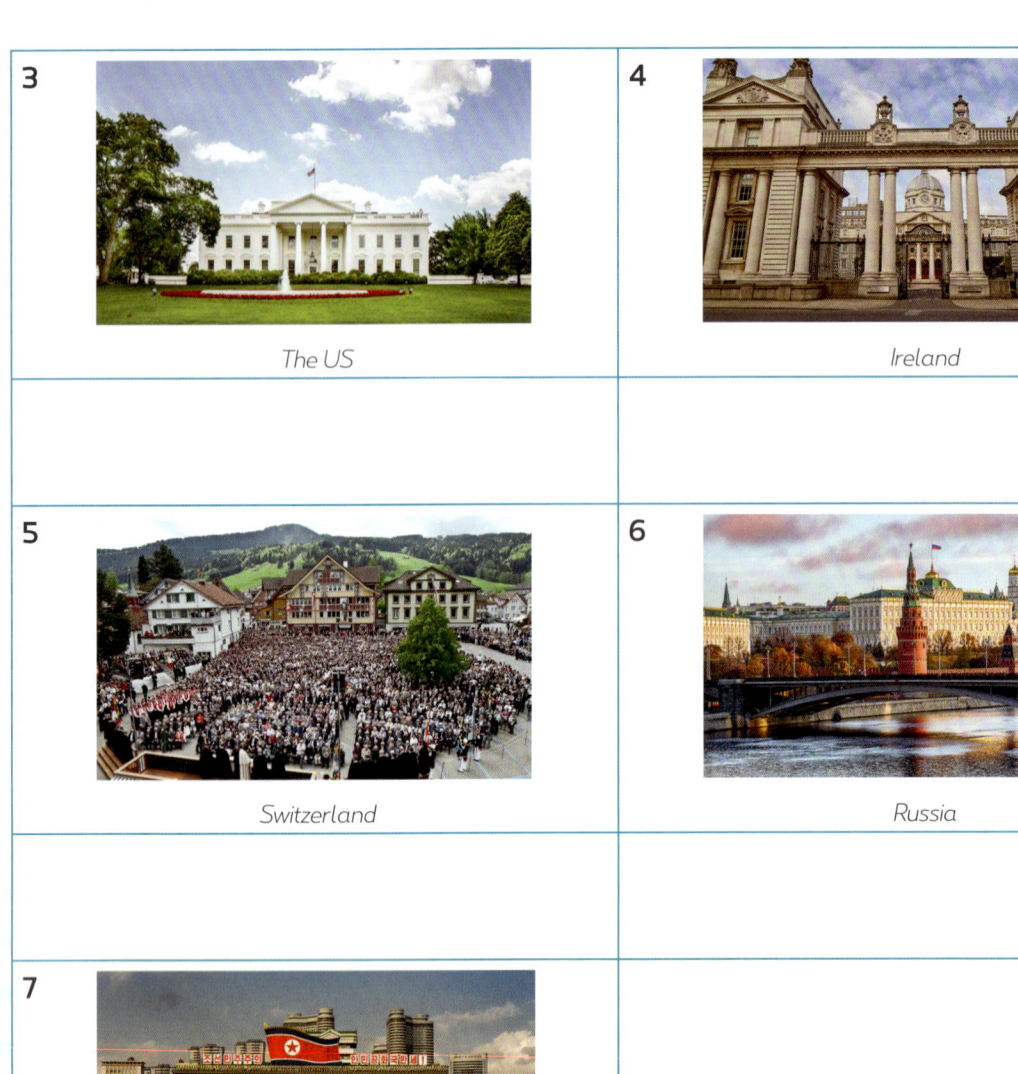

3	4
The US	Ireland

5	6
Switzerland	Russia

7	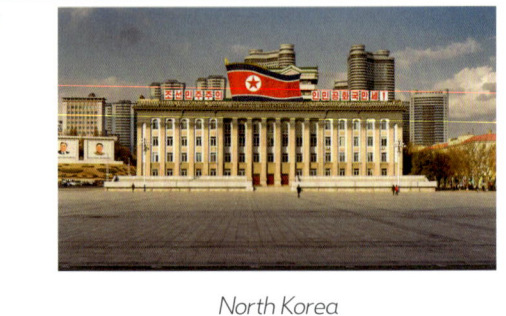
North Korea	

Exercise 71D **Understanding the difference between direct democracy and representative democracy**

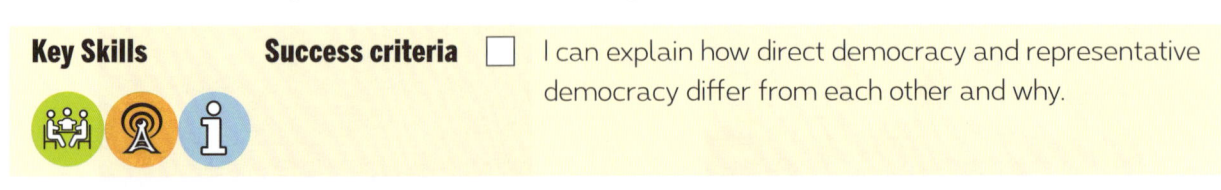

Key Skills **Success criteria** ☐ I can explain how direct democracy and representative democracy differ from each other and why.

Working in pairs, watch the video and answer the questions on the next page.

> YouTube — Go to YouTube and search for 'Contrasting Direct and Representative Democracy - A-Level Politics Revision Video - Study Rocket' (2:10).

Lesson 71: Systems of democratic government

1. What are the basic principles of democracy?

2. Where did direct democracy start?

3. What made it more manageable there?

4. What is a form of direct democracy we use in Ireland today?

5. What is representative, or indirect, democracy?

6. What happens if representatives do not represent the people who elected them?

7. Which form of democracy do you think is better? Why?

8. Do you think direct democracy could work in Ireland? Why?

Lesson 72

Case study: Turkmenistan

Learning outcome 3.5
Students should be able to compare two or more systems of government, taking particular note of the ways in which the state interacts with its citizens, and citizens can shape their state.

Exercise 72A Identifying similarities and differences between Turkmenistan and Ireland

Key Skills **Success criteria** ☐ I can identify similarities and differences between Turkmenistan and Ireland.

Turkmenistan is a country situated in central Asia with a population of 5.5 million people. Its largest natural resource is natural gas. Turkmenistan is a presidential republic, which means that the president is head of state and head of government. Since 2016, the president is elected for a seven-year term and a previous age limit of 70 has been removed.

Citizens are allowed to set up political parties under the Constitution of 2008. The Constitution also allows freedom of the press. Judges are appointed by the president for five-year periods. Turkmenistan's parliament has two houses. Forty-eight members of the 56-seat upper chamber are indirectly elected by regional electors and eight are selected by the president. The 125-seat lower chamber is elected by the people.

Lesson 72: Case study: Turkmenistan

Look at the information about Turkmenistan and answer the questions that follow.

1. How do the populations of Turkmenistan and Ireland compare?
   _____

2. Is Ireland a presidential republic? Explain your answer.
   _____

3. What are the similarities between the Irish and Turkmen constitutions in how the president is elected?
   _____

4. Does the Turkmen Constitution allow other political parties?
   _____

5. How are Turkmenistan and Ireland's parliaments similar?
   _____
   _____

Exercise 72B Analysing the presentation of the Turkmen president

Key Skills **Success criteria** ☐ I can identify propaganda in the presentation of the Turkmen president.

Gurbanguly Berdimuhamedov was elected President of Turkmenistan in 2007, with 89.23% of the vote. He was re-elected in 2012 with 97% of the vote and in 2017 with 97.69% of the vote. These very high figures suggest that the elections were not fair. The pictures below show a statue of President Berdimuhamedov on horseback on a marble cliff and public pictures of the president.

Watch the videos, look at the pictures and read the information on President Berdimuhamedov, then answer the questions that follow (questions 1–4 are based on the videos).

YouTube Go to YouTube and search for 'Turkmenistan's "action hero" president' (1:44) and 'Turkmen Auto-crat "Redesigns" Car' (1:43).

1. The President is a dentist, yet he is presented as an expert rally driver, mechanic and singer. Why do you think these areas are promoted?
   _____
   _____

325

● CALL TO ACTION | *Chapter 6*

2. Do you believe these claims? Why/why not?

3. Why do you think these videos were made?

4. What do these videos tell you about Turkmenistan?

5. What do the pictures of the President suggest to you?

6. Why do you think people might believe these videos?

Exercise 72C   Analysing media freedom in Turkmenistan

Key Skills

Success criteria ☐ I can identify how a lack of free media limits democracy.

The Turkmen government controls all the media and censors the internet. People must show identification before they go online in internet cafés. Journalists have been convicted of trumped-up charges if they fail to present the country in a positive light. In 2016, Khudayberdy Allashov, a contributor to Radio Free Europe/Radio Liberty, was beaten by police. He and his mother were charged with possessing chewing tobacco, which is illegal. Allashov and his mother spent over two months in prison and on release were kept under police surveillance and forbidden from using the internet or phones.

Reporters without Borders creates the **World Press Freedom Index** each year and ranks countries according to the level of press freedom. In the map, pale yellow means press freedom is good, yellow is fairly good, orange is problematic, red is bad and brown is very bad. In 2021, Norway ranked highest of all 180 countries, Switzerland came tenth, Ireland came twelfth and Turkmenistan came 178th.

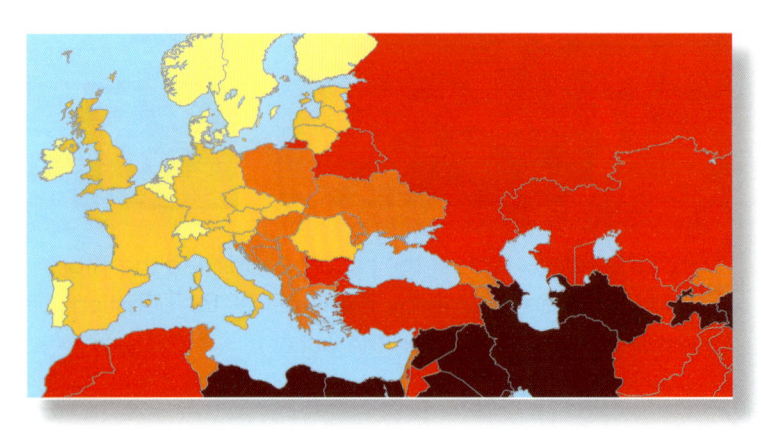

Working in pairs, look at the information on media in Turkmenistan and answer the questions below.

1. What colour is Ireland on the map? What does that tell you?

2. What colour is Turkmenistan? What does that tell you?

326

Lesson 72: Case study: Turkmenistan

3. Give an example of how the Turkmen police deal with journalists who do not present the country in a good light?

4. How else is media controlled in Turkmenistan?

5. Why is an independent media important in a democracy?

Exercise 72D Analysing corruption and wealth in Turkmenistan

Key Skills

Success criteria ☐ I can identify how unequal distribution of resources and corruption happen in an authoritarian system.

The corruption perception index ranks countries from 100 (very clean) to 0 (very corrupt). Working in pairs, look at the charts and answer the questions below.

Corruption perception index, 2017
- Switzerland: 85
- Ireland: 73
- Turkmenistan: 20

GDP per capita
- Ireland: $89,600
- Switzerland: $68,393
- Turkmenistan: $15,536 (2019)

1. According to the corruption perception index chart, which country is most corrupt?

2. Which is least corrupt? Why do you think this might be?

3. Turkmenistan has many natural resources. How does it compare in GDP per capita to the other countries on the chart?

4. What does this suggest?

5. What do these charts tell us about life in an authoritarian country?

327

Lesson 73: Strengths of democracy

Learning outcome 3.6
Students should be able to discuss the strengths and weaknesses of the democratic process.

Exercise 73A Examining the advent of democracy in different countries

Key Skills

Success criteria ☐ I can identify how democracy was not achieved in a similar fashion everywhere.

In a democracy, people can vote on issues directly or send someone that they elect to make decisions for them. The main feature of a democracy is that the people choose their leaders and get the chance to remove them if they are not happy with their performance.

Working in groups, match the following photos with the correct names and year in which they first achieved the right to vote.

People	A Saudi Arabian woman	a Swiss woman
	North Korean Park Sang Hak	Irishwoman Hanna Sheehy-Skeffington
	a 19th-century Irish peasant farmer	a black South African woman
	Australian Neville Bonner	an early 20th-century native American woman

Year	1884	1918	1956	1962	1971	1994	2015	Not in their lifetime

1	2	3	4

5	6	7	8

Lesson 73: Strengths of democracy

Exercise 73B Identifying leaders of government and their countries

Key Skills **Success criteria** ☐ I can identify autocratic leaders of governments and their countries.

Working in pairs, look at the photos of the following political leaders and match the countries they ran or run, then answer the questions that follow.

Countries
- Syria
- Kampuchea (Cambodia)
- Germany
- Belarus
- North Korea
- Uganda

1. Adolf Hitler	2. Pol Pot	3. Kim Jong-un

4. Idi Amin	5. Alexander Lukashenko	6. Bashar al-Assad

1. What do these men have in common?

2. How many of these people are still in power?

3. What do you know about life in their countries?

4. How does it differ from life in Ireland?

329

CALL TO ACTION | *Chapter 6*

Exercise 73C **Analysing the differences between democracy and authoritarianism**

Key Skills **Success criteria** ☐ I can identify differences between democracy and authoritarianism.

> **YouTube** Go to YouTube and search for 'Forms of Government – World101' (5:20).

Working in pairs, watch the video and answer the questions that follow.

1. How does direct democracy differ from representative democracy?

2. What are the three categories of democracies that can be found around the world today?

3. What two factors exist in a healthy democracy?

4. What is federalism?

5. How do authoritarian leaders use some of the same ideas as democratic leaders?

6. How are authoritarian governments different from democratic ones?

7. What is democratic backsliding?

Exercise 73D **Identifying the freedoms that are lost in an authoritarian society**

Key Skills **Success criteria** ☐ I can identify the freedoms that are lost in an authoritarianism state.

What are the strengths of a democracy?
- Every time a person votes they get the chance to express their opinion.
- People have an equal right to vote in a democracy – it does not matter whether they are rich or poor, etc.

Lesson 73: Strengths of democracy

- Wealth tends to be more fairly distributed in democratic countries.
- In democracies, there is less fear of the police or being arrested for criticising the government.
- Democracies are less likely to go to war with other countries.
- In order to get a majority of people to support them, governments in democracies are less likely to be extremist.

Working in pairs, look at the following scenario and answer the questions that follow.

> The Irish economy has gone into recession and people are very angry with the government. A small group of people have managed to overthrow the government by force. They must act quickly to keep their new power.

1. How can this group stop people communicating and organising overthrowing them?
   _____
   _____

2. How can they stop people criticising them in public?
   _____

3. How can they stop people criticising them in private?
   _____

4. How can they keep a close eye on the people?
   _____
   _____

5. What methods can they use to get people to support them?
   _____
   _____

6. What will change if they manage to stay in power?
   _____
   _____

Lesson 74: Weaknesses of democracy

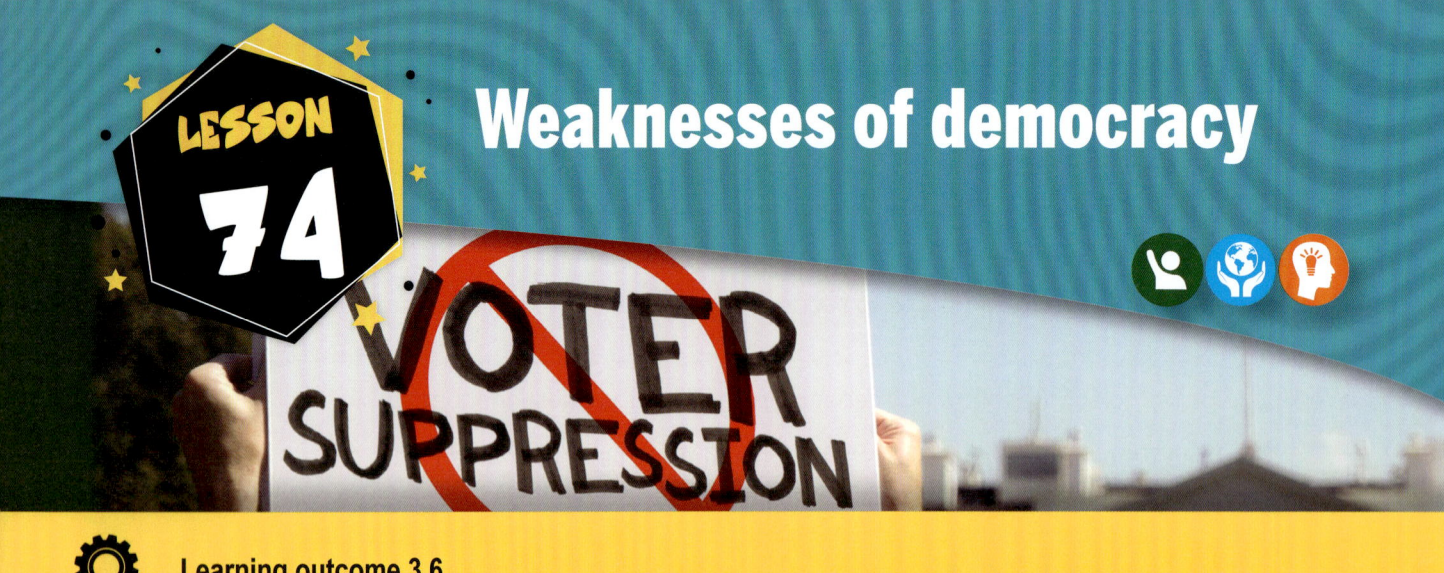

Learning outcome 3.6
Students should be able to discuss the strengths and weaknesses of the democratic process.

Exercise 74A — Examining quotes about democracy

Key Skills

Success criteria
☐ I can identify strengths and weaknesses of democracy by analysing quotes.

Working in pairs, read the quotes about democracy and answer the questions on the next page.

> Democracies, unlike dictatorships, are forgiving and generous, but they cannot survive unless they fight.
> *Jalal Talabani, President of Iraq, 2006–2014*

> The bedrock of our democracy is the rule of law and that means we have to have an independent judiciary – judges who can make decisions independent of the political winds that are blowing.
> *Caroline Kennedy, US lawyer and former Ambassador to Japan*

> The best argument against democracy is a five-minute conversation with the average voter.
> *Winston Churchill (1874–1965), British Prime Minister*

> In Italy, for 30 years under the Borgias, they had warfare, terror, murder and bloodshed, but they produced Michelangelo, Leonardo da Vinci and the Renaissance. In Switzerland they had brotherly love, they had 500 years of democracy and peace – and what did that produce? The cuckoo clock.
> *Graham Greene (1904–1991), English writer*

> This is why we feel that democracy's important: because democracy allows you to have small explosions and therefore avoid the bigger explosions.
> *Indira Gandhi (1917–1984), Indian Prime Minister*

> Democracy is not a spectator sport, it's a participatory event. If we don't participate in it, it ceases to be a democracy.
> *Michael Moore, US filmmaker and activist*

> Democracies succeed or fail based on their journalism.
> *Scott Pelley, US journalist*

> The problem of the world today is the people talk on and on about democracy, freedom, justice. But I don't give a damn about democracy if I am worried about survival.
> *Imelda Marcos, Philippine politician and widow of former dictator Ferdinand Marcos*

> I worry about a democracy having nuclear weapons as much as a dictatorship having nuclear weapons.
> *Mohamed ElBaradei, Director General of the International Atomic Energy Agency from 1997 to 2009*

Lesson 74: Weaknesses of democracy

1. The quotes by which people mention the strengths of democracy?
   _____
   _____

2. The quotes by which people mention the weaknesses of democracy?
   _____
   _____

3. What areas are mentioned as being important for democracy to succeed?
   _____
   _____

4. Research how one of these people contributed to or weakened democracy. Write your findings here.
   _____
   _____
   _____
   _____
   _____
   _____
   _____
   _____
   _____

Exercise 74B Analysing weaknesses of democracy

Key Skills **Success criteria** ☐ I can identify a key weakness of democracy and suggest how to overcome it.

The weaknesses of democracy include:
- It depends on the majority. Sometimes the majority make decisions that are not in the best interests of everyone. Slavery was acceptable to the majority for many years.
- It can be hard to reach decisions because there are so many different viewpoints.
- People tend to look after their own interests first and vote for politicians who promise to give them what they want.
- People sometimes have no idea what or who they are voting for.
- Politicians often promise to do things they cannot deliver and hope that people will forget by the time the next election comes around.
- Politicians often make decisions that have a short-term effect so they can point to their successes at election time. In many cases, long-term solutions would be the better option, but the person making these decisions would not get the credit for them.
- Election campaigns are very expensive to run.

■ CALL TO ACTION | *Chapter 6*

Look at the video about the philosopher Socrates's view of democracy and answer the questions that follow.

> **YouTube** Go to YouTube and search for 'Why Socrates Hated Democracy' (4:21).

1. What two achievements was Ancient Greece proud of?

2. Why did Socrates use the example of the ship?

3. What did Socrates say about voting?

4. How did Socrates have first-hand experience of voters' foolishness?

5. What is the difference between an intellectual democracy and a democracy by birthright?

6. What did Socrates give as examples of two types of candidates?

7. Of the two, who is more likely to be elected? Why?

8. What does this video tell you about the weaknesses of democracy?

Exercise 74C Analysing polarisation in the media

Key Skills   **Success criteria**   ☐ I can identify polarisation in media headlines.

Anti-democratic leaders exploit populism and polarisation. **Populism** involves appealing to ordinary people. Corrupt leaders often use populism to convince people to support them. **Polarisation** is the idea of two completely different views on topics. Anti-democratic leaders use this to split the people into two different groups in conflict with each other.

Polarisation is not used only by anti-democratic leaders. The Brexit vote when the UK voted to leave the EU was an example of polarisation in a democracy. Many voters were strongly on one side or the other. There was further division within political parties, with some MPs leaving their parties, a new party being set up and two prime ministers having to resign before the Brexit Bill was passed by parliament.

Lesson 74: Weaknesses of democracy

Look at the newspaper headlines and cartoons below and answer the questions that follow.

1. Which headline is pro-Brexit?

2. What methods does the newspaper use to show this?

3. What is the difference between the pro- and anti-Brexit headlines?

4. How are these examples of polarisation in politics?

5. Which cartoon is pro-Brexit and which one is anti-Brexit?

6. Both cartoons use the idea of boats at sea. What is the difference between them?

7. Are these examples of healthy debate? Why/why not?

8. How can polarisation be harmful to a democracy?

335

■ CALL TO ACTION | *Chapter 6*

Exercise 74D   Analysing problems in democracies

Key Skills   **Success criteria**   ☐ I can identify problems in democracies.

Watch the video and answer the questions that follow.

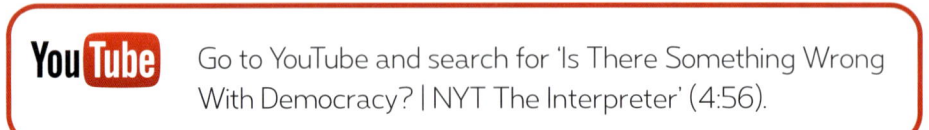

> **YouTube** Go to YouTube and search for 'Is There Something Wrong With Democracy? | NYT The Interpreter' (4:56).

1. What is the pattern for democracies?

2. How are China and Saudi Arabia exceptions to this pattern?

3. In what way are Russia and Venezuela also exceptions to this?

4. What has China put in place that appears democratic? Why?

5. When this does not work, what does China do instead?

6. How do countries slide back into dictatorships?

7. What does this video tell you about populism and polarisation?

8. What warning signs of dangers to democracy are emerging in the US?

336

Reflection: Reflecting on my learning about democracy

Learning outcome 3.14
Students should be able to reflect on their ongoing learning and what it means for them.

Key Skills

Success criteria ☐ I can give examples of how my thinking about democracy has developed.

Look back at the skills and knowledge you have developed in this chapter. It is important to identify what you have learned and where you could learn more. Use the following worksheet to guide your reflection on democracy. Then working in groups, discuss your responses to each of the questions.

1. Before looking at democracy, I thought …	
2. Things I learned about democracy	
3. Where I got my information from	
4. How I know the information was reliable	
5. The different types of sources I got my information from	
6. The most interesting thing I learned was …	
7. How the new information I have learned will change what I do	

337

Action: Running a mock election

A mock election campaign gives you the opportunity to see how candidates convince others to vote for them, how to vote and how the votes are counted. In Ireland, a general election must be held no less than three weeks from the day it is called. In the case of the mock election, it is a good idea to conduct it over three weeks. For the class election, you will elect members to a class council. Your teacher will give you a list of areas that the class council is responsible for. There will be three seats on the council elected by proportional representation single transferable vote (PR-STV).

Several roles are needed for the mock election:

- Candidates and campaign managers
- A returning officer and staff
- A person to organise the register of electors.

✓ Action 1 Organising a register of electors

Key Skills **Success criteria** ☐ I will organise the register of electors/I will ensure that my name is on the register of electors.

One student will organise a register of electors. All other students must check that they are on the register in order to vote in the election.

1. If you are the registrar, use the class list and organise a register. Students must come to you to sign it. Set a deadline for signing this.
2. If you are not the registrar, you must check that your name is on the register or you will not be able to vote.

✓ Action 2 Running an election campaign and preparing for an election

Key Skills **Success criteria** ☐ I will conduct the tasks needed to run an election campaign or prepare for an election.

You can set up political parties or run as independent candidates. The parties can devise slogans, symbols and **manifestos** (a list of the things you plan to do if elected). A returning officer should employ several staff to help with the jobs. This involves creating a nomination paper. Each candidate needs two nominations to run and nobody can nominate more than one person. This will prevent the election becoming unwieldy. The returning officer should also create a polling card and ensure that every voter receives one before the election. Students can create posters and newspaper reports.

Work in groups to conduct your tasks and answer the following questions:

1. What is my role?

2. What have I done?

3. What have I learned so far about voting and elections?

✓ Action 3   Voting

Key Skills   **Success criteria**   ☐ I will be able to vote in order of my preference.

All students will vote. The presiding officer and staff run the polling station. These people cannot be candidates. They must ensure the polling booth is private, stamp ballot papers and use a ballot box. Ballot papers should include candidates in alphabetical order, addresses (class address) and occupations, party affiliations and symbols.

✓ Action 4   Counting the vote

Key Skills   **Success criteria**   ☐ I will be able to count the votes in the election.

The returning officer and counting staff will count the votes, with help from your teacher. The results of the counts will be made public. Note the following points:

1. How many votes were cast?

2. Were any spoiled?

3. What was the total valid poll?

4. What was the quota?

5. Was anyone elected on the first count?

6. Who were the successful candidates?

7. How many counts were needed?

Once the election is complete and all votes have been counted, discuss as a class what you have learned about an election campaign.

Chapter 7 The Law and the Citizen

Rules or laws

LESSON 75

Learning outcome 3.7
Students should be able to identify laws that directly relate to their lives.

Exercise 75A — Identifying how school rules operate

Key Skills **Success criteria** ☐ I can identify how rules operate.

Working in pairs, discuss the following questions about the rules in your school and write the answers below.

1. List three school rules.

2. Why do you think these rules exist?

3. What would happen if they did not exist?

4. What would happen if you broke these rules?

5. Who decides what happens if a serious rule is broken?

6. Who makes the school rules?

7. Who is consulted when the rules are drawn up?

8. How could you change any rule you disagree with?

Lesson 75: Rules or laws

Exercise 75B Identifying features of laws and rules

Key Skills   **Success criteria** ☐ I can identify the differences between laws and school rules.

Rules are instructions about how to behave. There are rules in school, at home, in sports and leisure and at work. These rules vary from school to school, from house to house, etc. For example, in one house the children might be allowed to spend only 30 minutes per day on screens, whereas in another house they could spend as long as they want once they have finished their homework. There are also different results for breaking the rules. For example, in one school a student might get detention for not doing homework, whereas in another the student might have to do extra homework. A teacher might let one student off with a warning because it was unusual, whereas a student who never does homework gets detention.

Laws are different to rules because they are created by the Oireachtas and enforced by the courts. Laws say how everybody in the country should behave. They do not differ from place to place within a country and they have the same punishments for everybody. If a person breaks a law, a record is kept by the courts and gardaí.

Working in pairs, answer these questions about laws and school rules.

	Laws	School rules
1. Who creates them?		
2. Who enforces them?		
3. What happens if you break them?		

Exercise 75C Distinguishing between rules and laws

Key Skills   **Success criteria** ☐ I can identify rules or laws.

Working in pairs, identify whether the following are rules or laws.

1. You must make your bed when you get up in the morning.
   ___

2. You cannot drive without a licence.
   ___

3. You must not talk while a film is playing at the cinema.
   ___

4. You cannot drink alcohol if you are 15.
   ___

341

■ CALL TO ACTION | *Chapter 7*

5. You must not talk in a library.

6. You must not drive faster than 120 km per hour on the motorway.

7. You must not smoke in a workplace.

8. In a game of rugby, you must not throw the ball forward.

Exercise 75D Establishing laws on a new planet

Key Skills **Success criteria** ☐ I can identify the most important laws.

Laws are put in place to make people in a country behave in a certain way. They are enforced by the police and courts. All laws should be based on the idea of justice, which means that people are treated equally and fairly. In a just world there would be no violence, poverty, discrimination or persecution based on religion or ethnicity. Some of these things can be protected by laws, but not all of them are.

You are part of the crew of a spaceship on an international mission to explore a new planet. You are about to arrive at the planet. This planet can sustain human life, as it has water, good soil and a suitable climate. However, you have just been informed that the mission has been abandoned, as it is too costly and the countries involved cannot agree. You do not have enough fuel to return, but you have chickens and goats, seeds to grow plants and materials to make medicines. You also have a small number of weapons. The planet has never been lived on, so there are no laws and no history. In your group, you must draw up five essential laws for life on this planet, which will make it a safe and a fair place to live.

1. What are the five laws your group chooses?

2. Rank these in order of importance.

3. Can you think of any other important laws that could be included?

342

Lesson 76: Laws that relate to young people

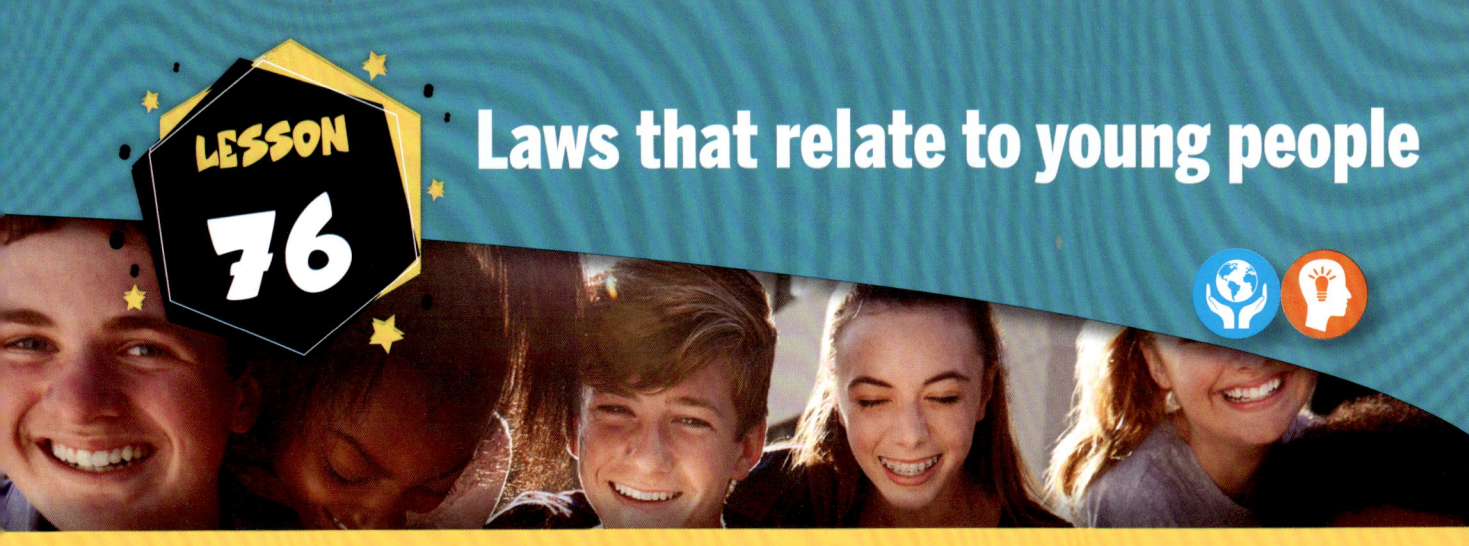

Learning outcome 3.7
Students should be able to identify laws that directly relate to their lives.

Exercise 76A — Identifying laws that apply to me

Key Skills

Success criteria ☐ I can identify how laws apply to me.

Working in pairs, write the correct age you have to be to do the following:

1. Buy alcohol in an off-licence   _____
2. Babysit   _____
3. Drive a car   _____
4. Book a flight   _____
5. Leave school   _____
6. Get a tattoo   _____
7. Work up to 7 hours a day during school holidays   _____
8. Get married   _____

Exercise 76B — Understanding the consequences of not having laws

Key Skills

Success criteria ☐ I can identify the consequences of not having laws.

When a law has been passed, the minister in charge has the power to add to the law. This is called a **statutory instrument**. The **Irish Statute Book** is a database of all Irish laws passed by the Oireachtas. It also contains the most recent version of the Constitution and statutory instruments.

Working in pairs, look at the laws on the Irish Statute book on the next page and discuss what the consequence would be if these laws did not exist. Write your answers. The first one has been done as an example.

343

CALL TO ACTION | Chapter 7

Law	Consequence of no law
Charities Act 2009 This law explains that charities only work to be of public benefit, must spend all their money on charity (except for wages and essential running costs) and do not use their money to pay benefits to members.	*People raising money for charity could decide to keep the money or spend it on themselves*
Control of Dogs Acts 1986–1992 Dog owners must have a dog licence and get their dog microchipped. County or city councils can appoint dog wardens, seize dogs, impose on-the-spot fines and run dog shelters.	
Non-Fatal Offences Against the Person Act 1997 This law says that areas such as assaults, threats of violence involving syringes/blood, stalking, debt collection with threats of harm and poisoning are criminal offences.	
Intoxicating Liquor Act 1998 (Age Card) Regulations 2007 People aged 18 and more can get age cards to show that they have reached the legal age for purchasing alcohol.	
Criminal Justice (Theft and Fraud Offences Act) 2001 This law covers the crimes of theft, burglary, robbery, obtaining goods by deception and the maximum sentence on conviction for each one.	

Exercise 76C Identifying education laws that apply to young people

Key Skills   **Success criteria**   ☐   I can identify education laws the apply to young people.

One of the main areas where laws apply to young people is in education. The right to education is contained in the Constitution. There are various Education Acts explaining how the education system operates.

Working in pairs, discuss whether each of the statements on the next page is true or false (you will probably have to guess some of the answers).

Source: Adapted from 'Rights and Entitlements for Young People', Citizens Information

344

Lesson 76: Laws that relate to young people

Statement	True	False
1. Children must attend school.		
2. The State is obliged to provide free primary education.		
3. Schools are obliged to accept all children who apply.		
4. Children must be educated between the ages of 6 and 16.		
5. Schools are responsible for making sure that children attend school.		
6. Parents can be fined or imprisoned for not sending their children to school.		
7. Children must have started school by the age of 6.		
8. Transition Year is compulsory.		

Exercise 76D Identifying how young people are affected by the law

Key Skills **Success criteria** ☐ I can identify cases of young people affected by the law.

Look at news sources (newspaper, TV news, online news, etc.) and identify as many issues as you can about young people and the law. Write them below. You can use the example as a guide.

Example

Sunday 4 August, www.thejournal.ie: A 16-year-old working as a waitress complained that she was asked to work more hours than legally allowed and was fired when she refused.

345

Lesson 77: How laws are made

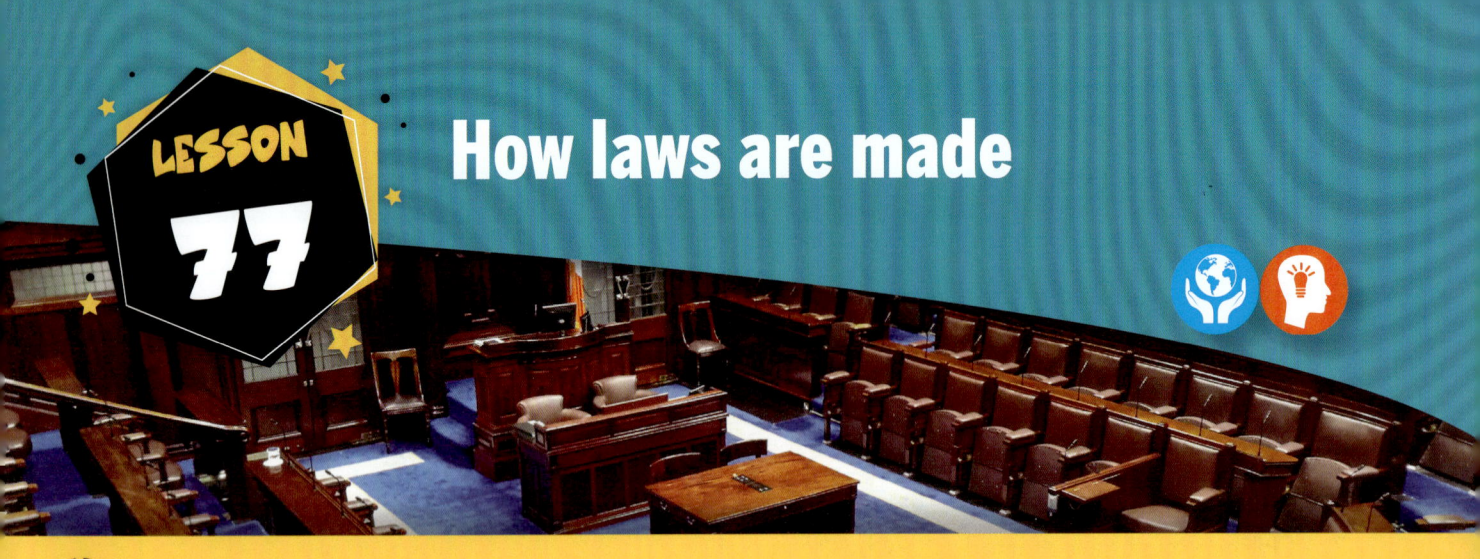

Learning outcome 3.8
Students should be able to explain how laws are made, enforced and evolve over time.

Exercise 77A Identifying sources of law

Key Skills **Success criteria** ☐ I can match situations with sources of law.

There are several sources of law in Ireland:
- The **Constitution** lists the rules for how the country is run and the rights that the government must provide for people.
- **Statute law** is all the laws passed by the Oireachtas.
- **Case law** is when a law that is unclear is tested in the courts. The court's findings decide how to interpret the law.
- Some **EU laws**, called regulations, must be accepted as law in all member states, including Ireland.
- Local authorities pass **bye-laws**. These cover areas such as littering, parking and control of dogs and horses.

Working in pairs, look at the following situations and identify whether the law comes from the Constitution, statute, case, EU law or a bye-law.

		Source of law
1.	In September 2020, Mr Justice Heslin in the High Court ruled in the M50 Skip Hire & Recycling Limited v. Commissioner for Environmental Information case that a member of the public, Mr XY, had the right to find out where certain waste was sent under the European Communities (Access to Information on the Environment) Regulations 2007–2018.	
2.	The Education (Welfare) Act 2000 was passed to provide for every child to receive a minimum education, to cover what is required for home-schooling and to collect information on when children have missed more than 20 school days in a year.	

3. The General Data Protection Regulation (GDPR) are data protection laws that apply to each EU country. In Ireland, the Data Protection Laws were changed to be the same as the GDPR. These laws mean that your personal data should be stored only when there is a legal reason.	
4. Nobody can park a vehicle in a car park in such a position that it would be likely to cause danger to other persons using the car park or to obstruct the entrance to or exit from the car park.	
5. Irish citizens are free to practise their religion and freedom of conscience under article 44 of the Constitution. The State cannot favour or discriminate against any religion.	

Exercise 77B Understanding how laws are made

Key Skills   Success criteria   ☐ I can explain how laws are made in Ireland.

The **Constitution (Bunreacht na hÉireann)** explains how the country is governed and the rights and fundamental freedoms of citizens. A **referendum** must be held in order to change or remove any article in the Constitution. The Constitution lists the main law-making roles of the different institutions.

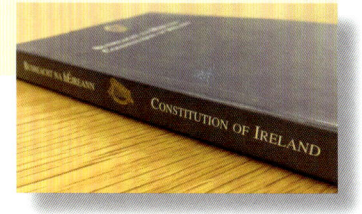

- Articles 15–27 give the Oireachtas the power to make and change laws.
- Article 28 of the Constitution gives the government the power to carry out the laws.
- Articles 34–37 of the Constitution give the courts the power to interpret and apply laws.

Amendments to the Constitution are required for EU treaties as these transfer some powers from national law to European law.

The Oireachtas

The main purpose of the Oireachtas is to make and revise laws. Any new law that is proposed is called a **bill**. A bill must be passed by both the Dáil and the Seanad.

The government can introduce bills for new laws, to change laws or to pass the budget. Individual TDs and senators can also introduce bills – these are called **Private Members' Bills**.

There are five stages in a bill passing through the Houses of the Oireachtas:

- **Stage 1** — The bill is introduced in either house
- **Stage 2** — The general principles of the bill are debated
- **Stage 3** — At the committee stage, there is a detailed examination of each section of the bill
- **Stage 4** — At the report stage, amendments from the committee stage are considered
- **Stage 5** — The bill is passed by the house and is sent to the other house, beginning again at stage 2.

Once the bill has been passed by both houses, it goes to the president to be signed into law. The president must sign a bill unless they decide to refer it to the Supreme Court to check if it is constitutional. When a bill is signed by the president, it becomes a law and is called an **act**. It is then added to the Statute Book.

● CALL TO ACTION | *Chapter 7*

The **Law Reform Commission** (LRC) is an independent organisation that examines laws and proposes changes.

Watch the video and answer the questions that follow.

> **YouTube** Go to YouTube and search for 'How laws are made – oireachtasfilm' (2:45).

1. What is the only body with the power to make laws in Ireland?

2. Who proposes the majority of bills?

3. What happens at stage 2?

4. At what stage are changes proposed?

5. What happens at stage 4?

6. What laws must start in the Dáil?

7. What must the president do before signing a bill?

Exercise 77C Reviewing the legislative process

Key Skills   **Success criteria**   ☐ I can summarise the legislative process.

Read the passage below and fill in the blanks by adding the correct words from the box below.

The only body with the power to make laws in Ireland is the _____.
A _____ is a proposed law. This is debated and must pass through both the _____ and the _____.
When it is signed into law by the _____ it becomes known as an _____. Most laws are proposed by the government, but a TD can also bring a _____ Bill before either house. If the president thinks a law might be unconstitutional, they can send it to the _____ to test if it is in line with the Constitution.

| Supreme Court | Dáil | Private Members' | bill |
| president | Oireachtas | Seanad | act |

348

Lesson 77: How laws are made

Exercise 77D **Understanding the president's role in the legislative process**

Key Skills **Success criteria** ☐ I can explain the president's role in making laws.

Read the legal opinion given below and answer the questions that follow.

Opinion: Those criticising the president for signing bills into law are overestimating his power

Dr Alan Greene

FOOTAGE RECENTLY emerged of President Michael D. Higgins being subjected to verbal abuse by anti-water charge protesters in Finglas, Dublin. It would appear that these protesters are angry at the president for signing the Water Services Act 2013 into law.

However, what other options were available to him?

Under Article 26 of the Constitution, the president may, prior to signing a bill into law, meet with his Council of State and refer the bill to the Supreme Court to test its constitutionality. If the bill is found to be unconstitutional, the president must decline to sign it and so it never becomes law. President Higgins could have made use of his power under Article 26.

If, on the other hand, the bill is found to be constitutional, the president must sign it into law. However, an act that has received the stamp of constitutionality after an Article 26 reference can never be challenged again. As a result, the Article 26 procedure is rarely used – there have been only 15 references.

President Higgins thus had no real option but to sign the Water Services Bill into law.

Source: TheJournal.ie

1. Why were the protesters annoyed with the president?

2. What other options did the president have?

3. What would have happened if the bill was found to be unconstitutional?

4. If it was found to be constitutional, what would have happened?

5. How do we know that presidents are unlikely to refer bills to the Supreme Court?

Lesson 78: Policing laws

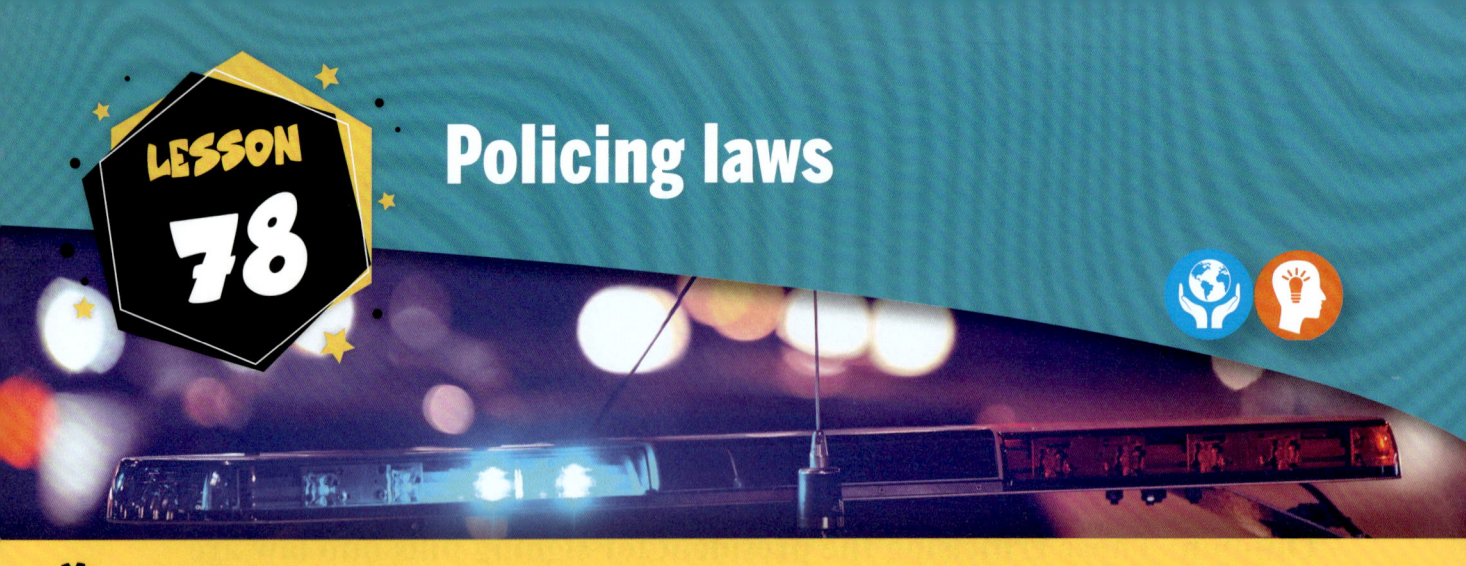

Learning outcome 3.8
Students should be able to explain how laws are made, enforced and evolve over time.

Exercise 78A   Identifying the different jobs the Gardaí do

Key Skills

Success criteria   ☐ I can identify the different elements of the job of a Garda.

The **Garda Síochána** was set up in 1923 as the national police service of Ireland. The Gardaí are in charge of all policing duties in the country. Some of their jobs include:

- Detecting and preventing crime
- Investigating crimes and preparing files for the Director of Public Prosecutions (DPP)
- Ensuring the nation's security
- Policing road safety
- Community policing

Working in pairs, look at the following pictures and identify what job the Gardaí are doing.

Can you think of any other jobs the Gardaí do that are not covered here?

Lesson 78: Policing laws

Exercise 78B — Identifying the work of different Garda units

Key Skills   **Success criteria**   ☐ I can identify the different units of the Gardaí and the jobs they do.

Look at the videos and answer the questions that follow.

> Go to YouTube and search for:
> 1. 'A Day with the Garda Dog Unit' (2:23)
> 2. 'Garda Air Support' (2:34)
> 3. 'VIDEO: A day in the life of Dublin's new armed guards' (1:00).

1. Name two jobs the dogs do. (Video 1)

2. What is the first task of the day for the Air Support Unit? (Video 2)

3. Why was the Air Support Unit called out in the case of the aggravated burglary shown in the video? (Video 2)

4. How long do they take to respond? (Video 2)

5. What does the Air Support Unit do while their colleagues are searching the forest? (Video 2)

6. Where is the Emergency Response Unit based? (Video 3)

7. What is its role? (Video 3)

8. What do the different units in the Gardaí tell you about their job?

9. Can you name any other Garda units?

Exercise 78C — Organising the investigation of a crime

Key Skills   **Success criteria**   ☐ I can identify the different teams required for analysing a crime.

351

Other Garda units include:

- The **Garda Mounted Unit** polices events such as matches and concerts, search for people in places where vehicles cannot go to and operate crowd control.
- The **Garda Water Unit** is used in murder and missing persons investigations and to recover evidence from the sea, rivers, lakes and other waterways.
- The **Technical Bureau** are skilled teams that investigate fingerprints, firearms, photography and mapping, documents and handwriting and facial identification. These Gardaí also interview victims or witnesses of a crime to produce a photo-fit of the person who committed the crime.
- The **Garda National Bureau of Criminal Investigation** conducts criminal investigations like murder, cold cases, extradition, stolen property, environmental waste, genocide, crimes against humanity, war crimes and passport fraud
- The **Garda National Cyber Crime Bureau (GNCCB)** examines computer media seized as part of a criminal investigation. They also investigate computer crimes such as hacking.

The **Garda Commissioner** is the person in charge of running the Garda Síochána. Since 2016 the **Policing Authority**, an independent body, oversees the performance of the Garda Síochána. The **Garda Reserve** are unpaid volunteers who provide extra support to the Gardaí when needed.

The **Garda Síochána Ombudsman Commission (GSOC)** is responsible for:

- Complaints about Garda conduct, for example, if a Garda is drunk while on duty
- Investigating circumstances where the conduct of a Garda or Gardaí has led to death or serious injury
- Investigating matters relating to the conduct of Gardaí if it is in the public interest
- Examining the practices, policies and procedures of the Gardaí.

Look at the following situation. Your group is the Garda team charged with investigating this crime. Decide what units you would need and how you would go about solving this crime.

> A major work of art has been stolen from the home of a member of the public. This woman had no CCTV in her home when it happened and was away at the time. Her home is located at the end of a long drive in the countryside. What units of the Gardaí might be involved in investigating this crime and why? You have a limited budget to solve this crime, so you can call in only the most suitable units to help you.

Lesson 78: Policing laws

Exercise 78D Examining the consequences of committing an offence

Key Skills **Success criteria** ☐ I can identify the consequences of various offences.

The consequences of committing an offence for young people

- An **informal caution** is usually given where no previous caution has been given. This type of caution is usually given by the Juvenile Liaison Officer in a Garda station, or in the young person's own home.
- **Anti-Social Behaviour Warnings** are either written or verbal and are given by a Garda Síochána to stop anti-social behaviour.
- A **caution** is a formal warning. It is given in the presence of parents/guardians in a Garda station. The caution can be given by a Garda Síochána who is an Inspector or higher rank or a Juvenile Liaison Officer. Every young person who receives a formal caution is placed under the **supervision** of a Juvenile Liaison Officer for 12 months.
- **Restorative caution** is where the victim may be present when a formal caution is given. This means the young person will have to face up to the effects of their behaviour. The young person can also be invited to apologise and to make up to the victim for the harm done.
- **Anti-Social Behaviour Orders** (ASBOs) are civil orders granted by the court to restrict or prevent certain behaviours. Breaking an ASBO is a criminal offence. The order usually requires the young person to do certain things, for example, attend school every day, or report to a Garda, a teacher or other person.
- The aim of the **Juvenile Diversion Programme** is to prevent young offenders from committing further offences. The programme is run by specially trained Gardaí called Juvenile Liaison Officers. A young person admitted to the programme may receive a 'caution', be placed under 'supervision' of a Juvenile Liaison Officer or be subject to a 'conference'.
- **Fines (court outcome)**: The young person has to pay a fine to the courts.
- **Sentence (court outcome)**: If an offence is very serious in nature, a young person might be sentenced to a period of time at Oberstown Children Detention Campus. This is a type of prison for young people.
- A **Juvenile Diversion Programme Conference** may be held if a young person has been formally cautioned and is being supervised by a Juvenile Liaison Officer. A conference usually looks at the young person's problems and reasons for offending. It will try to prevent the young person getting into trouble again and will discuss family support and community involvement.
- A **referral to Tusla** means the young person is referred to a social worker.

CALL TO ACTION | Chapter 7

Working in pairs, look at the offences committed below. Then try to match each one to one of the consequences on the previous page. Explain your choices.

Offence	Consequence	Reason for your choice
1. A 10-year-old boy smashes a shop window causing €1,000 worth of damage.		
2. A group of 12-year-old boys and girls have been reported to the Gardaí for damaging trees in a housing estate. They have been pulling off the branches and setting them alight, also causing damage to the grass in the area.		
3. A 13-year-old girl is reported to the Gardaí for deliberately pushing a teacher at her school. The push resulted in the teacher hitting her head on a door.		
4. A 12-year-old boy is caught shoplifting by a shopkeeper and is reported to the Gardaí. He has stolen two bottles of Coke and several chocolate bars.		
5. Two 15-year-old girls are caught selling ecstasy tablets to their friends and are reported to the Gardaí. They have previous convictions for this type of offence.		

Lesson 79: Criminal and civil cases

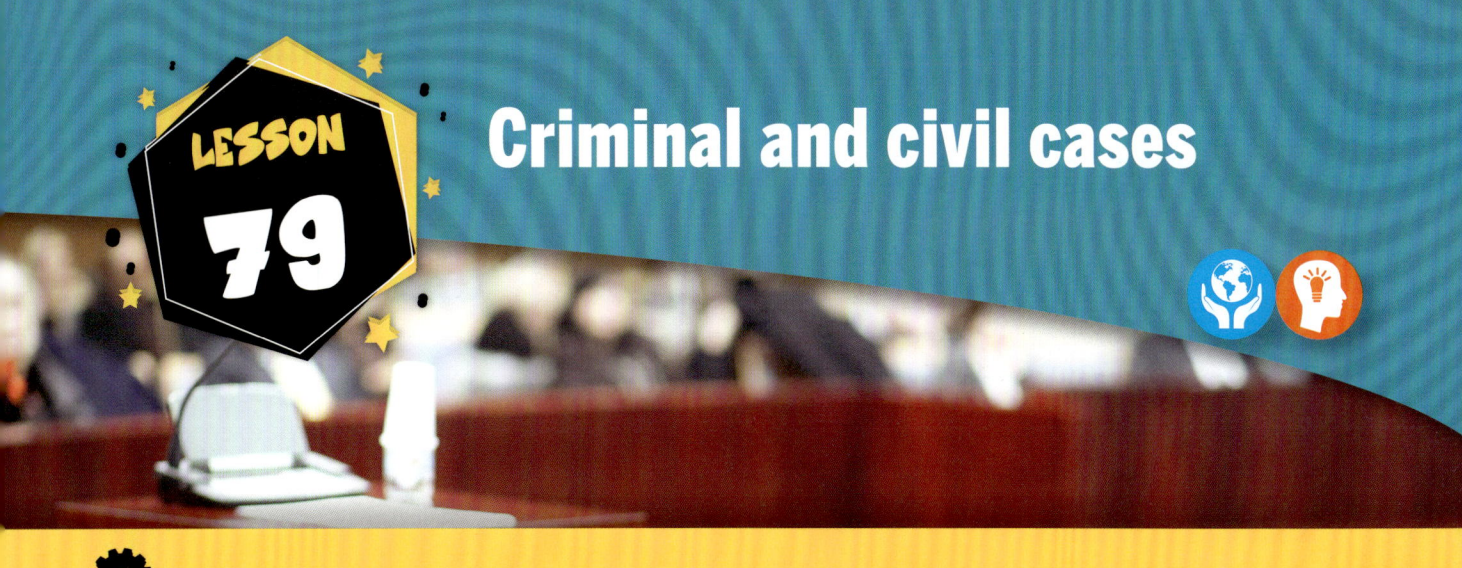

Learning outcome 3.9
Students should be able to explain the role and relevance of local, national and international courts.

Exercise 79A Classifying civil actions and criminal prosecutions

Key Skills **Success criteria** ☐ I can identify whether a case is civil or criminal.

There are two types of court case: **civil actions** and **criminal prosecutions**.

A **civil action** is taken by a person against other people or organisations to get compensation for what they have lost. Civil actions include:

- Property disputes (planning dispute, rights of way, ownership of property)
- Personal injury (traffic accidents, bullying, falling in a shop)
- Family law (separation, divorce, child custody)
- Employment law (unfair dismissal, breach of contract)
- Licensing laws (bars, lottery).

Criminal prosecutions are prosecuted by the State, usually through the DPP. They are taken to punish offenders for crimes such as murder, manslaughter, assault, theft, armed robbery and drink and drug driving. Minor cases such as less serious traffic offences are decided by judges sitting on their own, without a **jury**. Serious criminal cases and civil cases such as libel are tried by a judge and jury of 12 people. The judge guides the jury on the law, but the jury decides whether the person is guilty or not guilty.

Working in pairs, decide whether the following trials are civil or criminal cases.

Situation	Civil	Criminal
1. A man is caught driving at 150 km per hour on the motorway.		
2. Two neighbours are fighting over a hedge dividing their property.		
3. A woman is caught selling drugs to college students.		
4. A man applies to the court to stop his employer conducting an inquiry into his work (an injunction).		
5. A student is assaulted on their way home from a nightclub.		
6. A couple are in dispute over who should have custody of their children.		
7. A man buys a new phone but discovers it only has 30 minutes of battery life.		
8. A woman breaks into a family's home and steals their property.		

● CALL TO ACTION | *Chapter 7*

Exercise 79B Analysing a criminal case

Key Skills   **Success criteria** ☐ I can analyse a criminal case.

Suspects taken in for questioning in a criminal case must be told that they have the right to consult a solicitor and to have a solicitor present before questioning begins. After questioning, the Gardaí may submit a file to the DPP who will decide whether to prosecute.

Working in pairs, read the guide to a criminal case and answer the questions that follow.

A quick guide to a criminal case

Michael has been arrested and charged with intentionally causing serious harm to a shop assistant called Linda. The prosecution claims that Michael pushed Linda down on a counter and banged her head against it, fracturing her skull. Michael has told his lawyers that the shop assistant had accused him of trying to steal from her shop. He claims that Linda attacked him and fell over and that was how she was injured.

Michael's trial is held in the Circuit Court because of the seriousness of the offence. The State prosecutes the case and is represented by a barrister. A defence barrister represents Michael. The judge does not allow the State to give evidence that Michael had previous convictions for assault nor do they allow Michael's barrister to ask Michael the question: 'Didn't Linda accuse you of stealing from her shop?' A barrister is not allowed to ask **leading questions** (that is to say, questions which suggest the right answers) of their own witnesses.

The jury hears all the evidence put before them, including evidence from other eyewitnesses who were present in the shop at the time of the incident. The judge summarises the facts and explains the laws involved. In particular he explains that they cannot convict Michael unless they are satisfied of his guilt '**beyond reasonable doubt**'. The jury goes to a separate room and considers all of the evidence they have heard. When they return to the court the judge is informed that they have found Michael guilty of the offence with which he was charged. The judge must decide what sentence to impose up to the maximum permitted by law for the particular offence.

Source: The Courts Service of Ireland

1. Why is this a criminal case rather than a civil action?

2. Why is the case held in the Circuit Court?

3. The judge does not allow the State to give evidence that Michael has previous convictions for assault. Why do you think this is?

4. Why are barristers not allowed to ask leading questions?

5. What must the jury consider before making a decision?

6. Who decides the sentence?

Exercise 79C Analysing a civil case

Key Skills

Success criteria ☐ I can analyse a civil case.

Working in pairs, read the guide to a civil action and answer the questions that follow.

A quick guide to a civil case

Mary hired a firm of builders called Fab Construction to refurbish and extend her new home. On completion of the job Mary was dissatisfied with the quality of their work. She refused to pay the builders, who then instruct solicitors to sue her in the Circuit Court for the sum of €20,000 which they claim is owed under the terms of their written building contract with Mary.

In this action, Fab Construction is the **plaintiff** and Mary is the **defendant**. Before the case goes to court, Fab Construction's solicitors prepare a document called a civil bill, which is lodged in the Circuit Court office and which sets out the basis for their claim for payment. Mary's solicitors dispute the claim and prepare a document called a defence, which states that the builders have not completed the work the way Mary's specified and that, therefore, Mary does not owe the money.

Before the hearing date, Mary and Fab Construction organise a joint inspection of the property with their structural engineers. On the day of the hearing, barristers represent each party. Fab Construction calls their engineer as an expert witness to explain the work completed on Mary's house and to testify that the work was up to standard. Mary's engineer testifies that the house had not been properly damp-proofed in accordance with her instructions. In court, the judge listens to the evidence of both parties and to the legal arguments. He accepts Fab Construction's evidence that most of the work has been completed in accordance with the building contract. However, he also accepts Mary's evidence that there is still a problem with damp. Therefore, he allows a discount of €5,000 on the amount owed to the builders and orders Mary to pay €15,000 and the builder's legal costs in bringing the action.

In a civil trial, the plaintiff does not have to convince the judge that he or she is right 'beyond reasonable doubt'. It is enough to prove the case on the **balance of probabilities**. This means that the plaintiff must prove their version of events is more likely, or more believable, than the defendant's.

Source: The Courts Service of Ireland

1. Why is this a civil case rather than a criminal case?

2. What is a plaintiff?

3. Who decides the outcome of the trial in this case?

4. How is the decision-making part of the trial different in a criminal action than in a civil action?

5. Why do you think it is easier to prove a case in a civil action?

● CALL TO ACTION | *Chapter 7*

Exercise 79D Using the law to deal with littering

Key Skills

Success criteria ☐ I can explain how to use laws to solve a littering problem.

Rubbish left in an open or public place, such as paper wrappings, cigarette butts and dog fouling is litter. Local authorities are responsible for keeping public places litter free. They do this by providing and emptying bins, cleaning streets and taking legal action against people who break or ignore the law. The outdoor areas of property that people own or rent must be kept free of litter.

It is also illegal to burn household waste in a private garden. The local authority can issue a notice which tells a person to remove litter. If they fail to do so, the local authority can do whatever is necessary to clear it and the offender must pay the costs. Illegal dumping can be reported to the local authority who then investigate. They can ask for evidence of where a person is disposing of their waste and impose a fine.

Look at the following problem in a neighbourhood and then do the hot-seating exercise that follows.

A local resident describes a problem in her neighbourhood. Alex, 54, said, 'I have been living here for 20 years. There are trees, birds and flowers. But two years ago a family moved into the area. They do not use the refuse bins and instead dump their food in the back garden. Sometimes they burn the rubbish and there is black smoke and horrible smells coming from it. At first it was smelly especially in summer but recently we have noticed a problem with flies and other insects. This morning I saw rats running along the wall between our two gardens. Something needs to be done!'

The class will do a hot-seating exercise where a number of characters will take the hot seat to be interviewed. Write out the questions you would like to ask each of the following characters: Alex, a Garda who has been called out, a member of the Residents' Association and Sam, a member of the family causing the problem.

Alex	Garda	Residents' Association	Sam

Lesson 80: The role of Irish courts

Na Cúirteanna Breithiúnais Coiriúla
The Criminal Courts of Justice

Learning outcome 3.9
Students should be able to explain the role and relevance of local, national and international courts.

Exercise 80A Deciding which courts will try cases

Key Skills   Success criteria ☐ I can identify which courts which try various cases.

There are several different courts in the Irish legal system.

In the **District Court** a judge sitting without a jury decides on:

- **Civil actions** where the compensation claimed is not more than €15,000
- **Criminal matters** like drink driving, speeding, assault, criminal damage.

Sligo District Court

In the **Circuit Court**:

- A **judge and jury** decide on criminal cases except very serious cases such as murder
- **Civil cases** are tried by a judge sitting without a jury. These cases deal with compensation claims which do not exceed €75,000. The Circuit Court also deals with family law cases such as divorce.
- Appeals from the District Court are also heard.

In the **Special Criminal Court**, three judges sitting without a jury deal with criminal charges involving terrorist organisations and drug gangs.

In the **High Court**:

- A **judge** may sit with or without a jury in civil actions. The High Court deals with civil actions appealed from the Circuit Court or where the claim exceeds €38,000.
- Serious criminal offences, such as murder, are tried. A judge and jury try these cases. It is known as the Central Criminal Court when dealing with criminal cases.

The **Court of Appeal** hears appeals from the High Court, Circuit Court, Central Criminal Court and Special Criminal Court.

The **Supreme Court** is the highest court in Ireland. It hears appeals from the Court of Appeal and the High Court. Appeals cannot be taken further than the Supreme Court. Article 26 of the Constitution allows the president to refer any bill passed by the Oireachtas to the Supreme Court to decide whether it is constitutional.

■ CALL TO ACTION | *Chapter 7*

Look at the following cases, and decide which court you think cases are being tried in.

Case	Court
1. A man is claiming €2,500 compensation for a faulty boiler installed in his house.	
2. If this court decides that online material shared publicly and not just with the victim is considered harassment, the case cannot be appealed further.	
3. A crime gang member is being tried in this court because of the fear he would intimidate a jury.	
4. A couple are looking for a divorce.	
5. A famous actress is taking a libel case against a newspaper and seeking substantial damages.	
6. A woman convicted of murder is appealing the conviction.	

Exercise 80B **Understanding the various roles involved in a criminal trial**

Key Skills   **Success criteria**   ☐   I can identify the different roles in a criminal trial.

The main roles of people in the courtroom include the judge, defence and prosecution barristers, solicitors, jury and registrar.

Watch the video and answer the questions that follow:

> **You Tube** Go to YouTube and search for 'Lets Look at the Law: Who's Who in the Courtroom? The Courts Service of Ireland' (3:44).

1. Which courts deal with criminal cases without a jury?

2. What does the judge do?

3. Who is the prosecutor?

4. Who is the defendant?

5. What is the barrister's role?

6. What is the solicitor's role?

Lesson 80: The role of Irish courts

7. What is the jury's role?

8. What are the possible outcomes of a criminal case?

Exercise 80C Understanding how a court case operates

Key Skills **Success criteria** ☐ I can explain how a trial operates.

In a trial, **barristers** (sometimes called **counsel**) represent their clients, ask questions of the witnesses and argue their client's case. Barristers generally wear a black gown with a white collar and may wear a wig. A **junior counsel** prepares most of the paperwork and can represent clients in the District Court. A **senior counsel** is more experienced and represents clients in the High Court, Court of Appeal and Supreme Court. They are assisted by a junior counsel.

During a trial, the barristers for the prosecution and for the defence make an opening speech. The prosecution present their case first. They call their witnesses and conduct an **examination-in-chief**, which is direct questioning of a witness they call. The defence side then **cross-examine** the witness and this continues until all the prosecution witnesses have been called. The defence then present their case, calling their witnesses and conducting their examination-in-chief. The prosecution then cross-examine the witnesses. Finally, the prosecution and defence barristers make their closing speeches.

> **YouTube** Go to YouTube and search for 'Let's Look at Law: How Do You Run a Trial? The Courts Service of Ireland' (4:36).

Watch the video (stopping at 3 mins 35 secs) and answer the following questions.

1. What happens after the jury is sworn in?

2. What are the two types of questioning barristers use to examine witnesses?

■ CALL TO ACTION | *Chapter 7*

3. When does the defence make its case?

_____
_____

4. What happens once all the witnesses have given evidence?

_____
_____

5. What does the judge do?

_____
_____

Exercise 80D Examining the role and operation of prisons

Key Skills   Success criteria ☐ I can identify how prisons operate and how they provide rehabilitation..

When a person is found guilty of a crime, the judge decides the sentence. Sentences include:

- Prison or **suspended sentences**, which means that the person is sentenced to a period of time in prison but they do not need to go to prison if they do not commit a crime during this time
- Fines or paying compensation
- Community service orders, which involves cleaning up litter, gardening, painting and decorating in the community
- Curfews
- Disqualification from driving.

The judge considers several factors before sentencing. These include:

- The offender's personal circumstances, age, addiction issues, previous convictions, what they have lost because of the crime (job, friends, etc.)
- The offender's character
- How the crime happened, if the person was provoked or if it was an accident
- Whether anybody was injured or threatened, whether somebody's house was broken into or whether firearms or knives were used
- The value of the goods stolen and whether they were recovered
- Whether the offender admitted their crime and whether they were sorry
- The impact on the victim.

Prisons are used to punish and to rehabilitate offenders (help them return to society and prevent them reoffending).

There are 14 prisons in Ireland; 11 are closed (which have very strict security), two are open (which have no locks, bars or perimeter fences) and one is semi-open (which have very little internal security).

Lesson 80: The role of Irish courts

Watch the two videos and answer the questions that follow.

1. Go to YouTube and search for 'Inside Mountjoy Prison Newstalk' (6:20, start at 38 secs).

2. Go to www.irishprisons.ie and search for 'Midlands prison: life behind bars' (2:29).

Video 1

1. What are protection prisoners?

2. What questions are asked at the committal interview?

3. What is the challenging behaviour unit?

4. What measures are in place in Mountjoy to rehabilitate prisoners?

Video 2

5. What type of prison is Midlands Prison?

6. What incentives are given to encourage prisoners to attend education and training workshops?

7. Why do prisoners want to work in the kitchen?

8. What other training is available to prisoners?

9. What percentage of prisoners reoffend within a year of being released from prison?

10. What reasons are given for prisoners reoffending?

Lesson 81: International courts

Learning outcome 3.9
Students should be able to explain the role and relevance of local, national and international courts.

Exercise 81A — Examining the role of the EU Court of Justice

Key Skills

Success criteria ☐ I can explain the work of the EU Court of Justice.

The **Court of Justice of the European Union**, the **Supreme Court for EU law**, is based in Luxembourg. It interprets EU laws and makes sure that the law is implemented equally in all member states.

> **YouTube**: Go to YouTube and search for 'How the Court works the basics – Court of Justice of the European Union'. (2:46).

Court of Justice of the EU

Watch the video about the EU Court of Justice and answer the questions that follow.

1. How many courts are in the EU Court of Justice?
   _____

2. What does it mean if a lot of judges are hearing a case?
   _____
   _____

3. Name two areas dealt with by the Court of Justice.
   _____
   _____

4. When do individuals or companies take a case to the General Court?
   _____
   _____

Lesson 81: International courts

5. Who do member states bring cases against in the General Court?

6. What areas do member states bring to the General Court?

Exercise 81B Examining the impact of the European Court of Human Rights

Key Skills   **Success criteria** ☐ I can explain the impact of the European Court of Human Rights.

In Chapter 2, you learned about the **European Court of Human Rights**, which guarantees that the rights of citizens of Council of Europe member states are respected. The court deals only with rights protected under the European Convention on Human Rights (ECHR).

Working in pairs, read the Jabari vs Turkey case study and answer the questions that follow.

The European Court of Human Rights

Case Study

Jabari vs Turkey

Hoda Jabari was 22 when she fell in love with a man she met at college in Iran. The couple decided to get married. However, his parents stopped the marriage, and two years later he ended up marrying someone else. Ms Jabari continued to see him in secret. They were both arrested by the Iranian police. The officers suspected Ms Jabari of participating in adultery, for which she could be stoned to death under Iranian law.

With the help of her family, Hoda was released and fled to Istanbul. She tried to seek asylum in Turkey, but her request was denied because it had been made too late. The Turkish authorities were about to send her back to Iran when she appealed to the European Court of Human Rights for help.

The Court ruled that sending Hoda back to Iran to face a possible stoning would violate her basic rights. Hoda was not sent back to Iran. Following the court's ruling she was granted a residence permit in Turkey. She left to seek a new life in Canada in 2001.

Source: Council of Europe

1. What was the punishment for adultery under Iranian law?

2. Why was Hoda denied asylum in Turkey?

365

● CALL TO ACTION | *Chapter 7*

3. Why was she able to take the case in Turkey rather than in Iran?
   _____

4. Why did she win the case?
   _____
   _____

5. What does this case tell you about the European Court of Human Rights?
   _____
   _____

Exercise 81C Examining the role of the ICJ

Key Skills   **Success criteria** ☐ I can explain how the ICJ settles cases between member states and advises on international law.

The **International Court of Justice (ICJ)** is part of the UN. It is also called the World Court because it settles disputes between countries and gives opinions on international law. All UN member states can take cases against others at the ICJ. The ICJ has 15 judges elected for nine-year terms by the UN General Assembly and Security Council. It is based at the Peace Palace in the Hague in the Netherlands.

The Peace Palace

Working in pairs, read the case study on the Chagos Islands and answer the questions that follow.

Case Study

Legal Consequences of the Separation of the Chagos Archipelago from Mauritius (2019)

In 1965, Mauritius became independent from the UK. But part of the colony of Mauritius, the Chagos Islands, with a population of 1,500 to 2,000 people, were kept by the UK. Diego Garcia was the only inhabited Chagos Island. Between 1968 and 1973, British authorities began deporting the residents of Diego Garcia to build a US military base on the island. Islanders who left the island for medical reasons or to visit family were not allowed to return, pets were killed to scare people into leaving, food and medical supplies were restricted and finally the people who remained on the island were forced on to cargo ships going to Mauritius or the Seychelles.

Mauritius brought the case to the UN General Assembly in 2017. The General Assembly voted to refer the issue to the International Court of Justice. In 2019, the ICJ decided that the UK's separation of the Chagos Islands from the rest of Mauritius in 1965 was unlawful and was not 'based on a free and genuine expression of the people involved'. It said that the UK must 'end its administration of the Chagos Islands as rapidly as possible'. The General Assembly voted 116 to 6 in favour of welcoming the ICJ's advisory opinion. The UK noted the decision but did not accept it.

1. Why were people deported from the Chagos islands?

2. Do you think they wanted to leave? Why/why not?

3. Why did the ICJ find that the UK should 'end its administration' of the islands?

4. Was this decision well accepted by other countries? How do you know?

5. Do you think the court's findings will resolve the problem? Why/why not?

Exercise 81D   Analysing the ICC

Key Skills   **Success criteria**   ☐   I can identify the strengths and weaknesses of the ICC.

The **International Criminal Court (ICC)** was set up as a permanent court to try and punish people who have caused the most serious offences. These include:

- Genocide, which is aiming to destroy a national, ethnic or religious group
- War crimes, which involve torture, using child soldiers or targeting civilians by attacking schools, hospitals, etc.
- Crimes against humanity, which are large-scale attacks on civilians including murder, slavery, torture and imprisonment
- Aggression – using armed force against the political independence of another state.

Before the court was established in 2002, there had been no way of trying these crimes, apart from some international tribunals set up specifically to deal with cases such as the Nazis (Nuremburg) and Rwanda. The ICC is based in the Hague in the Netherlands. Currently 123 countries accept the jurisdiction of the court. Some countries such as China, India, Indonesia, North Korea, Saudi Arabia and Turkey have not signed the treaty and others such as the US, Israel, Russia and Iran signed the treaty but their parliaments did not ratify it. Two countries, Burundi and the Philippines, left when the court began investigating their governments.

The ICC deals with crimes:

- Committed on the territory of a state which accepts the authority of the ICC or by one of its nationals
- Referred to it by a prosecutor of the United Nations Security Council
- Only when national justice systems are genuinely not able or willing to carry out proceedings.

Unlike the International Court of Justice, the ICC can prosecute individuals.

CALL TO ACTION | *Chapter 7*

Members of International Criminal Court

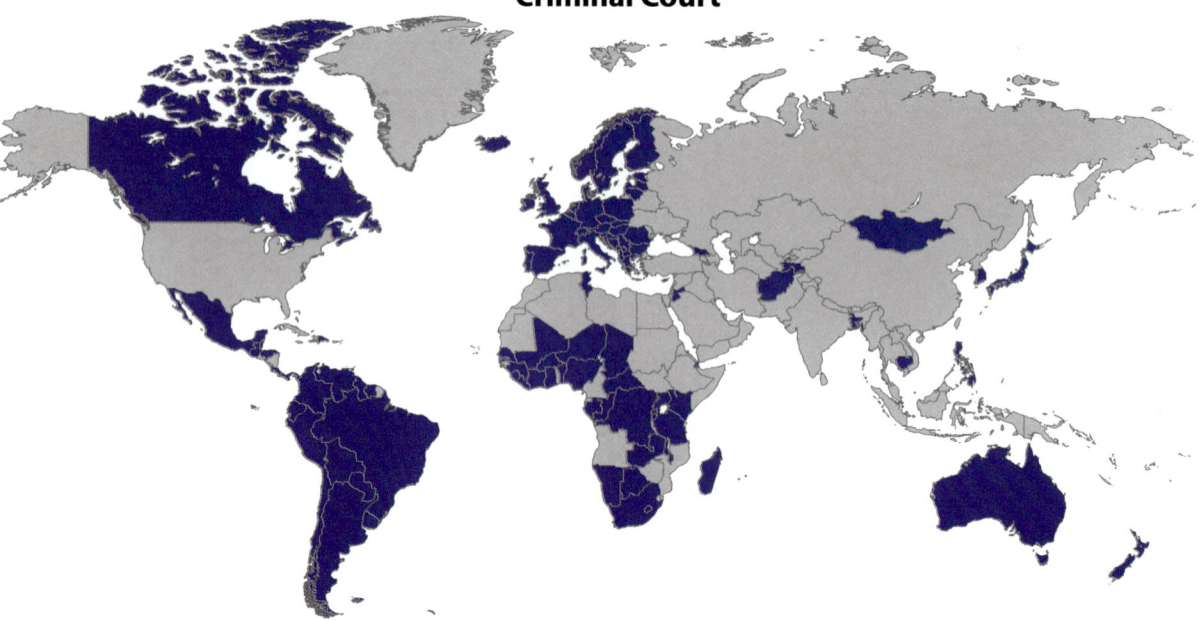

Working in pairs, answer the questions below.

1. Why was the International Criminal Court set up?

2. What types of crimes can it try?

3. Why is it important to have a court like this?

4. Can you identify any weaknesses of the court?

5. What type of people are tried in the ICC?

Lesson 82: Changing laws

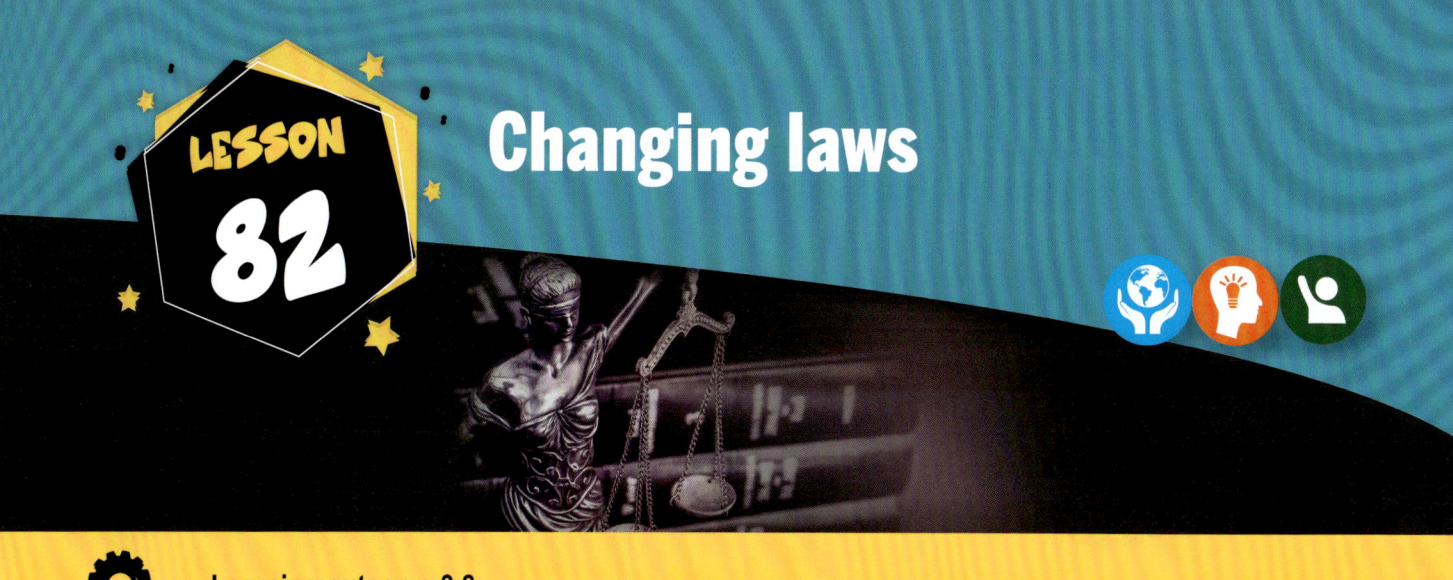

Learning outcome 3.8
Students should be able to explain how laws are made, enforced and evolve over time.

Exercise 82A Understanding legal and moral dilemmas

Key Skills

Success criteria
☐ I can explain how laws and morality come into conflict.

- **Legal duty** is a citizen's obligations under the law. For example, people must not drive over the speed limit or smoke in the workplace.
- **Moral responsibility** is the personal obligations people feel based on their beliefs about what is right and wrong.

Working in pairs read 'Heinz's Dilemma' and discuss the following questions. Write your answers below.

Heinz's Dilemma

In Europe, a woman was near death from a special kind of cancer. There was one drug that the doctors thought might save her. It was a form of radium that a druggist [*pharmacist*] in the same town had recently discovered. The drug was expensive to make, but the druggist was charging ten times what the drug cost him to make. He paid $400 for the radium and charged $4,000 for a small dose of the drug. The sick woman's husband, Heinz, went to everyone he knew to borrow the money and tried every legal means, but he could only get together about $2,000, which is half of what it cost. He told the druggist that his wife was dying, and asked him to sell it cheaper or let him pay later. But the druggist said, 'No, I discovered the drug and I'm going to make money from it.' So, having tried every legal means, Heinz gets desperate and considers breaking into the man's store to steal the drug for his wife.

Source: The College Theology Society, 1983

1. Heinz should steal the drugs because …

2. Heinz should not steal the drugs because …

3. What would you do if you were Heinz?

369

■ CALL TO ACTION | *Chapter 7*

Exercise 82B **Analysing the link between laws and morals**

Key Skills **Success criteria** ☐ I can explain how laws and morality are different and similar to each other.

Watch the video and answer the questions below.

> **YouTube** Go to YouTube and search for 'Legal vs. Moral: Written vs. Right – Political Philosophy Series – Academy 4 Social Change' (4:13).

1. What law did the pedestrian break?

2. What are the similarities between laws and morals?

3. What are the differences between laws and morals?

4. The law is binary. What does that mean?

5. Why is the Code of Ur-Nammu important?

6. Where did morality originally come from?

7. Give examples of how morals change.

8. How do morals and laws influence each other?

Lesson 82: Changing laws

Exercise 82C Examining the consequences of breaking unfair laws

Key Skills **Success criteria** ☐ I can explain how laws may need to be broken to change them.

Read the passage on Rosa Parks and answer the questions that follow.

Rosa Parks was born in Alabama in the USA in 1913. At that time, Alabama, like many other southern US states, had passed the Jim Crow Laws, which enforced racial segregation. The segregation laws meant that black and white people went to separate schools, restaurants, churches and even used separate waiting rooms. In many states black people could work only in low paid jobs.

On 1 December 1955, Rosa was returning home from work in Montgomery by bus. The segregation laws meant that black people had to sit in the back of the bus, the front seats were kept for white people. Rosa was sitting in the front row of seats reserved for black people when a white man got on the bus. He had no seat, so the driver asked the front row of black passengers to stand to create an extra row for white passengers. Three passengers got up, but Rosa refused. She was arrested for breaking the segregation laws.

The story spread and the black population of Montgomery began to boycott the buses. The boycott lasted over a year. A new association, the Montgomery Improvement Association (MIA), was set up with Dr Martin Luther King as its president. Rosa was found guilty of breaking the segregation laws, given a suspended sentence, fined and ordered to pay her court costs. She appealed right up to the US Supreme Court, which ruled that the segregation laws were unconstitutional.

During the boycott, Dr King's house was bombed and many black people had to walk long distances as they did not have cars. After receiving death threats, Rosa and her husband moved to Michigan, a northern US state.

Rosa died in 2005 aged 92.

> People always say that I didn't give up my seat because I was tired, but that isn't true. I was not tired physically – or no more tired than I usually was at the end of a working day. I was not old, although some people have an image of me as being old then. I was forty-two. No, the only tired I was, was tired of giving in.
> *Rosa Parks*

1. What was the impact of the Jim Crow laws?
   _____
   _____

2. How did Rosa break the law?
   _____

3. Why did she break the law?
   _____
   _____

4. How do you know that others supported her decision?
   _____

5. What was the eventual result for Rosa?
   _____

■ CALL TO ACTION | *Chapter 7*

6. How was this an example of breaking the law for moral reasons?

   _____

   _____

7. How did this protest make a difference?

   _____

   _____

Exercise 82D | **Identifying how to change laws that I do not agree with**

Key Skills   **Success criteria**   ☐ I can explain how I would change laws that I believe are not right.

There are several ways in which people can change laws. They can:

- Contact their local TD, senator or county councillor to say what they want. If a lot of people are contacting politicians, it makes them realise that this idea is popular with people.
- Organise a demonstration. Large numbers of people marching shows a lot of support for a cause.
- Make people aware of the problem by launching a campaign. This could be online through social media, in newspapers or on TV and radio.
- Organise a petition. It is easy to organise online petitions on websites like www.change.org. A lot of people signing a petition shows there is a lot of public interest in it.
- Organise strikes. Greta Thunberg's climate strike raised a lot of attention for her cause.

Look at the following situations where young people are not happy with the law. Do you agree with them or not? Why? What is the best way to change the law?

Situation	Do you agree?	Why/why not?	What is the best way to change this law?
1. I think it is ridiculous that I have to wait until I am 18 to vote in elections or referenda. In Scotland 16 and 17 year olds can vote.			
2. I'm 15, but I can only get 70% of the minimum wage for my part-time job. It's not fair.			
3. I'm 15 and I hate school. I shouldn't have to come to school.			
4. I live in the country and I take my mother's car to visit my grandmother up the road. I'm only 15, so I could get in trouble, but I'm a better driver than most adults.			

Lesson 83: The nine grounds of discrimination

Learning outcome 3.10
Students should be able to list the nine grounds under which discrimination is illegal in Irish law, with examples.

Exercise 83A Identifying situations where discrimination has occurred

Key Skills **Success criteria** ☐ I can explain where discrimination has occurred and why it is discrimination.

In Chapter 1, you learned that inequality is when money, property or other resources and opportunities are distributed unequally among different members of society. Discrimination happens when a person is treated less favourably than somebody else because of who they are. In Ireland, the Employment Equality Acts make it illegal to discriminate against or harass an employee because of:

1. Gender
2. Civil status (married, single, civil partnership)
3. Family status (children, pregnant, carer)
4. Sexual orientation
5. Religious belief
6. Age
7. Disability
8. Race, nationality
9. Membership of the Travelling Community.

These categories are referred to as the **nine grounds**.

The Equal Status Acts make it illegal to discriminate in providing services, accommodation, education and goods on the same nine grounds. In accommodation, people cannot be discriminated against because they are receiving social welfare payments. Adverts such as 'would suit professionals' or 'rent allowance not accepted' are examples of discriminatory adverts.

There are some exemptions such as:

- If a person is not able to afford to pay the rent it is not discriminatory to refuse to rent to them
- A sport club can hold an event for men only, but it must also hold an event for women
- Single sex boys' and girls' schools are allowed.

Anyone who thinks they have been discriminated against can make a complaint to the **Workplace Relations Commission (WRC)**.

Look at the scenarios on the next page and decide whether or not discrimination has occurred. Explain your response.

CALL TO ACTION | Chapter 7

Scenario	Discrimination: yes or no?	Why/Why not?
1. Noel is 58 and went for promotion to the job of regional manager in the company where he works. He was highly qualified and experienced, but the position went to Lisa, who was 26 and less qualified. When he questioned why he had not got the job, he was told that the travel element of the job made it more suited to a younger person.		
2. Sarah was looking for accommodation and went to see a house. The landlord was asking for €800 per month. Sarah could not afford to pay this much and was not offered the house. She heard later that a man was renting the house.		
3. During her interview for a job, Farah mentioned that she has just got married. The manager asked her if she planned on having a family soon, and Farah said no, but was embarrassed. The job was offered to Aoife who is single.		
4. Sam was refused entry to his local secondary school. When his mother asked to speak to the principal, she told her that the First Year pupils' classrooms were upstairs and not suited to somebody who used a wheelchair.		
5. At Seán's company, everybody got a Christmas bonus. This year the bonus was a weekend in a luxury hotel. Seán got a weekend for one person, but his married colleagues got a stay for two people.		

Exercise 83B Identifying groups affected by discrimination

Key Skills **Success criteria** ☐ I can explain, using statistics, which groups are affected by discrimination.

Working in pairs, look at the table and bar chart on the next page from the Central Statistics Office and answer the questions that follow.

374

Lesson 83: The nine grounds of discrimination

Quarter 1 2019

Percentage of persons who experienced discrimination[1]	
% of persons aged 18+	Q1 2019
State	17.7
Principal economic status	
At work	17.1
Unemployed	30.2
Student	21.9
Home duties	14.1
Retired	12.4
Others	24.1
LGBTI+	
LGBTI+	33.2
Non-LGBTI+	17.2
Nationality	
Irish	16.3
Non-Irish	26.7

[1] In the two years prior to interview

Discrimination by perceived grounds, 2019

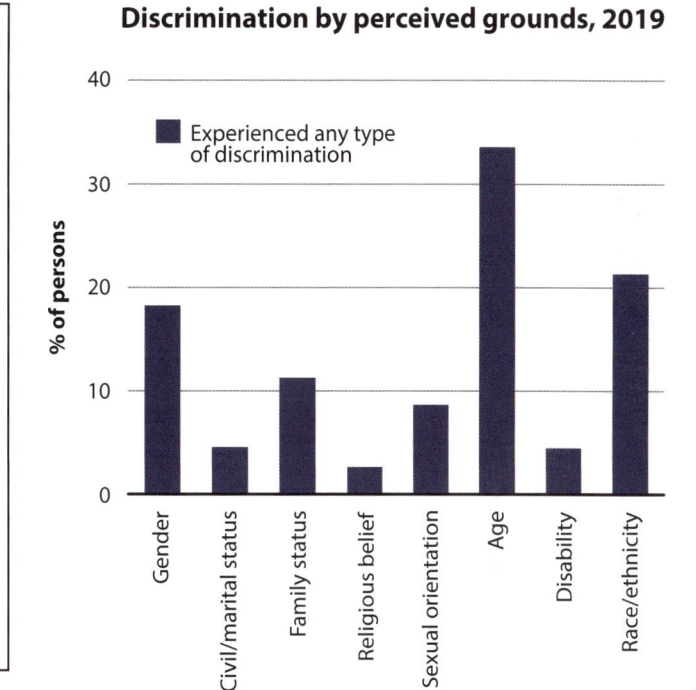

(Bar chart showing "Experienced any type of discrimination" across grounds: Gender, Civil/marital status, Family status, Religious belief, Sexual orientation, Age, Disability, Race/ethnicity)

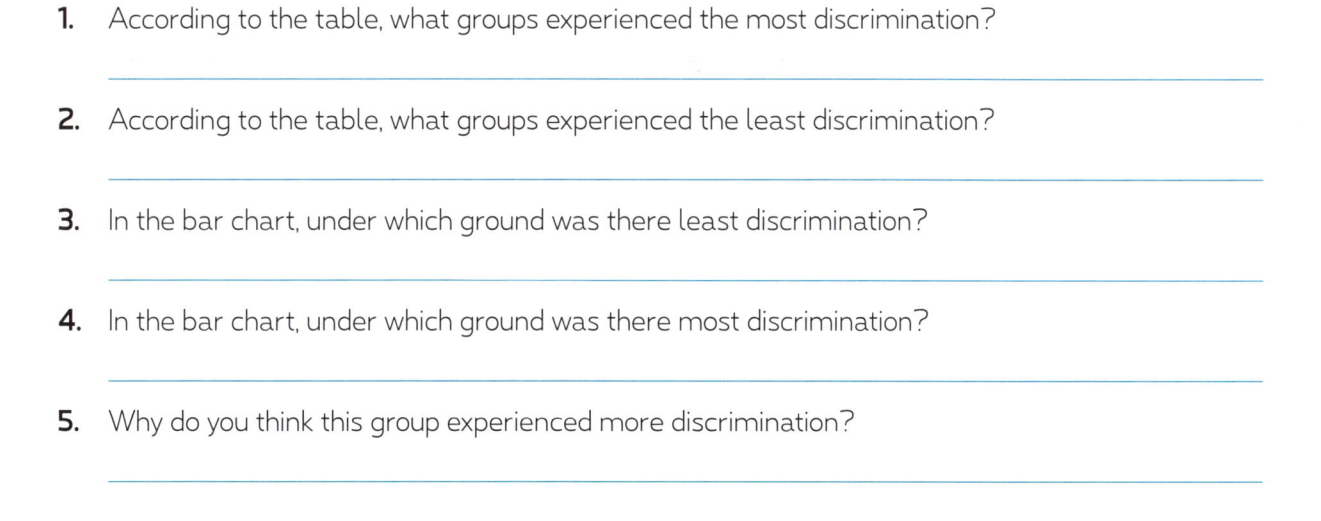

1. According to the table, what groups experienced the most discrimination?

2. According to the table, what groups experienced the least discrimination?

3. In the bar chart, under which ground was there least discrimination?

4. In the bar chart, under which ground was there most discrimination?

5. Why do you think this group experienced more discrimination?

Exercise 83C — Identifying different types of discrimination experienced by different groups

Key Skills

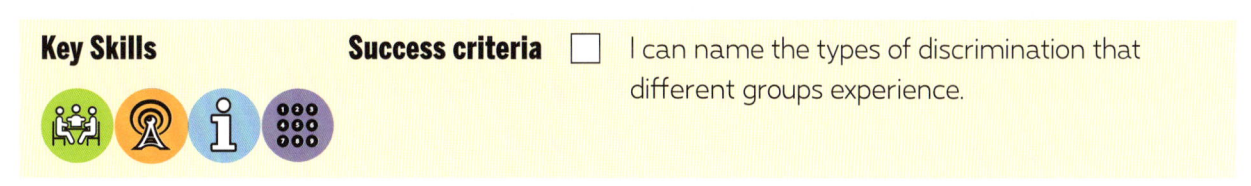

Success criteria ☐ I can name the types of discrimination that different groups experience.

Working in pairs, look at the table on the next page, which explains where people have experienced discrimination. Answer the questions that follow.

375

CALL TO ACTION | Chapter 7

Discrimination by social setting of discrimination and perceived grounds for discrimination, Q1 2019

% of persons aged 18+ who experienced discrimination

Social setting of discrimination	The workplace	Looking for work	Pubs and restaurants	Financial institutions	Health	Public transport	Education	Looking for accommodation	Contact with Gardaí
Gender	33.0	15.6	12.4	11.5	0.8	9.3	6.3	2.9	32.6
Civil or marital status	4.0	3.9	1.0	5.1	6.8	0.0	0.0	4.7	0.0
Family status	5.2	12.1	3.8	12.5	5.3	1.7	27.4	9.4	4.4
Religious belief	0.2	2.7	3.6	3.7	6.5	2.2	4.4	0.4	0.0
Sexual orientation	2.2	2.8	30.4	0.0	5.2	5.7	1.4	0.0	5.6
Age	25.9	35.3	18.1	35.2	16.2	5.2	38.2	19.2	26.2
Disability	2.8	1.5	2.8	7.1	2.0	34.7	6.3	2.2	1.2
Race/Skin colour/Ethnic group/Nationality	22.6	19.7	29.1	15.4	7.9	35.9	10.9	15.4	10.5
Membership of the Travelling Community	0.9	2.0	5.7	0.0	0.0	4.6	6.4	3.6	6.8

1. In which social settings was the most gender discrimination recorded?

2. In which social setting was the most discrimination based on sexual orientation recorded?

3. In which social setting was the most discrimination based on disability recorded?

4. In which social setting was the most discrimination based on membership of the Travelling Community recorded?

5. What groups experience most discrimination in accommodation?

6. Do any of these figures surprise you? Why/Why not?

Lesson 83: The nine grounds of discrimination

Exercise 83D Investigating how different cases apply to real people

Key Skills **Success criteria** ☐ I can identify the different types of cases taken and their resolution.

Mediation is when a neutral mediator helps two sides who are in dispute to come to an agreement without the need to go to court.

Look at the following cases which appeared before the WRC. Answer the questions on the next page.

Case	Topic	Outcome
A. A Tenant v. A Landlord	The woman contacted a landlord to view a rental property. The landlord asked whether she was in full-time employment. She said no, but she was in receipt of the Housing Assistance Payment (HAP) and was willing to pay an extra rent top-up of €100 per month. He said he did not want people on the HAP scheme.	The WRC ruled that the landlord's preference for non-HAP tenants was discriminatory. It ordered the landlord to pay a total of €750 in compensation to the woman.
B. A Prospective Employee v. A Recruitment Service	The complainant, a newly qualified man in his early thirties who is deaf, alleged discrimination on the disability ground. His interview offer with a recruitment service was withdrawn after he made basic reasonable accommodation (changes to make work conditions fair for a person with a disability) requests.	The complaint was resolved by mediation and included a written apology and a payment of €2,500 by the recruitment service. The recruitment service agreed to develop an Equality and Reasonable Accommodation Policy and to provide training to staff, once completed. The recruitment service further committed to providing staff with Deaf Awareness Training.
C. A Complainant v. A Limited Company	An estate agent declined to show a rental property to a member of the Travelling Community, saying that it was no longer available. However, when a friend of the woman, who is not a member of the Travelling Community, subsequently contacted the estate agent, the agent said that it was still available and arranged a viewing for them.	The Irish Human Rights and Equality Commission referred the matter to the WRC for mediation on behalf of the woman. It was resolved to the satisfaction of all parties involved.
D. A Service User v. An Airline	The complainant claimed that prior to boarding the flight she was requested by the airline's staff to move from her allocated seat in order to accommodate the religious beliefs of two men who had been allocated the seats beside her and who did not wish to sit beside a woman.	The complainant lodged a complaint with the WRC. The matter was resolved to the satisfaction of all parties following a mediation process facilitated by the Workplace Relations Commission.

Source: Irish Human Rights and Equality Commission

CALL TO ACTION | Chapter 7

1. Identify the type of discrimination in each case.

2. What services were involved in these cases?

3. Is there any case where rights come into conflict? If so, which one?

4. Many cases were resolved by mediation. What does that mean?

5. Why do you think that people were willing to solve cases by mediation?

Lesson 84: Legal case studies

No Smoking
Cosc ar thobac

Learning outcome 3.11
Students should be able to investigate how individuals or groups have used the law to bring about change in society.

Exercise 84A Investigating how ministers can change laws

Key Skills

Success criteria
☐ I can explain how ministers have the power to change laws.

There are many reasons why laws change. These include:
- Challenges are taken based on rights in the Constitution
- Technology changes and the laws need to change to keep up with this. For example, 40 years ago phones were not mobile devices.
- People's views change. For example, divorce was banned in Ireland until the 1990s.

Individuals and organisations also bring about changes in the law.

In 2004, smoking in the workplace was banned in Ireland. The Minister for Health at the time, Mícheál Martin, played a major role in changing this law.

Smoking! Ireland makes history with cigarette ban

Anita Guidera   **January 17 2014**

HISTORY was made in March 2004 when Ireland became the first country in the world to introduce comprehensive legislation banning smoking in workplaces. Overnight, ashtrays vanished from pubs, clubs and restaurants. Those caught smoking faced a hefty €3,000 fine. It soon became obvious that the ban had been a huge success. Cigarette sales fell by 60pc in bars and it was reported that 7,000 people gave up smoking in the first 12 months after the ban came into effect.

A recent study showed that an estimated 4,000 lives had been saved by its introduction and thousands of smokers successfully quit the habit. For months, Minister for Health and Children Mícheál Martin and his team of experts had worked hard to ensure the legislation was strong enough to withstand legal challenges, but they had no way of knowing how the public would react. 'The tobacco industry itself was very strongly against it. Publicans at the time were very much opposed to it. There was a big push to get a compromise, maybe part of the room or pub or restaurant to be dedicated as a smoking area, but of course that wouldn't have worked. Smoke drifts. It doesn't stay in a corner.

'TDs would tell stories of their clinics being full of publicans in the weeks and months leading up to it. I remember one deputy telling me they were queueing out the door. He just had to keep saying, "This man is not for turning".'

But Mr Martin was heartened by the response from the public and bowled over by the international media attention.

Source: *The Irish Independent*

● CALL TO ACTION | *Chapter 7*

Working in pairs, answer the following questions.

1. Why was the law banning smoking unusual at the time?

2. How do we know it was a success?

3. Was everyone in favour of it? How do you know?

4. Why did the minister not want a compromise?

5. How was he put under pressure to compromise?

6. Was it accepted by the public?

7. What were the benefits of this law?

Exercise 84B Investigating how individuals can change laws

Key Skills   **Success criteria** ☐ I can explain how individuals can use the courts to change laws.

Working in pairs, answer the following questions.

Case Study

Case Study: N.V.H v. Minister for Justice and Equality

N.V.H. was a Burmese man who applied for refugee status when he arrived in Ireland in 2008. This was refused and he appealed. While waiting for the appeal, he was offered a job in the direct provision centre where he was living. He applied to the Minister for Justice and Equality for permission to take up this job, but he was refused because the Refugee Act 1996 banned asylum seekers from working while waiting for their cases to be decided.

N.V.H. took a case to the High Court challenging the Minister's decision and saying it was against the European Convention on Human Rights and the Constitution. He lost the case and he lost his appeal in the Court of Appeal. He decided to appeal to the Supreme Court, but in the time before his case was heard he was given refugee status.

The State said that his appeal was **moot** (pointless). The Supreme Court agreed that the case was moot but still heard the case because of the claim that constitutional rights were challenged.

In 2018, the court found that the complete ban on asylum seekers working went against the constitutional right to seek employment. Mr Justice O'Donnell said:

'It simply doesn't make sense to prevent people from entering the labour market. People don't want to be reliant on the state... Allowing people to work would also be of benefit to the exchequer in terms of tax and spending power and would be of huge benefit to integration.'

The government allowed asylum seekers to work if they had been waiting nine months or more for their application for asylum. In 2021, this was reduced to six months.

Lesson 84: Legal case studies

1. Why was N.V.H. not allowed to work?

2. How do you know that N.V.H. was persistent?

3. Why was his case described as 'moot'?

4. According to Mr Justice O'Donnell, what are the benefits of the right to work?

5. How did N.V.H.'s case lead to a change in the law?

6. N.V.H. changed the law in a different way to Minster Martin. Explain the difference.

Exercise 84C — Assessing my knowledge of the legal system

Key Skills **Success criteria** ☐ I can answer questions on the legal system.

Complete the crossword on the next page.

Across

1 A lawyer who argues your case in court
4 Laws made by the local authority
9 The most important court in the country
10 The Irish Constitution (do not include the fada)
11 When a bill becomes a law it is called an ...
13 The ICJ and ICC are based in this country. The ....
14 A way of changing the Constitution
15 The person who runs a court case and issues sentences
16 People found guilty of a serious crime can be sent here

Down

2 If a person receives this, they are not sent to prison, but may have to go if they commit another offence
3 An EU decision that must become part of the laws of every member state
5 Where laws are made in Ireland
6 The head judge in Ireland
7 Twelve people who decide if a person is guilty in a trial
8 The nine grounds prevent this
12 The Irish police

CALL TO ACTION | *Chapter 7*

Lesson 84: Legal case studies

Exercise 84D Assessing my knowledge about law

Key Skills **Success criteria** ☐ I can answer questions about law.

Working in pairs, tick the correct answers in the quiz below.

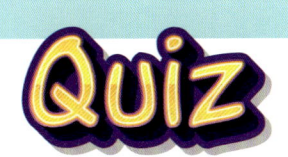

QUIZ

1. What is the most senior judge in Ireland called?
   - (a) The President of the High Court ☐
   - (b) The Master of the High Court ☐
   - (c) The Chief Justice ☐
   - (d) The President of the District Court ☐

2. Who advises the government on laws?
   - (a) The Chief Whip ☐
   - (b) The Attorney General ☐
   - (c) The Minister for Justice ☐
   - (d) The DPP ☐

3. What is unusual about the Special Criminal Court?
   - (a) It only meets once a year ☐
   - (b) It has no jury ☐
   - (c) It has no judge ☐
   - (d) It has no power ☐

4. This person's job is to decide whether a case should proceed to court.
   - (a) The Attorney General ☐
   - (b) The DPP ☐
   - (c) The Garda Commissioner ☐
   - (d) The Court Registrar ☐

5. The Irish Constitution is also known as...
   - (a) Bunreacht na hÉireann ☐
   - (b) The 1922 Constitution ☐
   - (c) The Magna Carta ☐
   - (d) The Bill of Rights ☐

6. What is a law passed by the Oireachtas called?
   - (a) An act ☐
   - (b) A bill ☐
   - (c) A sentence ☐
   - (d) A regulation ☐

7. What is required to change any article of the Constitution?
   - (a) A vote in the Oireachtas ☐
   - (b) The president's signature ☐
   - (c) A petition signed by over 50,000 people ☐
   - (d) A referendum ☐

Reflection: Reflecting on my learning about law

Learning outcome 3.14
Students should be able to reflect on their ongoing learning and what it means for them.

Key Skills

Success criteria ☐ I can give examples of how my thinking about the law has developed.

Look back at the skills and knowledge you have developed in this chapter. It is important to identify what you have learned and where you could learn more. Use the following worksheet to guide your reflection on the law. Then working in groups, discuss your responses for each of the questions below.

1. Before looking at the law, I thought …	
2. Things I learned about the law	
3. Where I got my information from	
4. How I know the information was reliable	
5. The different types of sources I got my information from	
6. The most interesting thing I learned was …	
7. How the new information I have learned will change what I do	

Action: Taking part in a mock trial

Having completed this chapter, you are now more aware of what a court case involves. You will now conduct a mock trial. The case before the court is as follows.

INDICTMENT

IN THE CIRCUIT CRIMINAL COURT,

CORK.

THE PEOPLE (AT THE SUIT OF THE DIRECTOR OF PUBLIC PROSECUTIONS)

v

DARA O'CONNOR

STATEMENT OF OFFENCE

Assault causing harm, contrary to Section 3 of the Non-Fatal Offences Against the Person Act 1997.

PARTICULARS OF OFFENCE

Dara O'Connor, on 24th September 2021 at Páirc Uí Chaoimh stadium, Cork you did assault Stevie Higgins catching his/her ankle and pushing him/her down steps causing him/her a serious back injury.

✓ Action 1 Understanding how to conduct a trial

Key Skills **Success criteria** ☐ I can identify how to conduct a criminal trial.

Watch the videos which show extracts from a mock criminal case and note the information you learn by answering the questions that follow.

> **YouTube** Go to YouTube and search for:
> 1. 'Lets Look at the Law: A Mock Trial in Action Part 1' (18:55).
> 2. 'Lets Look at the Law: A Mock Trial in Action Part 2' (5:26).

1. What do you notice about the layout of the court?

_____

_____

385

CALL TO ACTION | Chapter 7

2. How do the various people address the court?
   _____
   _____

3. What is not allowed?
   _____

✓ Action 2 Developing my role

Key Skills **Success criteria** ☐ I can list the information I need in order to make the trial a success.

The following roles need to be allocated for the trial:

Court staff	Judge, Registrar, Tipstaff/Judicial assistant, Stenographer
Prosecution	Senior counsel, Junior counsel, Solicitor
Defence	Senior counsel, Junior counsel, Solicitor
Prosecution witnesses	Stevie Higgins, Nollaig Moriarty, Alex Harris, Dr Walshe
Defence witnesses	Dara O'Connor, Cameron Smith
Reporters	12 members of the jury, including a chairperson

Once the roles have been allocated your teacher will give you additional information about your role. Use this to note how you will prepare for your trial. Note some of the key information you will need below.

_____
_____
_____
_____
_____
_____
_____
_____

✓ Action 3 Conducting the mock trial

Key Skills **Success criteria** ☐ I can play a role in a mock trial.

Conduct the trial.

Once the mock trial is complete and the judge has delivered their verdict, discuss as a class what you have learned about court cases.

Lesson 85

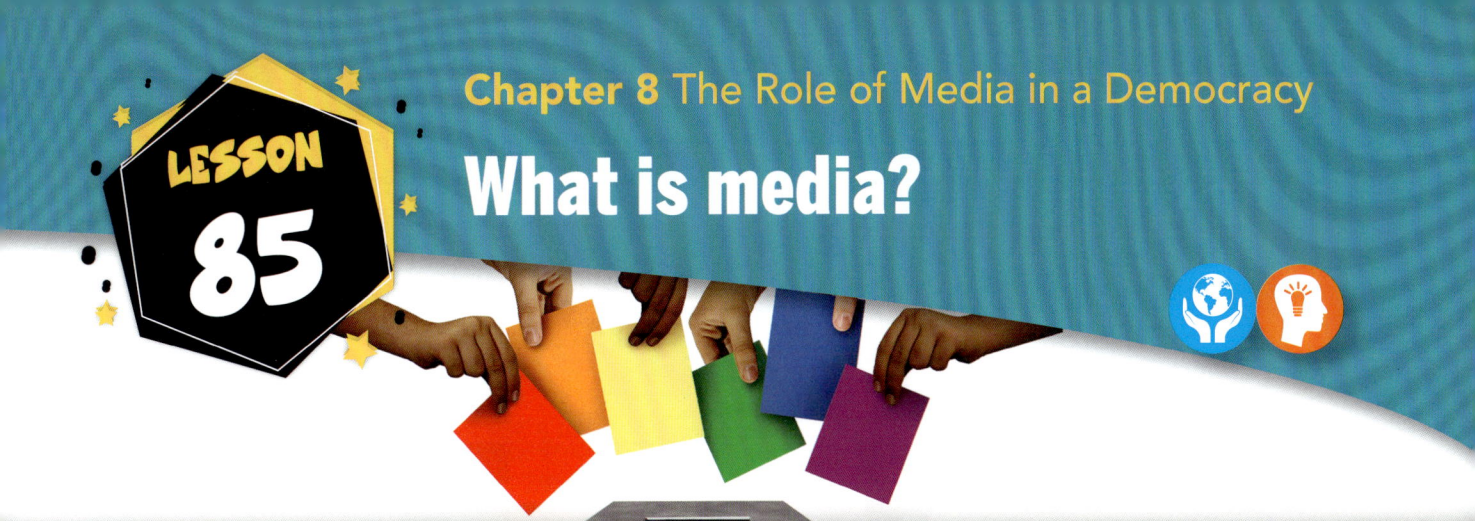

Chapter 8 The Role of Media in a Democracy

What is media?

Learning outcome 3.12

Students should be able to explore the role of different media in generating information and news and assess the pros and cons of each.

Exercise 85A Understanding a statistical report on media

Key Skills **Success criteria**
- I can explain, giving examples, whether or not a report is reliable.
- I can understand data presented in charts and explain what it means.

Media is a method of mass communication. This means that it delivers information to a large audience. There are three main ways of communicating:

1. **Broadcasting** (television and radio)
2. **Publishing** (newspapers and magazines)
3. **Internet** (websites, blogs, social media).

Media is important because it:

- Helps citizens to make responsible decisions based on facts rather than on opinions, which can be biased, uninformed or incorrect
- Investigates whether governments and powerful organisations and people in society are doing their jobs properly and acting within the law
- Can highlight injustices in society.

There are also disadvantages of media.

- Many media organisations are owned by companies whose main interest is making money.
- Some media are one-sided so do not present all sides of an issue.
- Some media report incorrect information (this may be intentional or unintentional).

In some countries the media is **censored**. This means that the media cannot print or broadcast certain information or opinions. Authoritarian governments censor the media to prevent journalists, organisations or other politicians from criticising them. These governments also use **propaganda** to make them appear in a positive light. Propaganda involves using information to influence other people's opinions. This information can be true or false.

■ CALL TO ACTION | *Chapter 8*

Look at the information below taken from the Reuters News Report for Ireland and answer the questions that follow:

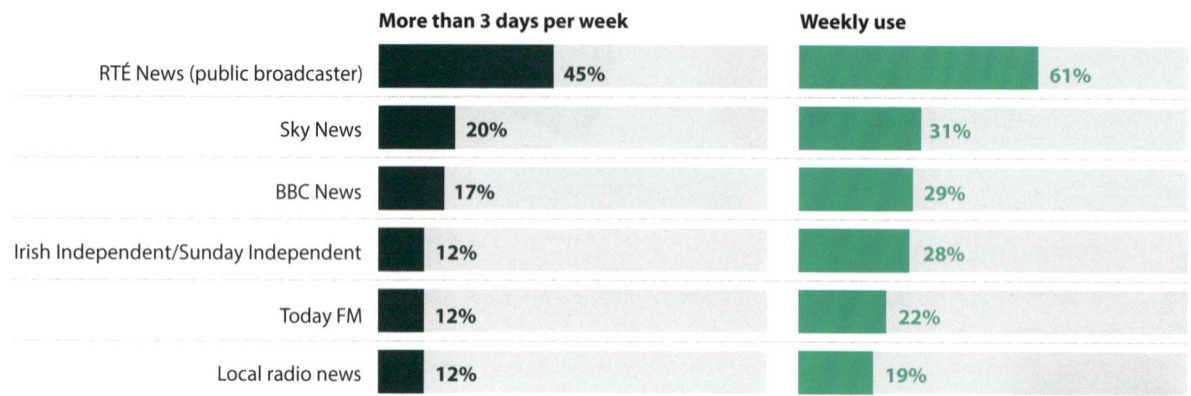

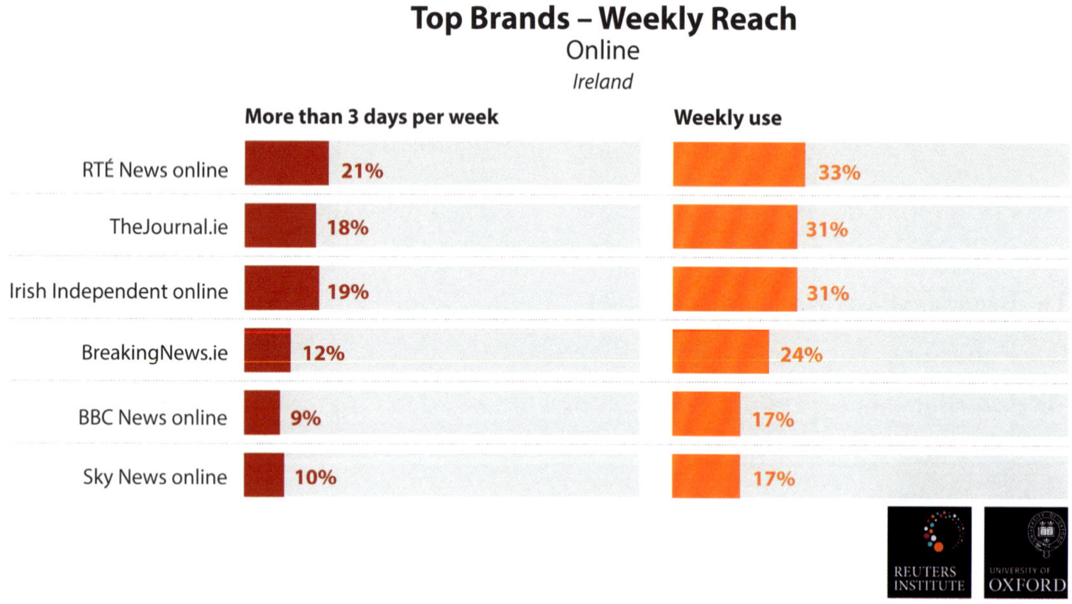

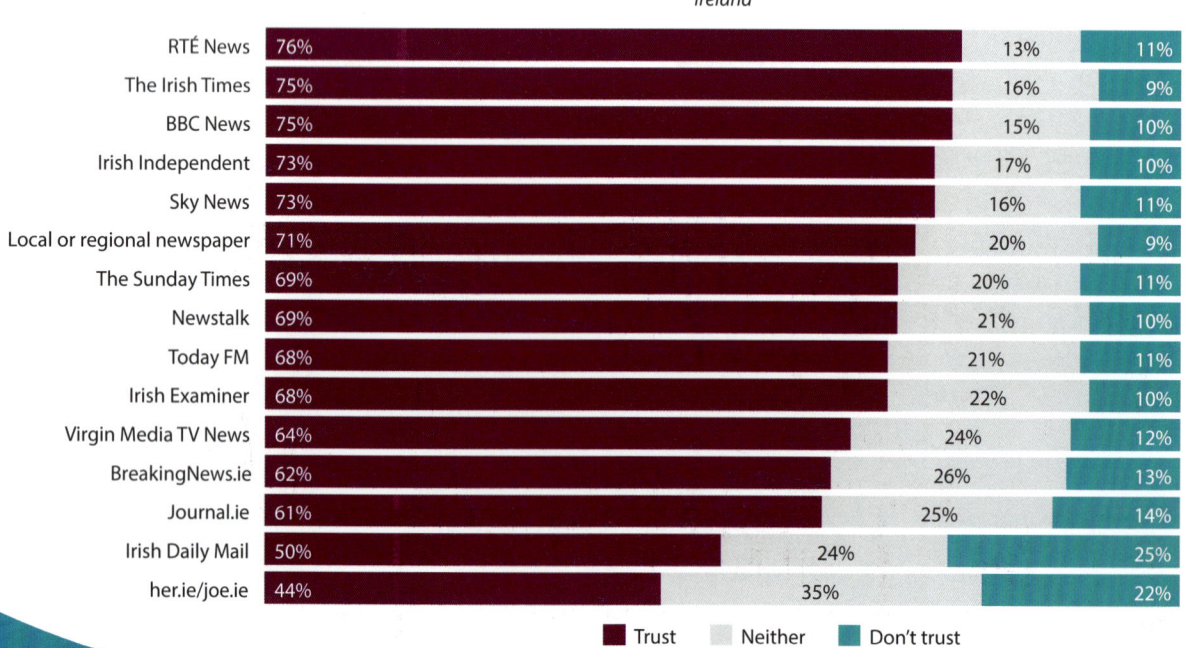

Top Brands – Weekly Reach
TV, Radio, Print
Ireland

More than 3 days per week

Brand	%
RTÉ News (public broadcaster)	45%
Sky News	20%
BBC News	17%
Irish Independent/Sunday Independent	12%
Today FM	12%
Local radio news	12%

Weekly use

Brand	%
RTÉ News (public broadcaster)	61%
Sky News	31%
BBC News	29%
Irish Independent/Sunday Independent	28%
Today FM	22%
Local radio news	19%

REUTERS INSTITUTE | UNIVERSITY OF OXFORD

Top Brands – Weekly Reach
Online
Ireland

More than 3 days per week

Brand	%
RTÉ News online	21%
TheJournal.ie	18%
Irish Independent online	19%
BreakingNews.ie	12%
BBC News online	9%
Sky News online	10%

Weekly use

Brand	%
RTÉ News online	33%
TheJournal.ie	31%
Irish Independent online	31%
BreakingNews.ie	24%
BBC News online	17%
Sky News online	17%

REUTERS INSTITUTE | UNIVERSITY OF OXFORD

Brand Trust
Ireland

Brand	Trust	Neither	Don't trust
RTÉ News	76%	13%	11%
The Irish Times	75%	16%	9%
BBC News	75%	15%	10%
Irish Independent	73%	17%	10%
Sky News	73%	16%	11%
Local or regional newspaper	71%	20%	9%
The Sunday Times	69%	20%	11%
Newstalk	69%	21%	10%
Today FM	68%	21%	11%
Irish Examiner	68%	22%	10%
Virgin Media TV News	64%	24%	12%
BreakingNews.ie	62%	26%	13%
Journal.ie	61%	25%	14%
Irish Daily Mail	50%	24%	25%
her.ie/joe.ie	44%	35%	22%

■ Trust   ■ Neither   ■ Don't trust

Source: Reuters Institute for the Study of Journalism

1. What evidence shows that this is a serious report?

2. Where do the largest number of people get their TV, radio or print news?

3. Which of the TV, radio or print news do you think are reliable? Why?

4. What are the top three sites from where people get their online news?

5. Which online news sites do you think are reliable? Why?

6. What are the three most trusted news organisations in Ireland?

7. Which news organisation is most distrusted?

8. Why do you think some brands are more trusted than others?

Exercise 85B Understanding how media freedom and democracy are linked

Key Skills   **Success criteria**
- ☐ I can name countries where there is media freedom and countries where media freedom is limited.
- ☐ I can explain why this has an impact on democracy in these countries.

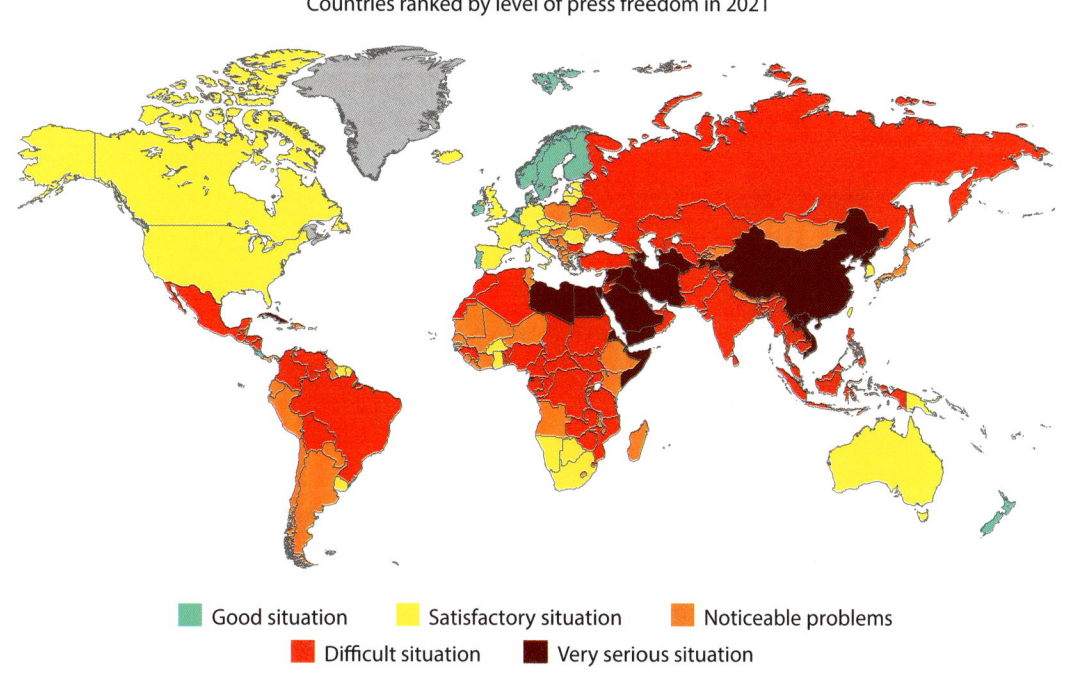

Look at the map on press freedom and answer the questions that follow.

The State of World Press Freedom
Countries ranked by level of press freedom in 2021

- Good situation
- Satisfactory situation
- Noticeable problems
- Difficult situation
- Very serious situation

■ CALL TO ACTION | *Chapter 8*

1. As well as having good or satisfactory levels of press freedom, what do most of the countries in green and yellow have in common?

2. What do the countries in red have in common?

3. Do you think this map is reliable? Why/why not?

4. Research one country on the map where the media is not free. Use three different sources.
   Country: _____
   Sources I used: _____

   (a) What type of government does this country have?

   (b) How is the media censored?

   (c) Give an example of how this censorship affects people.

Exercise 85C — Understanding the power of the internet

Key Skills   **Success criteria** ☐ I can explain why I think statistics are reliable or not.

There are many advantages of media freedom, but there are also disadvantages:
- Sometimes politicians use spin to make themselves appear better. Spin is a form of propaganda.
- The media often only give one side of an argument or leave out a major piece of information.
- The media often cover only topical subjects and ignore other important issues.
- Sometimes the media can intrude too much on people's personal lives.

Look at the figures below about internet use in August 2021. Answer the questions that follow.

- The internet has over 4 billion users.
- Facebook has 2.2 billion users.
- Snapchat has 280 million users.
- Google processes 228 million searches per hour.
- The average Twitter user has 707 followers.
- 300 hours of video are uploaded to YouTube every minute.
- Over two-thirds of Instagram users are under 35.
- 68% of Pinterest's users are under 49.
- The average CEO has 930 LinkedIn connections.

Source: www.statistica.com

Lesson 85: What is media?

1. Which of these websites/social networks do you use?
   _____
   _____

2. Which do you never use?
   _____
   _____

3. Which would you trust the most?
   _____

4. What makes you think that the figures given are reliable?
   _____
   _____

Exercise 85D Understanding the different purposes of media

Key Skills

Success criteria
- ☐ I can identify whether a piece of media is meant to inform, persuade or entertain.
- ☐ I can explain how I know the purpose of different pieces of media.

There are three main purposes of media: to **inform**, to **persuade** and to **entertain**.

Decide what the main purpose of each of the following pieces of media is. Then write what made you decide.

Media piece	Purpose	How you decided which type it is
1.		
2.		
3.		

391

■ CALL TO ACTION | *Chapter 8*

Exercise 85E Identifying the advantages/disadvantages of young people's news sources

Key Skills

Success criteria ☐ I can give some advantages and disadvantages of young people's news sources.

A US study found the most trusted sources of information for teenagers were:
- Trusted adults
- Blogs
- Social media
- Humorous current affairs programmes.

They liked these because they explained why things were good or bad and they were not **objective**. Objective means that you look at things from a neutral point of view and do not say whether they are good or bad. **Subjective** is when you have your own view, often based on feelings or emotions.

Fill in the grid below:

	Example	Advantage of this source	Disadvantage of this source
Trusted adults			
Blogs			
Social media			
Humorous current affairs programme			

1. Are these sources similar to your sources of news?

   _____

2. If not, what are your news sources?

   _____

Lesson 86: Types of media

Learning outcome 3.12
Students should be able to explore the role of different media in generating information and news and assess the pros and cons of each.

There are many different types of media which generate news and information.

Exercise 86A Understanding satire and why it is used

Key Skills   **Success criteria**
- ☐ I can explain, giving examples, why the reports are satirical.
- ☐ I can explain the advantages of using satire.

Satire is the use of irony (or sarcasm), humour or exaggeration to make fun of or expose people's stupidity or failings. Satire has long been used in fiction and more recently in satirical news. While satirical news is meant to be funny, it also normally has a political message. Satirical news is usually presented in the same way as real news, but it makes fun of the people or activities being satirised.

Look at these articles taken from satirical websites and answer the questions which follow.

GOP claims Biden is artificially inflating job approval rating by displaying competence

With a new Associated Press poll showing Joe Biden garnering a sixty-three-per-cent general-approval rating, Republicans are accusing the president of 'artificially inflating' that number through 'blatant displays of competence.' Senator Rand Paul said. 'If you want to get a high approval rating, all you have to do is do a job that people approve of.' Senator Ted Cruz agreed. 'Joe Biden is so desperate to have a high approval rating that he's been using every day in office to deliver results to the American people,' he charged. 'I for one find this behavior beneath contempt.' Representative Marjorie Taylor Greene called Biden's seventy-one-per-cent approval rating for his handling of the pandemic 'a joke,' noting, 'If all you care about is people liking the way you handle the pandemic, I guess you'd handle the pandemic all the livelong day. Big whoop.' The Senate Minority Leader, Mitch McConnell, said that Biden 'should take no comfort' in his high approval numbers. 'When people get tired of Biden's competence – and they will – they'll vote Republican,' he said.

Source: Andy Borowitz, *The New Yorker*

● CALL TO ACTION | *Chapter 8*

Scientists baffled after discovering adult human who is completely immune to people criticising things he likes

Simon Williams, 35, has been hailed a 'scientific marvel' for the way his brain just scrolls past posts designed to trigger his anger response, and researchers are keen to understand his secret. As one told us, 'We don't get it. When someone says something negative about something he likes, he just … well … *ignores* it. 'We're not quite sure how he does it, or how his brain is able to handle it, but it seems Simon is completely immune. And we mean *completely*. 'People with opinions completely opposed to his own, expressing them in his social media feeds has literally zero effect on him. We hope that by studying Simon we might be able to develop therapies to help those poor souls who are unable to browse past anything that mocks something they like without posting numerous comments explaining why the post is "wrong".' Williams told us, 'This all really flattering, but I don't see what all the fuss is about? Doesn't everyone ignore stuff they don't like? What, *no*? Err … why not? It's really easy, just a swipe of my thumb and the derogatory post about that thing I like is consigned to history and I can go about my day without even giving it a second thought. I mean, the world is full of different opinions, and it would be arrogant in the extreme to think that only my opinion can be the correct one, regardless of the subject. Right?'

Source: NewsThump

1. Do you think these articles are funny? Why/why not?

2. Did you understand their messages?

3. What made them effective?

4. Would you recommend them to others? Why/why not?

Exercise 86B Understanding how memes can be used to make an argument

Key Skills   **Success criteria**   ☐ I can explain the message of a meme.
                                               ☐ I can explain, giving examples, the reasons why a meme is effective.

Memes are often made for entertainment, but they can also be made to convince people or make a political statement.

Working in pairs, pick two of the following memes and answer the questions that follow.

394

Lesson 86: Types of media

	Meme ☐	Meme ☐
1. What is the meme about?		
2. What visual and verbal elements show the author's point of view?	1. Visual 2. Verbal	1. Visual 2. Verbal
3. Who do you think this meme is aimed at?		
4. Why do you think this group would like it?		
5. Why do you think this message was created?		
6. What are the potential beneficial effects of this message?		
7. What are the potential harmful effects of this message?		

395

■ CALL TO ACTION | *Chapter 8*

Exercise 86C — Creating a meme

Key Skills   **Success criteria**   ☐ I can create a meme and use text that makes it funny and makes a point that is easily understood by others.

Use PowerPoint or www.canva.com to create a meme about a topic that interests you. Print it out and stick it in the box below.

Exercise 86D — Understanding the power of social media posts

Key Skills   **Success criteria**   ☐ I can explain, giving examples, why a social media post is effective.

News sources such as blogs and social networks can report news faster than TV news, newspapers and their online sites. They are also generally free. TV news and newspapers have experienced journalists and editors to check a story before it is posted. Blogs and social networks often do not, and this can lead to incorrect information being posted.

Social media can be beneficial for making information available. During the Arab Spring in the early 2010s, people protested against authoritarian governments in North Africa and the Middle East. Information on when and where protests were taking place spread on social media. Social media in these countries was not controlled in the same way that newspapers and television were. The tweet on the right is an example of how social media was used:

> **Fawaz Rashed**
> @FawazRashed
>
> "We use Facebook to schedule the protests, Twitter to coordinate, and YouTube to tell the world." #egypt #jan25
>
> 11:04 PM · Mar 18, 2011 · Twitter Web Client

Lesson 86: Types of media

People who record events on their phones and post them are referred to as **citizen journalists** because they post information that is in the interest of the public and make it available to the public. They sometimes get paid for a story or earn money from advertising on their channel. But because they are not professional journalists, they might show only one side of a story or might not be aware of how their contribution can be misleading. Another problem is that people with extreme views can present their own opinions as facts and others believe them.

Look at the following examples of social media posts and, working in pairs. answer the questions.

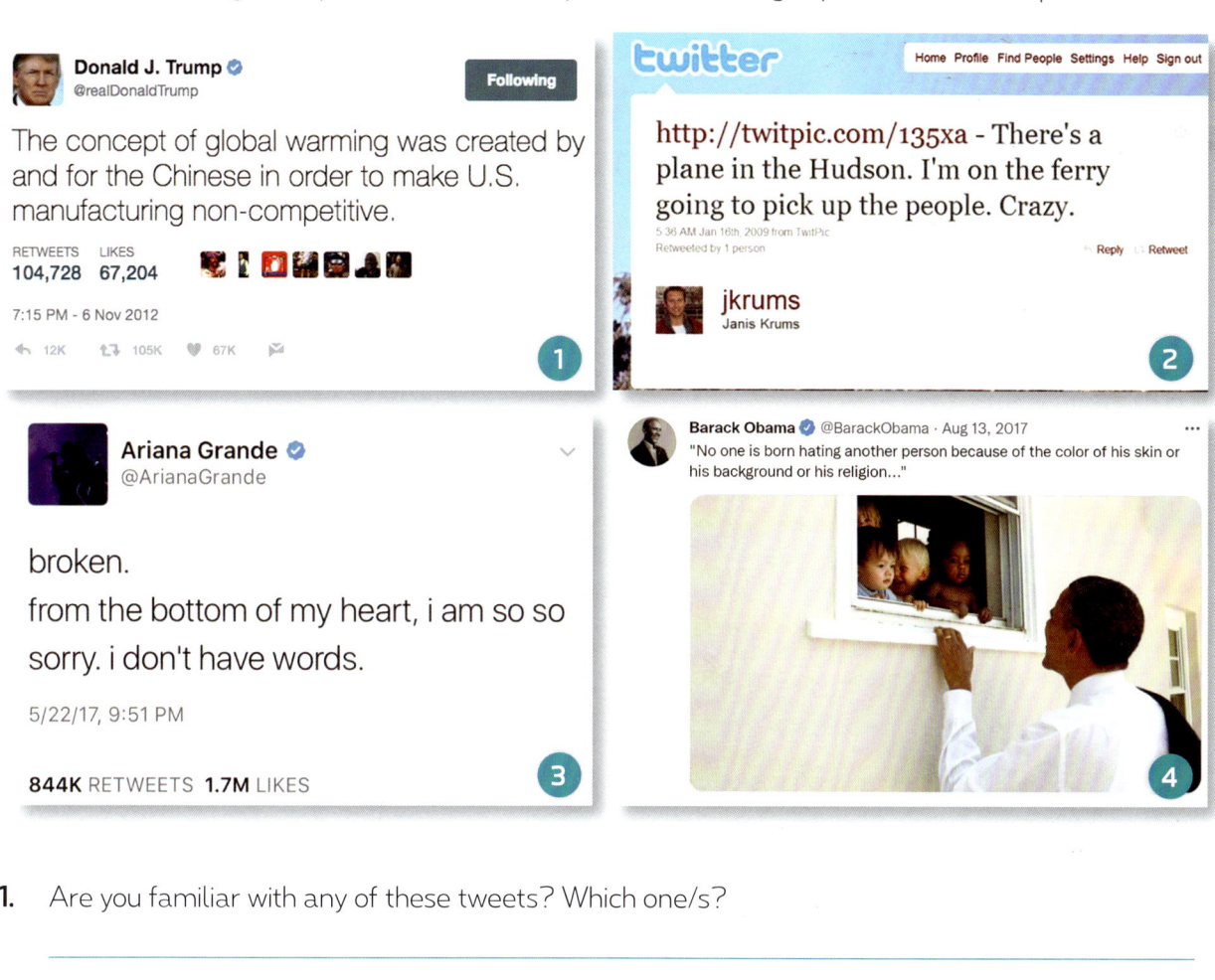

1. Donald J. Trump @realDonaldTrump — The concept of global warming was created by and for the Chinese in order to make U.S. manufacturing non-competitive. RETWEETS 104,728 LIKES 67,204 — 7:15 PM - 6 Nov 2012 — 12K 105K 67K

2. twitter — jkrums Janis Krums: http://twitpic.com/135xa - There's a plane in the Hudson. I'm on the ferry going to pick up the people. Crazy. 5:36 AM Jan 16th, 2009 from TwitPic. Retweeted by 1 person

3. Ariana Grande @ArianaGrande — broken. from the bottom of my heart, i am so so sorry. i don't have words. 5/22/17, 9:51 PM — 844K RETWEETS 1.7M LIKES

4. Barack Obama @BarackObama · Aug 13, 2017 — "No one is born hating another person because of the color of his skin or his background or his religion..."

1. Are you familiar with any of these tweets? Which one/s?

2. Do you think any of these tweets might be influential?

3. What makes it influential?

4. Do you think this posting was the action of a good citizen? Why/why not?

397

Lesson 87: Different perspectives

Learning outcome 3.12
Students should be able to explore the role of different media in generating information and news and assess the pros and cons of each.

Exercise 87A Identifying what makes information reliable in videos, news articles and memes

Key Skills **Success criteria**
- ☐ I can explain how different media can give information in different ways.
- ☐ I can give examples of features that make a report reliable.
- ☐ I can show how somebody's opinion can be different from facts.
- ☐ I can explain why people have different viewpoints.

People can have different views on topics depending on how they affect them. For example, look at the cube below. It is known as the Necker cube. Can you decide whether corner 1 or corner 2 is closer to you?

The answer depends on your **perspective**, which means the way you see things. Your perspective might be different from somebody else's because your experience is different to theirs. For example, if you had no home a small flat might seem wonderful, but if you lived in a mansion, the small flat might seem a terrible place to live.

Some people will see corner 1 of the Necker cube as closer, others will see corner 2 (some can see both as being closer, depending on how they look at it). All are correct, so it is important to consider that there may be more than one answer when making other decisions. It is rare that one side is completely right and the other side completely wrong. People have different reasons for having different viewpoints.

Go to YouTube and search for:
1. 'Causes and Effects of Climate Change | National Geographic' (3:04)
2. 'BILL NYE: SCIENCE GUY – Climate Change' (1:35)
3. 'Nature Is Speaking – Reese Witherspoon is Home – Conservation International' (1:00).

Lesson 87: Different perspectives

1. Watch the three videos, then answer the following questions:

	Video 1	Video 2	Video 3
(a) Do you know who made this video and why?			
(b) How does it attract and hold your attention?			
(c) Do you think different people would see it differently? Why?			
(d) What ideas are presented as important?			
(e) Was anything important missing/left out?			

2. Select one of the articles that your teacher gives you and answer the following questions:

   (a) What was effective about the piece you selected?
   _____

   (b) Was this piece made to inform, persuade or entertain?
   _____

   (c) Was anything important left out? If so, what?
   _____
   _____

3. Looking at the two sides presented in this article, what have you learned in favour and against this topic?
   _____
   _____

399

● CALL TO ACTION | *Chapter 8*

Exercise 87B Understanding the power of headlines

Key Skills **Success criteria** ☐ I can distinguish between objective and sensationalist headlines.
☐ I can explain the features that make headlines effective.

Headlines aim to sum up an article. They are the part of a media story that attracts people's attention. People often decide whether or not to read an article based on the headline. Headlines can be misleading as they may not describe what the article is actually about. They can also be **sensationalist**, which means they are presented in a way that is meant to shock or be overdramatic. The headline and photo on the right appeared on the Breitbart UK website in 2017. The photo and headline created the impression of refugees arriving to Spain on jet-skis. This was found to be a photo of the German footballer, Lukas Podolski, taken during the 2014 World Cup in Brazil.

Look at the headlines below and answer the questions that follow.

1. Write two headlines that you think are objective (neutral).
   _____
   _____

2. Why do you think they are objective?
   _____

3. Write two headlines that you think are sensationalist.
   _____
   _____

4. Why do you think they are sensationalist?
   _____

400

Lesson 87: Different perspectives

Exercise 87C — Understanding the power of advertisements

Key Skills | **Success criteria**
- [ ] I can identify the message in an advertisement.
- [ ] I can explain the hidden messages in advertisements.
- [ ] I can explain the factors that make advertisements effective.

Advertising is used to sell products or to encourage people to change behaviour. Advertisements often use a mix of persuasion, entertainment and information.

Choose two of the advertisements above and fill in the grid below.

	Advertisement 1	Advertisement 2
1. What makes this a good advertisement?		
2. What is the message of the advertisement?		
3. What could be included that might change your opinion?		

401

CALL TO ACTION | Chapter 8

Exercise 87D Designing an advertisement

Key Skills

Success criteria
- [ ] I can use data to create an advertisement.
- [ ] I can use design features to convince people to buy a product.
- [ ] I can explain how advertising uses information that persuades people.

Your class has been asked to design an advertisement for fruit smoothies to be sold to students in your school. If the advert is successful, it will be entered into a competition to design an advert for a big brand.

Before designing the advert, you decide to carry out some market research to find out more about students in your school: what they like, what might they buy and what they do not like. You send out surveys to all students and, once the surveys are complete, carry out interviews with smaller groups. You collect the data below:

Like	Dislike	Other considerations
Strawberries, raspberries, bananas, pears, oranges, blackberries and mangos	Pineapples, blackcurrants, watermelons, melons	Do not want something too sweet
Orange, red, pink, blue colours	Brown, green or grey colours	No additives
Thick	Watery	Good source of vitamins
Juice, milk, coconut water	Almond milk, rice milk	Dairy and nut allergies
Sunshine and bright fruits	Plain carton	Want it to be environmentally friendly

1. Based on the above information decide the following:

    (a) Which is the better choice as an ingredient for a smoothie – strawberries or melons?

    _____

    (b) Which is the better image – a tub of blackberries, mangos and raspberries or a green box?

    _____

    (c) Which would be the better colour for the smoothie – brown or red?

    _____

2. On the next page, create an advert for the smoothie using the information from your research. Include methods of persuading your customers, such as repetition, humour and testimonials. Put your completed advert in the box on the next page.

Lesson 87: Different perspectives

Lesson 88: Bias, propaganda and fake news

Learning outcome 3.12
Students should be able to explore the role of different media in generating information and news and assess the pros and cons of each.

Exercise 88A — Identifying the danger of hearing one viewpoint only

Key Skills

Success criteria ☐ I can identify problems caused by people not hearing alternative viewpoints.

Confirmation bias is when people accept information if it supports their own views. In order to avoid confirmation bias, you must be able to justify your opinion, consider someone else's viewpoint and reflect on your decision.

An **echo chamber** happens when everybody following a type of media has the same viewpoint and they never encounter opposing views. **Filter bubbles** happen when an algorithm suggests stories for you based on what you have read or watched in the past. These are both common online. Eventually you will only ever hear one side of the story.

Watch the videos on confirmation bias, echo chambers and filter bubbles and answer the following questions:

> Go to YouTube and search for:
> 1. 'How Filter Bubbles Isolate You' (2:37)
> 2. 'What is an Echo Chamber?' (2:16)
> 3. 'Filter Bubbles and Echo Chambers MinuteVideos' (3:17).

1. Can you think of an example of confirmation bias?

2. Do you think you get information from echo chambers? Why or why not?

3. Can you think of any examples of how you have been given information based on filter bubbles?

Lesson 88: Bias, propaganda and fake news

4. What do you think are the results of echo chambers and filter bubbles?
   _____
   _____

5. Can you give any examples of how these have led to problems?
   _____
   _____

Exercise 88B — Understanding how grammar can convey different impressions

Key Skills **Success criteria** ☐ I can explain by giving examples how grammar can change the meaning of a report.

Grammar can be used to give text a different meaning. It can be used to influence people reading the news.

Look at the following example from a study by Fausey & Matlock.

Paragraph 1

Mark Johnson is a Senator in the US Senate. He is up for re-election. He graduated from the University of Texas, Austin with a degree in political science. Mark's first term as a US Senator is almost complete. Last year, Mark had an affair with his assistant and took hush money from a prominent constituent.

Paragraph 2

Mark Johnson is a Senator in the US Senate. He is up for re-election. He graduated from the University of Texas, Austin with a degree in political science. Mark's first term as a US Senator is almost complete. Last year, Mark was having an affair with his assistant and was taking hush money from a prominent constituent.

1. Does the language used in the different paragraphs affect your impression of Senator Johnson?
   _____

2. Which paragraph leaves a more positive impression?
   _____

3. What do you think the difference was when people were asked whether Senator Johnson would be re-elected?
   _____
   _____

● CALL TO ACTION | *Chapter 8*

Exercise 88C Identifying how words are used to influence opinion

Key Skills   **Success criteria**   ☐ I can explain, giving examples, the differences between an objective and a subjective report.
☐ I can list words that influence people's opinions.

Read the news reports below, which both report on the same story. Then answer the questions following.

Shocked teenager fined £100 for feeding a chip to a pigeon

A teenager from Swansea has been fined £100 for feeding a McDonald's chip to a pigeon.

Lauren-Paige Smith, 19, was treating herself to a McDonald's for lunch, when she kindly offered one of her chips to a hungry bird.

She was immediately approached by a rude council worker who thoughtlessly issued her with a £25 fine for littering.

Animal-lover Lauren told the official that she hadn't been littering. She explained that the pigeon had eaten the whole chip so there was no litter left on the ground.

However, the harsh council worker still gave her the fine.

Lauren felt that she was being treated unfairly so she did not pay the fine. However, she was astonished to receive a letter last week summoning her to court along with a larger fine of £100.

Lauren said: 'I was feeding the pigeons some of my lunch when a man who worked for the council came out of nowhere and told me I was littering. And now I'm being hauled into court.'

Lauren added: 'I can't believe I'm being penalized for doing a kind act. I thought it was a wind up.'

Source: NewsWise

Woman facing £100 fine for feeding bird

On July 8, Lauren-Paige Smith, 19, of Rumney in Cardiff was finishing her lunch outside McDonald's restaurant on Castle Street in Swansea when she fed some chips to a pigeon. A litter enforcement officer saw Ms Smith feed the bird and approached her. He identified himself and charged her a fine of £25. Ms Smith refused to pay the fine and consequently appeared at Swansea's Magistrates Court charged with littering, an offence under Section 87 of the Environmental Protection Act.

A spokesperson for Swansea Council stated that the council was actively ensuring that food waste was discouraged because of the negative impact on the look of the city and because it has encouraged aggressive birds to attack shoppers. Before the hearing Ms Smith said that she was an animal-lover who had never been in trouble before this incident.

In bodycam footage taken from the litter warden, which was shown in court, the warden could be heard saying, 'You could feed them seeds, but not chips, that's human waste'. Ms Smith argued that the bird had eaten all the chips and there was no litter.

In court, Ms Smith said that she was not pleading either guilty or not guilty as she did not believe that a crime had been committed. A trial date was set for November 29.

1. Which of these accounts is more objective?

   _____

2. Give examples of how it is objective.

   _____
   _____

3. Can you find examples of how the other report is not objective?

   _____
   _____

406

Lesson 88: Bias, propaganda and fake news

Exercise 88D   Understanding the power of propaganda

Key Skills   **Success criteria**   ☐ I can explain, giving examples, what makes propaganda effective.

Propaganda is when information, opinions or even pictures are used with the intention of influencing people's opinions. These are generally biased and often false. They are designed to make one group or viewpoint look bad and another look good.

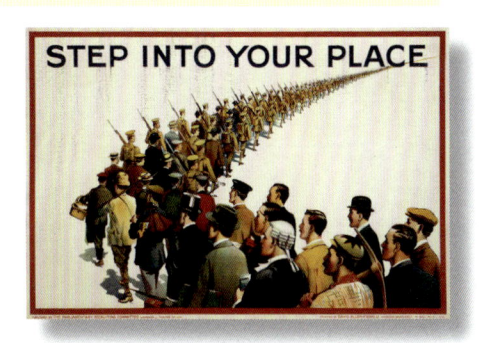

We often think of how Hitler and Mussolini used propaganda to get people to support them and turn against others, but they were not the only people to use propaganda. The image on the right was used to recruit soldiers in Britain for World War I. It creates the impression of men from many different professions joining together for a noble cause. It makes no reference to what the war really involved or that the obviously wealthy men were less likely to have to fight on the front line.

Propaganda can be in other formats. Some Hollywood films, such as *American Sniper* and *Zero Dark Thirty*, have been seen as propaganda for the US military. Both films present one side of complex issues and do not question whether it is acceptable to execute people without a trial.

Propaganda can also be used to positive effect, such as promoting health or environmental campaigns. The children's writer, Dr Seuss, wrote *The Lorax* as a tale about the dangers of destroying the environment. The poster shown on the right encouraged people to wear a mask during the Covid-19 pandemic.

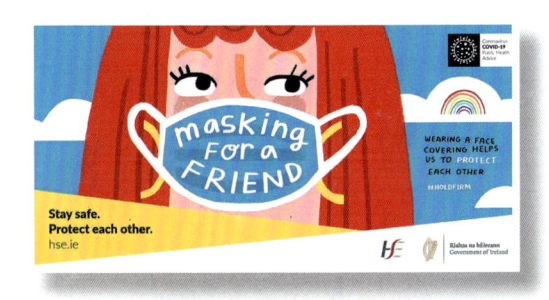

Look at the posters below and answer the following questions.

Translation:
We Cannot Allow This
(Iran)

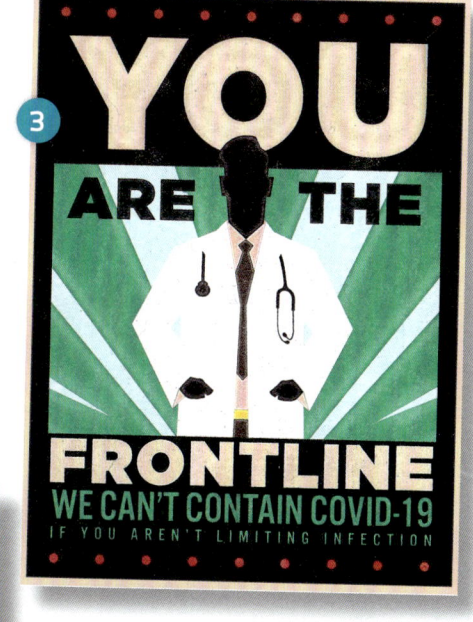

● CALL TO ACTION | *Chapter 8*

Select two of the propaganda posters and identify the features that make each an effective poster.

Poster	What makes it effective?

Exercise 88E Distinguishing between real and fake news

Key Skills **Success criteria**
- ☐ I can explain, giving reasons, why a news report is not reliable.
- ☐ I can identify a reliable news report, giving examples of features that explain why.

Fake news refers to news or stories that are intended to deliberately mislead readers or viewers. Fake news can take different forms. It can be:

- Obviously fake, often because it is satirical or funny
- Biased
- Intentionally false and misleading.

In reality, the fake news we see is more likely to be one of the first two types. The 1938 headline on the right from *The New York Times* shows how many listeners to a radio broadcast called *The War of the Worlds*, about a fictional invasion by Martians, believed it was true and panicked.

The image on the left was frequently used by Donald Trump supporters looking to build a wall along the US border with Mexico. It was supposed to show a caravan of male-only refugees trying to get into the United States. It was revealed to be a photo taken a few years earlier of Pakistani asylum seekers on the Greek island of Lesbos.

Sometimes **deep fake** videos are used. These generally show a video of famous person speaking but the words are spoken by somebody else.

408

Lesson 88: Bias, propaganda and fake news

How to identify fake news

When trying to identify whether or not a news report is fake, consider the following:

- Has the story been covered by other papers, websites or channels?
- Does the story come from a newspaper, magazine or website you have never heard of?
- Does it include a lot of advertisements?
- Is the journalist named? If so, do they have a good reputation?
- Are reputable experts quoted?
- Were reliable witnesses mentioned?
- Has the website/paper a history of publishing unreliable news items?
- Do a reverse image search to find the original source of an image using www.tineye.com.

Your teacher will now show you two videos and two articles. Using the guidelines above decide whether they are objective, satirical, biased or completely fake.

> Go to YouTube and search for:
> 1. 'House hippo 2.0' (0:52)
> 2. 'What's Real Evidence of Climate Change? – Let's Talk – NPR' (1:31).

	Type of report	Reasons for your decision
Video 1		
Video 2		
News article 1		
News article 2		

Lesson 89: My media actions

Learning outcome 3.12
Students should be able to explore the role of different media in generating information and news and assess the pros and cons of each.

Exercise 89A Using reliable websites when looking for information

Key Skills

Success criteria
- [ ] I can explain how I know that a website is current, reliable and accurate.
- [ ] I can explain the reason why a website exists.

When you are looking for information or researching a topic online, the **CRAP Test** is a useful way to inspect how reliable a website is. CRAP stands for Currency, Reliability, Accuracy and Purpose. The test works by answering the questions on each of the four sections.

Currency	Reliability
• How recent is the information? • How recently has it been updated?	• Does the website have facts or is it based on somebody's opinion? • Is it one-sided? • Are there sources for the facts/quotes/statistics?
Authority/Accuracy	**Purpose/Point of view**
• Did the person who created the website/article have enough experience to be a reliable source? • Is the publisher or sponsor reputable? • Does the publisher have an interest in showing one viewpoint over the other side? • Are there more advertisements than information or is an author trying to convince you to buy their book?	• Is the information written for educational reasons, for entertainment or for journalistic reasons? • Is it fair or biased? • Is the creator/author trying to sell you something?

It is also important to check the site's **web address**. An .edu or ac.uk (in the UK) is from a third-level institution and is normally reliable. An Irish government website has gov.ie or, in the UK, gov.uk. Websites ending in .com or .org or .ie can belong to anyone.

People sometimes think the first website they find in a Google search is the most reliable source but they are often advertising or the most popular, not necessarily the most accurate.

Lesson 89: My media actions

Watch the video on the CRAP Test. Your teacher will give you a list of websites to visit.

> **YouTube** Go to YouTube and search for 'The CRAP Test for Evaluating Websites' (5:45).

Choose two of the websites and evaluate them under the following headings:

	Currency	Reliability	Accuracy	Purpose
Website				
Website				

Exercise 89B Distinguishing between online consumption and contribution

Key Skills   **Success criteria**   ☐ I can name online consumption and contributions that I engage in.

When we use the internet we can **contribute**, which means we give something. An example of this would be posting a recipe online. This contributes something as other people can use the recipe. We also **consume**, which means we take things from the internet. For example, if we want to learn how to bake a chocolate cake, we can look for a recipe online. Without people both contributing and consuming, the internet will not work. There is no point looking for information if nobody posts it, and equally there is no point in posting information if nobody uses it.

Categorise the following options in the box below.

When I do the following actions do I contribute or consume?

Action	Contribute/Consume?
1. Check the menu for the local takeaway	
2. Read online news articles	
3. Create a video on how to apply make-up and post it on YouTube	
4. Create a website of my photos	
5. Correct mistakes about my local town on Wikipedia	
6. Follow a sportsperson on Twitter	
7. Write a report on basketball for the school website	
8. Use Google Maps to find a concert venue	
9. Do a sponsored race for a charity and post it online to raise money	
10. Post photos of a school tour on Instagram	

■ CALL TO ACTION | *Chapter 8*

Exercise 89C   Distinguishing between different types of online contributions

Key Skills   **Success criteria**
- ☐ I can give examples of positive online contributions and explain why they are positive.
- ☐ I can give examples of negative online contributions and explain why they are negative.
- ☐ I can give examples of neutral online contributions and explain why they are neutral.

Online contributions can be **positive** (good for ourselves and our community), **negative** (harmful) or **neutral** (neither helpful nor harmful).

Look at the following list and classify the contributions as positive, negative or neutral. Explain why you classified them in this way.

Contribution	Positive/ Negative/ Neutral?	Why?
1. Posting a recipe for strawberry tart		
2. Posting a photo of my new jacket		
3. Answering a question about my town posed on a forum		
4. Posting a photo of illegal dumping of rubbish on a local website		
5. Signing an online petition		
6. Emailing Google Maps to inform them about a mistake in their maps		
7. Posting a video of my friend singing out of tune at a school concert		

Exercise 89D   Distinguishing between effective and ineffective online discussion

Key Skills   **Success criteria**
- ☐ I can identify effective and ineffective online discussions and explain why they are effective or ineffective.

Online discussion is **effective** when it is helpful and something useful happens. On the other hand, **ineffective** discussion is where nothing of any use happens. It may even involve harmful discussion. People can contribute to online discussions by adding information that was missing, correcting something that was said, answering a question or expressing an opinion.

Effective discussion happens when:
- A moderator on the site checks that people are posting true information
- People read the original post carefully before posting a comment
- The language is respectful and easily understood
- People use evidence and personal experiences.

Lesson 89: My media actions

Ineffective discussion happens when:
- There is no moderator
- One person dominates the conversation and is not willing to hear new ideas
- People make typos and use slang that makes their point hard for others to understand
- Commentators stray from the original topic
- People (often using anonymous accounts) insult others who do not share their opinions

Look at the examples below of online discussions, then answer the questions.

A. This discussion is about an announcement by the government that the Covid-19 vaccines would not be delivered on time:

Pat B
27 mins ago

Moving the goalposts again

👍 255

Sarah C
6 mins ago

Ah yes, typical crap from government, only interested in their wealthy buddies.

👍 151

Superman
22 mins ago

As usual this fool out looking for attention, doesn't care if it is good or bad

👍 178

Lilly Perone
21 mins ago

Not the government's fault, big pharma not supplying enough. We just have to be patient. Not easy but we'll get there.

👍 21

Superman
20 mins ago

Ya, your clearly a stooge for the failed government, course its there fault that people are dying and there doing nothin

👍 36

Sally
15 mins ago

Shocking really, so many more will die because of this incompetence

👍 56

Mac 2020
11 mins ago

The people won't forget. We'll be waiting when they call at our doors.

👍 49

Winter Rain
9 mins ago

Problem is that everyone thinks this is a bad thing, the big companies are only looking to make money injecting poisons into everybody. There was a big report to say that these companies can use the vaccine to make people dependent on drugs, like an addiction. An who makes the $$$$???

👍 21

Superman
5 mins ago

Ah shut up you clown

👍 11

413

■ CALL TO ACTION | *Chapter 8*

B. The following is taken from a forum discussing combi boilers.

Mark Dwyer

Mon 5 April 18.30

Hi everyone, our boiler has been causing us trouble. We want to switch to a combi boiler but my father-in-law says it's a bad idea, but I like the idea of a new boiler and new water tank. I suppose it's cheaper to replace the two in one go????

Conor O'Connell

Mon 5 April 19.02

I got the combi boiler last year, huge savings on gas and the whole system is much quieter. I'd say go for it.

Mark Dwyer

Mon 5 April 20.30

Thanks @ConorO'Connell, that's great to know. Do you have a bath as my father-in-law says that the combi takes ages to fill them and that's putting us off.

Jill Kelleher

Wed 7 April 11.12

How many bathrooms do you have? If you have more than one you won't have enough water to run two showers.

Sean Murphy

Fri 9 April 18.17

We have a combi for a four bedroom, two bathroom house and we can use both showers without a problem, but one of the showers is electric. The only problem is it can take longer for the water to get to the downstairs shower, but not sure whether that's because of the combi or the location of the bathroom.

---

1. Which discussion is effective? Why?

   _____

   _____

2. Which discussion is ineffective? Why?

   _____

   _____

414

Lesson 89: My media actions

Exercise 89E — Understanding how sharing media shows my own beliefs

Key Skills   **Success criteria**   ☐ I can explain, giving reasons, why I would or would not share a piece of media.

The following posters are examples of the types of images shared online.

1. Dogs Die in Hot Cars (RSPCA)
2. MEN ~~DON'T~~ CRY
3. WHAT WOULD YOU DO? SHARE THIS IF YOU AGREE THAT ISRAEL HAS THE RIGHT TO SELF DEFENSE — ISRAEL DEFENSE FORCES
4. Benefits of RUNNING — Strengthen Muscles, Relieves Stress, Good for Lung, Healthy Heart, Strong Bones, Weight loss

1. Which poster would you share on your social network? Explain why you would be willing to share this.

   _____
   _____

2. Which poster would you not share with your social network? Explain why you would not be willing to share this.

   _____
   _____

415

Lesson 90

Case study: 2020 US presidential election

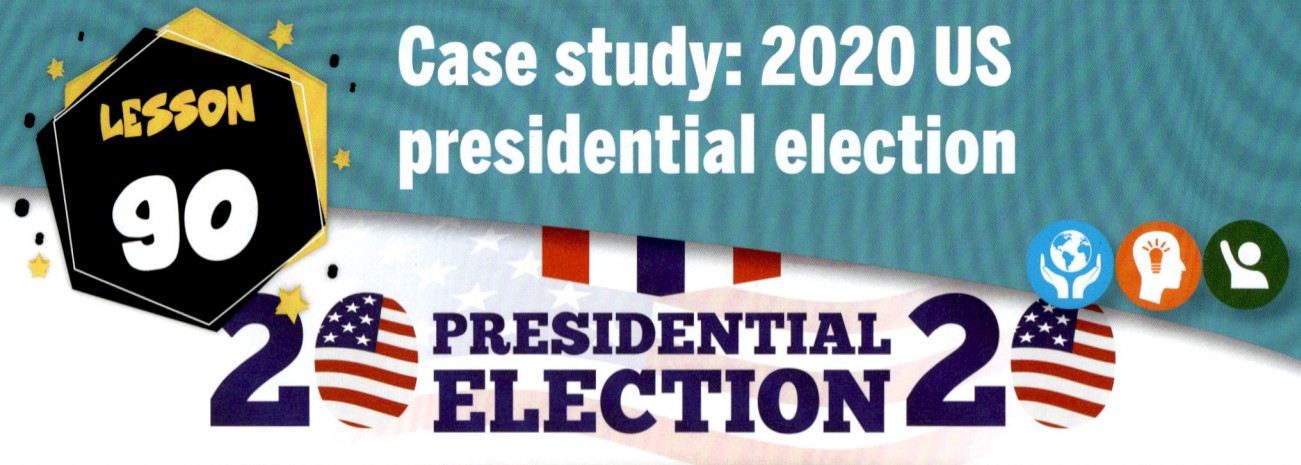

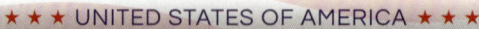

Learning outcome 3.13

Students will be able to examine case studies of the use of digital or other media in **one** of the following:
- a social justice movement
- a criminal investigation
- a political election or referendum
- an environmental movement.

Exercise 90A Evaluating video advertisements to see if they persuade people

Key Skills **Success criteria**
- [ ] I can identify advertisements that are one-sided.
- [ ] I can explain the factors that would successfully persuade people.

The 2020 US presidential election was very divisive. The sitting president, Republican Donald Trump, eventually lost to former vice president, Democrat Joe Biden. The election took place during the Covid-19 pandemic.

The counting of votes took longer than usual, and because of the pandemic many voters mailed in their votes. Trump took an early lead but in several states, the mail-in votes were counted last and most of these were from Biden supporters. This meant that Biden overtook Trump's early lead in these states. When Trump saw his lead disappear, he claimed that the election was fraudulent, and that he had really won. He posted messages on Twitter claiming to have won.

Opinion polls showed that 70% of voters from Trump's own Republican party believed that the election was fraudulent. This was despite legal challenges by Trump finding no evidence of fraud. It was a campaign of disinformation, which used lies and conspiracy theories to convince people. A campaign called Stop the Steal started on social media and was promoted by Trump supporters. On 6 January, 2021 Trump held a rally in Washington, DC where he repeated

Donald J. Trump ✓
@realDonaldTrump

I WON THE ELECTION!

ⓘ **Official sources called this election differently**

23:55 · 15 Nov 20 · Twitter for iPhone

Lesson 90: Case study: 2020 US presidential election

his claim that the election had been stolen from him. He called on the crowd to 'fight like hell'. Thousands of Trump supporters believed the fake news and attacked the US Capitol, where the Congress was meeting to certify the election results. The attack led to the death of five people and was an example of the danger of fake news. Many people continued to believe the election had been stolen even after the riot.

Watch the three advertisements, then answer the questions on the next page:

> Go to YouTube and search for:
> 1. 'Mourning in America The Lincoln Project' (1:00)
> 2. 'New Trump Ad: "The Bidening"' (1:28)
> 3. 'Laughed At – Joe Biden for President' (1:03).

	Mourning in America	The Bidening	Laughed At
1. Is this advertisement informative, persuasive or entertaining?			
2. If it is a mix of these, can you say why this is the case?			
3. Which parts are the most effective?			
4. Can you find any examples of bias?			
5. What idea does this advertisement give about the candidate?			
6. Which is the most effective advertisement? Explain why.			

417

CALL TO ACTION | Chapter 8

Exercise 90B Reading articles (including persuasive articles) with different perspectives

Key Skills **Success criteria**
- ☐ I can identify, giving examples, reports that are objective.
- ☐ I can identify, giving examples, reports that are persuasive.
- ☐ I can explain the effective persuasive factors used in news media.

Read the three reports below and answer the questions that follow.

Article 1: Trump v Biden: Final push in election campaign

27 Oct 2020 by Brian O'Donovan

Donald Trump continues to hold big rallies packed with thousands of people. He recently addressed one such event in Gastonia, North Carolina. It was held on the tarmac of an airport, but despite Covid-19 restrictions, thousands of people were packed together, many not wearing masks.

Many supporters said they were backing Donald Trump because of his success as a businessman. 'America is a corporation and it should be run as such, therefore he is the man for the job,' Tabatha Moses said. But what about recent media reports that the US President is hundreds of millions of dollars in debt and has avoided paying income tax? 'I don't care about all of that, it's what he has done for the country that matters,' Tabatha said. Theron Suddeth dismissed reports of Donald Trump's struggling businesses and tax avoidance as lies. 'He's the smartest man we've ever had as president, someone who builds skyscrapers. A man isn't going to have a plane and helicopters if he doesn't pay taxes, that's ridiculous,' he said.

Joe Biden also holds campaign rallies but they look very different to Donald Trump's. They tend to be smaller with just a handful of socially-distanced supporters. He often holds drive-in rallies, where attendees remain inside their cars. The Biden campaign also organises small, local events like 'Ridin' with Biden', when groups of cyclists get together wearing their Joe Biden t-shirts and ride their bikes to show their support for the Democratic candidate. There are plenty of virtual rallies too.

Source: RTÉ News

Article 2: Maureen Dowd: Biden the anti-venom for Trump's poisonous menace

Sun, Oct 25, 2020 by Maureen Dowd

You can only let King Kong, as Don McGahn, Donald Trump's first White House counsel, dubbed his former boss, smash up the metropolis for so long.

Trump does have a gift for symmetry, though, you must admit. He began his presidency with an epic tantrum about pictures showing that his inaugural crowd could not compare with Obama's. And now he could be ending his presidency with another epic tantrum about crowd size.

After interviewer Lesley Stahl trolled him during the taping of the 60 Minutes TV show, saying, 'You used to have bigger rallies', you could almost see steam pouring out of the president's ears. He stormed out of the interview a short while later.

Whatever Joe Biden's shortcomings, he is genuine when he says he will make his presidency about helping others. As the former vice-president vowed in a speech in Delaware, 'I'll listen to the American people, no matter what their politics'.

Biden's appeal comes from his own struggles. He was a working-class kid who stuttered. He was an adult who suffered terrible losses. He was not coddled by a rich father who was always there to bail him out of a jam.

Trump calls Biden gloomy but he's the one threatening the apocalypse if he loses …

'Wave bye-bye to your savings, cause it's going down the tubes,' he said at a rally in Florida on Friday, warning that Biden's climate aims might somehow deprive Floridians of air conditioning.

When asked about families living under the polluted clouds of oil refineries and chemical plants – made worse by his administration's constant rollback of regulations – the president said, all that smog is a small price to pay because the families 'are employed heavily and they are making a lot of money'.

'Normal life, that's all we want,' Trump said at the Florida rally. But his only normal is chaos.

Source: *The Irish Times*

Lesson 90: Case study: 2020 US presidential election

Article 3: Why I voted for Trump in 2016 and will vote for him again: Goodwin

By Michael Goodwin **October 24, 2020**

On Election Day (2016), I put aside concerns about whether Trump was ready and voted for him … In fact, the 2020 choice is much easier. There are two main reasons why I'm sticking with Trump. One is because of what he has done, and the other is because of what his opponents have done to sabotage and overthrow him. First, the primary yardstick of a president is whether he produces peace and prosperity. Trump achieved both until the pandemic sent the economy into recession. Thankfully, the recovery is happening and a vaccine should give it rocket fuel. Trump's most admirable trait is that he has kept his key promises. That is remarkable only because voters have too long tolerated politicians who sell one thing and deliver another. For all his flaws, the president has largely delivered what he promised. From the start, he was a jobs president and his polices benefited workers of every race and income level. His ironclad commitment to job creation was illustrated at last week's debate, where sharp contrasts with Joe Biden centered on the Democrat's pledge to raise taxes and 'transition away' from oil and gas. Trump correctly called both job killers.

Source: *The New York Post*

	O'Donovan article	Dowd article	Goodwin article
1. Decide whether each article is informative, persuasive or entertaining.			
2. If it is a mix of these, can you explain why?			
3. How do the reports differ from each other?			
4. What parts are the most effective?			
5. Can you find any examples of bias?			
6. Research the sites where these articles appeared. What did you learn about the sites?	www.rte.ie/news	www.irishtimes.com	www.nypost.com

■ CALL TO ACTION | *Chapter 8*

Exercise 90C — Understanding how memes persuade people

Key Skills **Success criteria** ☐ I can identify how people use memes to persuade others.

Look at the memes below and answer the questions that follow.

1. What impression does meme 1 give you of Joe Biden's ability?
   _____
   _____

2. What do you learn about the character of Donald Trump from meme 2?
   _____
   _____

3. Who do you think made each of these memes?
   (a) Biden meme: _____

   (b) Trump meme: _____

4. What was the purpose of each meme?
   (a) Biden meme: _____

   (b) Trump meme: _____

5. How are they effective/ineffective?
   (a) Biden meme: _____

   (b) Trump meme: _____

420

Reflection: Reflecting on my learning about the role of media in a democracy

Learning outcome 3.14
Students should be able to reflect on their ongoing learning and what it means for them.

Key Skills

Success criteria
- [ ] I can give examples of how my thinking about the media has developed.
- [ ] I can give examples of what I will do differently when engaging with the media.

Look back at the skills and knowledge you have developed in this chapter. It is important to identify what you have learned and where you could learn more. Use the following worksheet to guide your reflection on the role of media in society. Then working in groups, discuss your responses for each of the questions below.

1. Before looking at the media, I thought …	
2. Things I learned about the media	
3. Where I got my information from	
4. How I know the information was reliable	
5. The different types of sources I got my information from	
6. The most interesting thing I learned was …	
7. How the new information I have learned will change what I do	

421

Action: Conducting a survey

Before conducting a survey, look at how surveys are presented in the media. As a class, collect examples of how surveys have been reported in the media.

✓ Action 1 Understanding how media reports surveys

Key Skills **Success criteria**
- ☐ I can identify, giving examples, of how media report on survey results.
- ☐ I can give an example of inaccurate reporting of surveys.
- ☐ I can identify, giving examples, whether or not a report is reliable.

Answer the following questions.

1. Are all the reports on surveys reliable?
   _____
   _____

2. What are the things you would consider when judging whether or not a survey is reliable?
   _____
   _____

As a class, conduct an online survey on an issue in the media, for example, young people's use of social media, where people get their news.

1. Begin by deciding who you will survey. Will you poll your year group, your school, young people in your community or everybody in your community? When deciding who to poll, you must consider what answers you want. For example, if you decide to find out about young people's interest in media, you need to ask young people. Asking members of the local retirement club will give you some information, but it will not be as accurate as asking members of the local youth club.

2. Design your questions based on what you want to find out. Decide whether you want **open** or **closed** questions.

   - Open questions are ones where the person answering can write their own response. They are useful if you want to answer questions such as why and how. In this case, you will have to analyse what people are saying to see if there are patterns in their answers. For example, a lot of people answering used words that could be seen as angry, others were fed up, whereas others did not care.

   - With closed questions, the person answering chooses between options you have selected. Closed questions give results in percentages, so you can see what people as a group think about a topic. If you use online questionnaires like Google Forms or Survey Monkey, you will get immediate results in percentages. For example, 35% of people like television and 34% like social media, but only 4% play music.

3. Be careful to use respectful language in your questions.

Action 2 **Designing, conducting, analysing and reporting a survey**

Key Skills **Success criteria** ☐ I can conduct the tasks needed to design, conduct, analyse or report a survey.

Before conducting the survey, it is important to decide the roles people will play. The class works as groups with different responsibilities as below:

- Group 1: Question
- Group 2: Design
- Group 3: PR
- Group 4: Distribution
- Group 5: Collection
- Group 6: Analysis
- Group 7: Report

Once you have been assigned to a group, the group will meet up and decide what jobs need to be done and who will do them. Write these jobs below.

CALL TO ACTION | *Chapter 8*

✓ **Action 3** **Reflecting on what I have learned from conducting a survey**

Key Skills   **Success criteria**   ☐ I can answer questions that describe what I did and what I learned from carrying out the survey.

Answer the questions below.

1. What was my group's responsibility?
   _____
   _____

2. What jobs did I do?
   _____
   _____
   _____

3. What skills did I use?
   _____
   _____
   _____

4. What did I learn from the survey?
   _____
   _____
   _____

5. What did my group do well?
   _____
   _____
   _____

6. What would I do differently if I had to do it again?
   _____
   _____
   _____

7. What were the good things about working in a group?
   _____
   _____
   _____

8. What was hard about working in a group?
   _____
   _____

Chapter 9 Classroom-Based Assessment: My Citizenship Action Record

At the end of each chapter, you completed an action linked to the topic. One of the actions you completed in **Second** or **Third Year** can be used for your Classroom-Based Assessment (CBA) in CSPE.

The CBA in CSPE is a **Citizenship Action Record** which must:

- Show how you **personally** engaged in a citizenship action and describe what **you** did. The overall action was undertaken by the class, but you must create an individual Citizenship Action Record which shows the role you played in the action and what you learned from it.
- Have an **action** focus. A Citizenship Action Record must involve some action. For example, an awareness campaign involves telling others about something by making posters, deciding where to put them and discussing in groups what information to put on them. Research might be part of this, where you find out the key facts, but the action is deciding what to include in the poster, designing it and promoting it by working with others.
- Show **what you have learned** from doing the action.
- Describe the **skills** you used.
- Show **evidence** of the work you did at various stages. For example, if you organised a guest speaker you would include the emails you sent at different stages and the responses you received. This could include a thank you email received after the guest speaker had visited the school. Evidence can include photos, videos and screenshots.
- Show how you **reflected** on what you learned from taking part in the action.

In the actions you have completed in this book, you have agreed an issue, formed committees, planned tasks with the committees, completed the action and reflected on what you learned. This means that most of the work for your CBA has already been done and recorded. Using that information, you can now write the Citizenship Action Record.

The CBA will be awarded one of four descriptors given below.

1. **Exceptional**: The action record shows how the student fully and effectively engaged in meaningful action. The student's personal reflections on their learning are of excellent quality. The record is presented in a comprehensive, creative and highly effective manner.
2. **Above expectations**: The action record provides evidence of how the student engaged in meaningful action. The student's personal reflections on their learning are of good quality. The record is presented in an organised, creative and effective manner.
3. **In line with expectations**: The action record provides evidence of the student's engagement in the action. There is some evidence of personal reflection on their learning. The action record is presented in an organised manner with some creativity.
4. **Yet to meet expectations**: There is limited evidence of personal engagement in the action taken. There is very limited evidence of student reflection on learning. The action record provides a very basic summary of information although it may lack detail and creativity.

The Citizenship Action Record can be written (handwritten or typed), digital, visual, audio, a presentation, an interview, a poster presentation or a mix of these. On the following pages, you can write up your Citizenship Action Record. You may choose to convert this information into a PowerPoint, a poster, an infographic or something else, but you do not have to.

CALL TO ACTION | *Chapter 9*

1. Title of my Citizenship Action Record

This could be a simple title such as 'Organising a trip to a sustainable farm'. Just make sure the title explains what the action did. For example, a title of 'A sustainable farm' does not explain what the action was.

2. Reason for choosing this action

In this section, explain **why** the particular issue was chosen. For example, you might have decided to invite a guest speaker to talk to you about an issue that was topical in the news, or you might have decided to fundraise for an organisation helping with a specific area that interested you. Make clear how this area was something that you were **personally** engaged by.

3. Aim of my citizenship action

In this section, explain what the **purpose** of the action was. For example, you may have visited an eco-project because you wanted to begin an awareness campaign. You may have felt that you needed to learn how more about the topic before you could explain it to others.

4. How I contributed to the action

In this section, explain what **you** did in the action. Writing 'We were in charge of publicity' is not enough, because it says what the group did, not what *you* did. Your job might have been social media, whereas somebody else might have made a poster. Write clearly what *you* did explaining it in as much detail as you can.

5. Evidence

Because the CBA is a record, it needs to include evidence of the action. Include the evidence of your work here. This might be emails you sent, a screenshot, photos, the details of the money collected, notes you wrote, pictures of books you consulted, people you met, etc.

6. What I learned about the topic

In this section, write down what you learned about the topic and not what you learned about the process. If you were doing a survey, note the facts you found out rather than what you learned about doing a survey.

7. Wellbeing indicators

Mention the wellbeing indicators that you were aware of in doing the CBA. These could be:

- **Active** – were you physically active doing the CBA? For example, you set up the hall as a courtroom for the mock trial.

- **Aware** – were you aware of what was happening around you? For example, you realised that people were not going to be interested in the poster unless it was presented in a more appealing or entertaining way.

- **Connected** – did you understand how things were linked? For example, if you did not design the poster on time other people would not be able to promote it on social media.

- **Resilient** – were you able to overcome something? For example, the first time you had to speak to the classes about your plan was really hard, but you improved and became more confident as it went on.

- **Respected** – did you listen to others and did they listen to you? For example, you had to make a decision on who to invite. There were a lot of different opinions, but you discussed them calmly and each person explained and listened to each other before making a decision.

- **Responsible** – did you behave responsibly in the action? For example, you collected €500 and made sure it was kept safe.

8. The skills I used, why and how I used them

It is important to realise that you developed skills as part of the action. There are many different types of skills and these will be different depending on the job you did. Some of the skills you used might involve:

- **Working with others** (emailing, phone calls, working in groups, organising appointments)
- **Being creative** (designing a poster, infographic, role playing)
- **Communicating** (listening to others, discussing ideas, dividing tasks, public speaking, class presentations)
- **Managing information and thinking** (organising/summarising information, picking out keywords or sentences, examining different opinions)
- **Being literate** (researching, using the internet or library, asking questions, carrying out interviews or surveys, using computer skills)
- **Being numerate** (counting money, counting votes, analysing surveys, making bar charts, pie charts)
- **Managing myself** (reflecting, planning, choosing activities, deciding on a venue/checking its availability, allocating tasks)
- **Staying well** (valuing other people's opinions, ensuring respectful communication, providing refreshments, ensuring essential things are available, such as chairs, stage, costumes and a projector).

Once you have identified the skills you used, show **why** and **how** you used them, for example:

Skill: working with others, I made a phone call.

Why: before we decided where to go, I rang three sustainable projects to see whether they accept school tours because if they didn't there would be no point in researching the project.

How: I wrote out what I wanted to say and rang the organisation's landline because I wanted to speak to somebody in the office. I spoke politely and explained that we were interested in their work and would like to learn more about it and I wanted to know if they accepted school visits.

9. How my opinions or attitudes have changed, been challenged or confirmed

Identify any changes in your opinion or attitude you have noticed as a result of this action. For example, your attitude to bottled water could have changed. You had always thought bottled water was healthier but the guest speaker showed how it was no different to tap water. Now you use a reusable bottle for water.

You can also show how your opinions or attitudes have been confirmed. For example, you thought young people had little interest in politics and the results of your survey confirmed this.

CALL TO ACTION | Chapter 9

10. My overall reflections on my learning and what it means for me now and into the future

There are three parts to this.

1. Consider the following questions to help you reflect on your learning:
   - What did you enjoy or dislike about working in a team?
   - If a friend of yours wanted to do the same action, what advice would you give them?
   - What worked well and what would you do differently if you were doing this action again?
   - What have you learned from taking part in the action?
   - How do you know that you have learned something?

2. Then consider what this means for you now. For example, you could say that you were really excited by the awareness campaign you organised and you want to join an organisation promoting this topic.

3. Finally, consider how this learning will have an impact on you in the future. For example, you were involved in designing a poster and you enjoyed the process so much that you would like to study design in college. Or you were so interested in deforestation that you would like to work for an organisation like Friends of the Earth.

Congratulations, you have now completed your CSPE journey!